Ethical Problems in the Practice of Law: Model Rules, State Variations, and Practice Questions

2025 and 2026 Edition

Ethical Problems in the Practice of Law: Model Rules, State Variations, and Practice Questions

2025 and 2026 Edition

LISA G. LERMAN
Professor of Law Emerita
The Catholic University of America, Columbus School of Law

PHILIP G. SCHRAG
Delaney Family Professor of Public Interest Law
Georgetown University Law Center

ANJUM GUPTA
Professor of Law
Judge Chester J. Straub Scholar
Director, Immigrant Rights Clinic
Rutgers Law School

ASPEN PUBLISHING

To contact Customer Service, e-mail customer.service@aspenpublishing.com, call 1-800-950-5259, or mail correspondence to:

Aspen Publishing
Attn: Order Department
1 Wall Street
Burlington, MA 01803

Printed in the United States of America.

1 2 3 4 5 6 7 8 9 0

ISBN 979-8-8920-7766-8

About Aspen Publishing

Aspen Publishing is a leading provider of educational content and digital learning solutions to law schools in the U.S. and around the world. Aspen provides best-in-class solutions for legal education through authoritative textbooks, written by renowned authors, and breakthrough products such as Connected eBooks, Connected Quizzing, and PracticePerfect.

The Aspen Casebook Series (famously known among law faculty and students as the "red and black" casebooks) encompasses hundreds of highly regarded textbooks in more than eighty disciplines, from large enrollment courses, such as Torts and Contracts to emerging electives such as Sustainability and the Law of Policing. Study aids such as the *Examples & Explanations* and the *Emanuel Law Outlines* series, both highly popular collections, help law students master complex subject matter.

Major products, programs, and initiatives include:

- **Connected eBooks** are enhanced digital textbooks and study aids that come with a suite of online content and learning tools designed to maximize student success. Designed in collaboration with hundreds of faculty and students, the Connected eBook is a significant leap forward in the legal education learning tools available to students.
- **Connected Quizzing** is an easy-to-use formative assessment tool that tests law students' understanding and provides timely feedback to improve learning outcomes. Delivered through CasebookConnect.com, the learning platform already used by students to access their Aspen casebooks, Connected Quizzing is simple to implement and integrates seamlessly with law school course curricula.
- **PracticePerfect** is a visually engaging, interactive study aid to explain commonly encountered legal doctrines through easy-to-understand animated videos, illustrative examples, and numerous practice questions. Developed by a team of experts, PracticePerfect is the ideal study companion for today's law students.
- The **Aspen Learning Library** enables law schools to provide their students with access to the most popular study aids on the market across all of their courses. Available through an annual subscription, the online library consists of study aids in e-book, audio, and video formats with full text search, note-taking, and highlighting capabilities.
- Aspen's **Digital Bookshelf** is an institutional-level online education bookshelf, consolidating everything students and professors need to ensure success. This program ensures that every student has access to affordable course materials from day one.
- **Leading Edge** is a community centered on thinking differently about legal education and putting those thoughts into actionable strategies. At the core of the program is the Leading Edge Conference, an annual gathering of legal education thought leaders looking to pool ideas and identify promising directions of exploration.

Contents

Introduction

This book is one of several rules supplements for professional responsibility courses. Most of the others include a great deal of information that is rarely assigned to students. They include numerous other statutes and codes relevant to the course but often not assigned; these resources add to the weight and cost of the books. We wanted to offer a lower-cost supplement that includes only the resources that most students of professional responsibility need while taking the course. The most important resource is the Model Rules of Professional Conduct. The black-letter rules and the comments are reprinted in full in this supplement.[1]

We have included two other sections in this rules supplement. The first is a selection of rules from the state ethics codes that are significantly different from the Model Rules. These rules are intended to assist in studying the Model Rules. A professor or a student may compare an excerpted rule with the relevant Model Rule to explore the divergent policy choices. We added brief notes to many of the excerpted rules to highlight the differences between the state rule and the corresponding Model Rule. The point is that the Model Rules, like all statutes and regulations, are a compilation of policy choices, best understood through critical evaluation.

The third section of the supplement consists of complex multiple-choice questions, written by the authors, that students can use to test their understanding of the topics covered in the professional responsibility course. Like the questions on the Multistate Professional Responsibility Examination (MPRE), our questions have four possible answers, all of which at first reading seem plausibly correct. By working through these questions, students will become familiar with the format of the MPRE and will improve their skills in analyzing such questions correctly. At the back of the book, we have included answers to the questions and a detailed narrative explanation of each of the answers.

Many students will want to test themselves using the review questions after studying each unit of the course. Although different courses take up topics in different sequences, it should be easy for students to identify the relevant set of questions for each topic. Students should consult the Model Rules, including the comments, as they attempt to answer these questions. Rather than guessing which answer sounds most reasonable, a student should figure out which answer is correct and

1. This supplement does not include the ABA Model Code of Judicial Conduct, but it can be found at https://www.americanbar.org/groups/professional_responsibility/publications/model_code_of_judicial_conduct/.

why, as well as why each of the incorrect answers is incorrect. The questions are too difficult to be answered from memory; the answers to some of them depend on the exact wording of certain Model Rules and comments. Students will need to make notes to untangle some of the questions. Even though the MPRE does not permit consultation of the rules, the learning value of using these questions will be much greater if they are tackled with the rules in hand. Also: *resist* the temptation to look at the answers to the questions or to read the explanation for the answers until you have done your own rigorous analysis of each question. Once you have done so, it is well worth your while to study the explanations to see whether you have accurately analyzed each question.

This Model Rules Supplement has a companion website, at https://www.aspenpublishing.com/products/Supp-Lerman-EthicalProblems2025-2026. If the American Bar Association makes any changes to the Model Rules or the comments before the end of 2026, we will post those changes in the "Student Materials" link on that website. Similarly, if we discover a need to qualify or add to any answer to a practice question, we will post the additional explanation in that link.

We welcome feedback from professors and from students on the state variations section of the supplement and on the multiple-choice questions. We also would welcome the contribution of additional multiple-choice questions and annotated answers from users of this supplement. If we use a suggested question in the next edition, we will acknowledge the drafter in the book. Feedback, suggestions, and questions may be sent to Lisa Lerman at lerman@law.edu.

The authors would like to thank the American Bar Association for permission to reproduce the following material:

November 2024

Lisa G. Lerman
Philip G. Schrag
Anjum Gupta

American Bar Association
Model Rules of Professional Conduct
(as amended through August 2024, and Comments)

Contents

PREAMBLE AND SCOPE

PREAMBLE: A LAWYER'S RESPONSIBILITIES

[1] A lawyer, as a member of the legal profession, is a representative of clients, an officer of the legal system and a public citizen having special responsibility for the quality of justice.

[2] As a representative of clients, a lawyer performs various functions. As advisor, a lawyer provides a client with an informed understanding of the client's legal rights and obligations and explains their practical implications. As advocate, a lawyer zealously asserts the client's position under the rules of the adversary system. As negotiator, a lawyer seeks a result advantageous to the client but consistent with requirements of honest dealings with others. As an evaluator, a lawyer acts by examining a client's legal affairs and reporting about them to the client or to others.

[3] In addition to these representational functions, a lawyer may serve as a third-party neutral, a nonrepresentational role helping the parties to resolve a dispute or other matter. Some of these Rules apply directly to lawyers who are or have served as third-party neutrals. See, e.g., Rules 1.12 and 2.4. In addition, there are Rules that apply to lawyers who are not active in the practice of law or to practicing lawyers even when they are acting in a nonprofessional capacity. For example, a lawyer who commits fraud in the conduct of a business is subject to discipline for engaging in conduct involving dishonesty, fraud, deceit or misrepresentation. See Rule 8.4.

[4] In all professional functions a lawyer should be competent, prompt and diligent. A lawyer should maintain communication with a client concerning the representation. A lawyer should keep in confidence information relating to representation of a client except so far as disclosure is required or permitted by the Rules of Professional Conduct or other law.

[5] A lawyer's conduct should conform to the requirements of the law, both in professional service to clients and in the lawyer's business and personal affairs. A lawyer should use the law's procedures only for legitimate purposes and not to harass or intimidate others. A lawyer should demonstrate respect for the legal system and for those who serve it, including judges, other lawyers and public officials. While it is a lawyer's duty, when necessary, to challenge the rectitude of official action, it is also a lawyer's duty to uphold legal process.

[6] As a public citizen, a lawyer should seek improvement of the law, access to the legal system, the administration of justice and the quality of service rendered by the legal profession. As a member of a learned profession, a lawyer should cultivate knowledge of the law beyond its use for clients, employ that knowledge in reform of the law and work to strengthen legal education. In addition, a lawyer should further the public's understanding of and confidence in the rule of law and the justice system because legal institutions in a constitutional democracy depend on popular participation and support to maintain their authority. A lawyer should be mindful of deficiencies in the administration of justice and of the fact that the poor, and sometimes persons who are not poor, cannot afford adequate legal assistance. Therefore, all lawyers should devote professional time and resources and use civic

influence to ensure equal access to our system of justice for all those who because of economic or social barriers cannot afford or secure adequate legal counsel. A lawyer should aid the legal profession in pursuing these objectives and should help the bar regulate itself in the public interest.

[7] Many of a lawyer's professional responsibilities are prescribed in the Rules of Professional Conduct, as well as substantive and procedural law. However, a lawyer is also guided by personal conscience and the approbation of professional peers. A lawyer should strive to attain the highest level of skill, to improve the law and the legal profession and to exemplify the legal profession's ideals of public service.

[8] A lawyer's responsibilities as a representative of clients, an officer of the legal system and a public citizen are usually harmonious. Thus, when an opposing party is well represented, a lawyer can be a zealous advocate on behalf of a client and at the same time assume that justice is being done. So also, a lawyer can be sure that preserving client confidences ordinarily serves the public interest because people are more likely to seek legal advice, and thereby heed their legal obligations, when they know their communications will be private.

[9] In the nature of law practice, however, conflicting responsibilities are encountered. Virtually all difficult ethical problems arise from conflict between a lawyer's responsibilities to clients, to the legal system and to the lawyer's own interest in remaining an ethical person while earning a satisfactory living. The Rules of Professional Conduct often prescribe terms for resolving such conflicts. Within the framework of these Rules, however, many difficult issues of professional discretion can arise. Such issues must be resolved through the exercise of sensitive professional and moral judgment guided by the basic principles underlying the Rules. These principles include the lawyer's obligation zealously to protect and pursue a client's legitimate interests, within the bounds of the law, while maintaining a professional, courteous and civil attitude toward all persons involved in the legal system.

[10] The legal profession is largely self-governing. Although other professions also have been granted powers of self-government, the legal profession is unique in this respect because of the close relationship between the profession and the processes of government and law enforcement. This connection is manifested in the fact that ultimate authority over the legal profession is vested largely in the courts.

[11] To the extent that lawyers meet the obligations of their professional calling, the occasion for government regulation is obviated. Selfregulation also helps maintain the legal profession's independence from government domination. An independent legal profession is an important force in preserving government under law, for abuse of legal authority is more readily challenged by a profession whose members are not dependent on government for the right to practice.

[12] The legal profession's relative autonomy carries with it special responsibilities of self-government. The profession has a responsibility to assure that its regulations are conceived in the public interest and not in furtherance of parochial or self-interested concerns of the bar. Every lawyer is responsible for observance of the Rules of Professional Conduct. A lawyer should also aid in securing their

observance by other lawyers. Neglect of these responsibilities compromises the independence of the profession and the public interest which it serves.

[13] Lawyers play a vital role in the preservation of society. The fulfillment of this role requires an understanding by lawyers of their relationship to our legal system. The Rules of Professional Conduct, when properly applied, serve to define that relationship.

SCOPE

[14] The Rules of Professional Conduct are rules of reason. They should be interpreted with reference to the purposes of legal representation and of the law itself. Some of the Rules are imperatives, cast in the terms "shall" or "shall not." These define proper conduct for purposes of professional discipline. Others, generally cast in the term "may," are permissive and define areas under the Rules in which the lawyer has discretion to exercise professional judgment. No disciplinary action should be taken when the lawyer chooses not to act or acts within the bounds of such discretion. Other Rules define the nature of relationships between the lawyer and others. The Rules are thus partly obligatory and disciplinary and partly constitutive and descriptive in that they define a lawyer's professional role. Many of the Comments use the term "should." Comments do not add obligations to the Rules but provide guidance for practicing in compliance with the Rules.

[15] The Rules presuppose a larger legal context shaping the lawyer's role. That context includes court rules and statutes relating to matters of licensure, laws defining specific obligations of lawyers and substantive and procedural law in general. The Comments are sometimes used to alert lawyers to their responsibilities under such other law.

[16] Compliance with the Rules, as with all law in an open society, depends primarily upon understanding and voluntary compliance, secondarily upon reinforcement by peer and public opinion and finally, when necessary, upon enforcement through disciplinary proceedings. The Rules do not, however, exhaust the moral and ethical considerations that should inform a lawyer, for no worthwhile human activity can be completely defined by legal rules. The Rules simply provide a framework for the ethical practice of law.

[17] Furthermore, for purposes of determining the lawyer's authority and responsibility, principles of substantive law external to these Rules determine whether a client-lawyer relationship exists. Most of the duties flowing from the client-lawyer relationship attach only after the client has requested the lawyer to render legal services and the lawyer has agreed to do so. But there are some duties, such as that of confidentiality under Rule 1.6, that attach when the lawyer agrees to consider whether a client-lawyer relationship shall be established. See Rule 1.18. Whether a client-lawyer relationship exists for any specific purpose can depend on the circumstances and may be a question of fact.

[18] Under various legal provisions, including constitutional, statutory and common law, the responsibilities of government lawyers may include authority

concerning legal matters that ordinarily reposes in the client in private client-lawyer relationships. For example, a lawyer for a government agency may have authority on behalf of the government to decide upon settlement or whether to appeal from an adverse judgment. Such authority in various respects is generally vested in the attorney general and the state's attorney in state government, and their federal counterparts, and the same may be true of other government law officers. Also, lawyers under the supervision of these officers may be authorized to represent several government agencies in intragovernmental legal controversies in circumstances where a private lawyer could not represent multiple private clients. These Rules do not abrogate any such authority.

[19] Failure to comply with an obligation or prohibition imposed by a Rule is a basis for invoking the disciplinary process. The Rules presuppose that disciplinary assessment of a lawyer's conduct will be made on the basis of the facts and circumstances as they existed at the time of the conduct in question and in recognition of the fact that a lawyer often has to act upon uncertain or incomplete evidence of the situation. Moreover, the Rules presuppose that whether or not discipline should be imposed for a violation, and the severity of a sanction, depend on all the circumstances, such as the willfulness and seriousness of the violation, extenuating factors and whether there have been previous violations.

[20] Violation of a Rule should not itself give rise to a cause of action against a lawyer nor should it create any presumption in such a case that a legal duty has been breached. In addition, violation of a Rule does not necessarily warrant any other nondisciplinary remedy, such as disqualification of a lawyer in pending litigation. The Rules are designed to provide guidance to lawyers and to provide a structure for regulating conduct through disciplinary agencies. They are not designed to be a basis for civil liability. Furthermore, the purpose of the Rules can be subverted when they are invoked by opposing parties as procedural weapons. The fact that a Rule is a just basis for a lawyer's self-assessment, or for sanctioning a lawyer under the administration of a disciplinary authority, does not imply that an antagonist in a collateral proceeding or transaction has standing to seek enforcement of the Rule. Nevertheless, since the Rules do establish standards of conduct by lawyers, a lawyer's violation of a Rule may be evidence of breach of the applicable standard of conduct.

[21] The Comment accompanying each Rule explains and illustrates the meaning and purpose of the Rule. The Preamble and this note on Scope provide general orientation. The Comments are intended as guides to interpretation, but the text of each Rule is authoritative.

ARTICLE 1. CLIENT-LAWYER RELATIONSHIP

Rule 1.0 Terminology

(a) "Belief" or "believes" denotes that the person involved actually supposed the fact in question to be true. A person's belief may be inferred from circumstances.

(b) "Confirmed in writing," when used in reference to the informed consent of a person, denotes informed consent that is given in writing by the person or a writing that a lawyer promptly transmits to the person confirming an oral informed consent. See paragraph (e) for the definition of "informed consent." If it is not feasible to obtain or transmit the writing at the time the person gives informed consent, then the lawyer must obtain or transmit it within a reasonable time thereafter.

(c) "Firm" or "law firm" denotes a lawyer or lawyers in a law partnership, professional corporation, sole proprietorship or other association authorized to practice law; or lawyers employed in a legal services organization or the legal department of a corporation or other organization.

(d) "Fraud" or "fraudulent" denotes conduct that is fraudulent under the substantive or procedural law of the applicable jurisdiction and has a purpose to deceive.

(e) "Informed consent" denotes the agreement by a person to a proposed course of conduct after the lawyer has communicated adequate information and explanation about the material risks of and reasonably available alternatives to the proposed course of conduct.

(f) "Knowingly," "known," or "knows" denotes actual knowledge of the fact in question. A person's knowledge may be inferred from circumstances.

(g) "Partner" denotes a member of a partnership, a shareholder in a law firm organized as a professional corporation, or a member of an association authorized to practice law.

(h) "Reasonable" or "reasonably" when used in relation to conduct by a lawyer denotes the conduct of a reasonably prudent and competent lawyer.

(i) "Reasonable belief" or "reasonably believes" when used in reference to a lawyer denotes that the lawyer believes the matter in question and that the circumstances are such that the belief is reasonable.

(j) "Reasonably should know" when used in reference to a lawyer denotes that a lawyer of reasonable prudence and competence would ascertain the matter in question.

(k) "Screened" denotes the isolation of a lawyer from any participation in a matter through the timely imposition of procedures within a firm that are reasonably adequate under the circumstances to protect information that the isolated lawyer is obligated to protect under these Rules or other law.

(l) "Substantial" when used in reference to degree or extent denotes a material matter of clear and weighty importance.

(m) "Tribunal" denotes a court, an arbitrator in a binding arbitration proceeding or a legislative body, administrative agency or other body acting in an adjudicative capacity. A legislative body, administrative agency or other body acts in an adjudicative capacity when a neutral official, after the presentation of evidence or legal argument by a party or parties, will render a binding legal judgment directly affecting a party's interests in a particular matter.

(n) "Writing" or "written" denotes a tangible or electronic record of a communication or representation, including handwriting, typewriting, printing,

photostating, photography, audio or videorecording, and electronic communications. A "signed" writing includes an electronic sound, symbol or process attached to or logically associated with a writing and executed or adopted by a person with the intent to sign the writing.

Comment

Confirmed in Writing

[1] If it is not feasible to obtain or transmit a written confirmation at the time the client gives informed consent, then the lawyer must obtain or transmit it within a reasonable time thereafter. If a lawyer has obtained a client's informed consent, the lawyer may act in reliance on that consent so long as it is confirmed in writing within a reasonable time thereafter.

Firm

[2] Whether two or more lawyers constitute a firm within paragraph (c) can depend on the specific facts. For example, two practitioners who share office space and occasionally consult or assist each other ordinarily would not be regarded as constituting a firm. However, if they present themselves to the public in a way that suggests that they are a firm or conduct themselves as a firm, they should be regarded as a firm for purposes of the Rules. The terms of any formal agreement between associated lawyers are relevant in determining whether they are a firm, as is the fact that they have mutual access to information concerning the clients they serve. Furthermore, it is relevant in doubtful cases to consider the underlying purpose of the Rule that is involved. A group of lawyers could be regarded as a firm for purposes of the Rule that the same lawyer should not represent opposing parties in litigation, while it might not be so regarded for purposes of the Rule that information acquired by one lawyer is attributed to another.

[3] With respect to the law department of an organization, including the government, there is ordinarily no question that the members of the department constitute a firm within the meaning of the Rules of Professional Conduct. There can be uncertainty, however, as to the identity of the client. For example, it may not be clear whether the law department of a corporation represents a subsidiary or an affiliated corporation, as well as the corporation by which the members of the department are directly employed. A similar question can arise concerning an unincorporated association and its local affiliates.

[4] Similar questions can also arise with respect to lawyers in legal aid and legal services organizations. Depending upon the structure of the organization, the entire organization or different components of it may constitute a firm or firms for purposes of these Rules.

Fraud

[5] When used in these Rules, the terms "fraud" or "fraudulent" refer to conduct that is characterized as such under the substantive or procedural law of the applicable jurisdiction and has a purpose to deceive. This does not include merely

negligent misrepresentation or negligent failure to apprise another of relevant information. For purposes of these Rules, it is not necessary that anyone has suffered damages or relied on the misrepresentation or failure to inform.

Informed Consent

[6] Many of the Rules of Professional Conduct require the lawyer to obtain the informed consent of a client or other person (e.g., a former client or, under certain circumstances, a prospective client) before accepting or continuing representation or pursuing a course of conduct. See, e.g., Rules 1.2(c), 1.6(a) and 1.7(b). The communication necessary to obtain such consent will vary according to the Rule involved and the circumstances giving rise to the need to obtain informed consent. The lawyer must make reasonable efforts to ensure that the client or other person possesses information reasonably adequate to make an informed decision. Ordinarily, this will require communication that includes a disclosure of the facts and circumstances giving rise to the situation, any explanation reasonably necessary to inform the client or other person of the material advantages and disadvantages of the proposed course of conduct and a discussion of the client's or other person's options and alternatives. In some circumstances it may be appropriate for a lawyer to advise a client or other person to seek the advice of other counsel. A lawyer need not inform a client or other person of facts or implications already known to the client or other person; nevertheless, a lawyer who does not personally inform the client or other person assumes the risk that the client or other person is inadequately informed and the consent is invalid. In determining whether the information and explanation provided are reasonably adequate, relevant factors include whether the client or other person is experienced in legal matters generally and in making decisions of the type involved, and whether the client or other person is independently represented by other counsel in giving the consent. Normally, such persons need less information and explanation than others, and generally a client or other person who is independently represented by other counsel in giving the consent should be assumed to have given informed consent.

[7] Obtaining informed consent will usually require an affirmative response by the client or other person. In general, a lawyer may not assume consent from a client's or other person's silence. Consent may be inferred, however, from the conduct of a client or other person who has reasonably adequate information about the matter. A number of Rules require that a person's consent be confirmed in writing. See Rules 1.7(b) and 1.9(a). For a definition of "writing" and "confirmed in writing," see paragraphs (n) and (b). Other Rules require that a client's consent be obtained in a writing signed by the client. See, e.g., Rules 1.8(a) and (g). For a definition of "signed," see paragraph (n).

Screened

[8] This definition applies to situations where screening of a personally disqualified lawyer is permitted to remove imputation of a conflict of interest under Rules 1.10, 1.11, 1.12 or 1.18.

[9] The purpose of screening is to assure the affected parties that confidential information known by the personally disqualified lawyer remains protected. The personally disqualified lawyer should acknowledge the obligation not to communicate with any of the other lawyers in the firm with respect to the matter. Similarly, other lawyers in the firm who are working on the matter should be informed that the screening is in place and that they may not communicate with the personally disqualified lawyer with respect to the matter. Additional screening measures that are appropriate for the particular matter will depend on the circumstances. To implement, reinforce and remind all affected lawyers of the presence of the screening, it may be appropriate for the firm to undertake such procedures as a written undertaking by the screened lawyer to avoid any communication with other firm personnel and any contact with any firm files or other information, including information in electronic form, relating to the matter, written notice and instructions to all other firm personnel forbidding any communication with the screened lawyer relating to the matter, denial of access by the screened lawyer to firm files or other information, including information in electronic form, relating to the matter and periodic reminders of the screen to the screened lawyer and all other firm personnel.

[10] In order to be effective, screening measures must be implemented as soon as practical after a lawyer or law firm knows or reasonably should know that there is a need for screening.

Rule 1.1 Competence

A lawyer shall provide competent representation to a client. Competent representation requires the legal knowledge, skill, thoroughness and preparation reasonably necessary for the representation.

Comment

Legal Knowledge and Skill

[1] In determining whether a lawyer employs the requisite knowledge and skill in a particular matter, relevant factors include the relative complexity and specialized nature of the matter, the lawyer's general experience, the lawyer's training and experience in the field in question, the preparation and study the lawyer is able to give the matter and whether it is feasible to refer the matter to, or associate or consult with, a lawyer of established competence in the field in question. In many instances, the required proficiency is that of a general practitioner. Expertise in a particular field of law may be required in some circumstances.

[2] A lawyer need not necessarily have special training or prior experience to handle legal problems of a type with which the lawyer is unfamiliar. A newly admitted lawyer can be as competent as a practitioner with long experience. Some important legal skills, such as the analysis of precedent, the evaluation of evidence and legal drafting, are required in all legal problems. Perhaps the most fundamental legal skill consists of determining what kind of legal problems a situation may

involve, a skill that necessarily transcends any particular specialized knowledge. A lawyer can provide adequate representation in a wholly novel field through necessary study. Competent representation can also be provided through the association of a lawyer of established competence in the field in question.

[3] In an emergency a lawyer may give advice or assistance in a matter in which the lawyer does not have the skill ordinarily required where referral to or consultation or association with another lawyer would be impractical. Even in an emergency, however, assistance should be limited to that reasonably necessary in the circumstances, for ill-considered action under emergency conditions can jeopardize the client's interest.

[4] A lawyer may accept representation where the requisite level of competence can be achieved by reasonable preparation. This applies as well to a lawyer who is appointed as counsel for an unrepresented person. See also Rule 6.2.

Thoroughness and Preparation

[5] Competent handling of a particular matter includes inquiry into and analysis of the factual and legal elements of the problem, and use of methods and procedures meeting the standards of competent practitioners. It also includes adequate preparation. The required attention and preparation are determined in part by what is at stake; major litigation and complex transactions ordinarily require more extensive treatment than matters of lesser complexity and consequence. An agreement between the lawyer and the client regarding the scope of the representation may limit the matters for which the lawyer is responsible. See Rule 1.2(c).

Retaining or Contracting with Other Lawyers

[6] Before a lawyer retains or contracts with other lawyers outside the lawyer's own firm to provide or assist in the provision of legal services to a client, the lawyer should ordinarily obtain informed consent from the client and must reasonably believe that the other lawyers' services will contribute to the competent and ethical representation of the client. See also Rules 1.2 (allocation of authority), 1.4 (communication with client), 1.5(e) (fee sharing), 1.6 (confidentiality), and 5.5(a) (unauthorized practice of law). The reasonableness of the decision to retain or contract with other lawyers outside the lawyer's own firm will depend upon the circumstances, including the education, experience and reputation of the nonfirm lawyers; the nature of the services assigned to the nonfirm lawyers; and the legal protections, professional conduct rules, and ethical environments of the jurisdictions in which the services will be performed, particularly relating to confidential information.

[7] When lawyers from more than one law firm are providing legal services to the client on a particular matter, the lawyers ordinarily should consult with each other and the client about the scope of their respective representations and the allocation of responsibility among them. See Rule 1.2. When making allocations of responsibility in a matter pending before a tribunal, lawyers and parties may have additional obligations that are a matter of law beyond the scope of these Rules.

Maintaining Competence

[8] To maintain the requisite knowledge and skill, a lawyer should keep abreast of changes in the law and its practice, including the benefits and risks associated with relevant technology, engage in continuing study and education and comply with all continuing legal education requirements to which the lawyer is subject.

Definitional Cross-References

"Firm" See Rule 1.0(c)
"Informed consent" See Rule 1.0(e)
"Reasonably" See Rule 1.0(h)
"Reasonably believe" See Rule 1.0(i)

Rule 1.2 Scope of Representation and Allocation of Authority Between Client and Lawyer

(a) Subject to paragraphs (c) and (d), a lawyer shall abide by a client's decisions concerning the objectives of representation and, as required by Rule 1.4, shall consult with the client as to the means by which they are to be pursued. A lawyer may take such action on behalf of the client as is impliedly authorized to carry out the representation. A lawyer shall abide by a client's decision whether to settle a matter. In a criminal case, the lawyer shall abide by the client's decision, after consultation with the lawyer, as to a plea to be entered, whether to waive jury trial and whether the client will testify.

(b) A lawyer's representation of a client, including representation by appointment, does not constitute an endorsement of the client's political, economic, social or moral views or activities.

(c) A lawyer may limit the scope of the representation if the limitation is reasonable under the circumstances and the client gives informed consent.

(d) A lawyer shall not counsel a client to engage, or assist a client, in conduct that the lawyer knows is criminal or fraudulent, but a lawyer may discuss the legal consequences of any proposed course of conduct with a client and may counsel or assist a client to make a good faith effort to determine the validity, scope, meaning or application of the law.

Comment

Allocation of Authority between Client and Lawyer

[1] Paragraph (a) confers upon the client the ultimate authority to determine the purposes to be served by legal representation, within the limits imposed by law and the lawyer's professional obligations. The decisions specified in paragraph (a), such as whether to settle a civil matter, must also be made by the client. See Rule 1.4(a)(1) for the lawyer's duty to communicate with the client about such decisions. With respect to the means by which the client's objectives are to be pursued, the

lawyer shall consult with the client as required by Rule 1.4(a)(2) and may take such action as is impliedly authorized to carry out the representation.

[2] On occasion, however, a lawyer and a client may disagree about the means to be used to accomplish the client's objectives. Clients normally defer to the special knowledge and skill of their lawyer with respect to the means to be used to accomplish their objectives, particularly with respect to technical, legal and tactical matters. Conversely, lawyers usually defer to the client regarding such questions as the expense to be incurred and concern for third persons who might be adversely affected. Because of the varied nature of the matters about which a lawyer and client might disagree and because the actions in question may implicate the interests of a tribunal or other persons, this Rule does not prescribe how such disagreements are to be resolved. Other law, however, may be applicable and should be consulted by the lawyer. The lawyer should also consult with the client and seek a mutually acceptable resolution of the disagreement. If such efforts are unavailing and the lawyer has a fundamental disagreement with the client, the lawyer may withdraw from the representation. See Rule 1.16(b)(4). Conversely, the client may resolve the disagreement by discharging the lawyer. See Rule 1.16(a)(3).

[3] At the outset of a representation, the client may authorize the lawyer to take specific action on the client's behalf without further consultation. Absent a material change in circumstances and subject to Rule 1.4, a lawyer may rely on such an advance authorization. The client may, however, revoke such authority at any time.

[4] In a case in which the client appears to be suffering diminished capacity, the lawyer's duty to abide by the client's decisions is to be guided by reference to Rule 1.14.

Independence from Client's Views or Activities

[5] Legal representation should not be denied to people who are unable to afford legal services, or whose cause is controversial or the subject of popular disapproval. By the same token, representing a client does not constitute approval of the client's views or activities.

Agreements Limiting Scope of Representation

[6] The scope of services to be provided by a lawyer may be limited by agreement with the client or by the terms under which the lawyer's services are made available to the client. When a lawyer has been retained by an insurer to represent an insured, for example, the representation may be limited to matters related to the insurance coverage. A limited representation may be appropriate because the client has limited objectives for the representation. In addition, the terms upon which representation is undertaken may exclude specific means that might otherwise be used to accomplish the client's objectives. Such limitations may exclude actions that the client thinks are too costly or that the lawyer regards as repugnant or imprudent.

[7] Although this Rule affords the lawyer and client substantial latitude to limit the representation, the limitation must be reasonable under the circumstances. If, for example, a client's objective is limited to securing general information about

the law the client needs in order to handle a common and typically uncomplicated legal problem, the lawyer and client may agree that the lawyer's services will be limited to a brief telephone consultation. Such a limitation, however, would not be reasonable if the time allotted was not sufficient to yield advice upon which the client could rely. Although an agreement for a limited representation does not exempt a lawyer from the duty to provide competent representation, the limitation is a factor to be considered when determining the legal knowledge, skill, thoroughness and preparation reasonably necessary for the representation. See Rule 1.1.

[8] All agreements concerning a lawyer's representation of a client must accord with the Rules of Professional Conduct and other law. See, e.g., Rules 1.1, 1.8 and 5.6.

Criminal, Fraudulent and Prohibited Transactions

[9] Paragraph (d) prohibits a lawyer from knowingly counseling or assisting a client to commit a crime or fraud. This prohibition, however, does not preclude the lawyer from giving an honest opinion about the actual consequences that appear likely to result from a client's conduct. Nor does the fact that a client uses advice in a course of action that is criminal or fraudulent of itself make a lawyer a party to the course of action. There is a critical distinction between presenting an analysis of legal aspects of questionable conduct and recommending the means by which a crime or fraud might be committed with impunity.

[10] When the client's course of action has already begun and is continuing, the lawyer's responsibility is especially delicate. The lawyer is required to avoid assisting the client, for example, by drafting or delivering documents that the lawyer knows are fraudulent or by suggesting how the wrongdoing might be concealed. A lawyer may not continue assisting a client in conduct that the lawyer originally supposed was legally proper but then discovers is criminal or fraudulent. The lawyer must, therefore, withdraw from the representation of the client in the matter. See Rule 1.16(a). In some cases, withdrawal alone might be insufficient. It may be necessary for the lawyer to give notice of the fact of withdrawal and to disaffirm any opinion, document, affirmation or the like. See Rule 4.1.

[11] Where the client is a fiduciary, the lawyer may be charged with special obligations in dealings with a beneficiary.

[12] Paragraph (d) applies whether or not the defrauded party is a party to the transaction. Hence, a lawyer must not participate in a transaction to effectuate criminal or fraudulent avoidance of tax liability. Paragraph (d) does not preclude undertaking a criminal defense incident to a general retainer for legal services to a lawful enterprise. The last clause of paragraph (d) recognizes that determining the validity or interpretation of a statute or regulation may require a course of action involving disobedience of the statute or regulation or of the interpretation placed upon it by governmental authorities.

[13] If a lawyer comes to know or reasonably should know that a client expects assistance not permitted by the Rules of Professional Conduct or other law or if the lawyer intends to act contrary to the client's instructions, the lawyer

must consult with the client regarding the limitations on the lawyer's conduct. See Rule 1.4(a)(5).

Definitional Cross-References

"Fraudulent" *See* Rule 1.0(d)
"Informed consent" *See* Rule 1.0(e)
"Knows" *See* Rule 1.0(f)
"Reasonable" *See* Rule 1.0(h)

Rule 1.3 Diligence

A lawyer shall act with reasonable diligence and promptness in representing a client.

Comment

[1] A lawyer should pursue a matter on behalf of a client despite opposition, obstruction or personal inconvenience to the lawyer, and take whatever lawful and ethical measures are required to vindicate a client's cause or endeavor. A lawyer must also act with commitment and dedication to the interests of the client and with zeal in advocacy upon the client's behalf. A lawyer is not bound, however, to press for every advantage that might be realized for a client. For example, a lawyer may have authority to exercise professional discretion in determining the means by which a matter should be pursued. See Rule 1.2. The lawyer's duty to act with reasonable diligence does not require the use of offensive tactics or preclude the treating of all persons involved in the legal process with courtesy and respect.

[2] A lawyer's work load must be controlled so that each matter can be handled competently.

[3] Perhaps no professional shortcoming is more widely resented than procrastination. A client's interests often can be adversely affected by the passage of time or the change of conditions; in extreme instances, as when a lawyer overlooks a statute of limitations, the client's legal position may be destroyed. Even when the client's interests are not affected in substance, however, unreasonable delay can cause a client needless anxiety and undermine confidence in the lawyer's trustworthiness. A lawyer's duty to act with reasonable promptness, however, does not preclude the lawyer from agreeing to a reasonable request for a postponement that will not prejudice the lawyer's client.

[4] Unless the relationship is terminated as provided in Rule 1.16, a lawyer should carry through to conclusion all matters undertaken for a client. If a lawyer's employment is limited to a specific matter, the relationship terminates when the matter has been resolved. If a lawyer has served a client over a substantial period in a variety of matters, the client sometimes may assume that the lawyer will continue to serve on a continuing basis unless the lawyer gives notice of withdrawal. Doubt about whether a client-lawyer relationship still exists should be clarified by the lawyer, preferably in writing, so that the client will not mistakenly suppose the lawyer

is looking after the client's affairs when the lawyer has ceased to do so. For example, if a lawyer has handled a judicial or administrative proceeding that produced a result adverse to the client and the lawyer and the client have not agreed that the lawyer will handle the matter on appeal, the lawyer must consult with the client about the possibility of appeal before relinquishing responsibility for the matter. See Rule 1.4(a)(2). Whether the lawyer is obligated to prosecute the appeal for the client depends on the scope of the representation the lawyer has agreed to provide to the client. See Rule 1.2.

[5] To prevent neglect of client matters in the event of a sole practitioner's death or disability, the duty of diligence may require that each sole practitioner prepare a plan, in conformity with applicable rules, that designates another competent lawyer to review client files, notify each client of the lawyer's death or disability, and determine whether there is a need for immediate protective action. Cf. Rule 28 of the American Bar Association *Model Rules for Lawyer Disciplinary Enforcement* (providing for court appointment of a lawyer to inventory files and take other protective action in absence of a plan providing for another lawyer to protect the interests of the clients of a deceased or disabled lawyer).

Definitional Cross-References

"Reasonable" *See* Rule 1.0(h)

Rule 1.4 Communication

(a) A lawyer shall:

(1) promptly inform the client of any decision or circumstance with respect to which the client's informed consent, as defined in Rule 1.0(e), is required by these Rules;

(2) reasonably consult with the client about the means by which the client's objectives are to be accomplished;

(3) keep the client reasonably informed about the status of the matter;

(4) promptly comply with reasonable requests for information; and

(5) consult with the client about any relevant limitation on the lawyer's conduct when the lawyer knows that the client expects assistance not permitted by the Rules of Professional Conduct or other law.

(b) A lawyer shall explain a matter to the extent reasonably necessary to permit the client to make informed decisions regarding the representation.

Comment

[1] Reasonable communication between the lawyer and the client is necessary for the client effectively to participate in the representation.

Communicating with Client

[2] If these Rules require that a particular decision about the representation be made by the client, paragraph (a)(1) requires that the lawyer promptly consult

with and secure the client's consent prior to taking action unless prior discussions with the client have resolved what action the client wants the lawyer to take. For example, a lawyer who receives from opposing counsel an offer of settlement in a civil controversy or a proffered plea bargain in a criminal case must promptly inform the client of its substance unless the client has previously indicated that the proposal will be acceptable or unacceptable or has authorized the lawyer to accept or to reject the offer. See Rule 1.2(a).

[3] Paragraph (a)(2) requires the lawyer to reasonably consult with the client about the means to be used to accomplish the client's objectives. In some situations— depending on both the importance of the action under consideration and the feasibility of consulting with the client— this duty will require consultation prior to taking action. In other circumstances, such as during a trial when an immediate decision must be made, the exigency of the situation may require the lawyer to act without prior consultation. In such cases the lawyer must nonetheless act reasonably to inform the client of actions the lawyer has taken on the client's behalf. Additionally, paragraph (a)(3) requires that the lawyer keep the client reasonably informed about the status of the matter, such as significant developments affecting the timing or the substance of the representation.

[4] A lawyer's regular communication with clients will minimize the occasions on which a client will need to request information concerning the representation. When a client makes a reasonable request for information, however, paragraph (a)(4) requires prompt compliance with the request, or if a prompt response is not feasible, that the lawyer, or a member of the lawyer's staff, acknowledge receipt of the request and advise the client when a response may be expected. A lawyer should promptly respond to or acknowledge client communications.

Explaining Matters

[5] The client should have sufficient information to participate intelligently in decisions concerning the objectives of the representation and the means by which they are to be pursued, to the extent the client is willing and able to do so. Adequacy of communication depends in part on the kind of advice or assistance that is involved. For example, when there is time to explain a proposal made in a negotiation, the lawyer should review all important provisions with the client before proceeding to an agreement. In litigation a lawyer should explain the general strategy and prospects of success and ordinarily should consult the client on tactics that are likely to result in significant expense or to injure or coerce others. On the other hand, a lawyer ordinarily will not be expected to describe trial or negotiation strategy in detail. The guiding principle is that the lawyer should fulfill reasonable client expectations for information consistent with the duty to act in the client's best interests, and the client's overall requirements as to the character of representation. In certain circumstances, such as when a lawyer asks a client to consent to a representation affected by a conflict of interest, the client must give informed consent, as defined in Rule 1.0(e).

[6] Ordinarily, the information to be provided is that appropriate for a client who is a comprehending and responsible adult. However, fully informing the client

according to this standard may be impracticable, for example, where the client is a child or suffers from diminished capacity. See Rule 1.14. When the client is an organization or group, it is often impossible or inappropriate to inform every one of its members about its legal affairs; ordinarily, the lawyer should address communications to the appropriate officials of the organization. See Rule 1.13. Where many routine matters are involved, a system of limited or occasional reporting may be arranged with the client.

Withholding Information

[7] In some circumstances, a lawyer may be justified in delaying transmission of information when the client would be likely to react imprudently to an immediate communication. Thus, a lawyer might withhold a psychiatric diagnosis of a client when the examining psychiatrist indicates that disclosure would harm the client. A lawyer may not withhold information to serve the lawyer's own interest or convenience or the interests or convenience of another person. Rules or court orders governing litigation may provide that information supplied to a lawyer may not be disclosed to the client. Rule 3.4(c) directs compliance with such rules or orders.

Definitional Cross-References

"Informed consent" *See* Rule 1.0(e)
"Knows" *See* Rule 1.0(f)
"Reasonably" *See* Rule 1.0(h)

Rule 1.5 Fees

(a) A lawyer shall not make an agreement for, charge, or collect an unreasonable fee or an unreasonable amount for expenses. The factors to be considered in determining the reasonableness of a fee include the following:

(1) the time and labor required, the novelty and difficulty of the questions involved, and the skill requisite to perform the legal service properly;

(2) the likelihood, if apparent to the client, that the acceptance of the particular employment will preclude other employment by the lawyer;

(3) the fee customarily charged in the locality for similar legal services;

(4) the amount involved and the results obtained;

(5) the time limitations imposed by the client or by the circumstances;

(6) the nature and length of the professional relationship with the client;

(7) the experience, reputation, and ability of the lawyer or lawyers performing the services; and

(8) whether the fee is fixed or contingent.

(b) The scope of the representation and the basis or rate of the fee and expenses for which the client will be responsible shall be communicated to the client, preferably in writing, before or within a reasonable time after commencing the representation, except when the lawyer will charge a regularly represented client on the same basis or rate. Any changes in the basis or rate of the fee or expenses shall also be communicated to the client.

(c) A fee may be contingent on the outcome of the matter for which the service is rendered, except in a matter in which a contingent fee is prohibited by paragraph (d) or other law. A contingent fee agreement shall be in a writing signed by the client and shall state the method by which the fee is to be determined, including the percentage or percentages that shall accrue to the lawyer in the event of settlement, trial or appeal; litigation and other expenses to be deducted from the recovery; and whether such expenses are to be deducted before or after the contingent fee is calculated. The agreement must clearly notify the client of any expenses for which the client will be liable whether or not the client is the prevailing party. Upon conclusion of a contingent fee matter, the lawyer shall provide the client with a written statement stating the outcome of the matter and, if there is a recovery, showing the remittance to the client and the method of its determination.

(d) A lawyer shall not enter into an arrangement for, charge, or collect:

(1) any fee in a domestic relations matter, the payment or amount of which is contingent upon the securing of a divorce or upon the amount of alimony or support, or property settlement in lieu thereof; or

(2) a contingent fee for representing a defendant in a criminal case.

(e) A division of a fee between lawyers who are not in the same firm may be made only if:

(1) the division is in proportion to the services performed by each lawyer or each lawyer assumes joint responsibility for the representation;

(2) the client agrees to the arrangement, including the share each lawyer will receive, and the agreement is confirmed in writing; and

(3) the total fee is reasonable.

Comment

Reasonableness of Fee and Expenses

[1] Paragraph (a) requires that lawyers charge fees that are reasonable under the circumstances. The factors specified in (1) through (8) are not exclusive. Nor will each factor be relevant in each instance. Paragraph (a) also requires that expenses for which the client will be charged must be reasonable. A lawyer may seek reimbursement for the cost of services performed in-house, such as copying, or for other expenses incurred inhouse, such as telephone charges, either by charging a reasonable amount to which the client has agreed in advance or by charging an amount that reasonably reflects the cost incurred by the lawyer.

Basis or Rate of Fee

[2] When the lawyer has regularly represented a client, they ordinarily will have evolved an understanding concerning the basis or rate of the fee and the expenses for which the client will be responsible. In a new client-lawyer relationship, however, an understanding as to fees and expenses must be promptly established. Generally, it is desirable to furnish the client with at least a simple memorandum or copy of the lawyer's customary fee arrangements that states the general nature

of the legal services to be provided, the basis, rate or total amount of the fee and whether and to what extent the client will be responsible for any costs, expenses or disbursements in the course of the representation. A written statement concerning the terms of the engagement reduces the possibility of misunderstanding.

[3] Contingent fees, like any other fees, are subject to the reasonableness standard of paragraph (a) of this Rule. In determining whether a particular contingent fee is reasonable, or whether it is reasonable to charge any form of contingent fee, a lawyer must consider the factors that are relevant under the circumstances. Applicable law may impose limitations on contingent fees, such as a ceiling on the percentage allowable, or may require a lawyer to offer clients an alternative basis for the fee. Applicable law also may apply to situations other than a contingent fee, for example, government regulations regarding fees in certain tax matters.

Terms of Payment

[4] A lawyer may require advance payment of a fee, but is obliged to return any unearned portion. See Rule 1.16(d). A lawyer may accept property in payment for services, such as an ownership interest in an enterprise, providing this does not involve acquisition of a proprietary interest in the cause of action or subject matter of the litigation contrary to Rule 1.8 (i). However, a fee paid in property instead of money may be subject to the requirements of Rule 1.8(a) because such fees often have the essential qualities of a business transaction with the client.

[5] An agreement may not be made whose terms might induce the lawyer improperly to curtail services for the client or perform them in a way contrary to the client's interest. For example, a lawyer should not enter into an agreement whereby services are to be provided only up to a stated amount when it is foreseeable that more extensive services probably will be required, unless the situation is adequately explained to the client. Otherwise, the client might have to bargain for further assistance in the midst of a proceeding or transaction. However, it is proper to define the extent of services in light of the client's ability to pay. A lawyer should not exploit a fee arrangement based primarily on hourly charges by using wasteful procedures.

Prohibited Contingent Fees

[6] Paragraph (d) prohibits a lawyer from charging a contingent fee in a domestic relations matter when payment is contingent upon the securing of a divorce or upon the amount of alimony or support or property settlement to be obtained. This provision does not preclude a contract for a contingent fee for legal representation in connection with the recovery of post-judgment balances due under support, alimony or other financial orders because such contracts do not implicate the same policy concerns.

Division of Fee

[7] A division of fee is a single billing to a client covering the fee of two or more lawyers who are not in the same firm. A division of fee facilitates association of more than one lawyer in a matter in which neither alone could serve the client as

well, and most often is used when the fee is contingent and the division is between a referring lawyer and a trial specialist. Paragraph (e) permits the lawyers to divide a fee either on the basis of the proportion of services they render or if each lawyer assumes responsibility for the representation as a whole. In addition, the client must agree to the arrangement, including the share that each lawyer is to receive, and the agreement must be confirmed in writing. Contingent fee agreements must be in a writing signed by the client and must otherwise comply with paragraph (c) of this Rule. Joint responsibility for the representation entails financial and ethical responsibility for the representation as if the lawyers were associated in a partnership. A lawyer should only refer a matter to a lawyer whom the referring lawyer reasonably believes is competent to handle the matter. See Rule 1.1.

[8] Paragraph (e) does not prohibit or regulate division of fees to be received in the future for work done when lawyers were previously associated in a law firm.

Disputes over Fees

[9] If a procedure has been established for resolution of fee disputes, such as an arbitration or mediation procedure established by the bar, the lawyer must comply with the procedure when it is mandatory, and, even when it is voluntary, the lawyer should conscientiously consider submitting to it. Law may prescribe a procedure for determining a lawyer's fee, for example, in representation of an executor or administrator, a class or a person entitled to a reasonable fee as part of the measure of damages. The lawyer entitled to such a fee and a lawyer representing another party concerned with the fee should comply with the prescribed procedure.

Definitional Cross-References

"Confirmed in writing" *See* Rule 1.0(b)
"Firm" *See* Rule 1.0(c)
"Writing" and "Written" and "Signed" *See* Rule 1.0(n)

Rule 1.6 Confidentiality of Information

(a) A lawyer shall not reveal information relating to the representation of a client unless the client gives informed consent, the disclosure is impliedly authorized in order to carry out the representation or the disclosure is permitted by paragraph (b).

(b) A lawyer may reveal information relating to the representation of a client to the extent the lawyer reasonably believes necessary:

(1) to prevent reasonably certain death or substantial bodily harm;

(2) to prevent the client from committing a crime or fraud that is reasonably certain to result in substantial injury to the financial interests or property of another and in furtherance of which the client has used or is using the lawyer's services;

(3) to prevent, mitigate or rectify substantial injury to the financial interests or property of another that is reasonably certain to result or has

resulted from the client's commission of a crime or fraud in furtherance of which the client has used the lawyer's services;

(4) to secure legal advice about the lawyer's compliance with these Rules;

(5) to establish a claim or defense on behalf of the lawyer in a controversy between the lawyer and the client, to establish a defense to a criminal charge or civil claim against the lawyer based upon conduct in which the client was involved, or to respond to allegations in any proceeding concerning the lawyer's representation of the client;

(6) to comply with other law or a court order; or

(7) to detect and resolve conflicts of interest arising from the lawyer's change of employment or from changes in the composition or ownership of a firm, but only if the revealed information would not compromise the attorney-client privilege or otherwise prejudice the client.

(c) A lawyer shall make reasonable efforts to prevent the inadvertent or unauthorized disclosure of, or unauthorized access to, information relating to the representation of a client.

Comment

[1] This Rule governs the disclosure by a lawyer of information relating to the representation of a client during the lawyer's representation of the client. See Rule 1.18 for the lawyer's duties with respect to information provided to the lawyer by a prospective client, Rule 1.9(c)(2) for the lawyer's duty not to reveal information relating to the lawyer's prior representation of a former client and Rules 1.8(b) and 1.9(c)(1) for the lawyer's duties with respect to the use of such information to the disadvantage of clients and former clients.

[2] A fundamental principle in the client-lawyer relationship is that, in the absence of the client's informed consent, the lawyer must not reveal information relating to the representation. See Rule 1.0(e) for the definition of informed consent. This contributes to the trust that is the hallmark of the client-lawyer relationship. The client is thereby encouraged to seek legal assistance and to communicate fully and frankly with the lawyer even as to embarrassing or legally damaging subject matter. The lawyer needs this information to represent the client effectively and, if necessary, to advise the client to refrain from wrongful conduct. Almost without exception, clients come to lawyers in order to determine their rights and what is, in the complex of laws and regulations, deemed to be legal and correct. Based upon experience, lawyers know that almost all clients follow the advice given, and the law is upheld.

[3] The principle of client-lawyer confidentiality is given effect by related bodies of law: the attorney-client privilege, the work product doctrine and the rule of confidentiality established in professional ethics. The attorney-client privilege and work product doctrine apply in judicial and other proceedings in which a lawyer may be called as a witness or otherwise required to produce evidence concerning a client. The rule of client-lawyer confidentiality applies in situations other than those where evidence is sought from the lawyer through compulsion of law. The

confidentiality rule, for example, applies not only to matters communicated in confidence by the client but also to all information relating to the representation, whatever its source. A lawyer may not disclose such information except as authorized or required by the Rules of Professional Conduct or other law. See also Scope.

[4] Paragraph (a) prohibits a lawyer from revealing information relating to the representation of a client. This prohibition also applies to disclosures by a lawyer that do not in themselves reveal protected information but could reasonably lead to the discovery of such information by a third person. A lawyer's use of a hypothetical to discuss issues relating to the representation is permissible so long as there is no reasonable likelihood that the listener will be able to ascertain the identity of the client or the situation involved.

Authorized Disclosure

[5] Except to the extent that the client's instructions or special circumstances limit that authority, a lawyer is impliedly authorized to make disclosures about a client when appropriate in carrying out the representation. In some situations, for example, a lawyer may be impliedly authorized to admit a fact that cannot properly be disputed or to make a disclosure that facilitates a satisfactory conclusion to a matter. Lawyers in a firm may, in the course of the firm's practice, disclose to each other information relating to a client of the firm, unless the client has instructed that particular information be confined to specified lawyers.

Disclosure Adverse to Client

[6] Although the public interest is usually best served by a strict rule requiring lawyers to preserve the confidentiality of information relating to the representation of their clients, the confidentiality rule is subject to limited exceptions. Paragraph (b)(1) recognizes the overriding value of life and physical integrity and permits disclosure reasonably necessary to prevent reasonably certain death or substantial bodily harm. Such harm is reasonably certain to occur if it will be suffered imminently or if there is a present and substantial threat that a person will suffer such harm at a later date if the lawyer fails to take action necessary to eliminate the threat. Thus, a lawyer who knows that a client has accidentally discharged toxic waste into a town's water supply may reveal this information to the authorities if there is a present and substantial risk that a person who drinks the water will contract a life-threatening or debilitating disease and the lawyer's disclosure is necessary to eliminate the threat or reduce the number of victims.

[7] Paragraph (b)(2) is a limited exception to the rule of confidentiality that permits the lawyer to reveal information to the extent necessary to enable affected persons or appropriate authorities to prevent the client from committing a crime or fraud, as defined in Rule 1.0(d), that is reasonably certain to result in substantial injury to the financial or property interests of another and in furtherance of which the client has used or is using the lawyer's services. Such a serious abuse of the client-lawyer relationship by the client forfeits the protection of this Rule. The client can, of course, prevent such disclosure by refraining from the wrongful conduct. Although paragraph (b)(2) does not require the lawyer to reveal the client's

misconduct, the lawyer may not counsel or assist the client in conduct the lawyer knows is criminal or fraudulent. See Rule 1.2(d). See also Rule 1.16 with respect to the lawyer's obligation or right to withdraw from the representation of the client in such circumstances, and Rule 1.13(c), which permits the lawyer, where the client is an organization, to reveal information relating to the representation in limited circumstances.

[8] Paragraph (b)(3) addresses the situation in which the lawyer does not learn of the client's crime or fraud until after it has been consummated. Although the client no longer has the option of preventing disclosure by refraining from the wrongful conduct, there will be situations in which the loss suffered by the affected person can be prevented, rectified or mitigated. In such situations, the lawyer may disclose information relating to the representation to the extent necessary to enable the affected persons to prevent or mitigate reasonably certain losses or to attempt to recoup their losses. Paragraph (b)(3) does not apply when a person who has committed a crime or fraud thereafter employs a lawyer for representation concerning that offense.

[9] A lawyer's confidentiality obligations do not preclude a lawyer from securing confidential legal advice about the lawyer's personal responsibility to comply with these Rules. In most situations, disclosing information to secure such advice will be impliedly authorized for the lawyer to carry out the representation. Even when the disclosure is not impliedly authorized, paragraph (b)(4) permits such disclosure because of the importance of a lawyer's compliance with the Rules of Professional Conduct.

[10] Where a legal claim or disciplinary charge alleges complicity of the lawyer in a client's conduct or other misconduct of the lawyer involving representation of the client, the lawyer may respond to the extent the lawyer reasonably believes necessary to establish a defense. The same is true with respect to a claim involving the conduct or representation of a former client. Such a charge can arise in a civil, criminal, disciplinary or other proceeding and can be based on a wrong allegedly committed by the lawyer against the client or on a wrong alleged by a third person, for example, a person claiming to have been defrauded by the lawyer and client acting together. The lawyer's right to respond arises when an assertion of such complicity has been made. Paragraph (b)(5) does not require the lawyer to await the commencement of an action or proceeding that charges such complicity, so that the defense may be established by responding directly to a third party who has made such an assertion. The right to defend also applies, of course, where a proceeding has been commenced.

[11] A lawyer entitled to a fee is permitted by paragraph (b)(5) to prove the services rendered in an action to collect it. This aspect of the rule expresses the principle that the beneficiary of a fiduciary relationship may not exploit it to the detriment of the fiduciary.

[12] Other law may require that a lawyer disclose information about a client. Whether such a law supersedes Rule 1.6 is a question of law beyond the scope of these Rules. When disclosure of information relating to the representation appears to be required by other law, the lawyer must discuss the matter with the client to

the extent required by Rule 1.4. If, however, the other law supersedes this Rule and requires disclosure, paragraph (b)(6) permits the lawyer to make such disclosures as are necessary to comply with the law.

Detection of Conflicts of Interest

[13] Paragraph (b)(7) recognizes that lawyers in different firms may need to disclose limited information to each other to detect and resolve conflicts of interest, such as when a lawyer is considering an association with another firm, two or more firms are considering a merger, or a lawyer is considering the purchase of a law practice. See Rule 1.17, Comment [7]. Under these circumstances, lawyers and law firms are permitted to disclose limited information, but only once substantive discussions regarding the new relationship have occurred. Any such disclosure should ordinarily include no more than the identity of the persons and entities involved in a matter, a brief summary of the general issues involved, and information about whether the matter has terminated. Even this limited information, however, should be disclosed only to the extent reasonably necessary to detect and resolve conflicts of interest that might arise from the possible new relationship. Moreover, the disclosure of any information is prohibited if it would compromise the attorney-client privilege or otherwise prejudice the client (e.g., the fact that a corporate client is seeking advice on a corporate takeover that has not been publicly announced; that a person has consulted a lawyer about the possibility of divorce before the person's intentions are known to the person's spouse; or that a person has consulted a lawyer about a criminal investigation that has not led to a public charge). Under those circumstances, paragraph (a) prohibits disclosure unless the client or former client gives informed consent. A lawyer's fiduciary duty to the lawyer's firm may also govern a lawyer's conduct when exploring an association with another firm and is beyond the scope of these Rules.

[14] Any information disclosed pursuant to paragraph (b)(7) may be used or further disclosed only to the extent necessary to detect and resolve conflicts of interest. Paragraph (b)(7) does not restrict the use of information acquired by means independent of any disclosure pursuant to paragraph (b)(7). Paragraph (b)(7) also does not affect the disclosure of information within a law firm when the disclosure is otherwise authorized, see Comment [5], such as when a lawyer in a firm discloses information to another lawyer in the same firm to detect and resolve conflicts of interest that could arise in connection with undertaking a new representation.

[15] A lawyer may be ordered to reveal information relating to the representation of a client by a court or by another tribunal or governmental entity claiming authority pursuant to other law to compel the disclosure. Absent informed consent of the client to do otherwise, the lawyer should assert on behalf of the client all nonfrivolous claims that the order is not authorized by other law or that the information sought is protected against disclosure by the attorney-client privilege or other applicable law. In the event of an adverse ruling, the lawyer must consult with the client about the possibility of appeal to the extent required by Rule 1.4. Unless review is sought, however, paragraph (b)(6) permits the lawyer to comply with the court's order.

[16] Paragraph (b) permits disclosure only to the extent the lawyer reasonably believes the disclosure is necessary to accomplish one of the purposes specified. Where practicable, the lawyer should first seek to persuade the client to take suitable action to obviate the need for disclosure. In any case, a disclosure adverse to the client's interest should be no greater than the lawyer reasonably believes necessary to accomplish the purpose. If the disclosure will be made in connection with a judicial proceeding, the disclosure should be made in a manner that limits access to the information to the tribunal or other persons having a need to know it and appropriate protective orders or other arrangements should be sought by the lawyer to the fullest extent practicable.

[17] Paragraph (b) permits but does not require the disclosure of information relating to a client's representation to accomplish the purposes specified in paragraphs (b)(1) through (b)(6). In exercising the discretion conferred by this Rule, the lawyer may consider such factors as the nature of the lawyer's relationship with the client and with those who might be injured by the client, the lawyer's own involvement in the transaction and factors that may extenuate the conduct in question. A lawyer's decision not to disclose as permitted by paragraph (b) does not violate this Rule. Disclosure may be required, however, by other Rules. Some Rules require disclosure only if such disclosure would be permitted by paragraph (b). See Rules 1.2(d), 4.1(b), 8.1 and 8.3. Rule 3.3, on the other hand, requires disclosure in some circumstances regardless of whether such disclosure is permitted by this Rule. See Rule 3.3(c).

Acting Competently to Preserve Confidentiality

[18] Paragraph (c) requires a lawyer to act competently to safeguard information relating to the representation of a client against unauthorized access by third parties and against inadvertent or unauthorized disclosure by the lawyer or other persons who are participating in the representation of the client or who are subject to the lawyer's supervision. See Rules 1.1, 5.1 and 5.3. The unauthorized access to, or the inadvertent or unauthorized disclosure of, information relating to the representation of a client does not constitute a violation of paragraph (c) if the lawyer has made reasonable efforts to prevent the access or disclosure. Factors to be considered in determining the reasonableness of the lawyer's efforts include, but are not limited to, the sensitivity of the information, the likelihood of disclosure if additional safeguards are not employed, the cost of employing additional safeguards, the difficulty of implementing the safeguards, and the extent to which the safeguards adversely affect the lawyer's ability to represent clients (e.g., by making a device or important piece of software excessively difficult to use). A client may require the lawyer to implement special security measures not required by this Rule or may give informed consent to forgo security measures that would otherwise be required by this Rule. Whether a lawyer may be required to take additional steps to safeguard a client's information in order to comply with other law, such as state and federal laws that govern data privacy or that impose notification requirements upon the loss of, or unauthorized access to, electronic information, is beyond the scope of these Rules. For a lawyer's duties

when sharing information with nonlawyers outside the lawyer's own firm, see Rule 5.3, Comments [3]-[4].

[19] When transmitting a communication that includes information relating to the representation of a client, the lawyer must take reasonable precautions to prevent the information from coming into the hands of unintended recipients. This duty, however, does not require that the lawyer use special security measures if the method of communication affords a reasonable expectation of privacy. Special circumstances, however, may warrant special precautions. Factors to be considered in determining the reasonableness of the lawyer's expectation of confidentiality include the sensitivity of the information and the extent to which the privacy of the communication is protected by law or by a confidentiality agreement. A client may require the lawyer to implement special security measures not required by this Rule or may give informed consent to the use of a means of communication that would otherwise be prohibited by this Rule. Whether a lawyer may be required to take additional steps in order to comply with other law, such as state and federal laws that govern data privacy, is beyond the scope of these Rules.

Former Client

[20] The duty of confidentiality continues after the client-lawyer relationship has terminated. See Rule 1.9(c)(2). See Rule 1.9(c)(1) for the prohibition against using such information to the disadvantage of the former client.

Definitional Cross-References

"Firm" *See* Rule 1.0(c)
"Fraud" *See* Rule 1.0(d)
"Informed consent" *See* Rule 1.0(e)
"Reasonable" and "Reasonably" *See* Rule 1.0(h)
"Reasonably believes" *See* Rule 1.0(i)
"Substantial" *See* Rule 1.0(l)

Rule 1.7 Conflict of Interest: Current Clients

(a) Except as provided in paragraph (b), a lawyer shall not represent a client if the representation involves a concurrent conflict of interest. A concurrent conflict of interest exists if:

(1) the representation of one client will be directly adverse to another client; or

(2) there is a significant risk that the representation of one or more clients will be materially limited by the lawyer's responsibilities to another client, a former client or a third person or by a personal interest of the lawyer.

(b) Notwithstanding the existence of a concurrent conflict of interest under paragraph (a), a lawyer may represent a client if:

(1) the lawyer reasonably believes that the lawyer will be able to provide competent and diligent representation to each affected client;

(2) the representation is not prohibited by law;

(3) the representation does not involve the assertion of a claim by one client against another client represented by the lawyer in the same litigation or other proceeding before a tribunal; and

(4) each affected client gives informed consent, confirmed in writing.

Comment

General Principles

[1] Loyalty and independent judgment are essential elements in the lawyer's relationship to a client. Concurrent conflicts of interest can arise from the lawyer's responsibilities to another client, a former client or a third person or from the lawyer's own interests. For specific Rules regarding certain concurrent conflicts of interest, see Rule 1.8. For former client conflicts of interest, see Rule 1.9. For conflicts of interest involving prospective clients, see Rule 1.18. For definitions of "informed consent" and "confirmed in writing," see Rule 1.0(e) and (b).

[2] Resolution of a conflict of interest problem under this Rule requires the lawyer to: 1) clearly identify the client or clients; 2) determine whether a conflict of interest exists; 3) decide whether the representation may be undertaken despite the existence of a conflict, i.e., whether the conflict is consentable; and 4) if so, consult with the clients affected under paragraph (a) and obtain their informed consent, confirmed in writing. The clients affected under paragraph (a) include both of the clients referred to in paragraph (a)(1) and the one or more clients whose representation might be materially limited under paragraph (a)(2).

[3] A conflict of interest may exist before representation is undertaken, in which event the representation must be declined, unless the lawyer obtains the informed consent of each client under the conditions of paragraph (b). To determine whether a conflict of interest exists, a lawyer should adopt reasonable procedures, appropriate for the size and type of firm and practice, to determine in both litigation and non-litigation matters the persons and issues involved. See also Comment to Rule 5.1. Ignorance caused by a failure to institute such procedures will not excuse a lawyer's violation of this Rule. As to whether a client-lawyer relationship exists or, having once been established, is continuing, see Comment to Rule 1.3 and Scope.

[4] If a conflict arises after representation has been undertaken, the lawyer ordinarily must withdraw from the representation, unless the lawyer has obtained the informed consent of the client under the conditions of paragraph (b). See Rule 1.16. Where more than one client is involved, whether the lawyer may continue to represent any of the clients is determined both by the lawyer's ability to comply with duties owed to the former client and by the lawyer's ability to represent adequately the remaining client or clients, given the lawyer's duties to the former client. See Rule 1.9. See also Comments [5] and [29].

[5] Unforeseeable developments, such as changes in corporate and other organizational affiliations or the addition or realignment of parties in litigation, might create conflicts in the midst of a representation, as when a company sued by the lawyer on behalf of one client is bought by another client represented by the lawyer in an unrelated matter. Depending on the circumstances, the lawyer may have the

option to withdraw from one of the representations in order to avoid the conflict. The lawyer must seek court approval where necessary and take steps to minimize harm to the clients. See Rule 1.16. The lawyer must continue to protect the confidences of the client from whose representation the lawyer has withdrawn. See Rule 1.9(c).

Identifying Conflicts of Interest: Directly Adverse

[6] Loyalty to a current client prohibits undertaking representation directly adverse to that client without that client's informed consent. Thus, absent consent, a lawyer may not act as an advocate in one matter against a person the lawyer represents in some other matter, even when the matters are wholly unrelated. The client as to whom the representation is directly adverse is likely to feel betrayed, and the resulting damage to the client-lawyer relationship is likely to impair the lawyer's ability to represent the client effectively. In addition, the client on whose behalf the adverse representation is undertaken reasonably may fear that the lawyer will pursue that client's case less effectively out of deference to the other client, i.e., that the representation may be materially limited by the lawyer's interest in retaining the current client. Similarly, a directly adverse conflict may arise when a lawyer is required to cross-examine a client who appears as a witness in a lawsuit involving another client, as when the testimony will be damaging to the client who is represented in the lawsuit. On the other hand, simultaneous representation in unrelated matters of clients whose interests are only economically adverse, such as representation of competing economic enterprises in unrelated litigation, does not ordinarily constitute a conflict of interest and thus may not require consent of the respective clients.

[7] Directly adverse conflicts can also arise in transactional matters. For example, if a lawyer is asked to represent the seller of a business in negotiations with a buyer represented by the lawyer, not in the same transaction but in another, unrelated matter, the lawyer could not undertake the representation without the informed consent of each client.

Identifying Conflicts of Interest: Material Limitation

[8] Even where there is no direct adverseness, a conflict of interest exists if there is a significant risk that a lawyer's ability to consider, recommend or carry out an appropriate course of action for the client will be materially limited as a result of the lawyer's other responsibilities or interests. For example, a lawyer asked to represent several individuals seeking to form a joint venture is likely to be materially limited in the lawyer's ability to recommend or advocate all possible positions that each might take because of the lawyer's duty of loyalty to the others. The conflict in effect forecloses alternatives that would otherwise be available to the client. The mere possibility of subsequent harm does not itself require disclosure and consent. The critical questions are the likelihood that a difference in interests will eventuate and, if it does, whether it will materially interfere with the lawyer's independent professional judgment in considering alternatives or foreclose courses of action that reasonably should be pursued on behalf of the client.

Lawyer's Responsibilities to Former Clients and Other Third Persons

[9] In addition to conflicts with other current clients, a lawyer's duties of loyalty and independence may be materially limited by responsibilities to former clients under Rule 1.9 or by the lawyer's responsibilities to other persons, such as fiduciary duties arising from a lawyer's service as a trustee, executor or corporate director.

Personal Interest Conflicts

[10] The lawyer's own interests should not be permitted to have an adverse effect on representation of a client. For example, if the probity of a lawyer's own conduct in a transaction is in serious question, it may be difficult or impossible for the lawyer to give a client detached advice. Similarly, when a lawyer has discussions concerning possible employment with an opponent of the lawyer's client, or with a law firm representing the opponent, such discussions could materially limit the lawyer's representation of the client. In addition, a lawyer may not allow related business interests to affect representation, for example, by referring clients to an enterprise in which the lawyer has an undisclosed financial interest. See Rule 1.8 for specific Rules pertaining to a number of personal interest conflicts, including business transactions with clients. See also Rule 1.10 (personal interest conflicts under Rule 1.7 ordinarily are not imputed to other lawyers in a law firm).

[11] When lawyers representing different clients in the same matter or in substantially related matters are closely related by blood or marriage, there may be a significant risk that client confidences will be revealed and that the lawyer's family relationship will interfere with both loyalty and independent professional judgment. As a result, each client is entitled to know of the existence and implications of the relationship between the lawyers before the lawyer agrees to undertake the representation. Thus, a lawyer related to another lawyer, e.g., as parent, child, sibling or spouse, ordinarily may not represent a client in a matter where that lawyer is representing another party, unless each client gives informed consent. The disqualification arising from a close family relationship is personal and ordinarily is not imputed to members of firms with whom the lawyers are associated. See Rule 1.10.

[12] A lawyer is prohibited from engaging in sexual relationships with a client unless the sexual relationship predates the formation of the client-lawyer relationship. See Rule 1.8(j).

Interest of Person Paying for a Lawyer's Service

[13] A lawyer may be paid from a source other than the client, including a co-client, if the client is informed of that fact and consents and the arrangement does not compromise the lawyer's duty of loyalty or independent judgment to the client. See Rule 1.8(f). If acceptance of the payment from any other source presents a significant risk that the lawyer's representation of the client will be materially limited by the lawyer's own interest in accommodating the person paying the lawyer's fee or by the lawyer's responsibilities to a payer who is also a co-client, then the lawyer must comply with the requirements of paragraph (b) before accepting the representation, including determining whether the conflict is consentable and, if so, that the client has adequate information about the material risks of the representation.

Prohibited Representations

[14] Ordinarily, clients may consent to representation notwithstanding a conflict. However, as indicated in paragraph (b), some conflicts are nonconsentable, meaning that the lawyer involved cannot properly ask for such agreement or provide representation on the basis of the client's consent. When the lawyer is representing more than one client, the question of consentability must be resolved as to each client.

[15] Consentability is typically determined by considering whether the interests of the clients will be adequately protected if the clients are permitted to give their informed consent to representation burdened by a conflict of interest. Thus, under paragraph (b)(1), representation is prohibited if in the circumstances the lawyer cannot reasonably conclude that the lawyer will be able to provide competent and diligent representation. See Rule 1.1 (competence) and Rule 1.3 (diligence).

[16] Paragraph (b)(2) describes conflicts that are nonconsentable because the representation is prohibited by applicable law. For example, in some states substantive law provides that the same lawyer may not represent more than one defendant in a capital case, even with the consent of the clients, and under federal criminal statutes certain representations by a former government lawyer are prohibited, despite the informed consent of the former client. In addition, decisional law in some states limits the ability of a governmental client, such as a municipality, to consent to a conflict of interest.

[17] Paragraph (b)(3) describes conflicts that are nonconsentable because of the institutional interest in vigorous development of each client's position when the clients are aligned directly against each other in the same litigation or other proceeding before a tribunal. Whether clients are aligned directly against each other within the meaning of this paragraph requires examination of the context of the proceeding. Although this paragraph does not preclude a lawyer's multiple representation of adverse parties to a mediation (because mediation is not a proceeding before a "tribunal" under Rule 1.0(m)), such representation may be precluded by paragraph (b)(1).

Informed Consent

[18] Informed consent requires that each affected client be aware of the relevant circumstances and of the material and reasonably foreseeable ways that the conflict could have adverse effects on the interests of that client. See Rule 1.0(e) (informed consent). The information required depends on the nature of the conflict and the nature of the risks involved. When representation of multiple clients in a single matter is undertaken, the information must include the implications of the common representation, including possible effects on loyalty, confidentiality and the attorney-client privilege and the advantages and risks involved. See Comments [30] and [31] (effect of common representation on confidentiality).

[19] Under some circumstances it may be impossible to make the disclosure necessary to obtain consent. For example, when the lawyer represents different clients in related matters and one of the clients refuses to consent to the disclosure necessary to permit the other client to make an informed decision, the lawyer

cannot properly ask the latter to consent. In some cases the alternative to common representation can be that each party may have to obtain separate representation with the possibility of incurring additional costs. These costs, along with the benefits of securing separate representation, are factors that may be considered by the affected client in determining whether common representation is in the client's interests.

Consent Confirmed in Writing

[20] Paragraph (b) requires the lawyer to obtain the informed consent of the client, confirmed in writing. Such a writing may consist of a document executed by the client or one that the lawyer promptly records and transmits to the client following an oral consent. See Rule 1.0(b). See also Rule 1.0(n) (writing includes electronic transmission). If it is not feasible to obtain or transmit the writing at the time the client gives informed consent, then the lawyer must obtain or transmit it within a reasonable time thereafter. See Rule 1.0(b). The requirement of a writing does not supplant the need in most cases for the lawyer to talk with the client, to explain the risks and advantages, if any, of representation burdened with a conflict of interest, as well as reasonably available alternatives, and to afford the client a reasonable opportunity to consider the risks and alternatives and to raise questions and concerns. Rather, the writing is required in order to impress upon clients the seriousness of the decision the client is being asked to make and to avoid disputes or ambiguities that might later occur in the absence of a writing.

Revoking Consent

[21] A client who has given consent to a conflict may revoke the consent and, like any other client, may terminate the lawyer's representation at any time. Whether revoking consent to the client's own representation precludes the lawyer from continuing to represent other clients depends on the circumstances, including the nature of the conflict, whether the client revoked consent because of a material change in circumstances, the reasonable expectations of the other clients and whether material detriment to the other clients or the lawyer would result.

Consent to Future Conflict

[22] Whether a lawyer may properly request a client to waive conflicts that might arise in the future is subject to the test of paragraph (b). The effectiveness of such waivers is generally determined by the extent to which the client reasonably understands the material risks that the waiver entails. The more comprehensive the explanation of the types of future representations that might arise and the actual and reasonably foreseeable adverse consequences of those representations, the greater the likelihood that the client will have the requisite understanding. Thus, if the client agrees to consent to a particular type of conflict with which the client is already familiar, then the consent ordinarily will be effective with regard to that type of conflict. If the consent is general and open ended, then the consent ordinarily will be ineffective, because it is not reasonably likely that the client will have understood the material risks involved. On the other hand, if the client is an

experienced user of the legal services involved and is reasonably informed regarding the risk that a conflict may arise, such consent is more likely to be effective, particularly if, e.g., the client is independently represented by other counsel in giving consent and the consent is limited to future conflicts unrelated to the subject of the representation. In any case, advance consent cannot be effective if the circumstances that materialize in the future are such as would make the conflict nonconsentable under paragraph (b).

Conflicts in Litigation

[23] Paragraph (b)(3) prohibits representation of opposing parties in the same litigation, regardless of the clients' consent. On the other hand, simultaneous representation of parties whose interests in litigation may conflict, such as coplaintiffs or codefendants, is governed by paragraph (a)(2). A conflict may exist by reason of substantial discrepancy in the parties' testimony, incompatibility in positions in relation to an opposing party or the fact that there are substantially different possibilities of settlement of the claims or liabilities in question. Such conflicts can arise in criminal cases as well as civil. The potential for conflict of interest in representing multiple defendants in a criminal case is so grave that ordinarily a lawyer should decline to represent more than one codefendant. On the other hand, common representation of persons having similar interests in civil litigation is proper if the requirements of paragraph (b) are met.

[24] Ordinarily a lawyer may take inconsistent legal positions in different tribunals at different times on behalf of different clients. The mere fact that advocating a legal position on behalf of one client might create precedent adverse to the interests of a client represented by the lawyer in an unrelated matter does not create a conflict of interest. A conflict of interest exists, however, if there is a significant risk that a lawyer's action on behalf of one client will materially limit the lawyer's effectiveness in representing another client in a different case; for example, when a decision favoring one client will create a precedent likely to seriously weaken the position taken on behalf of the other client. Factors relevant in determining whether the clients need to be advised of the risk include: where the cases are pending, whether the issue is substantive or procedural, the temporal relationship between the matters, the significance of the issue to the immediate and long-term interests of the clients involved and the clients' reasonable expectations in retaining the lawyer. If there is significant risk of material limitation, then absent informed consent of the affected clients, the lawyer must refuse one of the representations or withdraw from one or both matters.

[25] When a lawyer represents or seeks to represent a class of plaintiffs or defendants in a class-action lawsuit, unnamed members of the class are ordinarily not considered to be clients of the lawyer for purposes of applying paragraph (a)(1) of this Rule. Thus, the lawyer does not typically need to get the consent of such a person before representing a client suing the person in an unrelated matter. Similarly, a lawyer seeking to represent an opponent in a class action does not typically need the consent of an unnamed member of the class whom the lawyer represents in an unrelated matter.

Nonlitigation Conflicts

[26] Conflicts of interest under paragraphs (a)(1) and (a)(2) arise in contexts other than litigation. For a discussion of directly adverse conflicts in transactional matters, see Comment [7]. Relevant factors in determining whether there is significant potential for material limitation include the duration and intimacy of the lawyer's relationship with the client or clients involved, the functions being performed by the lawyer, the likelihood that disagreements will arise and the likely prejudice to the client from the conflict. The question is often one of proximity and degree. See Comment [8].

[27] For example, conflict questions may arise in estate planning and estate administration. A lawyer may be called upon to prepare wills for several family members, such as husband and wife, and, depending upon the circumstances, a conflict of interest may be present. In estate administration the identity of the client may be unclear under the law of a particular jurisdiction. Under one view, the client is the fiduciary; under another view the client is the estate or trust, including its beneficiaries. In order to comply with conflict of interest rules, the lawyer should make clear the lawyer's relationship to the parties involved.

[28] Whether a conflict is consentable depends on the circumstances. For example, a lawyer may not represent multiple parties to a negotiation whose interests are fundamentally antagonistic to each other, but common representation is permissible where the clients are generally aligned in interest even though there is some difference in interest among them. Thus, a lawyer may seek to establish or adjust a relationship between clients on an amicable and mutually advantageous basis; for example, in helping to organize a business in which two or more clients are entrepreneurs, working out the financial reorganization of an enterprise in which two or more clients have an interest or arranging a property distribution in settlement of an estate. The lawyer seeks to resolve potentially adverse interests by developing the parties' mutual interests. Otherwise, each party might have to obtain separate representation, with the possibility of incurring additional cost, complication or even litigation. Given these and other relevant factors, the clients may prefer that the lawyer act for all of them.

Special Considerations in Common Representation

[29] In considering whether to represent multiple clients in the same matter, a lawyer should be mindful that if the common representation fails because the potentially adverse interests cannot be reconciled, the result can be additional cost, embarrassment and recrimination. Ordinarily, the lawyer will be forced to withdraw from representing all of the clients if the common representation fails. In some situations, the risk of failure is so great that multiple representation is plainly impossible. For example, a lawyer cannot undertake common representation of clients where contentious litigation or negotiations between them are imminent or contemplated. Moreover, because the lawyer is required to be impartial between commonly represented clients, representation of multiple clients is improper when it is unlikely that impartiality can be maintained. Generally, if the relationship between the parties has already assumed antagonism, the possibility that the

clients' interests can be adequately served by common representation is not very good. Other relevant factors are whether the lawyer subsequently will represent both parties on a continuing basis and whether the situation involves creating or terminating a relationship between the parties.

[30] A particularly important factor in determining the appropriateness of common representation is the effect on client-lawyer confidentiality and the attorney-client privilege. With regard to the attorney-client privilege, the prevailing rule is that, as between commonly represented clients, the privilege does not attach. Hence, it must be assumed that if litigation eventuates between the clients, the privilege will not protect any such communications, and the clients should be so advised.

[31] As to the duty of confidentiality, continued common representation will almost certainly be inadequate if one client asks the lawyer not to disclose to the other client information relevant to the common representation. This is so because the lawyer has an equal duty of loyalty to each client, and each client has the right to be informed of anything bearing on the representation that might affect that client's interests and the right to expect that the lawyer will use that information to that client's benefit. See Rule 1.4. The lawyer should, at the outset of the common representation and as part of the process of obtaining each client's informed consent, advise each client that information will be shared and that the lawyer will have to withdraw if one client decides that some matter material to the representation should be kept from the other. In limited circumstances, it may be appropriate for the lawyer to proceed with the representation when the clients have agreed, after being properly informed, that the lawyer will keep certain information confidential. For example, the lawyer may reasonably conclude that failure to disclose one client's trade secrets to another client will not adversely affect representation involving a joint venture between the clients and agree to keep that information confidential with the informed consent of both clients.

[32] When seeking to establish or adjust a relationship between clients, the lawyer should make clear that the lawyer's role is not that of partisanship normally expected in other circumstances and, thus, that the clients may be required to assume greater responsibility for decisions than when each client is separately represented. Any limitations on the scope of the representation made necessary as a result of the common representation should be fully explained to the clients at the outset of the representation. See Rule 1.2(c).

[33] Subject to the above limitations, each client in the common representation has the right to loyal and diligent representation and the protection of Rule 1.9 concerning the obligations to a former client. The client also has the right to discharge the lawyer as stated in Rule 1.16.

Organizational Clients

[34] A lawyer who represents a corporation or other organization does not, by virtue of that representation, necessarily represent any constituent or affiliated organization, such as a parent or subsidiary. See Rule 1.13(a). Thus, the lawyer for an organization is not barred from accepting representation adverse to an affiliate

in an unrelated matter, unless the circumstances are such that the affiliate should also be considered a client of the lawyer, there is an understanding between the lawyer and the organizational client that the lawyer will avoid representation adverse to the client's affiliates, or the lawyer's obligations to either the organizational client or the new client are likely to limit materially the lawyer's representation of the other client.

[35] A lawyer for a corporation or other organization who is also a member of its board of directors should determine whether the responsibilities of the two roles may conflict. The lawyer may be called on to advise the corporation in matters involving actions of the directors. Consideration should be given to the frequency with which such situations may arise, the potential intensity of the conflict, the effect of the lawyer's resignation from the board and the possibility of the corporation's obtaining legal advice from another lawyer in such situations. If there is material risk that the dual role will compromise the lawyer's independence of professional judgment, the lawyer should not serve as a director or should cease to act as the corporation's lawyer when conflicts of interest arise. The lawyer should advise the other members of the board that in some circumstances matters discussed at board meetings while the lawyer is present in the capacity of director might not be protected by the attorney-client privilege and that conflict of interest considerations might require the lawyer's recusal as a director or might require the lawyer and the lawyer's firm to decline representation of the corporation in a matter.

Definitional Cross-References

"Confirmed in writing" *See* Rule 1.0(b)
"Informed consent" *See* Rule 1.0(e)
"Reasonably believes" *See* Rule 1.0(i)
"Tribunal" *See* Rule 1.0(m)

Rule 1.8 Conflict of Interest: Current Clients: Specific Rules

(a) A lawyer shall not enter into a business transaction with a client or knowingly acquire an ownership, possessory, security or other pecuniary interest adverse to a client unless:

(1) the transaction and terms on which the lawyer acquires the interest are fair and reasonable to the client and are fully disclosed and transmitted in writing in a manner that can be reasonably understood by the client;

(2) the client is advised in writing of the desirability of seeking and is given a reasonable opportunity to seek the advice of independent legal counsel on the transaction; and

(3) the client gives informed consent, in a writing signed by the client, to the essential terms of the transaction and the lawyer's role in the transaction, including whether the lawyer is representing the client in the transaction.

(b) A lawyer shall not use information relating to representation of a client to the disadvantage of the client unless the client gives informed consent, except as permitted or required by these Rules.

(c) A lawyer shall not solicit any substantial gift from a client, including a testamentary gift, or prepare on behalf of a client an instrument giving the lawyer or a person related to the lawyer any substantial gift unless the lawyer or other recipient of the gift is related to the client. For purposes of this paragraph, related persons include a spouse, child, grandchild, parent, grandparent or other relative or individual with whom the lawyer or the client maintains a close, familial relationship.

(d) Prior to the conclusion of representation of a client, a lawyer shall not make or negotiate an agreement giving the lawyer literary or media rights to a portrayal or account based in substantial part on information relating to the representation.

(e) A lawyer shall not provide financial assistance to a client in connection with pending or contemplated litigation, except that:

(1) a lawyer may advance court costs and expenses of litigation, the repayment of which may be contingent on the outcome of the matter;

(2) a lawyer representing an indigent client may pay court costs and expenses of litigation on behalf of the client; and

(3) a lawyer representing an indigent client pro bono, a lawyer representing an indigent client pro bono through a nonprofit legal services or public interest organization and a lawyer representing an indigent client pro bono through a law school clinical or pro bono program may provide modest gifts to the client for food, rent, transportation, medicine and other basic living expenses. The lawyer:

(i) may not promise, assure or imply the availability of such gifts prior to retention or as an inducement to continue the client-lawyer relationship after retention;

(ii) may not seek or accept reimbursement from the client, a relative of the client or anyone affiliated with the client; and

(iii) may not publicize or advertise a willingness to provide such gifts to prospective clients.

Financial assistance under this Rule may be provided even if the representation is eligible for fees under a fee-shifting statute.

(f) A lawyer shall not accept compensation for representing a client from one other than the client unless:

(1) the client gives informed consent;

(2) there is no interference with the lawyer's independence of professional judgment or with the client-lawyer relationship; and

(3) information relating to representation of a client is protected as required by Rule 1.6.

(g) A lawyer who represents two or more clients shall not participate in making an aggregate settlement of the claims of or against the clients, or in a criminal case an aggregated agreement as to guilty or nolo contendere pleas, unless each client gives informed consent, in a writing signed by the client. The lawyer's disclosure shall include the existence and nature of all the claims or pleas involved and of the participation of each person in the settlement.

(h) A lawyer shall not:

(1) make an agreement prospectively limiting the lawyer's liability to a client for malpractice unless the client is independently represented in making the agreement; or

(2) settle a claim or potential claim for such liability with an unrepresented client or former client unless that person is advised in writing of the desirability of seeking and is given a reasonable opportunity to seek the advice of independent legal counsel in connection therewith.

(i) A lawyer shall not acquire a proprietary interest in the cause of action or subject matter of litigation the lawyer is conducting for a client, except that the lawyer may:

(1) acquire a lien authorized by law to secure the lawyer's fee or expenses; and

(2) contract with a client for a reasonable contingent fee in a civil case.

(j) A lawyer shall not have sexual relations with a client unless a consensual sexual relationship existed between them when the client-lawyer relationship commenced.

(k) While lawyers are associated in a firm, a prohibition in the foregoing paragraphs (a) through (i) that applies to any one of them shall apply to all of them.

Comment

Business Transactions between Client and Lawyer

[1] A lawyer's legal skill and training, together with the relationship of trust and confidence between lawyer and client, create the possibility of overreaching when the lawyer participates in a business, property or financial transaction with a client, for example, a loan or sales transaction or a lawyer investment on behalf of a client. The requirements of paragraph (a) must be met even when the transaction is not closely related to the subject matter of the representation, as when a lawyer drafting a will for a client learns that the client needs money for unrelated expenses and offers to make a loan to the client. The Rule applies to lawyers engaged in the sale of goods or services related to the practice of law, for example, the sale of title insurance or investment services to existing clients of the lawyer's legal practice. See Rule 5.7. It also applies to lawyers purchasing property from estates they represent. It does not apply to ordinary fee arrangements between client and lawyer, which are governed by Rule 1.5, although its requirements must be met when the lawyer accepts an interest in the client's business or other nonmonetary property as payment of all or part of a fee. In addition, the Rule does not apply to standard commercial transactions between the lawyer and the client for products or services that the client generally markets to others, for example, banking or brokerage services, medical services, products manufactured or distributed by the client, and utilities' services. In such transactions, the lawyer has no advantage in dealing with the client, and the restrictions in paragraph (a) are unnecessary and impracticable.

[2] Paragraph (a)(1) requires that the transaction itself be fair to the client and that its essential terms be communicated to the client, in writing, in a manner that can be reasonably understood. Paragraph (a)(2) requires that the client also be advised, in writing, of the desirability of seeking the advice of independent legal counsel. It also requires that the client be given a reasonable opportunity to obtain such advice. Paragraph (a)(3) requires that the lawyer obtain the client's informed consent, in a writing signed by the client, both to the essential terms of the transaction and to the lawyer's role. When necessary, the lawyer should discuss both the material risks of the proposed transaction, including any risk presented by the lawyer's involvement, and the existence of reasonably available alternatives and should explain why the advice of independent legal counsel is desirable. See Rule 1.0(e) (definition of informed consent).

[3] The risk to a client is greatest when the client expects the lawyer to represent the client in the transaction itself or when the lawyer's financial interest otherwise poses a significant risk that the lawyer's representation of the client will be materially limited by the lawyer's financial interest in the transaction. Here the lawyer's role requires that the lawyer must comply, not only with the requirements of paragraph (a), but also with the requirements of Rule 1.7. Under that Rule, the lawyer must disclose the risks associated with the lawyer's dual role as both legal adviser and participant in the transaction, such as the risk that the lawyer will structure the transaction or give legal advice in a way that favors the lawyer's interests at the expense of the client. Moreover, the lawyer must obtain the client's informed consent. In some cases, the lawyer's interest may be such that Rule 1.7 will preclude the lawyer from seeking the client's consent to the transaction.

[4] If the client is independently represented in the transaction, paragraph (a)(2) of this Rule is inapplicable, and the paragraph (a)(1) requirement for full disclosure is satisfied either by a written disclosure by the lawyer involved in the transaction or by the client's independent counsel. The fact that the client was independently represented in the transaction is relevant in determining whether the agreement was fair and reasonable to the client as paragraph (a)(1) further requires.

Use of Information Related to Representation

[5] Use of information relating to the representation to the disadvantage of the client violates the lawyer's duty of loyalty. Paragraph (b) applies when the information is used to benefit either the lawyer or a third person, such as another client or business associate of the lawyer. For example, if a lawyer learns that a client intends to purchase and develop several parcels of land, the lawyer may not use that information to purchase one of the parcels in competition with the client or to recommend that another client make such a purchase. The Rule does not prohibit uses that do not disadvantage the client. For example, a lawyer who learns a government agency's interpretation of trade legislation during the representation of one client may properly use that information to benefit other clients. Paragraph (b) prohibits disadvantageous use of client information unless the client gives informed consent, except as permitted or required by these Rules. See Rules 1.2(d), 1.6, 1.9(c), 3.3, 4.1(b), 8.1 and 8.3.

Gifts to Lawyers

[6] A lawyer may accept a gift from a client, if the transaction meets general standards of fairness. For example, a simple gift such as a present given at a holiday or as a token of appreciation is permitted. If a client offers the lawyer a more substantial gift, paragraph (c) does not prohibit the lawyer from accepting it, although such a gift may be voidable by the client under the doctrine of undue influence, which treats client gifts as presumptively fraudulent. In any event, due to concerns about overreaching and imposition on clients, a lawyer may not suggest that a substantial gift be made to the lawyer or for the lawyer's benefit, except where the lawyer is related to the client as set forth in paragraph (c).

[7] If effectuation of a substantial gift requires preparing a legal instrument such as a will or conveyance, the client should have the detached advice that another lawyer can provide. The sole exception to this Rule is where the client is a relative of the donee.

[8] This Rule does not prohibit a lawyer from seeking to have the lawyer or a partner or associate of the lawyer named as executor of the client's estate or to another potentially lucrative fiduciary position. Nevertheless, such appointments will be subject to the general conflict of interest provision in Rule 1.7 when there is a significant risk that the lawyer's interest in obtaining the appointment will materially limit the lawyer's independent professional judgment in advising the client concerning the choice of an executor or other fiduciary. In obtaining the client's informed consent to the conflict, the lawyer should advise the client concerning the nature and extent of the lawyer's financial interest in the appointment, as well as the availability of alternative candidates for the position.

Literary Rights

[9] An agreement by which a lawyer acquires literary or media rights concerning the conduct of the representation creates a conflict between the interests of the client and the personal interests of the lawyer. Measures suitable in the representation of the client may detract from the publication value of an account of the representation. Paragraph (d) does not prohibit a lawyer representing a client in a transaction concerning literary property from agreeing that the lawyer's fee shall consist of a share in ownership in the property, if the arrangement conforms to Rule 1.5 and paragraphs (a) and (i).

Financial Assistance

[10] Lawyers may not subsidize lawsuits or administrative proceedings brought on behalf of their clients, including making or guaranteeing loans to their clients for living expenses, because to do so would encourage clients to pursue lawsuits that might not otherwise be brought and because such assistance gives lawyers too great a financial stake in the litigation. These dangers do not warrant a prohibition on a lawyer lending a client court costs and litigation expenses, including the expenses of medical examination and the costs of obtaining and presenting evidence, because these advances are virtually indistinguishable from contingent fees and help ensure access to the courts. Similarly, an exception allowing lawyers

representing indigent clients to pay court costs and litigation expenses regardless of whether these funds will be repaid is warranted.

[11] Paragraph (e)(3) provides another exception. A lawyer representing an indigent client without fee, a lawyer representing an indigent client pro bono through a nonprofit legal services or public interest organization and a lawyer representing an indigent client pro bono through a law school clinical or pro bono program may give the client modest gifts Gifts permitted under paragraph (e)(3) include modest contributions for food, rent, transportation, medicine and similar basic necessities of life. If the gift may have consequences for the client, including, e.g., for receipt of government benefits, social services, or tax liability, the lawyer should consult with the client about these. See Rule 1.4.

[12] The paragraph (e)(3) exception is narrow. Modest gifts are allowed in specific circumstances where it is unlikely to create conflicts of interest or invite abuse. Paragraph (e)(3) prohibits the lawyer from (i) promising, assuring or implying the availability of financial assistance prior to retention or as an inducement to continue the client-lawyer relationship after retention; (ii) seeking or accepting reimbursement from the client, a relative of the client or anyone affiliated with the client; and (iii) publicizing or advertising a willingness to provide gifts to prospective to clients beyond court costs and expenses of litigation in connection with contemplated or pending litigation or administrative proceedings.

[13] Financial assistance, including modest gifts pursuant to paragraph (e)(3), may be provided even if the representation is eligible for fees under a fee-shifting statute. However, paragraph (e)(3) does not permit lawyers to provide assistance in other contemplated or pending litigation in which the lawyer may eventually recover a fee, such as contingent-fee personal injury cases or cases in which fees may be available under a contractual fee-shifting provision, even if the lawyer does not eventually receive a fee.

Person Paying for a Lawyer's Services

[14] Lawyers are frequently asked to represent a client under circumstances in which a third person will compensate the lawyer, in whole or in part. The third person might be a relative or friend, an indemnitor (such as a liability insurance company) or a co-client (such as a corporation sued along with one or more of its employees). Because third-party payers frequently have interests that differ from those of the client, including interests in minimizing the amount spent on the representation and in learning how the representation is progressing, lawyers are prohibited from accepting or continuing such representations unless the lawyer determines that there will be no interference with the lawyer's independent professional judgment and there is informed consent from the client. See also Rule 5.4(c) (prohibiting interference with a lawyer's professional judgment by one who recommends, employs or pays the lawyer to render legal services for another).

[15] Sometimes, it will be sufficient for the lawyer to obtain the client's informed consent regarding the fact of the payment and the identity of the third-party payer. If, however, the fee arrangement creates a conflict of interest for the lawyer, then the lawyer must comply with Rule 1.7. The lawyer must also conform to the

requirements of Rule 1.6 concerning confidentiality. Under Rule 1.7(a), a conflict of interest exists if there is significant risk that the lawyer's representation of the client will be materially limited by the lawyer's own interest in the fee arrangement or by the lawyer's responsibilities to the third-party payer (for example, when the third-party payer is a co-client). Under Rule 1.7(b), the lawyer may accept or continue the representation with the informed consent of each affected client, unless the conflict is nonconsentable under that paragraph. Under Rule 1.7(b), the informed consent must be confirmed in writing.

Aggregate Settlements

[16] Differences in willingness to make or accept an offer of settlement are among the risks of common representation of multiple clients by a single lawyer. Under Rule 1.7, this is one of the risks that should be discussed before undertaking the representation, as part of the process of obtaining the clients' informed consent. In addition, Rule 1.2(a) protects each client's right to have the final say in deciding whether to accept or reject an offer of settlement and in deciding whether to enter a guilty or nolo contendere plea in a criminal case. The rule stated in this paragraph is a corollary of both these Rules and provides that, before any settlement offer or plea bargain is made or accepted on behalf of multiple clients, the lawyer must inform each of them about all the material terms of the settlement, including what the other clients will receive or pay if the settlement or plea offer is accepted. See also Rule 1.0(e) (definition of informed consent). Lawyers representing a class of plaintiffs or defendants, or those proceeding derivatively, may not have a full client-lawyer relationship with each member of the class; nevertheless, such lawyers must comply with applicable rules regulating notification of class members and other procedural requirements designed to ensure adequate protection of the entire class.

Limiting Liability and Settling Malpractice Claims

[17] Agreements prospectively limiting a lawyer's liability for malpractice are prohibited unless the client is independently represented in making the agreement because they are likely to undermine competent and diligent representation. Also, many clients are unable to evaluate the desirability of making such an agreement before a dispute has arisen, particularly if they are then represented by the lawyer seeking the agreement. This paragraph does not, however, prohibit a lawyer from entering into an agreement with the client to arbitrate legal malpractice claims, provided such agreements are enforceable and the client is fully informed of the scope and effect of the agreement. Nor does this paragraph limit the ability of lawyers to practice in the form of a limited-liability entity, where permitted by law, provided that each lawyer remains personally liable to the client for his or her own conduct and the firm complies with any conditions required by law, such as provisions requiring client notification or maintenance of adequate liability insurance. Nor does it prohibit an agreement in accordance with Rule 1.2 that defines the scope of the representation, although a definition of scope that makes the obligations of representation illusory will amount to an attempt to limit liability.

[18] Agreements settling a claim or a potential claim for malpractice are not prohibited by this Rule. Nevertheless, in view of the danger that a lawyer will take unfair advantage of an unrepresented client or former client, the lawyer must first advise such a person in writing of the appropriateness of independent representation in connection with such a settlement. In addition, the lawyer must give the client or former client a reasonable opportunity to find and consult independent counsel.

Acquiring Proprietary Interest in Litigation

[19] Paragraph (i) states the traditional general rule that lawyers are prohibited from acquiring a proprietary interest in litigation. Like paragraph (e), the general rule has its basis in common law champerty and maintenance and is designed to avoid giving the lawyer too great an interest in the representation. In addition, when the lawyer acquires an ownership interest in the subject of the representation, it will be more difficult for a client to discharge the lawyer if the client so desires. The Rule is subject to specific exceptions developed in decisional law and continued in these Rules. The exception for certain advances of the costs of litigation is set forth in paragraph (e). In addition, paragraph (i) sets forth exceptions for liens authorized by law to secure the lawyer's fees or expenses and contracts for reasonable contingent fees. The law of each jurisdiction determines which liens are authorized by law. These may include liens granted by statute, liens originating in common law and liens acquired by contract with the client. When a lawyer acquires by contract a security interest in property other than that recovered through the lawyer's efforts in the litigation, such an acquisition is a business or financial transaction with a client and is governed by the requirements of paragraph (a). Contracts for contingent fees in civil cases are governed by Rule 1.5.

Client-Lawyer Sexual Relationships

[20] The relationship between lawyer and client is a fiduciary one in which the lawyer occupies the highest position of trust and confidence. The relationship is almost always unequal; thus, a sexual relationship between lawyer and client can involve unfair exploitation of the lawyer's fiduciary role, in violation of the lawyer's basic ethical obligation not to use the trust of the client to the client's disadvantage. In addition, such a relationship presents a significant danger that, because of the lawyer's emotional involvement, the lawyer will be unable to represent the client without impairment of the exercise of independent professional judgment. Moreover, a blurred line between the professional and personal relationships may make it difficult to predict to what extent client confidences will be protected by the attorney-client evidentiary privilege, since client confidences are protected by privilege only when they are imparted in the context of the client-lawyer relationship. Because of the significant danger of harm to client interests and because the client's own emotional involvement renders it unlikely that the client could give adequate informed consent, this Rule prohibits the lawyer from having sexual relations with a client regardless of whether the relationship is consensual and regardless of the absence of prejudice to the client.

[21] Sexual relationships that predate the client-lawyer relationship are not prohibited. Issues relating to the exploitation of the fiduciary relationship and client dependency are diminished when the sexual relationship existed prior to the commencement of the client-lawyer relationship. However, before proceeding with the representation in these circumstances, the lawyer should consider whether the lawyer's ability to represent the client will be materially limited by the relationship. See Rule 1.7(a)(2).

[22] When the client is an organization, paragraph (j) of this Rule prohibits a lawyer for the organization (whether inside counsel or outside counsel) from having a sexual relationship with a constituent of the organization who supervises, directs or regularly consults with that lawyer concerning the organization's legal matters.

Imputation of Prohibitions

[23] Under paragraph (k), a prohibition on conduct by an individual lawyer in paragraphs (a) through (i) also applies to all lawyers associated in a firm with the personally prohibited lawyer. For example, one lawyer in a firm may not enter into a business transaction with a client of another member of the firm without complying with paragraph (a), even if the first lawyer is not personally involved in the representation of the client. The prohibition set forth in paragraph (j) is personal and is not applied to associated lawyers.

Definitional Cross-References

"Firm" *See* Rule 1.0(c)
"Informed consent" *See* Rule 1.0(e)
"Knowingly" *See* Rule 1.0(f)
"Substantial" *See* Rule 1.0(l)
"Writing" and "Signed" *See* Rule 1.0(n)

Rule 1.9 Duties to Former Clients

(a) A lawyer who has formerly represented a client in a matter shall not thereafter represent another person in the same or a substantially related matter in which that person's interests are materially adverse to the interests of the former client unless the former client gives informed consent, confirmed in writing.

(b) A lawyer shall not knowingly represent a person in the same or a substantially related matter in which a firm with which the lawyer formerly was associated had previously represented a client

(1) whose interests are materially adverse to that person; and

(2) about whom the lawyer had acquired information protected by Rules 1.6 and 1.9(c) that is material to the matter; unless the former client gives informed consent, confirmed in writing.

(c) A lawyer who has formerly represented a client in a matter or whose present or former firm has formerly represented a client in a matter shall not thereafter:

(1) use information relating to the representation to the disadvantage of the former client except as these Rules would permit or require with respect to a client, or when the information has become generally known; or

(2) **reveal information relating to the representation except as these Rules would permit or require with respect to a client.**

Comment

[1] After termination of a client-lawyer relationship, a lawyer has certain continuing duties with respect to confidentiality and conflicts of interest and thus may not represent another client except in conformity with this Rule. Under this Rule, for example, a lawyer could not properly seek to rescind on behalf of a new client a contract drafted on behalf of the former client. So also a lawyer who has prosecuted an accused person could not properly represent the accused in a subsequent civil action against the government concerning the same transaction. Nor could a lawyer who has represented multiple clients in a matter represent one of the clients against the others in the same or a substantially related matter after a dispute arose among the clients in that matter, unless all affected clients give informed consent. See Comment [9]. Current and former government lawyers must comply with this Rule to the extent required by Rule 1.11.

[2] The scope of a "matter" for purposes of this Rule depends on the facts of a particular situation or transaction. The lawyer's involvement in a matter can also be a question of degree. When a lawyer has been directly involved in a specific transaction, subsequent representation of other clients with materially adverse interests in that transaction clearly is prohibited. On the other hand, a lawyer who recurrently handled a type of problem for a former client is not precluded from later representing another client in a factually distinct problem of that type even though the subsequent representation involves a position adverse to the prior client. Similar considerations can apply to the reassignment of military lawyers between defense and prosecution functions within the same military jurisdictions. The underlying question is whether the lawyer was so involved in the matter that the subsequent representation can be justly regarded as a changing of sides in the matter in question.

[3] Matters are "substantially related" for purposes of this Rule if they involve the same transaction or legal dispute or if there otherwise is a substantial risk that confidential factual information as would normally have been obtained in the prior representation would materially advance the client's position in the subsequent matter. For example, a lawyer who has represented a businessperson and learned extensive private financial information about that person may not then represent that person's spouse in seeking a divorce. Similarly, a lawyer who has previously represented a client in securing environmental permits to build a shopping center would be precluded from representing neighbors seeking to oppose rezoning of the property on the basis of environmental considerations; however, the lawyer would not be precluded, on the grounds of substantial relationship, from defending a tenant of the completed shopping center in resisting eviction for nonpayment of rent. Information that has been disclosed to the public or to other parties adverse to the former client ordinarily will not be disqualifying. Information acquired in a prior representation may have been rendered obsolete by the passage of time, a circumstance that may be relevant in determining whether two representations are

substantially related. In the case of an organizational client, general knowledge of the client's policies and practices ordinarily will not preclude a subsequent representation; on the other hand, knowledge of specific facts gained in a prior representation that are relevant to the matter in question ordinarily will preclude such a representation. A former client is not required to reveal the confidential information learned by the lawyer in order to establish a substantial risk that the lawyer has confidential information to use in the subsequent matter. A conclusion about the possession of such information may be based on the nature of the services the lawyer provided the former client and information that would in ordinary practice be learned by a lawyer providing such services.

Lawyers Moving Between Firms

[4] When lawyers have been associated within a firm but then end their association, the question of whether a lawyer should undertake representation is more complicated. There are several competing considerations. First, the client previously represented by the former firm must be reasonably assured that the principle of loyalty to the client is not compromised. Second, the rule should not be so broadly cast as to preclude other persons from having reasonable choice of legal counsel. Third, the rule should not unreasonably hamper lawyers from forming new associations and taking on new clients after having left a previous association. In this connection, it should be recognized that today many lawyers practice in firms, that many lawyers to some degree limit their practice to one field or another, and that many move from one association to another several times in their careers. If the concept of imputation were applied with unqualified rigor, the result would be radical curtailment of the opportunity of lawyers to move from one practice setting to another and of the opportunity of clients to change counsel.

[5] Paragraph (b) operates to disqualify the lawyer only when the lawyer involved has actual knowledge of information protected by Rules 1.6 and 1.9(c). Thus, if a lawyer while with one firm acquired no knowledge or information relating to a particular client of the firm, and that lawyer later joined another firm, neither the lawyer individually nor the second firm is disqualified from representing another client in the same or a related matter even though the interests of the two clients conflict. See Rule 1.10(b) for the restrictions on a firm once a lawyer has terminated association with the firm.

[6] Application of paragraph (b) depends on a situation's particular facts, aided by inferences, deductions or working presumptions that reasonably may be made about the way in which lawyers work together. A lawyer may have general access to files of all clients of a law firm and may regularly participate in discussions of their affairs; it should be inferred that such a lawyer in fact is privy to all information about all the firm's clients. In contrast, another lawyer may have access to the files of only a limited number of clients and participate in discussions of the affairs of no other clients; in the absence of information to the contrary, it should be inferred that such a lawyer in fact is privy to information about the clients actually served but not those of other clients. In such an inquiry, the burden of proof should rest upon the firm whose disqualification is sought.

[7] Independent of the question of disqualification of a firm, a lawyer changing professional association has a continuing duty to preserve confidentiality of information about a client formerly represented. See Rules 1.6 and 1.9(c).

[8] Paragraph (c) provides that information acquired by the lawyer in the course of representing a client may not subsequently be used or revealed by the lawyer to the disadvantage of the client. However, the fact that a lawyer has once served a client does not preclude the lawyer from using generally known information about that client when later representing another client.

[9] The provisions of this Rule are for the protection of former clients and can be waived if the client gives informed consent, which consent must be confirmed in writing under paragraphs (a) and (b). See Rule 1.0(e). With regard to the effectiveness of an advance waiver, see Comment [22] to Rule 1.7. With regard to disqualification of a firm with which a lawyer is or was formerly associated, see Rule 1.10.

Definitional Cross-References

"Confirmed in writing" *See* Rule 1.0(b)
"Firm" *See* Rule 1.0(c)
"Informed consent" *See* Rule 1.0(e)
"Knowingly" and "Known" *See* Rule 1.0(f)
"Writing" *See* Rule 1.0(n)

Rule 1.10 Imputation of Conflicts of Interest: General Rule

(a) While lawyers are associated in a firm, none of them shall knowingly represent a client when any one of them practicing alone would be prohibited from doing so by Rules 1.7 or 1.9, unless

(1) the prohibition is based on a personal interest of the disqualified lawyer and does not present a significant risk of materially limiting the representation of the client by the remaining lawyers in the firm; or

(2) the prohibition is based upon Rule 1.9(a) or (b), and arises out of the disqualified lawyer's association with a prior firm, and

(i) the disqualified lawyer is timely screened from any participation in the matter and is apportioned no part of the fee therefrom;

(ii) written notice is promptly given to any affected former client to enable the former client to ascertain compliance with the provisions of this Rule, which shall include a description of the screening procedures employed; a statement of the firm's and of the screened lawyer's compliance with these Rules; a statement that review may be available before a tribunal; and an agreement by the firm to respond promptly to any written inquiries or objections by the former client about the screening procedures; and

(iii) certifications of compliance with these Rules and with the screening procedures are provided to the former client by the screened lawyer and by a partner of the firm, at reasonable intervals upon the

former client's written request and upon termination of the screening procedures.

(b) When a lawyer has terminated an association with a firm, the firm is not prohibited from thereafter representing a person with interests materially adverse to those of a client represented by the formerly associated lawyer and not currently represented by the firm, unless:

(1) the matter is the same or substantially related to that in which the formerly associated lawyer represented the client; and

(2) any lawyer remaining in the firm has information protected by Rules 1.6 and 1.9(c) that is material to the matter.

(c) A disqualification prescribed by this Rule may be waived by the affected client under the conditions stated in Rule 1.7.

(d) The disqualification of lawyers associated in a firm with former or current government lawyers is governed by Rule 1.11.

Comment

Definition of "Firm"

[1] For purposes of the Rules of Professional Conduct, the term "firm" denotes lawyers in a law partnership, professional corporation, sole proprietorship or other association authorized to practice law; or lawyers employed in a legal services organization or the legal department of a corporation or other organization. See Rule 1.0(c). Whether two or more lawyers constitute a firm within this definition can depend on the specific facts. See Rule 1.0, Comments [2]–[4].

Principles of Imputed Disqualification

[2] The rule of imputed disqualification stated in paragraph (a) gives effect to the principle of loyalty to the client as it applies to lawyers who practice in a law firm. Such situations can be considered from the premise that a firm of lawyers is essentially one lawyer for purposes of the rules governing loyalty to the client, or from the premise that each lawyer is vicariously bound by the obligation of loyalty owed by each lawyer with whom the lawyer is associated. Paragraph (a)(1) operates only among the lawyers currently associated in a firm. When a lawyer moves from one firm to another, the situation is governed by Rules 1.9(b) and 1.10(a)(2) and 1.10(b).

[3] The rule in paragraph (a) does not prohibit representation where neither questions of client loyalty nor protection of confidential information are presented. Where one lawyer in a firm could not effectively represent a given client because of strong political beliefs, for example, but that lawyer will do no work on the case and the personal beliefs of the lawyer will not materially limit the representation by others in the firm, the firm should not be disqualified. On the other hand, if an opposing party in a case were owned by a lawyer in the law firm, and others in the firm would be materially limited in pursuing the matter because of loyalty to that lawyer, the personal disqualification of the lawyer would be imputed to all others in the firm.

[4] The rule in paragraph (a) also does not prohibit representation by others in the law firm where the person prohibited from involvement in a matter is a nonlawyer, such as a paralegal or legal secretary. Nor does paragraph (a) prohibit representation if the lawyer is prohibited from acting because of events before the person became a lawyer, for example, work that the person did while a law student. Such persons, however, ordinarily must be screened from any personal participation in the matter to avoid communication to others in the firm of confidential information that both the nonlawyers and the firm have a legal duty to protect. See Rules 1.0(k) and 5.3.

[5] Rule 1.10(b) operates to permit a law firm, under certain circumstances, to represent a person with interests directly adverse to those of a client represented by a lawyer who formerly was associated with the firm. The Rule applies regardless of when the formerly associated lawyer represented the client. However, the law firm may not represent a person with interests adverse to those of a present client of the firm, which would violate Rule 1.7. Moreover, the firm may not represent the person where the matter is the same or substantially related to that in which the formerly associated lawyer represented the client and any other lawyer currently in the firm has material information protected by Rules 1.6 and 1.9(c).

[6] Rule 1.10(c) removes imputation with the informed consent of the affected client or former client under the conditions stated in Rule 1.7. The conditions stated in Rule 1.7 require the lawyer to determine that the representation is not prohibited by Rule 1.7(b) and that each affected client or former client has given informed consent to the representation, confirmed in writing. In some cases, the risk may be so severe that the conflict may not be cured by client consent. For a discussion of the effectiveness of client waivers of conflicts that might arise in the future, see Rule 1.7, Comment [22]. For a definition of informed consent, see Rule 1.0(e).

[7] Rule 1.10(a)(2) similarly removes the imputation otherwise required by Rule 1.10(a), but unlike section (c), it does so without requiring that there be informed consent by the former client. Instead, it requires that the procedures laid out in sections (a)(2)(i)-(iii) be followed. A description of effective screening mechanisms appears in Rule 1.0(k). Lawyers should be aware, however, that, even where screening mechanisms have been adopted, tribunals may consider additional factors in ruling upon motions to disqualify a lawyer from pending litigation.

[8] Paragraph (a)(2)(i) does not prohibit the screened lawyer from receiving a salary or partnership share established by prior independent agreement, but that lawyer may not receive compensation directly related to the matter in which the lawyer is disqualified.

[9] The notice required by paragraph (a)(2)(ii) generally should include a description of the screened lawyer's prior representation and be given as soon as practicable after the need for screening becomes apparent. It also should include a statement by the screened lawyer and the firm that the client's material confidential information has not been disclosed or used in violation of the Rules. The notice is intended to enable the former client to evaluate and comment upon the effectiveness of the screening procedures.

[10] The certifications required by paragraph (a)(2)(iii) give the former client assurance that the client's material confidential information has not been disclosed or used inappropriately, either prior to timely implementation of a screen or thereafter. If compliance cannot be certified, the certificate must describe the failure to comply.

[11] Where a lawyer has joined a private firm after having represented the government, imputation is governed by Rule 1.11(b) and (c), not this Rule. Under Rule 1.11(d), where a lawyer represents the government after having served clients in private practice, nongovernmental employment or in another government agency, former-client conflicts are not imputed to government lawyers associated with the individually disqualified lawyer.

[12] Where a lawyer is prohibited from engaging in certain transactions under Rule 1.8, paragraph (k) of that Rule, and not this Rule, determines whether that prohibition also applies to other lawyers associated in a firm with the personally prohibited lawyer.

Definitional Cross-References

"Firm" *See* Rule 1.0(c)
"Knowingly" *See* Rule 1.0(f)
"Partner" *See* Rule 1.0(g)
"Screened" *See* Rule 1.0(k)
"Tribunal" *See* Rule 1.0(m)
"Written" *See* Rule 1.0(n)

Rule 1.11 Special Conflicts of Interest for Former and Current Government Officers and Employees

(a) Except as law may otherwise expressly permit, a lawyer who has formerly served as a public officer or employee of the government:

(1) is subject to Rule 1.9(c); and

(2) shall not otherwise represent a client in connection with a matter in which the lawyer participated personally and substantially as a public officer or employee, unless the appropriate government agency gives its informed consent, confirmed in writing, to the representation.

(b) When a lawyer is disqualified from representation under paragraph (a), no lawyer in a firm with which that lawyer is associated may knowingly undertake or continue representation in such a matter unless:

(1) the disqualified lawyer is timely screened from any participation in the matter and is apportioned no part of the fee therefrom; and

(2) written notice is promptly given to the appropriate government agency to enable it to ascertain compliance with the provisions of this Rule.

(c) Except as law may otherwise expressly permit, a lawyer having information that the lawyer knows is confidential government information about a person acquired when the lawyer was a public officer or employee, may not represent a private client whose interests are adverse to that person in a matter

in which the information could be used to the material disadvantage of that person. As used in this Rule, the term "confidential government information" means information that has been obtained under governmental authority and which, at the time this Rule is applied, the government is prohibited by law from disclosing to the public or has a legal privilege not to disclose and which is not otherwise available to the public. A firm with which that lawyer is associated may undertake or continue representation in the matter only if the disqualified lawyer is timely screened from any participation in the matter and is apportioned no part of the fee therefrom.

(d) Except as law may otherwise expressly permit, a lawyer currently serving as a public officer or employee:

(1) is subject to Rules 1.7 and 1.9; and

(2) shall not:

(i) participate in a matter in which the lawyer participated personally and substantially while in private practice or nongovernmental employment, unless the appropriate government agency gives its informed consent, confirmed in writing; or

(ii) negotiate for private employment with any person who is involved as a party or as lawyer for a party in a matter in which the lawyer is participating personally and substantially, except that a lawyer serving as a law clerk to a judge, other adjudicative officer or arbitrator may negotiate for private employment as permitted by Rule 1.12(b) and subject to the conditions stated in Rule 1.12(b).

(e) As used in this Rule, the term "matter" includes:

(1) any judicial or other proceeding, application, request for a ruling or other determination, contract, claim, controversy, investigation, charge, accusation, arrest or other particular matter involving a specific party or parties, and

(2) any other matter covered by the conflict of interest rules of the appropriate government agency.

Comment

[1] A lawyer who has served or is currently serving as a public officer or employee is personally subject to the Rules of Professional Conduct, including the prohibition against concurrent conflicts of interest stated in Rule 1.7. In addition, such a lawyer may be subject to statutes and government regulations regarding conflict of interest. Such statutes and regulations may circumscribe the extent to which the government agency may give consent under this Rule. See Rule 1.0(e) for the definition of informed consent.

[2] Paragraphs (a)(1), (a)(2) and (d)(1) restate the obligations of an individual lawyer who has served or is currently serving as an officer or employee of the government toward a former government or private client. Rule 1.10 is not applicable to the conflicts of interest addressed by this Rule. Rather, paragraph (b) sets forth a special imputation rule for former government lawyers that provides for screening and

notice. Because of the special problems raised by imputation within a government agency, paragraph (d) does not impute the conflicts of a lawyer currently serving as an officer or employee of the government to other associated government officers or employees, although ordinarily it will be prudent to screen such lawyers.

[3] Paragraphs (a)(2) and (d)(2) apply regardless of whether a lawyer is adverse to a former client and are thus designed not only to protect the former client, but also to prevent a lawyer from exploiting public office for the advantage of another client. For example, a lawyer who has pursued a claim on behalf of the government may not pursue the same claim on behalf of a later private client after the lawyer has left government service, except when authorized to do so by the government agency under paragraph (a). Similarly, a lawyer who has pursued a claim on behalf of a private client may not pursue the claim on behalf of the government, except when authorized to do so by paragraph (d). As with paragraphs (a)(1) and (d)(1), Rule 1.10 is not applicable to the conflicts of interest addressed by these paragraphs.

[4] This Rule represents a balancing of interests. On the one hand, where the successive clients are a government agency and another client, public or private, the risk exists that power or discretion vested in that agency might be used for the special benefit of the other client. A lawyer should not be in a position where benefit to the other client might affect performance of the lawyer's professional functions on behalf of the government. Also, unfair advantage could accrue to the other client by reason of access to confidential government information about the client's adversary obtainable only through the lawyer's government service. On the other hand, the rules governing lawyers presently or formerly employed by a government agency should not be so restrictive as to inhibit transfer of employment to and from the government. The government has a legitimate need to attract qualified lawyers as well as to maintain high ethical standards. Thus a former government lawyer is disqualified only from particular matters in which the lawyer participated personally and substantially. The provisions for screening and waiver in paragraph (b) are necessary to prevent the disqualification rule from imposing too severe a deterrent against entering public service. The limitation of disqualification in paragraphs (a)(2) and (d)(2) to matters involving a specific party or parties, rather than extending disqualification to all substantive issues on which the lawyer worked, serves a similar function.

[5] When a lawyer has been employed by one government agency and then moves to a second government agency, it may be appropriate to treat that second agency as another client for purposes of this Rule, as when a lawyer is employed by a city and subsequently is employed by a federal agency. However, because the conflict of interest is governed by paragraph (d), the latter agency is not required to screen the lawyer as paragraph (b) requires a law firm to do. The question of whether two government agencies should be regarded as the same or different clients for conflict of interest purposes is beyond the scope of these Rules. See Rule 1.13 Comment [9].

[6] Paragraphs (b) and (c) contemplate a screening arrangement. See Rule 1.0(k) (requirements for screening procedures). These paragraphs do not prohibit a lawyer from receiving a salary or partnership share established by prior independent

agreement, but that lawyer may not receive compensation directly relating the lawyer's compensation to the fee in the matter in which the lawyer is disqualified.

[7] Notice, including a description of the screened lawyer's prior representation and of the screening procedures employed, generally should be given as soon as practicable after the need for screening becomes apparent.

[8] Paragraph (c) operates only when the lawyer in question has knowledge of the information, which means actual knowledge; it does not operate with respect to information that merely could be imputed to the lawyer.

[9] Paragraphs (a) and (d) do not prohibit a lawyer from jointly representing a private party and a government agency when doing so is permitted by Rule 1.7 and is not otherwise prohibited by law.

[10] For purposes of paragraph (e) of this Rule, a "matter" may continue in another form. In determining whether two particular matters are the same, the lawyer should consider the extent to which the matters involve the same basic facts, the same or related parties, and the time elapsed.

Definitional Cross-References

"Confirmed in writing" *See* Rule 1.0(b)
"Firm" *See* Rule 1.0(c)
"Informed consent" *See* Rule 1.0(e)
"Knowingly" and "Knows" *See* Rule 1.0(f)
"Screened" *See* Rule 1.0(k)
"Written" *See* Rule 1.0(n)

Rule 1.12 Former Judge, Arbitrator, Mediator or Other Third-Party Neutral

(a) Except as stated in paragraph (d), a lawyer shall not represent anyone in connection with a matter in which the lawyer participated personally and substantially as a judge or other adjudicative officer or law clerk to such a person or as an arbitrator, mediator or other third-party neutral, unless all parties to the proceeding give informed consent, confirmed in writing.

(b) A lawyer shall not negotiate for employment with any person who is involved as a party or as lawyer for a party in a matter in which the lawyer is participating personally and substantially as a judge or other adjudicative officer or as an arbitrator, mediator or other third-party neutral. A lawyer serving as a law clerk to a judge or other adjudicative officer may negotiate for employment with a party or lawyer involved in a matter in which the clerk is participating personally and substantially, but only after the lawyer has notified the judge or other adjudicative officer.

(c) If a lawyer is disqualified by paragraph (a), no lawyer in a firm with which that lawyer is associated may knowingly undertake or continue representation in the matter unless:

(1) the disqualified lawyer is timely screened from any participation in the matter and is apportioned no part of the fee therefrom; and

(2) written notice is promptly given to the parties and any appropriate tribunal to enable them to ascertain compliance with the provisions of this Rule.

(d) An arbitrator selected as a partisan of a party in a multimember arbitration panel is not prohibited from subsequently representing that party.

Comment

[1] This Rule generally parallels Rule 1.11. The term "personally and substantially" signifies that a judge who was a member of a multimember court, and thereafter left judicial office to practice law, is not prohibited from representing a client in a matter pending in the court, but in which the former judge did not participate. So also the fact that a former judge exercised administrative responsibility in a court does not prevent the former judge from acting as a lawyer in a matter where the judge had previously exercised remote or incidental administrative responsibility that did not affect the merits. Compare the Comment to Rule 1.11. The term "adjudicative officer" includes such officials as judges pro tempore, referees, special masters, hearing officers and other parajudicial officers, and also lawyers who serve as part-time judges. Paragraphs C(2), D(2) and E(2) of the Application Section of the Model Code of Judicial Conduct provide that a part-time judge, judge pro tempore or retired judge recalled to active service, shall not "act as a lawyer in a proceeding in which the judge has served as a judge or in any other proceeding related thereto." Although phrased differently from this Rule, those Rules correspond in meaning.

[2] Like former judges, lawyers who have served as arbitrators, mediators or other third-party neutrals may be asked to represent a client in a matter in which the lawyer participated personally and substantially. This Rule forbids such representation unless all of the parties to the proceedings give their informed consent, confirmed in writing. See Rule 1.0(e) and (b). Other law or codes of ethics governing third-party neutrals may impose more stringent standards of personal or imputed disqualification. See Rule 2.4.

[3] Although lawyers who serve as third-party neutrals do not have information concerning the parties that is protected under Rule 1.6, they typically owe the parties an obligation of confidentiality under law or codes of ethics governing third-party neutrals. Thus, paragraph (c) provides that conflicts of the personally disqualified lawyer will be imputed to other lawyers in a law firm unless the conditions of this paragraph are met.

[4] Requirements for screening procedures are stated in Rule 1.0(k). Paragraph (c)(1) does not prohibit the screened lawyer from receiving a salary or partnership share established by prior independent agreement, but that lawyer may not receive compensation directly related to the matter in which the lawyer is disqualified.

[5] Notice, including a description of the screened lawyer's prior representation and of the screening procedures employed, generally should be given as soon as practicable after the need for screening becomes apparent.

Definitional Cross-References

"Confirmed in writing" *See* Rule 1.0(b)
"Firm" *See* Rule 1.0(c)
"Informed consent" *See* Rule 1.0(e)
"Knowingly" *See* Rule 1.0(f)
"Screened" *See* Rule 1.0(k)
"Tribunal" *See* Rule 1.0(m)
"Writing" and "Written" *See* Rule 1.0(n)

Rule 1.13 Organization as Client

(a) A lawyer employed or retained by an organization represents the organization acting through its duly authorized constituents.

(b) If a lawyer for an organization knows that an officer, employee or other person associated with the organization is engaged in action, intends to act or refuses to act in a matter related to the representation that is a violation of a legal obligation to the organization, or a violation of law that reasonably might be imputed to the organization, and that is likely to result in substantial injury to the organization, then the lawyer shall proceed as is reasonably necessary in the best interest of the organization. Unless the lawyer reasonably believes that it is not necessary in the best interest of the organization to do so, the lawyer shall refer the matter to higher authority in the organization, including, if warranted by the circumstances, to the highest authority that can act on behalf of the organization as determined by applicable law.

(c) Except as provided in paragraph (d), if

(1) despite the lawyer's efforts in accordance with paragraph (b) the highest authority that can act on behalf of the organization insists upon or fails to address in a timely and appropriate manner an action or a refusal to act, that is clearly a violation of law; and

(2) the lawyer reasonably believes that the violation is reasonably certain to result in substantial injury to the organization, then the lawyer may reveal information relating to the representation whether or not Rule 1.6 permits such disclosure, but only if and to the extent the lawyer reasonably believes necessary to prevent substantial injury to the organization.

(d) Paragraph (c) shall not apply with respect to information relating to a lawyer's representation of an organization to investigate an alleged violation of law, or to defend the organization or an officer, employee or other constituent associated with the organization against a claim arising out of an alleged violation of law.

(e) A lawyer who reasonably believes that he or she has been discharged because of the lawyer's actions taken pursuant to paragraphs (b) or (c), or who withdraws under circumstances that require or permit the lawyer to take action under either of those paragraphs, shall proceed as the lawyer reasonably believes necessary to assure that the organization's highest authority is informed of the lawyer's discharge or withdrawal.

(f) In dealing with an organization's directors, officers, employees, members, shareholders or other constituents, a lawyer shall explain the identity of the client when the lawyer knows or reasonably should know that the organization's interests are adverse to those of the constituents with whom the lawyer is dealing.

(g) A lawyer representing an organization may also represent any of its directors, officers, employees, members, shareholders or other constituents, subject to the provisions of Rule 1.7. If the organization's consent to the dual representation is required by Rule 1.7, the consent shall be given by an appropriate official of the organization other than the individual who is to be represented, or by the shareholders.

Comment

The Entity as the Client

[1] An organizational client is a legal entity, but it cannot act except through its officers, directors, employees, shareholders and other constituents. Officers, directors, employees and shareholders are the constituents of the corporate organizational client. The duties defined in this Comment apply equally to unincorporated associations. "Other constituents" as used in this Comment means the positions equivalent to officers, directors, employees and shareholders held by persons acting for organizational clients that are not corporations.

[2] When one of the constituents of an organizational client communicates with the organization's lawyer in that person's organizational capacity, the communication is protected by Rule 1.6. Thus, by way of example, if an organizational client requests its lawyer to investigate allegations of wrongdoing, interviews made in the course of that investigation between the lawyer and the client's employees or other constituents are covered by Rule 1.6. This does not mean, however, that constituents of an organizational client are the clients of the lawyer. The lawyer may not disclose to such constituents information relating to the representation except for disclosures explicitly or impliedly authorized by the organizational client in order to carry out the representation or as otherwise permitted by Rule 1.6.

[3] When constituents of the organization make decisions for it, the decisions ordinarily must be accepted by the lawyer even if their utility or prudence is doubtful. Decisions concerning policy and operations, including ones entailing serious risk, are not as such in the lawyer's province. Paragraph (b) makes clear, however, that when the lawyer knows that the organization is likely to be substantially injured by action of an officer or other constituent that violates a legal obligation to the organization or is in violation of law that might be imputed to the organization, the lawyer must proceed as is reasonably necessary in the best interest of the organization. As defined in Rule 1.0(f), knowledge can be inferred from circumstances, and a lawyer cannot ignore the obvious.

[4] In determining how to proceed under paragraph (b), the lawyer should give due consideration to the seriousness of the violation and its consequences, the responsibility in the organization and the apparent motivation of the person

involved, the policies of the organization concerning such matters, and any other relevant considerations. Ordinarily, referral to a higher authority would be necessary. In some circumstances, however, it may be appropriate for the lawyer to ask the constituent to reconsider the matter; for example, if the circumstances involve a constituent's innocent misunderstanding of law and subsequent acceptance of the lawyer's advice, the lawyer may reasonably conclude that the best interest of the organization does not require that the matter be referred to higher authority. If a constituent persists in conduct contrary to the lawyer's advice, it will be necessary for the lawyer to take steps to have the matter reviewed by a higher authority in the organization. If the matter is of sufficient seriousness and importance or urgency to the organization, referral to higher authority in the organization may be necessary even if the lawyer has not communicated with the constituent. Any measures taken should, to the extent practicable, minimize the risk of revealing information relating to the representation to persons outside the organization. Even in circumstances where a lawyer is not obligated by Rule 1.13 to proceed, a lawyer may bring to the attention of an organizational client, including its highest authority, matters that the lawyer reasonably believes to be of sufficient importance to warrant doing so in the best interest of the organization.

[5] Paragraph (b) also makes clear that when it is reasonably necessary to enable the organization to address the matter in a timely and appropriate manner, the lawyer must refer the matter to higher authority, including, if warranted by the circumstances, the highest authority that can act on behalf of the organization under applicable law. The organization's highest authority to whom a matter may be referred ordinarily will be the board of directors or similar governing body. However, applicable law may prescribe that under certain conditions the highest authority reposes elsewhere, for example, in the independent directors of a corporation.

Relation to Other Rules

[6] The authority and responsibility provided in this Rule are concurrent with the authority and responsibility provided in other Rules. In particular, this Rule does not limit or expand the lawyer's responsibility under Rules 1.8, 1.16, 3.3 or 4.1. Paragraph (c) of this Rule supplements Rule 1.6(b) by providing an additional basis upon which the lawyer may reveal information relating to the representation, but does not modify, restrict, or limit the provisions of Rule 1.6(b)(1) – (6). Under paragraph (c) the lawyer may reveal such information only when the organization's highest authority insists upon or fails to address threatened or ongoing action that is clearly a violation of law, and then only to the extent the lawyer reasonably believes necessary to prevent reasonably certain substantial injury to the organization. It is not necessary that the lawyer's services be used in furtherance of the violation, but it is required that the matter be related to the lawyer's representation of the organization. If the lawyer's services are being used by an organization to further a crime or fraud by the organization, Rules 1.6(b)(2) and 1.6(b)(3) may permit the lawyer to disclose confidential information. In such circumstances Rule 1.2(d) may also be applicable, in which event, withdrawal from the representation under Rule 1.16(a)(1) may be required.

[7] Paragraph (d) makes clear that the authority of a lawyer to disclose information relating to a representation in circumstances described in paragraph (c) does not apply with respect to information relating to a lawyer's engagement by an organization to investigate an alleged violation of law or to defend the organization or an officer, employee or other person associated with the organization against a claim arising out of an alleged violation of law. This is necessary in order to enable organizational clients to enjoy the full benefits of legal counsel in conducting an investigation or defending against a claim.

[8] A lawyer who reasonably believes that he or she has been discharged because of the lawyer's actions taken pursuant to paragraph (b) or (c), or who withdraws in circumstances that require or permit the lawyer to take action under either of these paragraphs, must proceed as the lawyer reasonably believes necessary to assure that the organization's highest authority is informed of the lawyer's discharge or withdrawal.

Government Agency

[9] The duty defined in this Rule applies to governmental organizations. Defining precisely the identity of the client and prescribing the resulting obligations of such lawyers may be more difficult in the government context and is a matter beyond the scope of these Rules. See Scope [18]. Although in some circumstances the client may be a specific agency, it may also be a branch of government, such as the executive branch, or the government as a whole. For example, if the action or failure to act involves the head of a bureau, either the department of which the bureau is a part or the relevant branch of government may be the client for purposes of this Rule. Moreover, in a matter involving the conduct of government officials, a government lawyer may have authority under applicable law to question such conduct more extensively than that of a lawyer for a private organization in similar circumstances. Thus, when the client is a governmental organization, a different balance may be appropriate between maintaining confidentiality and assuring that the wrongful act is prevented or rectified, for public business is involved. In addition, duties of lawyers employed by the government or lawyers in military service may be defined by statutes and regulation. This Rule does not limit that authority. See Scope.

Clarifying the Lawyer's Role

[10] There are times when the organization's interest may be or become adverse to those of one or more of its constituents. In such circumstances the lawyer should advise any constituent, whose interest the lawyer finds adverse to that of the organization of the conflict or potential conflict of interest, that the lawyer cannot represent such constituent, and that such person may wish to obtain independent representation. Care must be taken to assure that the individual understands that, when there is such adversity of interest, the lawyer for the organization cannot provide legal representation for that constituent individual, and that discussions between the lawyer for the organization and the individual may not be privileged.

[11] Whether such a warning should be given by the lawyer for the organization to any constituent individual may turn on the facts of each case.

Dual Representation

[12] Paragraph (g) recognizes that a lawyer for an organization may also represent a principal officer or major shareholder.

Derivative Actions

[13] Under generally prevailing law, the shareholders or members of a corporation may bring suit to compel the directors to perform their legal obligations in the supervision of the organization. Members of unincorporated associations have essentially the same right. Such an action may be brought nominally by the organization, but usually is, in fact, a legal controversy over management of the organization.

[14] The question can arise whether counsel for the organization may defend such an action. The proposition that the organization is the lawyer's client does not alone resolve the issue. Most derivative actions are a normal incident of an organization's affairs, to be defended by the organization's lawyer like any other suit. However, if the claim involves serious charges of wrongdoing by those in control of the organization, a conflict may arise between the lawyer's duty to the organization and the lawyer's relationship with the board. In those circumstances, Rule 1.7 governs who should represent the directors and the organization.

Definitional Cross-References

"Knows" *See* Rule 1.0(f)
"Reasonably" *See* Rule 1.0(h)
"Reasonably believes" *See* Rule 1.0(i)
"Reasonably should know" *See* Rule 1.0(j)
"Substantial" *See* Rule 1.0(l)

Rule 1.14 Client With Diminished Capacity

(a) When a client's capacity to make adequately considered decisions in connection with a representation is diminished, whether because of minority, mental impairment or for some other reason, the lawyer shall, as far as reasonably possible, maintain a normal client-lawyer relationship with the client.

(b) When the lawyer reasonably believes that the client has diminished capacity, is at risk of substantial physical, financial or other harm unless action is taken and cannot adequately act in the client's own interest, the lawyer may take reasonably necessary protective action, including consulting with individuals or entities that have the ability to take action to protect the client and, in appropriate cases, seeking the appointment of a guardian ad litem, conservator or guardian.

(c) Information relating to the representation of a client with diminished capacity is protected by Rule 1.6. When taking protective action pursuant to paragraph (b), the lawyer is impliedly authorized under Rule 1.6(a) to reveal information about the client, but only to the extent reasonably necessary to protect the client's interests.

Comment

[1] The normal client-lawyer relationship is based on the assumption that the client, when properly advised and assisted, is capable of making decisions about important matters. When the client is a minor or suffers from a diminished mental capacity, however, maintaining the ordinary client-lawyer relationship may not be possible in all respects. In particular, a severely incapacitated person may have no power to make legally binding decisions. Nevertheless, a client with diminished capacity often has the ability to understand, deliberate upon, and reach conclusions about matters affecting the client's own well-being. For example, children as young as five or six years of age, and certainly those of ten or twelve, are regarded as having opinions that are entitled to weight in legal proceedings concerning their custody. So also, it is recognized that some persons of advanced age can be quite capable of handling routine financial matters while needing special legal protection concerning major transactions.

[2] The fact that a client suffers a disability does not diminish the lawyer's obligation to treat the client with attention and respect. Even if the person has a legal representative, the lawyer should as far as possible accord the represented person the status of client, particularly in maintaining communication.

[3] The client may wish to have family members or other persons participate in discussions with the lawyer. When necessary to assist in the representation, the presence of such persons generally does not affect the applicability of the attorney-client evidentiary privilege. Nevertheless, the lawyer must keep the client's interests foremost and, except for protective action authorized under paragraph (b), must look to the client, and not family members, to make decisions on the client's behalf.

[4] If a legal representative has already been appointed for the client, the lawyer should ordinarily look to the representative for decisions on behalf of the client. In matters involving a minor, whether the lawyer should look to the parents as natural guardians may depend on the type of proceeding or matter in which the lawyer is representing the minor. If the lawyer represents the guardian as distinct from the ward, and is aware that the guardian is acting adversely to the ward's interest, the lawyer may have an obligation to prevent or rectify the guardian's misconduct. See Rule 1.2(d).

Taking Protective Action

[5] If a lawyer reasonably believes that a client is at risk of substantial physical, financial or other harm unless action is taken, and that a normal client-lawyer relationship cannot be maintained as provided in paragraph (a) because the client lacks sufficient capacity to communicate or to make adequately considered decisions in connection with the representation, then paragraph (b) permits the lawyer to take protective measures deemed necessary. Such measures could include: consulting with family members, using a reconsideration period to permit clarification or improvement of circumstances, using voluntary surrogate decisionmaking tools such as durable powers of attorney or consulting with support groups, professional services, adult-protective agencies or other individuals or entities that have the ability to protect the client. In taking any protective action, the lawyer should be

guided by such factors as the wishes and values of the client to the extent known, the client's best interests and the goals of intruding into the client's decisionmaking autonomy to the least extent feasible, maximizing client capacities and respecting the client's family and social connections.

[6] In determining the extent of the client's diminished capacity, the lawyer should consider and balance such factors as: the client's ability to articulate reasoning leading to a decision, variability of state of mind and ability to appreciate consequences of a decision; the substantive fairness of a decision; and the consistency of a decision with the known long-term commitments and values of the client. In appropriate circumstances, the lawyer may seek guidance from an appropriate diagnostician.

[7] If a legal representative has not been appointed, the lawyer should consider whether appointment of a guardian ad litem, conservator or guardian is necessary to protect the client's interests. Thus, if a client with diminished capacity has substantial property that should be sold for the client's benefit, effective completion of the transaction may require appointment of a legal representative. In addition, rules of procedure in litigation sometimes provide that minors or persons with diminished capacity must be represented by a guardian or next friend if they do not have a general guardian. In many circumstances, however, appointment of a legal representative may be more expensive or traumatic for the client than circumstances in fact require. Evaluation of such circumstances is a matter entrusted to the professional judgment of the lawyer. In considering alternatives, however, the lawyer should be aware of any law that requires the lawyer to advocate the least restrictive action on behalf of the client.

Disclosure of the Client's Condition

[8] Disclosure of the client's diminished capacity could adversely affect the client's interests. For example, raising the question of diminished capacity could, in some circumstances, lead to proceedings for involuntary commitment. Information relating to the representation is protected by Rule 1.6. Therefore, unless authorized to do so, the lawyer may not disclose such information. When taking protective action pursuant to paragraph (b), the lawyer is impliedly authorized to make the necessary disclosures, even when the client directs the lawyer to the contrary. Nevertheless, given the risks of disclosure, paragraph (c) limits what the lawyer may disclose in consulting with other individuals or entities or seeking the appointment of a legal representative. At the very least, the lawyer should determine whether it is likely that the person or entity consulted with will act adversely to the client's interests before discussing matters related to the client. The lawyer's position in such cases is an unavoidably difficult one.

Emergency Legal Assistance

[9] In an emergency where the health, safety or a financial interest of a person with seriously diminished capacity is threatened with imminent and irreparable harm, a lawyer may take legal action on behalf of such a person even though the person is unable to establish a client-lawyer relationship or to make or express considered judgments about the matter, when the person or another acting in

good faith on that person's behalf has consulted with the lawyer. Even in such an emergency, however, the lawyer should not act unless the lawyer reasonably believes that the person has no other lawyer, agent or other representative available. The lawyer should take legal action on behalf of the person only to the extent reasonably necessary to maintain the status quo or otherwise avoid imminent and irreparable harm. A lawyer who undertakes to represent a person in such an exigent situation has the same duties under these Rules as the lawyer would with respect to a client.

[10] A lawyer who acts on behalf of a person with seriously diminished capacity in an emergency should keep the confidences of the person as if dealing with a client, disclosing them only to the extent necessary to accomplish the intended protective action. The lawyer should disclose to any tribunal involved and to any other counsel involved the nature of his or her relationship with the person. The lawyer should take steps to regularize the relationship or implement other protective solutions as soon as possible. Normally, a lawyer would not seek compensation for such emergency actions taken.

Definitional Cross-References

"Reasonably" *See* Rule 1.0(h)
"Reasonably believes" *See* Rule 1.0(i)
"Substantial" *See* Rule 1.0(l)

Rule 1.15 Safekeeping Property

(a) A lawyer shall hold property of clients or third persons that is in a lawyer's possession in connection with a representation separate from the lawyer's own property. Funds shall be kept in a separate account maintained in the state where the lawyer's office is situated, or elsewhere with the consent of the client or third person. Other property shall be identified as such and appropriately safeguarded. Complete records of such account funds and other property shall be kept by the lawyer and shall be preserved for a period of [five years] after termination of the representation.

(b) A lawyer may deposit the lawyer's own funds in a client trust account for the sole purpose of paying bank service charges on that account, but only in an amount necessary for that purpose.

(c) A lawyer shall deposit into a client trust account legal fees and expenses that have been paid in advance, to be withdrawn by the lawyer only as fees are earned or expenses incurred.

(d) Upon receiving funds or other property in which a client or third person has an interest, a lawyer shall promptly notify the client or third person. Except as stated in this Rule or otherwise permitted by law or by agreement with the client, a lawyer shall promptly deliver to the client or third person any funds or other property that the client or third person is entitled to receive and, upon request by the client or third person, shall promptly render a full accounting regarding such property.

(e) **When in the course of representation a lawyer is in possession of property in which two or more persons (one of whom may be the lawyer) claim interests, the property shall be kept separate by the lawyer until the dispute is resolved. The lawyer shall promptly distribute all portions of the property as to which the interests are not in dispute.**

Comment

[1] A lawyer should hold property of others with the care required of a professional fiduciary. Securities should be kept in a safe deposit box, except when some other form of safekeeping is warranted by special circumstances. All property that is the property of clients or third persons, including prospective clients, must be kept separate from the lawyer's business and personal property and, if monies, in one or more trust accounts. Separate trust accounts may be warranted when administering estate monies or acting in similar fiduciary capacities. A lawyer should maintain on a current basis books and records in accordance with generally accepted accounting practice and comply with any recordkeeping rules established by law or court order. See, e.g., ABA *Model Rules for Client Trust Account Records*.

[2] While normally it is impermissible to commingle the lawyer's own funds with client funds, paragraph (b) provides that it is permissible when necessary to pay bank service charges on that account. Accurate records must be kept regarding which part of the funds are the lawyer's.

[3] Lawyers often receive funds from which the lawyer's fee will be paid. The lawyer is not required to remit to the client funds that the lawyer reasonably believes represent fees owed. However, a lawyer may not hold funds to coerce a client into accepting the lawyer's contention. The disputed portion of the funds must be kept in a trust account and the lawyer should suggest means for prompt resolution of the dispute, such as arbitration. The undisputed portion of the funds shall be promptly distributed.

[4] Paragraph (e) also recognizes that third parties may have lawful claims against specific funds or other property in a lawyer's custody, such as a client's creditor who has a lien on funds recovered in a personal injury action. A lawyer may have a duty under applicable law to protect such third-party claims against wrongful interference by the client. In such cases, when the third-party claim is not frivolous under applicable law, the lawyer must refuse to surrender the property to the client until the claims are resolved. A lawyer should not unilaterally assume to arbitrate a dispute between the client and the third party, but, when there are substantial grounds for dispute as to the person entitled to the funds, the lawyer may file an action to have a court resolve the dispute.

[5] The obligations of a lawyer under this Rule are independent of those arising from activity other than rendering legal services. For example, a lawyer who serves only as an escrow agent is governed by the applicable law relating to fiduciaries even though the lawyer does not render legal services in the transaction and is not governed by this Rule.

[6] A lawyers' fund for client protection provides a means through the collective efforts of the bar to reimburse persons who have lost money or property as a result of dishonest conduct of a lawyer. Where such a fund has been established, a lawyer must participate where it is mandatory, and, even when it is voluntary, the lawyer should participate.

Rule 1.16 Declining or Terminating Representation

(a) A lawyer shall inquire into and assess the facts and circumstances of each representation to determine whether the lawyer may accept or continue the representation. Except as stated in paragraph (c), a lawyer shall not represent a client or, where representation has commenced, shall withdraw from the representation of a client if:

(1) the representation will result in violation of the Rules of Professional Conduct or other law;

(2) the lawyer's physical or mental condition materially impairs the lawyer's ability to represent the client;

(3) the lawyer is discharged; or

(4) the client or prospective client seeks to use or persists in using the lawyer's services to commit or further a crime or fraud, despite the lawyer's discussion pursuant to Rules 1.2(d) and 1.4(a)(5) regarding the limitations on the lawyer assisting with the proposed conduct.

(b) Except as stated in paragraph (c), a lawyer may withdraw from representing a client if:

(1) withdrawal can be accomplished without material adverse effect on the interests of the client;

(2) the client persists in a course of action involving the lawyer's services that the lawyer reasonably believes is criminal or fraudulent;

(3) the client has used the lawyer's services to perpetrate a crime or fraud;

(4) the client insists upon taking action that the lawyer considers repugnant or with which the lawyer has a fundamental disagreement;

(5) the client fails substantially to fulfill an obligation to the lawyer regarding the lawyer's services and has been given reasonable warning that the lawyer will withdraw unless the obligation is fulfilled;

(6) the representation will result in an unreasonable financial burden on the lawyer or has been rendered unreasonably difficult by the client; or

(7) other good cause for withdrawal exists.

(c) A lawyer must comply with applicable law requiring notice to or permission of a tribunal when terminating a representation. When ordered to do so by a tribunal, a lawyer shall continue representation notwithstanding good cause for terminating the representation.

(d) Upon termination of representation, a lawyer shall take steps to the extent reasonably practicable to protect a client's interests, such as giving reasonable notice to the client, allowing time for employment of other counsel, surrendering papers and property to which the client is entitled and refunding

any advance payment of fee or expense that has not been earned or incurred. The lawyer may retain papers relating to the client to the extent permitted by other law.

Comment

[1] Paragraph (a) imposes an obligation on a lawyer to inquire into and assess the facts and circumstances of the representation before accepting it. The obligation imposed by paragraph (a) continues throughout the representation. A change in the facts and circumstances relating to the representation may trigger a lawyer's need to make further inquiry and assessment. For example, a client traditionally uses a lawyer to acquire local real estate through the use of domestic limited liability companies, with financing from a local bank. The same client then asks the lawyer to create a multi-tier corporate structure, formed in another state to acquire property in a third jurisdiction, and requests to route the transaction's funding through the lawyer's trust account. Another example is when, during the course of a representation, a new party is named or a new entity becomes involved. A lawyer should not accept representation in a matter unless it can be performed competently, promptly, without improper conflict of interest and to completion. Ordinarily, a representation in a matter is completed when the agreed-upon assistance has been concluded. See Rules 1.1, 1.2(c), and 6.5. See also Rule 1.3, Comment [4].

Mandatory Withdrawal

[2] A lawyer ordinarily must decline or withdraw from representation if the client demands that the lawyer engage in conduct that is illegal or violates the Rules of Professional Conduct or other law. The lawyer is not obliged to decline or withdraw simply because the client suggests such a course of conduct; a client may make such a suggestion in the hope that a lawyer will not be constrained by a professional obligation. Under paragraph (a)(4), the lawyer's inquiry into and assessment of the facts and circumstances will be informed by the risk that the client or prospective client seeks to use or persists in using the lawyer's services to commit or further a crime or fraud. This analysis means that the required level of a lawyer's inquiry and assessment will vary for each client or prospective client, depending on the nature of the risk posed by each situation. Factors to be considered in determining the level of risk may include: (i) the identity of the client, such as whether the client is a natural person or an entity and, if an entity, the beneficial owners of that entity; (ii) the lawyer's experience and familiarity with the client; (iii) the nature of the requested legal services; (iv) the relevant jurisdictions involved in the representation (for example, whether a jurisdiction is considered at high risk for money laundering or terrorist financing); and (v) the identities of those depositing into or receiving funds from the lawyer's client trust account, or any other accounts in which client funds are held. For further guidance assessing risk, see, e.g., as amended or updated, Financial Action Task Force Guidance for a Risk-Based Approach for Legal Professionals, the ABA Voluntary Good Practices Guidance for Lawyers to Detect and Combat Money Laundering and Terrorist Financing, A Lawyer's Guide

to Detecting and Preventing Money Laundering (a collaborative publication of the International Bar Association, the American Bar Association, and the Council of Bars and Law Societies of Europe), the Organization for Economic Cooperation and Development (OECD) Due Diligence Guidance for Responsible Business Conduct, and the U.S. Department of Treasury Specially Designated Nationals and Blocked Persons List.

[3] When a lawyer has been appointed to represent a client, withdrawal ordinarily requires approval of the appointing authority. See also Rule 6.2. Similarly, court approval or notice to the court is often required by applicable law before a lawyer withdraws from pending litigation. Difficulty may be encountered if withdrawal is based on the client's demand that the lawyer engage in unprofessional conduct. The court may request an explanation for the withdrawal, while the lawyer may be bound to keep confidential the facts that would constitute such an explanation. The lawyer's statement that professional considerations require termination of the representation ordinarily should be accepted as sufficient. Lawyers should be mindful of their obligations to both clients and the court under Rules 1.6 and 3.3.

Discharge

[4] A client has a right to discharge a lawyer at any time, with or without cause, subject to liability for payment for the lawyer's services. Where future dispute about the withdrawal may be anticipated, it may be advisable to prepare a written statement reciting the circumstances.

[5] Whether a client can discharge appointed counsel may depend on applicable law. A client seeking to do so should be given a full explanation of the consequences. These consequences may include a decision by the appointing authority that appointment of successor counsel is unjustified, thus requiring self-representation by the client.

[6] If the client has severely diminished capacity, the client may lack the legal capacity to discharge the lawyer, and in any event the discharge may be seriously adverse to the client's interests. The lawyer should make special effort to help the client consider the consequences and may take reasonably necessary protective action as provided in Rule 1.14.

Optional Withdrawal

[7] A lawyer may withdraw from representation in some circumstances. The lawyer has the option to withdraw if it can be accomplished without material adverse effect on the client's interests. Withdrawal is also justified if the client persists in a course of action that the lawyer reasonably believes is criminal or fraudulent, for a lawyer is not required to be associated with such conduct even if the lawyer does not further it. Withdrawal is also permitted if the lawyer's services were misused in the past even if that would materially prejudice the client. The lawyer may also withdraw where the client insists on taking action that the lawyer considers repugnant or with which the lawyer has a fundamental disagreement.

[8] A lawyer may withdraw if the client refuses to abide by the terms of an agreement relating to the representation, such as an agreement concerning fees or court costs or an agreement limiting the objectives of the representation.

Assisting the Client upon Withdrawal

[9] Even if the lawyer has been unfairly discharged by the client, a lawyer must take all reasonable steps to mitigate the consequences to the client. The lawyer may retain papers as security for a fee only to the extent permitted by law. See Rule 1.15.

Definitional Cross-References

"Fraud" and "Fraudulent" *See* Rule 1.0(d)
"Reasonable" *See* Rule 1.0(h)
"Reasonably believes" *See* Rule 1.0(i)
"Tribunal" *See* Rule 1.0(m)

Rule 1.17 Sale of Law Practice

A lawyer or a law firm may sell or purchase a law practice, or an area of law practice, including good will, if the following conditions are satisfied:

(a) The seller ceases to engage in the private practice of law, or in the area of practice that has been sold, [in the geographic area] [in the jurisdiction] (a jurisdiction may elect either version) in which the practice has been conducted;

(b) The entire practice, or the entire area of practice, is sold to one or more lawyers or law firms;

(c) The seller gives written notice to each of the seller's clients regarding:

(1) the proposed sale;

(2) the client's right to retain other counsel or to take possession of the file; and

(3) the fact that the client's consent to the transfer of the client's files will be presumed if the client does not take any action or does not otherwise object within ninety (90) days of receipt of the notice.

If a client cannot be given notice, the representation of that client may be transferred to the purchaser only upon entry of an order so authorizing by a court having jurisdiction. The seller may disclose to the court in camera information relating to the representation only to the extent necessary to obtain an order authorizing the transfer of a file.

(d) The fees charged clients shall not be increased by reason of the sale.

Comment

[1] The practice of law is a profession, not merely a business. Clients are not commodities that can be purchased and sold at will. Pursuant to this Rule, when a lawyer or an entire firm ceases to practice, or ceases to practice in an area of law, and other lawyers or firms take over the representation, the selling lawyer or firm may obtain compensation for the reasonable value of the practice as may withdrawing partners of law firms. See Rules 5.4 and 5.6.

Termination of Practice by the Seller

[2] The requirement that all of the private practice, or all of an area of practice, be sold is satisfied if the seller in good faith makes the entire practice, or the area of practice, available for sale to the purchasers. The fact that a number of the seller's clients decide not to be represented by the purchasers but take their matters elsewhere, therefore, does not result in a violation. Return to private practice as a result of an unanticipated change in circumstances does not necessarily result in a violation. For example, a lawyer who has sold the practice to accept an appointment to judicial office does not violate the requirement that the sale be attendant to cessation of practice if the lawyer later resumes private practice upon being defeated in a contested or a retention election for the office or resigns from a judiciary position.

[3] The requirement that the seller cease to engage in the private practice of law does not prohibit employment as a lawyer on the staff of a public agency or a legal services entity that provides legal services to the poor, or as in-house counsel to a business.

[4] The Rule permits a sale of an entire practice attendant upon retirement from the private practice of law within the jurisdiction. Its provisions, therefore, accommodate the lawyer who sells the practice on the occasion of moving to another state. Some states are so large that a move from one locale therein to another is tantamount to leaving the jurisdiction in which the lawyer has engaged in the practice of law. To also accommodate lawyers so situated, states may permit the sale of the practice when the lawyer leaves the geographical area rather than the jurisdiction. The alternative desired should be indicated by selecting one of the two provided for in Rule 1.17(a).

[5] This Rule also permits a lawyer or law firm to sell an area of practice. If an area of practice is sold and the lawyer remains in the active practice of law, the lawyer must cease accepting any matters in the area of practice that has been sold, either as counsel or co-counsel or by assuming joint responsibility for a matter in connection with the division of a fee with another lawyer as would otherwise be permitted by Rule 1.5(e). For example, a lawyer with a substantial number of estate planning matters and a substantial number of probate administration cases may sell the estate planning portion of the practice but remain in the practice of law by concentrating on probate administration; however, that practitioner may not thereafter accept any estate planning matters. Although a lawyer who leaves a jurisdiction or geographical area typically would sell the entire practice, this Rule permits the lawyer to limit the sale to one or more areas of the practice, thereby preserving the lawyer's right to continue practice in the areas of the practice that were not sold.

Sale of Entire Practice or Entire Area of Practice

[6] The Rule requires that the seller's entire practice, or an entire area of practice, be sold. The prohibition against sale of less than an entire practice area protects those clients whose matters are less lucrative and who might find it difficult to

secure other counsel if a sale could be limited to substantial fee-generating matters. The purchasers are required to undertake all client matters in the practice or practice area, subject to client consent. This requirement is satisfied, however, even if a purchaser is unable to undertake a particular client matter because of a conflict of interest.

Client Confidences, Consent and Notice

[7] Negotiations between seller and prospective purchaser prior to disclosure of information relating to a specific representation of an identifiable client no more violate the confidentiality provisions of Model Rule 1.6 than do preliminary discussions concerning the possible association of another lawyer or mergers between firms, with respect to which client consent is not required. See Rule 1.6(b)(7). Providing the purchaser access to detailed information relating to the representation, such as the client's file, however, requires client consent. The Rule provides that before such information can be disclosed by the seller to the purchaser the client must be given actual written notice of the contemplated sale, including the identity of the purchaser, and must be told that the decision to consent or make other arrangements must be made within 90 days. If nothing is heard from the client within that time, consent to the sale is presumed.

[8] A lawyer or law firm ceasing to practice cannot be required to remain in practice because some clients cannot be given actual notice of the proposed purchase. Since these clients cannot themselves consent to the purchase or direct any other disposition of their files, the Rule requires an order from a court having jurisdiction authorizing their transfer or other disposition. The court can be expected to determine whether reasonable efforts to locate the client have been exhausted, and whether the absent client's legitimate interests will be served by authorizing the transfer of the file so that the purchaser may continue the representation. Preservation of client confidences requires that the petition for a court order be considered in camera. (A procedure by which such an order can be obtained needs to be established in jurisdictions in which it presently does not exist).

[9] All elements of client autonomy, including the client's absolute right to discharge a lawyer and transfer the representation to another, survive the sale of the practice or area of practice.

Fee Arrangements Between Client and Purchaser

[10] The sale may not be financed by increases in fees charged the clients of the practice. Existing arrangements between the seller and the client as to fees and the scope of the work must be honored by the purchaser.

Other Applicable Ethical Standards

[11] Lawyers participating in the sale of a law practice or a practice area are subject to the ethical standards applicable to involving another lawyer in the representation of a client. These include, for example, the seller's obligation to exercise

competence in identifying a purchaser qualified to assume the practice and the purchaser's obligation to undertake the representation competently (see Rule 1.1); the obligation to avoid disqualifying conflicts, and to secure the client's informed consent for those conflicts that can be agreed to (see Rule 1.7 regarding conflicts and Rule 1.0(e) for the definition of informed consent); and the obligation to protect information relating to the representation (see Rules 1.6 and 1.9).

[12] If approval of the substitution of the purchasing lawyer for the selling lawyer is required by the rules of any tribunal in which a matter is pending, such approval must be obtained before the matter can be included in the sale (see Rule 1.16).

Applicability of the Rule

[13] This Rule applies to the sale of a law practice of a deceased, disabled or disappeared lawyer. Thus, the seller may be represented by a non-lawyer representative not subject to these Rules. Since, however, no lawyer may participate in a sale of a law practice which does not conform to the requirements of this Rule, the representatives of the seller as well as the purchasing lawyer can be expected to see to it that they are met.

[14] Admission to or retirement from a law partnership or professional association, retirement plans and similar arrangements, and a sale of tangible assets of a law practice, do not constitute a sale or purchase governed by this Rule.

[15] This Rule does not apply to the transfers of legal representation between lawyers when such transfers are unrelated to the sale of a practice or an area of practice.

Definitional Cross-References

"Law firm" *See* Rule 1.0(c)
"Written" *See* Rule 1.0(n)

Rule 1.18 Duties to Prospective Client

(a) A person who consults with a lawyer about the possibility of forming a client-lawyer relationship with respect to a matter is a prospective client.

(b) Even when no client-lawyer relationship ensues, a lawyer who has learned information from a prospective client shall not use or reveal that information, except as Rule 1.9 would permit with respect to information of a former client.

(c) A lawyer subject to paragraph (b) shall not represent a client with interests materially adverse to those of a prospective client in the same or a substantially related matter if the lawyer received information from the prospective client that could be significantly harmful to that person in the matter, except as provided in paragraph (d). If a lawyer is disqualified from representation under this paragraph, no lawyer in a firm with which that lawyer is associated may knowingly undertake or continue representation in such a matter, except as provided in paragraph (d).

(d) When the lawyer has received disqualifying information as defined in paragraph (c), representation is permissible if:

(1) both the affected client and the prospective client have given informed consent, confirmed in writing; or:

(2) the lawyer who received the information took reasonable measures to avoid exposure to more disqualifying information than was reasonably necessary to determine whether to represent the prospective client; and

(i) the disqualified lawyer is timely screened from any participation in the matter and is apportioned no part of the fee therefrom; and

(ii) written notice is promptly given to the prospective client.

Comment

[1] Prospective clients, like clients, may disclose information to a lawyer, place documents or other property in the lawyer's custody, or rely on the lawyer's advice. A lawyer's consultations with a prospective client usually are limited in time and depth and leave both the prospective client and the lawyer free (and sometimes required) to proceed no further. Hence, prospective clients should receive some but not all of the protection afforded clients.

[2] A person becomes a prospective client by consulting with a lawyer about the possibility of forming a client-lawyer relationship with respect to a matter. Whether communications, including written, oral, or electronic communications, constitute a consultation depends on the circumstances. For example, a consultation is likely to have occurred if a lawyer, either in person or through the lawyer's advertising in any medium, specifically requests or invites the submission of information about a potential representation without clear and reasonably understandable warnings and cautionary statements that limit the lawyer's obligations, and a person provides information in response. See also Comment [4]. In contrast, a consultation does not occur if a person provides information to a lawyer in response to advertising that merely describes the lawyer's education, experience, areas of practice, and contact information, or provides legal information of general interest. Such a person communicates information unilaterally to a lawyer, without any reasonable expectation that the lawyer is willing to discuss the possibility of forming a client-lawyer relationship, and is thus not a "prospective client." Moreover, a person who communicates with a lawyer for the purpose of disqualifying the lawyer is not a "prospective client."

[3] It is often necessary for a prospective client to reveal information to the lawyer during an initial consultation prior to the decision about formation of a client-lawyer relationship. The lawyer often must learn such information to determine whether there is a conflict of interest with an existing client and whether the matter is one that the lawyer is willing to undertake. Paragraph (b) prohibits the lawyer from using or revealing that information, except as permitted by Rule 1.9, even if the client or lawyer decides not to proceed with the representation. The duty exists regardless of how brief the initial conference may be.

[4] In order to avoid acquiring disqualifying information from a prospective client, a lawyer considering whether or not to undertake a new matter should limit the initial consultation to only such information as reasonably appears necessary for that purpose. Where the information indicates that a conflict of interest or other reason for non-representation exists, the lawyer should so inform the prospective client or decline the representation. If the prospective client wishes to retain the lawyer, and if consent is possible under Rule 1.7, then consent from all affected present or former clients must be obtained before accepting the representation.

[5] A lawyer may condition a consultation with a prospective client on the person's informed consent that no information disclosed during the consultation will prohibit the lawyer from representing a different client in the matter. See Rule 1.0(e) for the definition of informed consent. If the agreement expressly so provides, the prospective client may also consent to the lawyer's subsequent use of information received from the prospective client.

[6] Even in the absence of an agreement, under paragraph (c), the lawyer is not prohibited from representing a client with interests adverse to those of the prospective client in the same or a substantially related matter unless the lawyer has received from the prospective client information that could be significantly harmful if used in the matter.

[7] Under paragraph (c), the prohibition in this Rule is imputed to other lawyers as provided in Rule 1.10, but, under paragraph (d)(1), imputation may be avoided if the lawyer obtains the informed consent, confirmed in writing, of both the prospective and affected clients. In the alternative, imputation may be avoided if the conditions of paragraph (d)(2) are met and all disqualified lawyers are timely screened and written notice is promptly given to the prospective client. See Rule 1.0(k) (requirements for screening procedures). Paragraph (d)(2)(i) does not prohibit the screened lawyer from receiving a salary or partnership share established by prior independent agreement, but that lawyer may not receive compensation directly related to the matter in which the lawyer is disqualified.

[8] Notice, including a general description of the subject matter about which the lawyer was consulted, and of the screening procedures employed, generally should be given as soon as practicable after the need for screening becomes apparent.

[9] For the duty of competence of a lawyer who gives assistance on the merits of a matter to a prospective client, see Rule 1.1. For a lawyer's duties when a prospective client entrusts valuables or papers to the lawyer's care, see Rule 1.15.

Definitional Cross-References

"Confirmed in writing" *See* Rule 1.0(b)
"Firm" *See* Rule 1.0(c)
"Informed consent" *See* Rule 1.0(e)
"Knowingly" *See* Rule 1.0(f)
"Reasonable" and "Reasonably" *See* Rule 1.0(h)
"Screened" *See* Rule 1.0(k)
"Written" *See* Rule 1.0(n)

ARTICLE 2. COUNSELOR

Rule 2.1 Advisor

In representing a client, a lawyer shall exercise independent professional judgment and render candid advice. In rendering advice, a lawyer may refer not only to law but to other considerations such as moral, economic, social and political factors, that may be relevant to the client's situation.

Comment

Scope of Advice

[1] A client is entitled to straightforward advice expressing the lawyer's honest assessment. Legal advice often involves unpleasant facts and alternatives that a client may be disinclined to confront. In presenting advice, a lawyer endeavors to sustain the client's morale and may put advice in as acceptable a form as honesty permits. However, a lawyer should not be deterred from giving candid advice by the prospect that the advice will be unpalatable to the client.

[2] Advice couched in narrow legal terms may be of little value to a client, especially where practical considerations, such as cost or effects on other people, are predominant. Purely technical legal advice, therefore, can sometimes be inadequate. It is proper for a lawyer to refer to relevant moral and ethical considerations in giving advice. Although a lawyer is not a moral advisor as such, moral and ethical considerations impinge upon most legal questions and may decisively influence how the law will be applied.

[3] A client may expressly or impliedly ask the lawyer for purely technical advice. When such a request is made by a client experienced in legal matters, the lawyer may accept it at face value. When such a request is made by a client inexperienced in legal matters, however, the lawyer's responsibility as advisor may include indicating that more may be involved than strictly legal considerations.

[4] Matters that go beyond strictly legal questions may also be in the domain of another profession. Family matters can involve problems within the professional competence of psychiatry, clinical psychology or social work; business matters can involve problems within the competence of the accounting profession or of financial specialists. Where consultation with a professional in another field is itself something a competent lawyer would recommend, the lawyer should make such a recommendation. At the same time, a lawyer's advice at its best often consists of recommending a course of action in the face of conflicting recommendations of experts.

Offering Advice

[5] In general, a lawyer is not expected to give advice until asked by the client. However, when a lawyer knows that a client proposes a course of action that is likely to result in substantial adverse legal consequences to the client, the lawyer's duty to the client under Rule 1.4 may require that the lawyer offer advice if the

client's course of action is related to the representation. Similarly, when a matter is likely to involve litigation, it may be necessary under Rule 1.4 to inform the client of forms of dispute resolution that might constitute reasonable alternatives to litigation. A lawyer ordinarily has no duty to initiate investigation of a client's affairs or to give advice that the client has indicated is unwanted, but a lawyer may initiate advice to a client when doing so appears to be in the client's interest.

Rule 2.2 (Deleted 2002)

Rule 2.3 Evaluation for Use by Third Persons

(a) A lawyer may provide an evaluation of a matter affecting a client for the use of someone other than the client if the lawyer reasonably believes that making the evaluation is compatible with other aspects of the lawyer's relationship with the client.

(b) When the lawyer knows or reasonably should know that the evaluation is likely to affect the client's interests materially and adversely, the lawyer shall not provide the evaluation unless the client gives informed consent.

(c) Except as disclosure is authorized in connection with a report of an evaluation, information relating to the evaluation is otherwise protected by Rule 1.6.

Comment

Definition

[1] An evaluation may be performed at the client's direction or when impliedly authorized in order to carry out the representation. See Rule 1.2. Such an evaluation may be for the primary purpose of establishing information for the benefit of third parties; for example, an opinion concerning the title of property rendered at the behest of a vendor for the information of a prospective purchaser, or at the behest of a borrower for the information of a prospective lender. In some situations, the evaluation may be required by a government agency; for example, an opinion concerning the legality of the securities registered for sale under the securities laws. In other instances, the evaluation may be required by a third person, such as a purchaser of a business.

[2] A legal evaluation should be distinguished from an investigation of a person with whom the lawyer does not have a client-lawyer relationship. For example, a lawyer retained by a purchaser to analyze a vendor's title to property does not have a client-lawyer relationship with the vendor. So also, an investigation into a person's affairs by a government lawyer or by special counsel employed by the government, is not an evaluation as that term is used in this Rule. The question is whether the lawyer is retained by the person whose affairs are being examined. When the lawyer is retained by that person, the general rules concerning loyalty to client and preservation of confidences apply, which is not the case if the lawyer is retained by someone else. For this reason, it is essential to identify the person by whom the

lawyer is retained. This should be made clear not only to the person under examination, but also to others to whom the results are to be made available.

Duties Owed to Third Person and Client

[3] When the evaluation is intended for the information or use of a third person, a legal duty to that person may or may not arise. That legal question is beyond the scope of this Rule. However, since such an evaluation involves a departure from the normal client-lawyer relationship, careful analysis of the situation is required. The lawyer must be satisfied as a matter of professional judgment that making the evaluation is compatible with other functions undertaken in behalf of the client. For example, if the lawyer is acting as advocate in defending the client against charges of fraud, it would normally be incompatible with that responsibility for the lawyer to perform an evaluation for others concerning the same or a related transaction. Assuming no such impediment is apparent, however, the lawyer should advise the client of the implications of the evaluation, particularly the lawyer's responsibilities to third persons and the duty to disseminate the findings.

Access to and Disclosure of Information

[4] The quality of an evaluation depends on the freedom and extent of the investigation upon which it is based. Ordinarily a lawyer should have whatever latitude of investigation seems necessary as a matter of professional judgment. Under some circumstances, however, the terms of the evaluation may be limited. For example, certain issues or sources may be categorically excluded, or the scope of search may be limited by time constraints or the noncooperation of persons having relevant information. Any such limitations that are material to the evaluation should be described in the report. If after a lawyer has commenced an evaluation, the client refuses to comply with the terms upon which it was understood the evaluation was to have been made, the lawyer's obligations are determined by law, having reference to the terms of the client's agreement and the surrounding circumstances. In no circumstances is the lawyer permitted to knowingly make a false statement of material fact or law in providing an evaluation under this Rule. See Rule 4.1.

Obtaining Client's Informed Consent

[5] Information relating to an evaluation is protected by Rule 1.6. In many situations, providing an evaluation to a third party poses no significant risk to the client; thus, the lawyer may be impliedly authorized to disclose information to carry out the representation. See Rule 1.6(a). Where, however, it is reasonably likely that providing the evaluation will affect the client's interests materially and adversely, the lawyer must first obtain the client's consent after the client has been adequately informed concerning the important possible effects on the client's interests. See Rules 1.6(a) and 1.0(e).

Financial Auditors' Requests for Information

[6] When a question concerning the legal situation of a client arises at the instance of the client's financial auditor and the question is referred to the lawyer,

the lawyer's response may be made in accordance with procedures recognized in the legal profession. Such a procedure is set forth in the American Bar Association Statement of Policy Regarding Lawyers' Responses to Auditors' Requests for Information, adopted in 1975.

Definitional Cross-References

"Informed consent" *See* Rule 1.0(e)
"Knows" *See* Rule 1.0(f)
"Reasonably believes" *See* Rule 1.0(i)
"Reasonably should know" *See* Rule 1.0(j)

Rule 2.4 Lawyer Serving as Third-Party Neutral

(a) A lawyer serves as a third-party neutral when the lawyer assists two or more persons who are not clients of the lawyer to reach a resolution of a dispute or other matter that has arisen between them. Service as a third-party neutral may include service as an arbitrator, a mediator or in such other capacity as will enable the lawyer to assist the parties to resolve the matter.

(b) A lawyer serving as a third-party neutral shall inform unrepresented parties that the lawyer is not representing them. When the lawyer knows or reasonably should know that a party does not understand the lawyer's role in the matter, the lawyer shall explain the difference between the lawyer's role as a third-party neutral and a lawyer's role as one who represents a client.

Comment

[1] Alternative dispute resolution has become a substantial part of the civil justice system. Aside from representing clients in dispute-resolution processes, lawyers often serve as third-party neutrals. A third-party neutral is a person, such as a mediator, arbitrator, conciliator or evaluator, who assists the parties, represented or unrepresented, in the resolution of a dispute or in the arrangement of a transaction. Whether a third-party neutral serves primarily as a facilitator, evaluator or decisionmaker depends on the particular process that is either selected by the parties or mandated by a court.

[2] The role of a third-party neutral is not unique to lawyers, although, in some court-connected contexts, only lawyers are allowed to serve in this role or to handle certain types of cases. In performing this role, the lawyer may be subject to court rules or other law that apply either to third-party neutrals generally or to lawyers serving as third-party neutrals. Lawyer-neutrals may also be subject to various codes of ethics, such as the Code of Ethics for Arbitrators in Commercial Disputes prepared by a joint committee of the American Bar Association and the American Arbitration Association or the Model Standards of Conduct for Mediators jointly prepared by the American Bar Association, the American Arbitration Association and the Society of Professionals in Dispute Resolution.

[3] Unlike nonlawyers who serve as third-party neutrals, lawyers serving in this role may experience unique problems as a result of differences between the role of

a third-party neutral and a lawyer's service as a client representative. The potential for confusion is significant when the parties are unrepresented in the process. Thus, paragraph (b) requires a lawyer-neutral to inform unrepresented parties that the lawyer is not representing them. For some parties, particularly parties who frequently use dispute-resolution processes, this information will be sufficient. For others, particularly those who are using the process for the first time, more information will be required. Where appropriate, the lawyer should inform unrepresented parties of the important differences between the lawyer's role as third-party neutral and a lawyer's role as a client representative, including the inapplicability of the attorney-client evidentiary privilege. The extent of disclosure required under this paragraph will depend on the particular parties involved and the subject matter of the proceeding, as well as the particular features of the dispute-resolution process selected.

[4] A lawyer who serves as a third-party neutral subsequently may be asked to serve as a lawyer representing a client in the same matter. The conflicts of interest that arise for both the individual lawyer and the lawyer's law firm are addressed in Rule 1.12.

[5] Lawyers who represent clients in alternative dispute-resolution processes are governed by the Rules of Professional Conduct. When the dispute-resolution process takes place before a tribunal, as in binding arbitration (see Rule 1.0(m)), the lawyer's duty of candor is governed by Rule 3.3. Otherwise, the lawyer's duty of candor toward both the third-party neutral and other parties is governed by Rule 4.1.

Definitional Cross-References

"Knows" *See* Rule 1.0(f)
"Reasonably should know" *See* Rule 1.0(j)

ARTICLE 3. ADVOCATE

Rule 3.1 Meritorious Claims and Contentions

A lawyer shall not bring or defend a proceeding, or assert or controvert an issue therein, unless there is a basis in law and fact for doing so that is not frivolous, which includes a good faith argument for an extension, modification or reversal of existing law. A lawyer for the defendant in a criminal proceeding, or the respondent in a proceeding that could result in incarceration, may nevertheless so defend the proceeding as to require that every element of the case be established.

Comment

[1] The advocate has a duty to use legal procedure for the fullest benefit of the client's cause, but also a duty not to abuse legal procedure. The law, both procedural and substantive, establishes the limits within which an advocate may proceed.

However, the law is not always clear and never is static. Accordingly, in determining the proper scope of advocacy, account must be taken of the law's ambiguities and potential for change.

[2] The filing of an action or defense or similar action taken for a client is not frivolous merely because the facts have not first been fully substantiated or because the lawyer expects to develop vital evidence only by discovery. What is required of lawyers, however, is that they inform themselves about the facts of their clients' cases and the applicable law and determine that they can make good faith arguments in support of their clients' positions. Such action is not frivolous even though the lawyer believes that the client's position ultimately will not prevail. The action is frivolous, however, if the lawyer is unable either to make a good faith argument on the merits of the action taken or to support the action taken by a good faith argument for an extension, modification or reversal of existing law.

[3] The lawyer's obligations under this Rule are subordinate to federal or state constitutional law that entitles a defendant in a criminal matter to the assistance of counsel in presenting a claim or contention that otherwise would be prohibited by this Rule.

Rule 3.2 Expediting Litigation

A lawyer shall make reasonable efforts to expedite litigation consistent with the interests of the client.

Comment

[1] Dilatory practices bring the administration of justice into disrepute. Although there will be occasions when a lawyer may properly seek a postponement for personal reasons, it is not proper for a lawyer to routinely fail to expedite litigation solely for the convenience of the advocates. Nor will a failure to expedite be reasonable if done for the purpose of frustrating an opposing party's attempt to obtain rightful redress or repose. It is not a justification that similar conduct is often tolerated by the bench and bar. The question is whether a competent lawyer acting in good faith would regard the course of action as having some substantial purpose other than delay. Realizing financial or other benefit from otherwise improper delay in litigation is not a legitimate interest of the client.

Definitional Cross-Reference

"Reasonable" *See* Rule 1.0(h)

Rule 3.3 Candor Toward the Tribunal

(a) A lawyer shall not knowingly:

(1) make a false statement of fact or law to a tribunal or fail to correct a false statement of material fact or law previously made to the tribunal by the lawyer;

(2) fail to disclose to the tribunal legal authority in the controlling jurisdiction known to the lawyer to be directly adverse to the position of the client and not disclosed by opposing counsel; or

(3) offer evidence that the lawyer knows to be false. If a lawyer, the lawyer's client, or a witness called by the lawyer, has offered material evidence and the lawyer comes to know of its falsity, the lawyer shall take reasonable remedial measures, including, if necessary, disclosure to the tribunal. A lawyer may refuse to offer evidence, other than the testimony of a defendant in a criminal matter, that the lawyer reasonably believes is false.

(b) A lawyer who represents a client in an adjudicative proceeding and who knows that a person intends to engage, is engaging or has engaged in criminal or fraudulent conduct related to the proceeding shall take reasonable remedial measures, including, if necessary, disclosure to the tribunal.

(c) The duties stated in paragraphs (a) and (b) continue to the conclusion of the proceeding, and apply even if compliance requires disclosure of information otherwise protected by Rule 1.6.

(d) In an ex parte proceeding, a lawyer shall inform the tribunal of all material facts known to the lawyer that will enable the tribunal to make an informed decision, whether or not the facts are adverse.

Comment

[1] This Rule governs the conduct of a lawyer who is representing a client in the proceedings of a tribunal. See Rule 1.0(m) for the definition of "tribunal." It also applies when the lawyer is representing a client in an ancillary proceeding conducted pursuant to the tribunal's adjudicative authority, such as a deposition. Thus, for example, paragraph (a) (3) requires a lawyer to take reasonable remedial measures if the lawyer comes to know that a client who is testifying in a deposition has offered evidence that is false.

[2] This Rule sets forth the special duties of lawyers as officers of the court to avoid conduct that undermines the integrity of the adjudicative process. A lawyer acting as an advocate in an adjudicative proceeding has an obligation to present the client's case with persuasive force. Performance of that duty while maintaining confidences of the client, however, is qualified by the advocate's duty of candor to the tribunal. Consequently, although a lawyer in an adversary proceeding is not required to present an impartial exposition of the law or to vouch for the evidence submitted in a cause, the lawyer must not allow the tribunal to be misled by false statements of law or fact or evidence that the lawyer knows to be false.

Representations by a Lawyer

[3] An advocate is responsible for pleadings and other documents prepared for litigation, but is usually not required to have personal knowledge of matters asserted therein, for litigation documents ordinarily present assertions by the client, or by someone on the client's behalf, and not assertions by the lawyer. Compare Rule 3.1. However, an assertion purporting to be on the lawyer's own knowledge, as in an affidavit by the lawyer or in a statement in open court, may properly be

made only when the lawyer knows the assertion is true or believes it to be true on the basis of a reasonably diligent inquiry. There are circumstances where failure to make a disclosure is the equivalent of an affirmative misrepresentation. The obligation prescribed in Rule 1.2(d) not to counsel a client to commit or assist the client in committing a fraud applies in litigation. Regarding compliance with Rule 1.2(d), see the Comment to that Rule. See also the Comment to Rule 8.4(b).

Legal Argument

[4] Legal argument based on a knowingly false representation of law constitutes dishonesty toward the tribunal. A lawyer is not required to make a disinterested exposition of the law, but must recognize the existence of pertinent legal authorities. Furthermore, as stated in paragraph (a)(2), an advocate has a duty to disclose directly adverse authority in the controlling jurisdiction that has not been disclosed by the opposing party. The underlying concept is that legal argument is a discussion seeking to determine the legal premises properly applicable to the case.

Offering Evidence

[5] Paragraph (a)(3) requires that the lawyer refuse to offer evidence that the lawyer knows to be false, regardless of the client's wishes. This duty is premised on the lawyer's obligation as an officer of the court to prevent the trier of fact from being misled by false evidence. A lawyer does not violate this Rule if the lawyer offers the evidence for the purpose of establishing its falsity.

[6] If a lawyer knows that the client intends to testify falsely or wants the lawyer to introduce false evidence, the lawyer should seek to persuade the client that the evidence should not be offered. If the persuasion is ineffective and the lawyer continues to represent the client, the lawyer must refuse to offer the false evidence. If only a portion of a witness's testimony will be false, the lawyer may call the witness to testify but may not elicit or otherwise permit the witness to present the testimony that the lawyer knows is false.

[7] The duties stated in paragraphs (a) and (b) apply to all lawyers, including defense counsel in criminal cases. In some jurisdictions, however, courts have required counsel to present the accused as a witness or to give a narrative statement if the accused so desires, even if counsel knows that the testimony or statement will be false. The obligation of the advocate under the Rules of Professional Conduct is subordinate to such requirements. See also Comment [9].

[8] The prohibition against offering false evidence only applies if the lawyer knows that the evidence is false. A lawyer's reasonable belief that evidence is false does not preclude its presentation to the trier of fact. A lawyer's knowledge that evidence is false, however, can be inferred from the circumstances. See Rule 1.0(f). Thus, although a lawyer should resolve doubts about the veracity of testimony or other evidence in favor of the client, the lawyer cannot ignore an obvious falsehood.

[9] Although paragraph (a)(3) only prohibits a lawyer from offering evidence the lawyer knows to be false, it permits the lawyer to refuse to offer testimony or other proof that the lawyer reasonably believes is false. Offering such proof may reflect adversely on the lawyer's ability to discriminate in the quality of evidence

and thus impair the lawyer's effectiveness as an advocate. Because of the special protections historically provided criminal defendants, however, this Rule does not permit a lawyer to refuse to offer the testimony of such a client where the lawyer reasonably believes but does not know that the testimony will be false. Unless the lawyer knows the testimony will be false, the lawyer must honor the client's decision to testify. See also Comment [7].

Remedial Measures

[10] Having offered material evidence in the belief that it was true, a lawyer may subsequently come to know that the evidence is false. Or, a lawyer may be surprised when the lawyer's client, or another witness called by the lawyer, offers testimony the lawyer knows to be false, either during the lawyer's direct examination or in response to cross-examination by the opposing lawyer. In such situations or if the lawyer knows of the falsity of testimony elicited from the client during a deposition, the lawyer must take reasonable remedial measures. In such situations, the advocate's proper course is to remonstrate with the client confidentially, advise the client of the lawyer's duty of candor to the tribunal and seek the client's cooperation with respect to the withdrawal or correction of the false statements or evidence. If that fails, the advocate must take further remedial action. If withdrawal from the representation is not permitted or will not undo the effect of the false evidence, the advocate must make such disclosure to the tribunal as is reasonably necessary to remedy the situation, even if doing so requires the lawyer to reveal information that otherwise would be protected by Rule 1.6. It is for the tribunal then to determine what should be done — making a statement about the matter to the trier of fact, ordering a mistrial or perhaps nothing.

[11] The disclosure of a client's false testimony can result in grave consequences to the client, including not only a sense of betrayal but also loss of the case and perhaps a prosecution for perjury. But the alternative is that the lawyer cooperate in deceiving the court, thereby subverting the truth-finding process which the adversary system is designed to implement. See Rule 1.2(d). Furthermore, unless it is clearly understood that the lawyer will act upon the duty to disclose the existence of false evidence, the client can simply reject the lawyer's advice to reveal the false evidence and insist that the lawyer keep silent. Thus the client could in effect coerce the lawyer into being a party to fraud on the court.

Preserving Integrity of Adjudicative Process

[12] Lawyers have a special obligation to protect a tribunal against criminal or fraudulent conduct that undermines the integrity of the adjudicative process, such as bribing, intimidating or otherwise unlawfully communicating with a witness, juror, court official or other participant in the proceeding, unlawfully destroying or concealing documents or other evidence or failing to disclose information to the tribunal when required by law to do so. Thus, paragraph (b) requires a lawyer to take reasonable remedial measures, including disclosure if necessary, whenever the lawyer knows that a person, including the lawyer's client, intends to engage, is engaging or has engaged in criminal or fraudulent conduct related to the proceeding.

Duration of Obligation

[13] A practical time limit on the obligation to rectify false evidence or false statements of law and fact has to be established. The conclusion of the proceeding is a reasonably definite point for the termination of the obligation. A proceeding has concluded within the meaning of this Rule when a final judgment in the proceeding has been affirmed on appeal or the time for review has passed.

Ex Parte Proceedings

[14] Ordinarily, an advocate has the limited responsibility of presenting one side of the matters that a tribunal should consider in reaching a decision; the conflicting position is expected to be presented by the opposing party. However, in any ex parte proceeding, such as an application for a temporary restraining order, there is no balance of presentation by opposing advocates. The object of an ex parte proceeding is nevertheless to yield a substantially just result. The judge has an affirmative responsibility to accord the absent party just consideration. The lawyer for the represented party has the correlative duty to make disclosures of material facts known to the lawyer and that the lawyer reasonably believes are necessary to an informed decision.

Withdrawal

[15] Normally, a lawyer's compliance with the duty of candor imposed by this Rule does not require that the lawyer withdraw from the representation of a client whose interests will be or have been adversely affected by the lawyer's disclosure. The lawyer may, however, be required by Rule 1.16(a) to seek permission of the tribunal to withdraw if the lawyer's compliance with this Rule's duty of candor results in such an extreme deterioration of the client-lawyer relationship that the lawyer can no longer competently represent the client. Also see Rule 1.16(b) for the circumstances in which a lawyer will be permitted to seek a tribunal's permission to withdraw. In connection with a request for permission to withdraw that is premised on a client's misconduct, a lawyer may reveal information relating to the representation only to the extent reasonably necessary to comply with this Rule or as otherwise permitted by Rule 1.6.

Definitional Cross-References

"Fraudulent" *See* Rule 1.0(d)
"Knowingly," "Known," and "Knows" *See* Rule 1.0(f)
"Reasonable" *See* Rule 1.0(h)
"Reasonably believes" *See* Rule 1.0(i)
"Tribunal" *See* Rule 1.0(m)

Rule 3.4 Fairness to Opposing Party and Counsel

A lawyer shall not:

(a) unlawfully obstruct another party's access to evidence or unlawfully alter, destroy or conceal a document or other material having potential

evidentiary value. A lawyer shall not counsel or assist another person to do any such act;

(b) falsify evidence, counsel or assist a witness to testify falsely, or offer an inducement to a witness that is prohibited by law;

(c) knowingly disobey an obligation under the rules of a tribunal, except for an open refusal based on an assertion that no valid obligation exists;

(d) in pretrial procedure, make a frivolous discovery request or fail to make reasonably diligent effort to comply with a legally proper discovery request by an opposing party;

(e) in trial, allude to any matter that the lawyer does not reasonably believe is relevant or that will not be supported by admissible evidence, assert personal knowledge of facts in issue except when testifying as a witness, or state a personal opinion as to the justness of a cause, the credibility of a witness, the culpability of a civil litigant or the guilt or innocence of an accused; or

(f) request a person other than a client to refrain from voluntarily giving relevant information to another party unless:

(1) the person is a relative or an employee or other agent of a client; and

(2) the lawyer reasonably believes that the person's interests will not be adversely affected by refraining from giving such information.

Comment

[1] The procedure of the adversary system contemplates that the evidence in a case is to be marshalled competitively by the contending parties. Fair competition in the adversary system is secured by prohibitions against destruction or concealment of evidence, improperly influencing witnesses, obstructive tactics in discovery procedure, and the like.

[2] Documents and other items of evidence are often essential to establish a claim or defense. Subject to evidentiary privileges, the right of an opposing party, including the government, to obtain evidence through discovery or subpoena is an important procedural right. The exercise of that right can be frustrated if relevant material is altered, concealed or destroyed. Applicable law in many jurisdictions makes it an offense to destroy material for purpose of impairing its availability in a pending proceeding or one whose commencement can be foreseen. Falsifying evidence is also generally a criminal offense. Paragraph (a) applies to evidentiary material generally, including computerized information. Applicable law may permit a lawyer to take temporary possession of physical evidence of client crimes for the purpose of conducting a limited examination that will not alter or destroy material characteristics of the evidence. In such a case, applicable law may require the lawyer to turn the evidence over to the police or other prosecuting authority, depending on the circumstances.

[3] With regard to paragraph (b), it is not improper to pay a witness's expenses or to compensate an expert witness on terms permitted by law. The common law rule in most jurisdictions is that it is improper to pay an occurrence witness any fee for testifying and that it is improper to pay an expert witness a contingent fee.

[4] Paragraph (f) permits a lawyer to advise employees of a client to refrain from giving information to another party, for the employees may identify their interests with those of the client. See also Rule 4.2.

Definitional Cross-References

"Knowingly" *See* Rule 1.0(f)
"Reasonably" *See* Rule 1.0(h)
"Reasonably believes" *See* Rule 1.0(i)
"Tribunal" *See* Rule 1.0(m)

Rule 3.5 Impartiality and Decorum of the Tribunal

A lawyer shall not:

(a) seek to influence a judge, juror, prospective juror or other official by means prohibited by law;

(b) communicate ex parte with such a person during the proceeding unless authorized to do so by law or court order;

(c) communicate with a juror or prospective juror after discharge of the jury if:

(1) the communication is prohibited by law or court order;

(2) the juror has made known to the lawyer a desire not to communicate; or

(3) the communication involves misrepresentation, coercion, duress or harassment; or

(d) engage in conduct intended to disrupt a tribunal.

Comment

[1] Many forms of improper influence upon a tribunal are proscribed by criminal law. Others are specified in the ABA Model Code of Judicial Conduct, with which an advocate should be familiar. A lawyer is required to avoid contributing to a violation of such provisions.

[2] During a proceeding a lawyer may not communicate ex parte with persons serving in an official capacity in the proceeding, such as judges, masters or jurors, unless authorized to do so by law or court order.

[3] A lawyer may on occasion want to communicate with a juror or prospective juror after the jury has been discharged. The lawyer may do so unless the communication is prohibited by law or a court order but must respect the desire of the juror not to talk with the lawyer. The lawyer may not engage in improper conduct during the communication.

[4] The advocate's function is to present evidence and argument so that the cause may be decided according to law. Refraining from abusive or obstreperous conduct is a corollary of the advocate's right to speak on behalf of litigants. A lawyer may stand firm against abuse by a judge but should avoid reciprocation; the

judge's default is no justification for similar dereliction by an advocate. An advocate can present the cause, protect the record for subsequent review and preserve professional integrity by patient firmness no less effectively than by belligerence or theatrics.

[5] The duty to refrain from disruptive conduct applies to any proceeding of a tribunal, including a deposition. See Rule 1.0(m).

Definitional Cross-References

"Known" *See* Rule 1.0(f)
"Tribunal" *See* Rule 1.0(m)

Rule 3.6 Trial Publicity

(a) A lawyer who is participating or has participated in the investigation or litigation of a matter shall not make an extrajudicial statement that the lawyer knows or reasonably should know will be disseminated by means of public communication and will have a substantial likelihood of materially prejudicing an adjudicative proceeding in the matter.

(b) Notwithstanding paragraph (a), a lawyer may state:

(1) the claim, offense or defense involved and, except when prohibited by law, the identity of the persons involved;

(2) information contained in a public record;

(3) that an investigation of a matter is in progress;

(4) the scheduling or result of any step in litigation;

(5) a request for assistance in obtaining evidence and information necessary thereto;

(6) a warning of danger concerning the behavior of a person involved, when there is reason to believe that there exists the likelihood of substantial harm to an individual or to the public interest; and

(7) in a criminal case, in addition to subparagraphs (1) through (6):

(i) the identity, residence, occupation and family status of the accused;

(ii) if the accused has not been apprehended, information necessary to aid in apprehension of that person;

(iii) the fact, time and place of arrest; and

(iv) the identity of investigating and arresting officers or agencies and the length of the investigation.

(c) Notwithstanding paragraph (a), a lawyer may make a statement that a reasonable lawyer would believe is required to protect a client from the substantial undue prejudicial effect of recent publicity not initiated by the lawyer or the lawyer's client. A statement made pursuant to this paragraph shall be limited to such information as is necessary to mitigate the recent adverse publicity.

(d) No lawyer associated in a firm or government agency with a lawyer subject to paragraph (a) shall make a statement prohibited by paragraph (a).

Comment

[1] It is difficult to strike a balance between protecting the right to a fair trial and safeguarding the right of free expression. Preserving the right to a fair trial necessarily entails some curtailment of the information that may be disseminated about a party prior to trial, particularly where trial by jury is involved. If there were no such limits, the result would be the practical nullification of the protective effect of the rules of forensic decorum and the exclusionary rules of evidence. On the other hand, there are vital social interests served by the free dissemination of information about events having legal consequences and about legal proceedings themselves. The public has a right to know about threats to its safety and measures aimed at assuring its security. It also has a legitimate interest in the conduct of judicial proceedings, particularly in matters of general public concern. Furthermore, the subject matter of legal proceedings is often of direct significance in debate and deliberation over questions of public policy.

[2] Special rules of confidentiality may validly govern proceedings in juvenile, domestic relations and mental disability proceedings, and perhaps other types of litigation. Rule 3.4(c) requires compliance with such rules.

[3] The Rule sets forth a basic general prohibition against a lawyer's making statements that the lawyer knows or should know will have a substantial likelihood of materially prejudicing an adjudicative proceeding. Recognizing that the public value of informed commentary is great and the likelihood of prejudice to a proceeding by the commentary of a lawyer who is not involved in the proceeding is small, the Rule applies only to lawyers who are, or who have been involved in the investigation or litigation of a case, and their associates.

[4] Paragraph (b) identifies specific matters about which a lawyer's statements would not ordinarily be considered to present a substantial likelihood of material prejudice, and should not in any event be considered prohibited by the general prohibition of paragraph (a). Paragraph (b) is not intended to be an exhaustive listing of the subjects upon which a lawyer may make a statement, but statements on other matters may be subject to paragraph (a).

[5] There are, on the other hand, certain subjects that are more likely than not to have a material prejudicial effect on a proceeding, particularly when they refer to a civil matter triable to a jury, a criminal matter, or any other proceeding that could result in incarceration. These subjects relate to:

(1) the character, credibility, reputation or criminal record of a party, suspect in a criminal investigation or witness, or the identity of a witness, or the expected testimony of a party or witness;

(2) in a criminal case or proceeding that could result in incarceration, the possibility of a plea of guilty to the offense or the existence or contents of any confession, admission, or statement given by a defendant or suspect or that person's refusal or failure to make a statement;

(3) the performance or results of any examination or test or the refusal or failure of a person to submit to an examination or test, or the identity or nature of physical evidence expected to be presented;

(4) any opinion as to the guilt or innocence of a defendant or suspect in a criminal case or proceeding that could result in incarceration;

(5) information that the lawyer knows or reasonably should know is likely to be inadmissible as evidence in a trial and that would, if disclosed, create a substantial risk of prejudicing an impartial trial; or

(6) the fact that a defendant has been charged with a crime, unless there is included therein a statement explaining that the charge is merely an accusation and that the defendant is presumed innocent until and unless proven guilty.

[6] Another relevant factor in determining prejudice is the nature of the proceeding involved. Criminal jury trials will be most sensitive to extrajudicial speech. Civil trials may be less sensitive. Non-jury hearings and arbitration proceedings may be even less affected. The Rule will still place limitations on prejudicial comments in these cases, but the likelihood of prejudice may be different depending on the type of proceeding.

[7] Finally, extrajudicial statements that might otherwise raise a question under this Rule may be permissible when they are made in response to statements made publicly by another party, another party's lawyer, or third persons, where a reasonable lawyer would believe a public response is required in order to avoid prejudice to the lawyer's client. When prejudicial statements have been publicly made by others, responsive statements may have the salutary effect of lessening any resulting adverse impact on the adjudicative proceeding. Such responsive statements should be limited to contain only such information as is necessary to mitigate undue prejudice created by the statements made by others.

[8] See Rule 3.8(f) for additional duties of prosecutors in connection with extrajudicial statements about criminal proceedings.

Definitional Cross-References

"Firm" *See* Rule 1.0(c)
"Knows" *See* Rule 1.0(f)
"Reasonable" *See* Rule 1.0(h)
"Reasonably should know" *See* Rule 1.0(j)
"Substantial" *See* Rule 1.0(l)

Rule 3.7 Lawyer as Witness

(a) A lawyer shall not act as advocate at a trial in which the lawyer is likely to be a necessary witness unless:

(1) the testimony relates to an uncontested issue;

(2) the testimony relates to the nature and value of legal services rendered in the case; or

(3) disqualification of the lawyer would work substantial hardship on the client.

(b) A lawyer may act as advocate in a trial in which another lawyer in the lawyer's firm is likely to be called as a witness unless precluded from doing so by Rule 1.7 or Rule 1.9.

Comment

[1] Combining the roles of advocate and witness can prejudice the tribunal and the opposing party and can also involve a conflict of interest between the lawyer and client.

Advocate-Witness Rule

[2] The tribunal has proper objection when the trier of fact may be confused or misled by a lawyer serving as both advocate and witness. The opposing party has proper objection where the combination of roles may prejudice that party's rights in the litigation. A witness is required to testify on the basis of personal knowledge, while an advocate is expected to explain and comment on evidence given by others. It may not be clear whether a statement by an advocate-witness should be taken as proof or as an analysis of the proof.

[3] To protect the tribunal, paragraph (a) prohibits a lawyer from simultaneously serving as advocate and necessary witness except in those circumstances specified in paragraphs (a)(1) through (a)(3). Paragraph (a)(1) recognizes that if the testimony will be uncontested, the ambiguities in the dual role are purely theoretical. Paragraph (a)(2) recognizes that where the testimony concerns the extent and value of legal services rendered in the action in which the testimony is offered, permitting the lawyers to testify avoids the need for a second trial with new counsel to resolve that issue. Moreover, in such a situation the judge has firsthand knowledge of the matter in issue; hence, there is less dependence on the adversary process to test the credibility of the testimony.

[4] Apart from these two exceptions, paragraph (a)(3) recognizes that a balancing is required between the interests of the client and those of the tribunal and the opposing party. Whether the tribunal is likely to be misled or the opposing party is likely to suffer prejudice depends on the nature of the case, the importance and probable tenor of the lawyer's testimony, and the probability that the lawyer's testimony will conflict with that of other witnesses. Even if there is risk of such prejudice, in determining whether the lawyer should be disqualified, due regard must be given to the effect of disqualification on the lawyer's client. It is relevant that one or both parties could reasonably foresee that the lawyer would probably be a witness. The conflict of interest principles stated in Rules 1.7, 1.9 and 1.10 have no application to this aspect of the problem.

[5] Because the tribunal is not likely to be misled when a lawyer acts as advocate in a trial in which another lawyer in the lawyer's firm will testify as a necessary witness, paragraph (b) permits the lawyer to do so except in situations involving a conflict of interest.

Conflict of Interest

[6] In determining if it is permissible to act as advocate in a trial in which the lawyer will be a necessary witness, the lawyer must also consider that the dual role may give rise to a conflict of interest that will require compliance with Rules 1.7 or 1.9. For example, if there is likely to be substantial conflict between the testimony of the client and that of the lawyer the representation involves a conflict of interest

that requires compliance with Rule 1.7. This would be true even though the lawyer might not be prohibited by paragraph (a) from simultaneously serving as advocate and witness because the lawyer's disqualification would work a substantial hardship on the client. Similarly, a lawyer who might be permitted to simultaneously serve as an advocate and a witness by paragraph (a)(3) might be precluded from doing so by Rule 1.9. The problem can arise whether the lawyer is called as a witness on behalf of the client or is called by the opposing party. Determining whether or not such a conflict exists is primarily the responsibility of the lawyer involved. If there is a conflict of interest, the lawyer must secure the client's informed consent, confirmed in writing. In some cases, the lawyer will be precluded from seeking the client's consent. See Rule 1.7. See Rule 1.0(b) for the definition of "confirmed in writing" and Rule 1.0(e) for the definition of "informed consent."

[7] Paragraph (b) provides that a lawyer is not disqualified from serving as an advocate because a lawyer with whom the lawyer is associated in a firm is precluded from doing so by paragraph (a). If, however, the testifying lawyer would also be disqualified by Rule 1.7 or Rule 1.9 from representing the client in the matter, other lawyers in the firm will be precluded from representing the client by Rule 1.10 unless the client gives informed consent under the conditions stated in Rule 1.7.

Definitional Cross-References

"Firm" *See* Rule 1.0(c)
"Substantial" *See* Rule 1.0(l)

Rule 3.8 Special Responsibilities of a Prosecutor

The prosecutor in a criminal case shall:

(a) refrain from prosecuting a charge that the prosecutor knows is not supported by probable cause;

(b) make reasonable efforts to assure that the accused has been advised of the right to, and the procedure for obtaining, counsel and has been given reasonable opportunity to obtain counsel;

(c) not seek to obtain from an unrepresented accused a waiver of important pretrial rights, such as the right to a preliminary hearing;

(d) make timely disclosure to the defense of all evidence or information known to the prosecutor that tends to negate the guilt of the accused or mitigates the offense, and, in connection with sentencing, disclose to the defense and to the tribunal all unprivileged mitigating information known to the prosecutor, except when the prosecutor is relieved of this responsibility by a protective order of the tribunal;

(e) not subpoena a lawyer in a grand jury or other criminal proceeding to present evidence about a past or present client unless the prosecutor reasonably believes:

(1) the information sought is not protected from disclosure by any applicable privilege;

(2) the evidence sought is essential to the successful completion of an ongoing investigation or prosecution; and

(3) there is no other feasible alternative to obtain the information;

(f) except for statements that are necessary to inform the public of the nature and extent of the prosecutor's action and that serve a legitimate law enforcement purpose, refrain from making extrajudicial comments that have a substantial likelihood of heightening public condemnation of the accused and exercise reasonable care to prevent investigators, law enforcement personnel, employees or other persons assisting or associated with the prosecutor in a criminal case from making an extrajudicial statement that the prosecutor would be prohibited from making under Rule 3.6 or this Rule.

(g) When a prosecutor knows of new, credible and material evidence creating a reasonable likelihood that a convicted defendant did not commit an offense of which the defendant was convicted, the prosecutor shall:

(1) promptly disclose that evidence to an appropriate court or authority, and

(2) if the conviction was obtained in the prosecutor's jurisdiction,

(i) promptly disclose that evidence to the defendant unless a court authorizes delay, and

(ii) undertake further investigation, or make reasonable efforts to cause an investigation, to determine whether the defendant was convicted of an offense that the defendant did not commit.

(h) When a prosecutor knows of clear and convincing evidence establishing that a defendant in the prosecutor's jurisdiction was convicted of an offense that the defendant did not commit, the prosecutor shall seek to remedy the conviction.

Comment

[1] A prosecutor has the responsibility of a minister of justice and not simply that of an advocate. This responsibility carries with it specific obligations to see that the defendant is accorded procedural justice, that guilt is decided upon the basis of sufficient evidence, and that special precautions are taken to prevent and to rectify the conviction of innocent persons. The extent of mandated remedial action is a matter of debate and varies in different jurisdictions. Many jurisdictions have adopted the ABA Standards for Criminal Justice Relating to the Prosecution Function, which are the product of prolonged and careful deliberation by lawyers experienced in both criminal prosecution and defense. Competent representation of the sovereignty may require a prosecutor to undertake some procedural and remedial measures as a matter of obligation. Applicable law may require other measures by the prosecutor and knowing disregard of those obligations or a systematic abuse of prosecutorial discretion could constitute a violation of Rule 8.4.

[2] In some jurisdictions, a defendant may waive a preliminary hearing and thereby lose a valuable opportunity to challenge probable cause. Accordingly, prosecutors should not seek to obtain waivers of preliminary hearings or other

important pretrial rights from unrepresented accused persons. Paragraph (c) does not apply, however, to an accused appearing *pro se* with the approval of the tribunal. Nor does it forbid the lawful questioning of an uncharged suspect who has knowingly waived the rights to counsel and silence.

[3] The exception in paragraph (d) recognizes that a prosecutor may seek an appropriate protective order from the tribunal if disclosure of information to the defense could result in substantial harm to an individual or to the public interest.

[4] Paragraph (e) is intended to limit the issuance of lawyer subpoenas in grand jury and other criminal proceedings to those situations in which there is a genuine need to intrude into the client-lawyer relationship.

[5] Paragraph (f) supplements Rule 3.6, which prohibits extrajudicial statements that have a substantial likelihood of prejudicing an adjudicatory proceeding. In the context of a criminal prosecution, a prosecutor's extrajudicial statement can create the additional problem of increasing public condemnation of the accused. Although the announcement of an indictment, for example, will necessarily have severe consequences for the accused, a prosecutor can, and should, avoid comments which have no legitimate law enforcement purpose and have a substantial likelihood of increasing public opprobrium of the accused. Nothing in this Comment is intended to restrict the statements which a prosecutor may make which comply with Rule 3.6(b) or 3.6(c).

[6] Like other lawyers, prosecutors are subject to Rules 5.1 and 5.3, which relate to responsibilities regarding lawyers and nonlawyers who work for or are associated with the lawyer's office. Paragraph (f) reminds the prosecutor of the importance of these obligations in connection with the unique dangers of improper extrajudicial statements in a criminal case. In addition, paragraph (f) requires a prosecutor to exercise reasonable care to prevent persons assisting or associated with the prosecutor from making improper extrajudicial statements, even when such persons are not under the direct supervision of the prosecutor. Ordinarily, the reasonable care standard will be satisfied if the prosecutor issues the appropriate cautions to law enforcement personnel and other relevant individuals.

[7] When a prosecutor knows of new, credible and material evidence creating a reasonable likelihood that a person outside the prosecutor's jurisdiction was convicted of a crime that the person did not commit, paragraph (g) requires prompt disclosure to the court or other appropriate authority, such as the chief prosecutor of the jurisdiction where the conviction occurred. If the conviction was obtained in the prosecutor's jurisdiction, paragraph (g) requires the prosecutor to examine the evidence and undertake further investigation to determine whether the defendant is in fact innocent or make reasonable efforts to cause another appropriate authority to undertake the necessary investigation, and to promptly disclose the evidence to the court and, absent court-authorized delay, to the defendant. Consistent with the objectives of Rules 4.2 and 4.3, disclosure to a represented defendant must be made through the defendant's counsel, and, in the case of an unrepresented defendant, would ordinarily be accompanied by a request to a court for the appointment of counsel to assist the defendant in taking such legal measures as may be appropriate.

[8] Under paragraph (h), once the prosecutor knows of clear and convincing evidence that the defendant was convicted of an offense that the defendant did not commit, the prosecutor must seek to remedy the conviction. Necessary steps may include disclosure of the evidence to the defendant, requesting that the court appoint counsel for an unrepresented indigent defendant and, where appropriate, notifying the court that the prosecutor has knowledge that the defendant did not commit the offense of which the defendant was convicted.

[9] A prosecutor's independent judgment, made in good faith, that the new evidence is not of such nature as to trigger the obligations of sections (g) and (h), though subsequently determined to have been erroneous, does not constitute a violation of this Rule.

Definitional Cross-References

"Known" and "Knows" *See* Rule 1.0(f)
"Reasonable" *See* Rule 1.0(h)
"Reasonably believes" *See* Rule 1.0(i)
"Substantial" *See* Rule 1.0(l)
"Tribunal" *See* Rule 1.0(m)

Rule 3.9 Advocate in Nonadjudicative Proceedings

A lawyer representing a client before a legislative body or administrative agency in a nonadjudicative proceeding shall disclose that the appearance is in a representative capacity and shall conform to the provisions of Rules 3.3(a) through (c), 3.4(a) through (c), and 3.5.

Comment

[1] In representation before bodies such as legislatures, municipal councils, and executive and administrative agencies acting in a rule-making or policy-making capacity, lawyers present facts, formulate issues and advance argument in the matters under consideration. The decisionmaking body, like a court, should be able to rely on the integrity of the submissions made to it. A lawyer appearing before such a body must deal with it honestly and in conformity with applicable rules of procedure. See Rules 3.3(a) through (c), 3.4(a) through (c) and 3.5.

[2] Lawyers have no exclusive right to appear before nonadjudicative bodies, as they do before a court. The requirements of this Rule therefore may subject lawyers to regulations inapplicable to advocates who are not lawyers. However, legislatures and administrative agencies have a right to expect lawyers to deal with them as they deal with courts.

[3] This Rule only applies when a lawyer represents a client in connection with an official hearing or meeting of a governmental agency or a legislative body to which the lawyer or the lawyer's client is presenting evidence or argument. It does not apply to representation of a client in a negotiation or

other bilateral transaction with a governmental agency or in connection with an application for a license or other privilege or the client's compliance with generally applicable reporting requirements, such as the filing of income-tax returns. Nor does it apply to the representation of a client in connection with an investigation or examination of the client's affairs conducted by government investigators or examiners. Representation in such matters is governed by Rules 4.1 through 4.4.

ARTICLE 4. TRANSACTIONS WITH PERSONS OTHER THAN CLIENTS

Rule 4.1 Truthfulness in Statements to Others

In the course of representing a client a lawyer shall not knowingly:

(a) make a false statement of material fact or law to a third person; or

(b) fail to disclose a material fact when disclosure is necessary to avoid assisting a criminal or fraudulent act by a client, unless disclosure is prohibited by Rule 1.6.

Comment

Misrepresentation

[1] A lawyer is required to be truthful when dealing with others on a client's behalf, but generally has no affirmative duty to inform an opposing party of relevant facts. A misrepresentation can occur if the lawyer incorporates or affirms a statement of another person that the lawyer knows is false. Misrepresentations can also occur by partially true but misleading statements or omissions that are the equivalent of affirmative false statements. For dishonest conduct that does not amount to a false statement or for misrepresentations by a lawyer other than in the course of representing a client, see Rule 8.4.

Statements of Fact

[2] This Rule refers to statements of fact. Whether a particular statement should be regarded as one of fact can depend on the circumstances. Under generally accepted conventions in negotiation, certain types of statements ordinarily are not taken as statements of material fact. Estimates of price or value placed on the subject of a transaction and a party's intentions as to an acceptable settlement of a claim are ordinarily in this category, and so is the existence of an undisclosed principal except where nondisclosure of the principal would constitute fraud. Lawyers should be mindful of their obligations under applicable law to avoid criminal and tortious misrepresentation.

Crime or Fraud by Client

[3] Under Rule 1.2(d), a lawyer is prohibited from counseling or assisting a client in conduct that the lawyer knows is criminal or fraudulent. Paragraph

(b) states a specific application of the principle set forth in Rule 1.2(d) and addresses the situation where a client's crime or fraud takes the form of a lie or misrepresentation. Ordinarily, a lawyer can avoid assisting a client's crime or fraud by withdrawing from the representation. Sometimes it may be necessary for the lawyer to give notice of the fact of withdrawal and to disaffirm an opinion, document, affirmation or the like. In extreme cases, substantive law may require a lawyer to disclose information relating to the representation to avoid being deemed to have assisted the client's crime or fraud. If the lawyer can avoid assisting a client's crime or fraud only by disclosing this information, then under paragraph (b) the lawyer is required to do so, unless the disclosure is prohibited by Rule 1.6.

Definitional Cross-References

"Fraudulent" *See* Rule 1.0(d)
"Knowingly" *See* Rule 1.0(f)

Rule 4.2 Communication with Person Represented by Counsel

In representing a client, a lawyer shall not communicate about the subject of the representation with a person the lawyer knows to be represented by another lawyer in the matter, unless the lawyer has the consent of the other lawyer or is authorized to do so by law or a court order.

Comment

[1] This Rule contributes to the proper functioning of the legal system by protecting a person who has chosen to be represented by a lawyer in a matter against possible overreaching by other lawyers who are participating in the matter, interference by those lawyers with the client-lawyer relationship and the uncounselled disclosure of information relating to the representation.

[2] This Rule applies to communications with any person who is represented by counsel concerning the matter to which the communication relates.

[3] The Rule applies even though the represented person initiates or consents to the communication. A lawyer must immediately terminate communication with a person if, after commencing communication, the lawyer learns that the person is one with whom communication is not permitted by this Rule.

[4] This Rule does not prohibit communication with a represented person, or an employee or agent of such a person, concerning matters outside the representation. For example, the existence of a controversy between a government agency and a private party, or between two organizations, does not prohibit a lawyer for either from communicating with nonlawyer representatives of the other regarding a separate matter. Nor does this Rule preclude communication with a represented person who is seeking advice from a lawyer who is not otherwise representing a client in the matter. A lawyer may not make a communication prohibited by this Rule

through the acts of another. See Rule 8.4(a). Parties to a matter may communicate directly with each other, and a lawyer is not prohibited from advising a client concerning a communication that the client is legally entitled to make. Also, a lawyer having independent justification or legal authorization for communicating with a represented person is permitted to do so.

[5] Communications authorized by law may include communications by a lawyer on behalf of a client who is exercising a constitutional or other legal right to communicate with the government. Communications authorized by law may also include investigative activities of lawyers representing governmental entities, directly or through investigative agents, prior to the commencement of criminal or civil enforcement proceedings. When communicating with the accused in a criminal matter, a government lawyer must comply with this Rule in addition to honoring the constitutional rights of the accused. The fact that a communication does not violate a state or federal constitutional right is insufficient to establish that the communication is permissible under this Rule.

[6] A lawyer who is uncertain whether a communication with a represented person is permissible may seek a court order. A lawyer may also seek a court order in exceptional circumstances to authorize a communication that would otherwise be prohibited by this Rule, for example, where communication with a person represented by counsel is necessary to avoid reasonably certain injury.

[7] In the case of a represented organization, this Rule prohibits communications with a constituent of the organization who supervises, directs or regularly consults with the organization's lawyer concerning the matter or has authority to obligate the organization with respect to the matter or whose act or omission in connection with the matter may be imputed to the organization for purposes of civil or criminal liability. Consent of the organization's lawyer is not required for communication with a former constituent. If a constituent of the organization is represented in the matter by his or her own counsel, the consent by that counsel to a communication will be sufficient for purposes of this Rule. Compare Rule 3.4(f). In communicating with a current or former constituent of an organization, a lawyer must not use methods of obtaining evidence that violate the legal rights of the organization. See Rule 4.4.

[8] The prohibition on communications with a represented person only applies in circumstances where the lawyer knows that the person is in fact represented in the matter to be discussed. This means that the lawyer has actual knowledge of the fact of the representation; but such actual knowledge may be inferred from the circumstances. See Rule 1.0(f). Thus, the lawyer cannot evade the requirement of obtaining the consent of counsel by closing eyes to the obvious.

[9] In the event the person with whom the lawyer communicates is not known to be represented by counsel in the matter, the lawyer's communications are subject to Rule 4.3.

Definitional Cross-Reference

"Knows" *See* Rule 1.0(f)

Rule 4.3 Dealing with Unrepresented Person

In dealing on behalf of a client with a person who is not represented by counsel, a lawyer shall not state or imply that the lawyer is disinterested. When the lawyer knows or reasonably should know that the unrepresented person misunderstands the lawyer's role in the matter, the lawyer shall make reasonable efforts to correct the misunderstanding. The lawyer shall not give legal advice to an unrepresented person, other than the advice to secure counsel, if the lawyer knows or reasonably should know that the interests of such a person are or have a reasonable possibility of being in conflict with the interests of the client.

Comment

[1] An unrepresented person, particularly one not experienced in dealing with legal matters, might assume that a lawyer is disinterested in loyalties or is a disinterested authority on the law even when the lawyer represents a client. In order to avoid a misunderstanding, a lawyer will typically need to identify the lawyer's client and, where necessary, explain that the client has interests opposed to those of the unrepresented person. For misunderstandings that sometimes arise when a lawyer for an organization deals with an unrepresented constituent, see Rule 1.13(f).

[2] The Rule distinguishes between situations involving unrepresented persons whose interests may be adverse to those of the lawyer's client and those in which the person's interests are not in conflict with the client's. In the former situation, the possibility that the lawyer will compromise the unrepresented person's interests is so great that the Rule prohibits the giving of any advice, apart from the advice to obtain counsel. Whether a lawyer is giving impermissible advice may depend on the experience and sophistication of the unrepresented person, as well as the setting in which the behavior and comments occur. This Rule does not prohibit a lawyer from negotiating the terms of a transaction or settling a dispute with an unrepresented person. So long as the lawyer has explained that the lawyer represents an adverse party and is not representing the person, the lawyer may inform the person of the terms on which the lawyer's client will enter into an agreement or settle a matter, prepare documents that require the person's signature and explain the lawyer's own view of the meaning of the document or the lawyer's view of the underlying legal obligations.

Definitional Cross-References

"Knows" *See* Rule 1.0(f)
"Reasonable" *See* Rule 1.0(h)
"Reasonably should know" *See* Rule 1.0(j)

Rule 4.4 Respect for Rights of Third Persons

(a) **In representing a client, a lawyer shall not use means that have no substantial purpose other than to embarrass, delay, or burden a third person, or use methods of obtaining evidence that violate the legal rights of such a person.**

(b) **A lawyer who receives a document or electronically stored information relating to the representation of the lawyer's client and knows or reasonably should know that the document or electronically stored information was inadvertently sent shall promptly notify the sender.**

Comment

[1] Responsibility to a client requires a lawyer to subordinate the interests of others to those of the client, but that responsibility does not imply that a lawyer may disregard the rights of third persons. It is impractical to catalogue all such rights, but they include legal restrictions on methods of obtaining evidence from third persons and unwarranted intrusions into privileged relationships, such as the client-lawyer relation- ship.

[2] Paragraph (b) recognizes that lawyers sometimes receive a document or electronically stored information that was mistakenly sent or produced by opposing parties or their lawyers. A document or electronically stored information is inadvertently sent when it is accidentally transmitted, such as when an email or letter is misaddressed or a document or electronically stored information is accidentally included with information that was intentionally transmitted. If a lawyer knows or reasonably should know that such a document or electronically stored information was sent inadvertently, then this Rule requires the lawyer to promptly notify the sender in order to permit that person to take protective measures. Whether the lawyer is required to take additional steps, such as returning the document or deleting electronically stored information, is a matter of law beyond the scope of these Rules, as is the question of whether the privileged status of a document or electronically stored information has been waived. Similarly, this Rule does not address the legal duties of a lawyer who receives a document or electronically stored information that the lawyer knows or reasonably should know may have been inappropriately obtained by the sending person. For purposes of this Rule, "document or electronically stored information" includes, in addition to paper documents, email and other forms of electronically stored information, including embedded data (commonly referred to as "metadata"), that is subject to being read or put into readable form. Metadata in electronic documents creates an obligation under this Rule only if the receiving lawyer knows or reasonably should know that the metadata was inadvertently sent to the receiving lawyer.

[3] Some lawyers may choose to return a document or delete electronically stored information unread, for example, when the lawyer learns before receiving it that it was inadvertently sent. Where a lawyer is not required by applicable law to do so, the decision to voluntarily return such a document or delete electronically stored information is a matter of professional judgment ordinarily reserved to the lawyer. See Rules 1.2 and 1.4.

Definitional Cross-References

"Knows" *See* Rule 1.0(f)
"Reasonably should know" *See* Rule 1.0(j)
"Substantial" *See* Rule 1.0(l)

ARTICLE 5. LAW FIRMS AND ASSOCIATIONS

Rule 5.1 Responsibilities of Partners, Managers, and Supervisory Lawyers

(a) A partner in a law firm, and a lawyer who individually or together with other lawyers possesses comparable managerial authority in a law firm, shall make reasonable efforts to ensure that the firm has in effect measures giving reasonable assurance that all lawyers in the firm conform to the Rules of Professional Conduct.

(b) A lawyer having direct supervisory authority over another lawyer shall make reasonable efforts to ensure that the other lawyer conforms to the Rules of Professional Conduct.

(c) A lawyer shall be responsible for another lawyer's violation of the Rules of Professional Conduct if:

(1) the lawyer orders or, with knowledge of the specific conduct, ratifies the conduct involved; or

(2) the lawyer is a partner or has comparable managerial authority in the law firm in which the other lawyer practices, or has direct supervisory authority over the other lawyer, and knows of the conduct at a time when its consequences can be avoided or mitigated but fails to take reasonable remedial action.

Comment

[1] Paragraph (a) applies to lawyers who have managerial authority over the professional work of a firm. See Rule 1.0(c). This includes members of a partnership, the shareholders in a law firm organized as a professional corporation, and members of other associations authorized to practice law; lawyers having comparable managerial authority in a legal services organization or a law department of an enterprise or government agency; and lawyers who have intermediate managerial responsibilities in a firm. Paragraph (b) applies to lawyers who have supervisory authority over the work of other lawyers in a firm.

[2] Paragraph (a) requires lawyers with managerial authority within a firm to make reasonable efforts to establish internal policies and procedures designed to provide reasonable assurance that all lawyers in the firm will conform to the Rules of Professional Conduct. Such policies and procedures include those designed to detect and resolve conflicts of interest, identify dates by which actions must be taken in pending matters, account for client funds and property and ensure that inexperienced lawyers are properly supervised.

[3] Other measures that may be required to fulfill the responsibility prescribed in paragraph (a) can depend on the firm's structure and the nature of its practice. In a small firm of experienced lawyers, informal supervision and periodic review of compliance with the required systems ordinarily will suffice. In a large firm, or in practice situations in which difficult ethical problems frequently arise, more elaborate measures may be necessary. Some firms, for example, have a procedure

whereby junior lawyers can make confidential referral of ethical problems directly to a designated senior partner or special committee. See Rule 5.2. Firms, whether large or small, may also rely on continuing legal education in professional ethics. In any event, the ethical atmosphere of a firm can influence the conduct of all its members, and the partners may not assume that all lawyers associated with the firm will inevitably conform to the Rules.

[4] Paragraph (c) expresses a general principle of personal responsibility for acts of another. See also Rule 8.4(a).

[5] Paragraph (c)(2) defines the duty of a partner or other lawyer having comparable managerial authority in a law firm, as well as a lawyer who has direct supervisory authority over performance of specific legal work by another lawyer. Whether a lawyer has supervisory authority in particular circumstances is a question of fact. Partners and lawyers with comparable authority have at least indirect responsibility for all work being done by the firm, while a partner or manager in charge of a particular matter ordinarily also has supervisory responsibility for the work of other firm lawyers engaged in the matter. Appropriate remedial action by a partner or managing lawyer would depend on the immediacy of that lawyer's involvement and the seriousness of the misconduct. A supervisor is required to intervene to prevent avoidable consequences of misconduct if the supervisor knows that the misconduct occurred. Thus, if a supervising lawyer knows that a subordinate misrepresented a matter to an opposing party in negotiation, the supervisor as well as the subordinate has a duty to correct the resulting misapprehension.

[6] Professional misconduct by a lawyer under supervision could reveal a violation of paragraph (b) on the part of the supervisory lawyer even though it does not entail a violation of paragraph (c) because there was no direction, ratification or knowledge of the violation.

[7] Apart from this Rule and Rule 8.4(a), a lawyer does not have disciplinary liability for the conduct of a partner, associate or subordinate. Whether a lawyer may be liable civilly or criminally for another lawyer's conduct is a question of law beyond the scope of these Rules.

[8] The duties imposed by this Rule on managing and supervising lawyers do not alter the personal duty of each lawyer in a firm to abide by the Rules of Professional Conduct. See Rule 5.2(a).

Definitional Cross-References

"Firm" and "Law firm" *See* Rule 1.0(c)
"Knows" *See* Rule 1.0(f)
"Partner" *See* Rule 1.0(g)
"Reasonable" *See* Rule 1.0(h)

Rule 5.2 Responsibilities of a Subordinate lawyer

(a) A lawyer is bound by the Rules of Professional Conduct notwithstanding that the lawyer acted at the direction of another person.

(b) A subordinate lawyer does not violate the Rules of Professional Conduct if that lawyer acts in accordance with a supervisory lawyer's reasonable resolution of an arguable question of professional duty.

Comment

[1] Although a lawyer is not relieved of responsibility for a violation by the fact that the lawyer acted at the direction of a supervisor, that fact may be relevant in determining whether a lawyer had the knowledge required to render conduct a violation of the Rules. For example, if a subordinate filed a frivolous pleading at the direction of a supervisor, the subordinate would not be guilty of a professional violation unless the subordinate knew of the document's frivolous character.

[2] When lawyers in a supervisor-subordinate relationship encounter a matter involving professional judgment as to ethical duty, the supervisor may assume responsibility for making the judgment. Otherwise a consistent course of action or position could not be taken. If the question can reasonably be answered only one way, the duty of both lawyers is clear and they are equally responsible for fulfilling it. However, if the question is reasonably arguable, someone has to decide upon the course of action. That authority ordinarily reposes in the supervisor, and a subordinate may be guided accordingly. For example, if a question arises whether the interests of two clients conflict under Rule 1.7, the supervisor's reasonable resolution of the question should protect the subordinate professionally if the resolution is subsequently challenged.

Definitional Cross-References

"Reasonable" *See* Rule 1.0(h)

Rule 5.3 Responsibilities Regarding Nonlawyer Assistance

With respect to a nonlawyer employed or retained by or associated with a lawyer:

(a) a partner, and a lawyer who individually or together with other lawyers possesses comparable managerial authority in a law firm shall make reasonable efforts to ensure that the firm has in effect measures giving reasonable assurance that the person's conduct is compatible with the professional obligations of the lawyer;

(b) a lawyer having direct supervisory authority over the nonlawyer shall make reasonable efforts to ensure that the person's conduct is compatible with the professional obligations of the lawyer; and

(c) a lawyer shall be responsible for conduct of such a person that would be a violation of the Rules of Professional Conduct if engaged in by a lawyer if:

(1) the lawyer orders or, with the knowledge of the specific conduct, ratifies the conduct involved; or

(2) the lawyer is a partner or has comparable managerial authority in the law firm in which the person is employed, or has direct supervisory

authority over the person, and knows of the conduct at a time when its consequences can be avoided or mitigated but fails to take reasonable remedial action.

Comment

[1] Paragraph (a) requires lawyers with managerial authority within a law firm to make reasonable efforts to ensure that the firm has in effect measures giving reasonable assurance that nonlawyers in the firm and nonlawyers outside the firm who work on firm matters act in a way compatible with the professional obligations of the lawyer. See Comment [6] to Rule 1.1 (retaining lawyers outside the firm) and Comment [1] to Rule 5.1 (responsibilities with respect to lawyers within a firm). Paragraph (b) applies to lawyers who have supervisory authority over such nonlawyers within or outside the firm. Paragraph (c) specifies the circumstances in which a lawyer is responsible for the conduct of such nonlawyers within or outside the firm that would be a violation of the Rules of Professional Conduct if engaged in by a lawyer.

Nonlawyers Within the Firm

[2] Lawyers generally employ assistants in their practice, including secretaries, investigators, law student interns, and paraprofessionals. Such assistants, whether employees or independent contractors, act for the lawyer in rendition of the lawyer's professional services. A lawyer must give such assistants appropriate instruction and supervision concerning the ethical aspects of their employment, particularly regarding the obligation not to disclose information relating to representation of the client, and should be responsible for their work product. The measures employed in supervising nonlawyers should take account of the fact that they do not have legal training and are not subject to professional discipline.

Nonlawyers Outside the Firm

[3] A lawyer may use nonlawyers outside the firm to assist the lawyer in rendering legal services to the client. Examples include the retention of an investigative or paraprofessional service, hiring a document management company to create and maintain a database for complex litigation, sending client documents to a third party for printing or scanning, and using an Internet-based service to store client information. When using such services outside the firm, a lawyer must make reasonable efforts to ensure that the services are provided in a manner that is compatible with the lawyer's professional obligations. The extent of this obligation will depend upon the circumstances, including the education, experience and reputation of the nonlawyer; the nature of the services involved; the terms of any arrangements concerning the protection of client information; and the legal and ethical environments of the jurisdictions in which the services will be performed, particularly with regard to confidentiality. See also Rules 1.1 (competence), 1.2 (allocation of authority), 1.4 (communication with client), 1.6 (confidentiality), 5.4(a) (professional independence of the lawyer), and 5.5(a) (unauthorized practice of law). When retaining or directing a nonlawyer outside the firm, a lawyer should

communicate directions appropriate under the circumstances to give reasonable assurance that the nonlawyer's conduct is compatible with the professional obligations of the lawyer.

[4] Where the client directs the selection of a particular nonlawyer service provider outside the firm, the lawyer ordinarily should agree with the client concerning the allocation of responsibility for monitoring as between the client and the lawyer. See Rule 1.2. When making such an allocation in a matter pending before a tribunal, lawyers and parties may have additional obligations that are a matter of law beyond the scope of these Rules.

Definitional Cross-References

"Firm" and "Law firm" *See* Rule 1.0(c)
"Knows" *See* Rule 1.0(f)
"Partner" *See* Rule 1.0(g)
"Reasonable" *See* Rule 1.0(h)

Rule 5.4 Professional Independence of a Lawyer

(a) A lawyer or law firm shall not share legal fees with a nonlawyer, except that:

(1) an agreement by a lawyer with the lawyer's firm, partner, or associate may provide for the payment of money, over a reasonable period of time after the lawyer's death, to the lawyer's estate or to one or more specified persons;

(2) a lawyer who purchases the practice of a deceased, disabled, or disappeared lawyer may, pursuant to the provisions of Rule 1.17, pay to the estate or other representative of that lawyer the agreed-upon purchase price;

(3) a lawyer or law firm may include nonlawyer employees in a compensation or retirement plan, even though the plan is based in whole or in part on a profit-sharing arrangement; and

(4) a lawyer may share court-awarded legal fees with a nonprofit organization that employed, retained or recommended employment of the lawyer in the matter.

(b) A lawyer shall not form a partnership with a nonlawyer if any of the activities of the partnership consist of the practice of law.

(c) A lawyer shall not permit a person who recommends, employs, or pays the lawyer to render legal services for another to direct or regulate the lawyer's professional judgment in rendering such legal services.

(d) A lawyer shall not practice with or in the form of a professional corporation or association authorized to practice law for a profit, if:

(1) a nonlawyer owns any interest therein, except that a fiduciary representative of the estate of a lawyer may hold the stock or interest of the lawyer for a reasonable time during administration;

(2) a nonlawyer is a corporate director or officer thereof or occupies the position of similar responsibility in any form of association other than a corporation; or

(3) a nonlawyer has the right to direct or control the professional judgment of a lawyer.

Comment

[1] The provisions of this Rule express traditional limitations on sharing fees. These limitations are to protect the lawyer's professional independence of judgment. Where someone other than the client pays the lawyer's fee or salary, or recommends employment of the lawyer, that arrangement does not modify the lawyer's obligation to the client. As stated in paragraph (c), such arrangements should not interfere with the lawyer's professional judgment.

[2] This Rule also expresses traditional limitations on permitting a third party to direct or regulate the lawyer's professional judgment in rendering legal services to another. See also Rule 1.8(f) (lawyer may accept compensation from a third party as long as there is no interference with the lawyer's independent professional judgment and the client gives informed consent).

Definitional Cross-References

"Firm" and "Law firm" *See* Rule 1.0(c)
"Partner" *See* Rule 1.0(g)

Rule 5.5 Unauthorized Practice of Law; Multijurisdictional Practice of law

(a) A lawyer shall not practice law in a jurisdiction in violation of the regulation of the legal profession in that jurisdiction, or assist another in doing so.

(b) A lawyer who is not admitted to practice in this jurisdiction shall not:

(1) except as authorized by these Rules or other law, establish an office or other systematic and continuous presence in this jurisdiction for the practice of law; or

(2) hold out to the public or otherwise represent that the lawyer is admitted to practice law in this jurisdiction.

(c) A lawyer admitted in another United States jurisdiction, and not disbarred or suspended from practice in any jurisdiction, may provide legal services on a temporary basis in this jurisdiction that:

(1) are undertaken in association with a lawyer who is admitted to practice in this jurisdiction and who actively participates in the matter;

(2) are in or reasonably related to a pending or potential proceeding before a tribunal in this or another jurisdiction, if the lawyer, or a person the lawyer is assisting, is authorized by law or order to appear in such proceeding or reasonably expects to be so authorized;

(3) are in or reasonably related to a pending or potential arbitration, mediation, or other alternative dispute resolution proceeding in this or another jurisdiction, if the services arise out of or are reasonably related to the lawyer's practice in a jurisdiction in which the lawyer is admitted

to practice and are not services for which the forum requires pro hac vice admission; or

(4) are not within paragraphs (c)(2) or (c)(3) and arise out of or are reasonably related to the lawyer's practice in a jurisdiction in which the lawyer is admitted to practice.

(d) A lawyer admitted in another United States jurisdiction or in a foreign jurisdiction, and not disbarred or suspended from practice in any jurisdiction or the equivalent thereof, or a person otherwise lawfully practicing as an in-house counsel under the laws of a foreign jurisdiction, may provide legal services through an office or other systematic and continuous presence in this jurisdiction that:

(1) are provided to the lawyer's employer or its organizational affiliates; are not services for which the forum requires pro hac vice admission; and, when performed by a foreign lawyer and requires advice on the law of this or another jurisdiction or of the United States, such advice shall be based upon the advice of a lawyer who is duly licensed and authorized by the jurisdiction to provide such advice; or

(2) are services that the lawyer is authorized by federal law or other law or rule to provide in this jurisdiction.

(e) For purposes of paragraph (d):

(1) the foreign lawyer must be a member in good standing of a recognized legal profession in a foreign jurisdiction, the members of which are admitted to practice as lawyers or counselors at law or the equivalent, and subject to effective regulation and discipline by a duly constituted professional body or a public authority; or

(2) the person otherwise lawfully practicing as an in-house counsel under the laws of a foreign jurisdiction must be authorized to practice under this Rule by, in the exercise of its discretion, [the highest court of this jurisdiction].

Comment

[1] A lawyer may practice law only in a jurisdiction in which the lawyer is authorized to practice. A lawyer may be admitted to practice law in a jurisdiction on a regular basis or may be authorized by court rule or order or by law to practice for a limited purpose or on a restricted basis. Paragraph (a) applies to unauthorized practice of law by a lawyer, whether through the lawyer's direct action or by the lawyer assisting another person. For example, a lawyer may not assist a person in practicing law in violation of the rules governing professional conduct in that person's jurisdiction.

[2] The definition of the practice of law is established by law and varies from one jurisdiction to another. Whatever the definition, limiting the practice of law to members of the bar protects the public against rendition of legal services by unqualified persons. This Rule does not prohibit a lawyer from employing the services of paraprofessionals and delegating functions to them, so long as the lawyer supervises the delegated work and retains responsibility for their work. See Rule 5.3.

[3] A lawyer may provide professional advice and instruction to nonlawyers whose employment requires knowledge of the law; for example, claims adjusters, employees of financial or commercial institutions, social workers, accountants and persons employed in government agencies. Lawyers also may assist independent nonlawyers, such as paraprofessionals, who are authorized by the law of a jurisdiction to provide particular law-related services. In addition, a lawyer may counsel nonlawyers who wish to proceed pro se.

[4] Other than as authorized by law or this Rule, a lawyer who is not admitted to practice generally in this jurisdiction violates paragraph (b)(1) if the lawyer establishes an office or other systematic and continuous presence in this jurisdiction for the practice of law. Presence may be systematic and continuous even if the lawyer is not physically present here. Such a lawyer must not hold out to the public or otherwise represent that the lawyer is admitted to practice law in this jurisdiction. See also Rule 7.1.

[5] There are occasions in which a lawyer admitted to practice in another United States jurisdiction, and not disbarred or suspended from practice in any jurisdiction, may provide legal services on a temporary basis in this jurisdiction under circumstances that do not create an unreasonable risk to the interests of their clients, the public or the courts. Paragraph (c) identifies four such circumstances. The fact that conduct is not so identified does not imply that the conduct is or is not authorized. With the exception of paragraphs (d)(1) and (d)(2), this Rule does not authorize a U.S. or foreign lawyer to establish an office or other systematic and continuous presence in this jurisdiction without being admitted to practice generally here.

[6] There is no single test to determine whether a lawyer's services are provided on a "temporary basis" in this jurisdiction, and may therefore be permissible under paragraph (c). Services may be "temporary" even though the lawyer provides services in this jurisdiction on a recurring basis, or for an extended period of time, as when the lawyer is representing a client in a single lengthy negotiation or litigation.

[7] Paragraphs (c) and (d) apply to lawyers who are admitted to practice law in any United States jurisdiction, which includes the District of Columbia and any state, territory or commonwealth of the United States. Paragraph (d) also applies to lawyers admitted in a foreign jurisdiction. The word "admitted" in paragraphs (c), (d) and (e) contemplates that the lawyer is authorized to practice in the jurisdiction in which the lawyer is admitted and excludes a lawyer who while technically admitted is not authorized to practice, because, for example, the lawyer is on inactive status.

[8] Paragraph (c)(1) recognizes that the interests of clients and the public are protected if a lawyer admitted only in another jurisdiction associates with a lawyer licensed to practice in this jurisdiction. For this paragraph to apply, however, the lawyer admitted to practice in this jurisdiction must actively participate in and share responsibility for the representation of the client.

[9] Lawyers not admitted to practice generally in a jurisdiction may be authorized by law or order of a tribunal or an administrative agency to appear before the tribunal or agency. This authority may be granted pursuant to formal rules governing

admission pro hac vice or pursuant to informal practice of the tribunal or agency. Under paragraph (c)(2), a lawyer does not violate this Rule when the lawyer appears before a tribunal or agency pursuant to such authority. To the extent that a court rule or other law of this jurisdiction requires a lawyer who is not admitted to practice in this jurisdiction to obtain admission pro hac vice before appearing before a tribunal or administrative agency, this Rule requires the lawyer to obtain that authority.

[10] Paragraph (c)(2) also provides that a lawyer rendering services in this jurisdiction on a temporary basis does not violate this Rule when the lawyer engages in conduct in anticipation of a proceeding or hearing in a jurisdiction in which the lawyer is authorized to practice law or in which the lawyer reasonably expects to be admitted pro hac vice. Examples of such conduct include meetings with the client, interviews of potential witnesses, and the review of documents. Similarly, a lawyer admitted only in another jurisdiction may engage in conduct temporarily in this jurisdiction in connection with pending litigation in another jurisdiction in which the lawyer is or reasonably expects to be authorized to appear, including taking depositions in this jurisdiction.

[11] When a lawyer has been or reasonably expects to be admitted to appear before a court or administrative agency, paragraph (c)(2) also permits conduct by lawyers who are associated with that lawyer in the matter, but who do not expect to appear before the court or administrative agency. For example, subordinate lawyers may conduct research, review documents, and attend meetings with witnesses in support of the lawyer responsible for the litigation.

[12] Paragraph (c)(3) permits a lawyer admitted to practice law in another jurisdiction to perform services on a temporary basis in this jurisdiction if those services are in or reasonably related to a pending or potential arbitration, mediation, or other alternative dispute resolution proceeding in this or another jurisdiction, if the services arise out of or are reasonably related to the lawyer's practice in a jurisdiction in which the lawyer is admitted to practice. The lawyer, however, must obtain admission pro hac vice in the case of a court-annexed arbitration or mediation or otherwise if court rules or law so require.

[13] Paragraph (c)(4) permits a lawyer admitted in another jurisdiction to provide certain legal services on a temporary basis in this jurisdiction that arise out of or are reasonably related to the lawyer's practice in a jurisdiction in which the lawyer is admitted but are not within paragraphs (c)(2) or (c)(3). These services include both legal services and services that nonlawyers may perform but that are considered the practice of law when performed by lawyers.

[14] Paragraphs (c)(3) and (c)(4) require that the services arise out of or be reasonably related to the lawyer's practice in a jurisdiction in which the lawyer is admitted. A variety of factors evidence such a relationship. The lawyer's client may have been previously represented by the lawyer, or may be resident in or have substantial contacts with the jurisdiction in which the lawyer is admitted. The matter, although involving other jurisdictions, may have a significant connection with that jurisdiction. In other cases, significant aspects of the lawyer's work might be conducted in that jurisdiction or a significant aspect of the matter may involve the law of that jurisdiction. The necessary relationship might arise when the client's activities or the legal

issues involve multiple jurisdictions, such as when the officers of a multinational corporation survey potential business sites and seek the services of their lawyer in assessing the relative merits of each. In addition, the services may draw on the lawyer's recognized expertise developed through the regular practice of law on behalf of clients in matters involving a particular body of federal, nationally-uniform, foreign, or international law. Lawyers desiring to provide pro bono legal services on a temporary basis in a jurisdiction that has been affected by a major disaster, but in which they are not otherwise authorized to practice law, as well as lawyers from the affected jurisdiction who seek to practice law temporarily in another jurisdiction, but in which they are not otherwise authorized to practice law, should consult the [*Model Court Rule on Provision of Legal Services Following Determination of Major Disaster*].

[15] Paragraph (d) identifies two circumstances in which a lawyer who is admitted to practice in another United States or a foreign jurisdiction, and is not disbarred or suspended from practice in any jurisdiction, or the equivalent thereof, may establish an office or other systematic and continuous presence in this jurisdiction for the practice of law. Pursuant to paragraph (c) of this Rule, a lawyer admitted in any U.S. jurisdiction may also provide legal services in this jurisdiction on a temporary basis. See also *Model Rule on Temporary Practice by Foreign Lawyers.* Except as provided in paragraphs (d)(1) and (d)(2), a lawyer who is admitted to practice law in another United States or foreign jurisdiction and who establishes an office or other systematic or continuous presence in this jurisdiction must become admitted to practice law generally in this jurisdiction.

[16] Paragraph (d)(1) applies to a U.S. or foreign lawyer who is employed by a client to provide legal services to the client or its organizational affiliates, i.e., entities that control, are controlled by, or are under common control with the employer. This paragraph does not authorize the provision of personal legal services to the employer's officers or employees. The paragraph applies to in-house corporate lawyers, government lawyers and others who are employed to render legal services to the employer. The lawyer's ability to represent the employer outside the jurisdiction in which the lawyer is licensed generally serves the interests of the employer and does not create an unreasonable risk to the client and others because the employer is well situated to assess the lawyer's qualifications and the quality of the lawyer's work. To further decrease any risk to the client, when advising on the domestic law of a United States jurisdiction or on the law of the United States, the foreign lawyer authorized to practice under paragraph (d)(1) of this Rule needs to base that advice on the advice of a lawyer licensed and authorized by the jurisdiction to provide it.

[17] If an employed lawyer establishes an office or other systematic presence in this jurisdiction for the purpose of rendering legal services to the employer, the lawyer may be subject to registration or other requirements, including assessments for client protection funds and mandatory continuing legal education. See *Model Rule for Registration of In-House Counsel.*

[18] Paragraph (d)(2) recognizes that a U.S. or foreign lawyer may provide legal services in a jurisdiction in which the lawyer is not licensed when authorized to do so by federal or other law, which includes statute, court rule, executive regulation or judicial precedent. See, e.g., *Model Rule on Practice Pending Admission.*

[19] A lawyer who practices law in this jurisdiction pursuant to paragraphs (c) or (d) or otherwise is subject to the disciplinary authority of this jurisdiction. See Rule 8.5(a).

[20] In some circumstances, a lawyer who practices law in this jurisdiction pursuant to paragraphs (c) or (d) may have to inform the client that the lawyer is not licensed to practice law in this jurisdiction. For example, that may be required when the representation occurs primarily in this jurisdiction and requires knowledge of the law of this jurisdiction. See Rule 1.4(b).

[21] Paragraphs (c) and (d) do not authorize communications advertising legal services in this jurisdiction by lawyers who are admitted to practice in other jurisdictions. Whether and how lawyers may communicate the availability of their services in this jurisdiction is governed by Rules 7.1 to 7.3.

Definitional Cross-References

"Reasonably" *See* Rule 1.0(h)
"Tribunal" *See* Rule 1.0(m)

Rule 5.6 Restrictions on Right to Practice

A lawyer shall not participate in offering or making:

(a) a partnership, shareholders, operating, employment, or other similar type of agreement that restricts the right of a lawyer to practice after termination of the relationship, except an agreement concerning benefits upon retirement; or

(b) an agreement in which a restriction on the lawyer's right to practice is part of the settlement of a client controversy.

Comment

[1] An agreement restricting the right of lawyers to practice after leaving a firm not only limits their professional autonomy but also limits the freedom of clients to choose a lawyer. Paragraph (a) prohibits such agreements except for restrictions incident to provisions concerning retirement benefits for service with the firm.

[2] Paragraph (b) prohibits a lawyer from agreeing not to represent other persons in connection with settling a claim on behalf of a client.

[3] This Rule does not apply to prohibit restrictions that may be included in the terms of the sale of a law practice pursuant to Rule 1.17.

Rule 5.7 Responsibilities Regarding Law-Related Services

(a) A lawyer shall be subject to the Rules of Professional Conduct with respect to the provision of law-related services, as defined in paragraph (b), if the law-related services are provided:

(1) by the lawyer in circumstances that are not distinct from the lawyer's provision of legal services to clients; or

(2) in other circumstances by an entity controlled by the lawyer individually or with others if the lawyer fails to take reasonable measures to assure that a person obtaining the law-related services knows that the services are not legal services and that the protections of the client-lawyer relationship do not exist.

(b) The term "law-related services" denotes services that might reasonably be performed in conjunction with and in substance are related to the provision of legal services, and that are not prohibited as unauthorized practice of law when provided by a nonlawyer.

Comment

[1] When a lawyer performs law-related services or controls an organization that does so, there exists the potential for ethical problems. Principal among these is the possibility that the person for whom the law-related services are performed fails to understand that the services may not carry with them the protections normally afforded as part of the client-lawyer relationship. The recipient of the law-related services may expect, for example, that the protection of client confidences, prohibitions against representation of persons with conflicting interests, and obligations of a lawyer to maintain professional independence apply to the provision of law-related services when that may not be the case.

[2] Rule 5.7 applies to the provision of law-related services by a lawyer even when the lawyer does not provide any legal services to the person for whom the law-related services are performed and whether the law-related services are performed through a law firm or a separate entity. The Rule identifies the circumstances in which all of the Rules of Professional Conduct apply to the provision of law-related services. Even when those circumstances do not exist, however, the conduct of a lawyer involved in the provision of law-related services is subject to those Rules that apply generally to lawyer conduct, regardless of whether the conduct involves the provision of legal services. See, e.g., Rule 8.4.

[3] When law-related services are provided by a lawyer under circumstances that are not distinct from the lawyer's provision of legal services to clients, the lawyer in providing the law-related services must adhere to the requirements of the Rules of Professional Conduct as provided in paragraph (a)(1). Even when the law-related and legal services are provided in circumstances that are distinct from each other, for example through separate entities or different support staff within the law firm, the Rules of Professional Conduct apply to the lawyer as provided in paragraph (a)(2) unless the lawyer takes reasonable measures to assure that the recipient of the law-related services knows that the services are not legal services and that the protections of the client-lawyer relationship do not apply.

[4] Law-related services also may be provided through an entity that is distinct from that through which the lawyer provides legal services. If the lawyer individually or with others has control of such an entity's operations, the Rule requires the lawyer to take reasonable measures to assure that each person using the services of the entity knows that the services provided by the entity are not legal services and

that the Rules of Professional Conduct that relate to the client-lawyer relationship do not apply. A lawyer's control of an entity extends to the ability to direct its operation. Whether a lawyer has such control will depend upon the circumstances of the particular case.

[5] When a client-lawyer relationship exists with a person who is referred by a lawyer to a separate law-related service entity controlled by the lawyer, individually or with others, the lawyer must comply with Rule 1.8(a).

[6] In taking the reasonable measures referred to in paragraph (a)(2) to assure that a person using law-related services understands the practical effect or significance of the inapplicability of the Rules of Professional Conduct, the lawyer should communicate to the person receiving the law-related services, in a manner sufficient to assure that the person understands the significance of the fact, that the relationship of the person to the business entity will not be a client-lawyer relationship. The communication should be made before entering into an agreement for provision of or providing law-related services, and preferably should be in writing.

[7] The burden is upon the lawyer to show that the lawyer has taken reasonable measures under the circumstances to communicate the desired understanding. For instance, a sophisticated user of law-related services, such as a publicly held corporation, may require a lesser explanation than someone unaccustomed to making distinctions between legal services and law-related services, such as an individual seeking tax advice from a lawyer-accountant or investigative services in connection with a lawsuit.

[8] Regardless of the sophistication of potential recipients of law-related services, a lawyer should take special care to keep separate the provision of law-related and legal services in order to minimize the risk that the recipient will assume that the law-related services are legal services. The risk of such confusion is especially acute when the lawyer renders both types of services with respect to the same matter. Under some circumstances the legal and law-related services may be so closely entwined that they cannot be distinguished from each other, and the requirement of disclosure and consultation imposed by paragraph (a)(2) of the Rule cannot be met. In such a case a lawyer will be responsible for assuring that both the lawyer's conduct and, to the extent required by Rule 5.3, that of nonlawyer employees in the distinct entity that the lawyer controls complies in all respects with the Rules of Professional Conduct.

[9] A broad range of economic and other interests of clients may be served by lawyers' engaging in the delivery of law-related services. Examples of law-related services include providing title insurance, financial planning, accounting, trust services, real estate counseling, legislative lobbying, economic analysis, social work, psychological counseling, tax preparation, and patent, medical or environmental consulting.

[10] When a lawyer is obliged to accord the recipients of such services the protections of those Rules that apply to the client-lawyer relationship, the lawyer must take special care to heed the proscriptions of the Rules addressing conflict of interest (Rules 1.7 through 1.11, especially Rules 1.7(a)(2) and 1.8(a), (b) and (f)), and

to scrupulously adhere to the requirements of Rule 1.6 relating to disclosure of confidential information. The promotion of the law-related services must also in all respects comply with Rules 7.1 through 7.3, dealing with advertising and solicitation. In that regard, lawyers should take special care to identify the obligations that may be imposed as a result of a jurisdiction's decisional law.

[11] When the full protections of all of the Rules of Professional Conduct do not apply to the provision of law-related services, principles of law external to the Rules, for example, the law of principal and agent, govern the legal duties owed to those receiving the services. Those other legal principles may establish a different degree of protection for the recipient with respect to confidentiality of information, conflicts of interest and permissible business relationships with clients. See also Rule 8.4 (Misconduct).

Definitional Cross-References

"Knows" *See* Rule 1.0(f)
"Reasonable" *See* Rule 1.0(h)

ARTICLE 6. PUBLIC SERVICE

Rule 6.1 Voluntary Pro Bono Publico Service

Every lawyer has a professional responsibility to provide legal services to those unable to pay. A lawyer should aspire to render at least (50) hours of pro bono publico legal services per year. In fulfilling this responsibility, the lawyer should:

(a) provide a substantial majority of the (50) hours of legal services without fee or expectation of fee to:

(1) persons of limited means; or

(2) charitable, religious, civic, community, governmental and educational organizations in matters that are designed primarily to address the needs of persons of limited means; and

(b) provide any additional services through:

(1) delivery of legal services at no fee or substantially reduced fee to individuals, groups or organizations seeking to secure or protect civil rights, civil liberties or public rights, or charitable, religious, civic, community, governmental and educational organizations in matters in furtherance of their organizational purposes, where the payment of standard legal fees would significantly deplete the organization's economic resources or would be otherwise inappropriate;

(2) delivery of legal services at a substantially reduced fee to persons of limited means; or

(3) participation in activities for improving the law, the legal system or the legal profession.

In addition, a lawyer should voluntarily contribute financial support to organizations that provide legal services to persons of limited means.

Comment

[1] Every lawyer, regardless of professional prominence or professional work load, has a responsibility to provide legal services to those unable to pay, and personal involvement in the problems of the disadvantaged can be one of the most rewarding experiences in the life of a lawyer. The American Bar Association urges all lawyers to provide a minimum of 50 hours of pro bono services annually. States, however, may decide to choose a higher or lower number of hours of annual service (which may be expressed as a percentage of a lawyer's professional time) depending upon local needs and local conditions. It is recognized that in some years a lawyer may render greater or fewer hours than the annual standard specified, but during the course of his or her legal career, each lawyer should render on average per year, the number of hours set forth in this Rule. Services can be performed in civil matters or in criminal or quasi-criminal matters for which there is no government obligation to provide funds for legal representation, such as post-conviction death penalty appeal cases.

[2] Paragraphs (a)(1) and (2) recognize the critical need for legal services that exists among persons of limited means by providing that a substantial majority of the legal services rendered annually to the disadvantaged be furnished without fee or expectation of fee. Legal services under these paragraphs consist of a full range of activities, including individual and class representation, the provision of legal advice, legislative lobbying, administrative rule making and the provision of free training or mentoring to those who represent persons of limited means. The variety of these activities should facilitate participation by government lawyers, even when restrictions exist on their engaging in the outside practice of law.

[3] Persons eligible for legal services under paragraphs (a)(1) and (2) are those who qualify for participation in programs funded by the Legal Services Corporation and those whose incomes and financial resources are slightly above the guidelines utilized by such programs but nevertheless, cannot afford counsel. Legal services can be rendered to individuals or to organizations such as homeless shelters, battered women's centers and food pantries that serve those of limited means. The term "governmental organizations" includes, but is not limited to, public protection programs and sections of governmental or public sector agencies.

[4] Because service must be provided without fee or expectation of fee, the intent of the lawyer to render free legal services is essential for the work performed to fall within the meaning of paragraphs (a)(1) and (2). Accordingly, services rendered cannot be considered pro bono if an anticipated fee is uncollected, but the award of statutory attorneys' fees in a case originally accepted as pro bono would not disqualify such services from inclusion under this section. Lawyers who do receive fees in such cases are encouraged to contribute an appropriate portion of such fees to organizations or projects that benefit persons of limited means.

[5] While it is possible for a lawyer to fulfill the annual responsibility to perform pro bono services exclusively through activities described in paragraphs (a)(1) and (2), to the extent that any hours of service remained unfulfilled, the remaining commitment can be met in a variety of ways as set forth in paragraph (b).

Constitutional, statutory or regulatory restrictions may prohibit or impede government and public sector lawyers and judges from performing the pro bono services outlined in paragraphs (a) (1) and (2). Accordingly, where those restrictions apply, government and public sector lawyers and judges may fulfill their pro bono responsibility by performing services outlined in paragraph (b).

[6] Paragraph (b)(1) includes the provision of certain types of legal services to those whose incomes and financial resources place them above limited means. It also permits the pro bono lawyer to accept a substantially reduced fee for services. Examples of the types of issues that may be addressed under this paragraph include First Amendment claims, Title VII claims and environmental protection claims. Additionally, a wide range of organizations may be represented, including social service, medical research, cultural and religious groups.

[7] Paragraph (b)(2) covers instances in which lawyers agree to and receive a modest fee for furnishing legal services to persons of limited means. Participation in judicare programs and acceptance of court appointments in which the fee is substantially below a lawyer's usual rate are encouraged under this section.

[8] Paragraph (b)(3) recognizes the value of lawyers engaging in activities that improve the law, the legal system or the legal profession. Serving on bar association committees, serving on boards of pro bono or legal services programs, taking part in Law Day activities, acting as a continuing legal education instructor, a mediator or an arbitrator and engaging in legislative lobbying to improve the law, the legal system or the profession are a few examples of the many activities that fall within this paragraph.

[9] Because the provision of pro bono services is a professional responsibility, it is the individual ethical commitment of each lawyer. Nevertheless, there may be times when it is not feasible for a lawyer to engage in pro bono services. At such times a lawyer may discharge the pro bono responsibility by providing financial support to organizations providing free legal services to persons of limited means. Such financial support should be reasonably equivalent to the value of the hours of service that would have otherwise been provided. In addition, at times it may be more feasible to satisfy the pro bono responsibility collectively, as by a firm's aggregate pro bono activities.

[10] Because the efforts of individual lawyers are not enough to meet the need for free legal services that exists among persons of limited means, the government and the profession have instituted additional programs to provide those services. Every lawyer should financially support such programs, in addition to either providing direct pro bono services or making financial contributions when pro bono service is not feasible.

[11] Law firms should act reasonably to enable and encourage all lawyers in the firm to provide the pro bono legal services called for by this Rule.

[12] The responsibility set forth in this Rule is not intended to be enforced through disciplinary process.

Definitional Cross-Reference

"Substantial" *See* Rule 1.0(l)

Rule 6.2 Accepting Appointments

A lawyer shall not seek to avoid appointment by a tribunal to represent a person except for good cause, such as:

(a) representing the client is likely to result in violation of the Rules of Professional Conduct or other law;

(b) representing the client is likely to result in an unreasonable financial burden on the lawyer; or

(c) the client or the cause is so repugnant to the lawyer as to be likely to impair the client-lawyer relationship or the lawyer's ability to represent the client.

Comment

[1] A lawyer ordinarily is not obliged to accept a client whose character or cause the lawyer regards as repugnant. The lawyer's freedom to select clients is, however, qualified. All lawyers have a responsibility to assist in providing pro bono publico service. See Rule 6.1. An individual lawyer fulfills this responsibility by accepting a fair share of unpopular matters or indigent or unpopular clients. A lawyer may also be subject to appointment by a court to serve unpopular clients or persons unable to afford legal services.

Appointed Counsel

[2] For good cause a lawyer may seek to decline an appointment to represent a person who cannot afford to retain counsel or whose cause is unpopular. Good cause exists if the lawyer could not handle the matter competently, see Rule 1.1, or if undertaking the representation would result in an improper conflict of interest, for example, when the client or the cause is so repugnant to the lawyer as to be likely to impair the client-lawyer relationship or the lawyer's ability to represent the client. A lawyer may also seek to decline an appointment if acceptance would be unreasonably burdensome, for example, when it would impose a financial sacrifice so great as to be unjust.

[3] An appointed lawyer has the same obligations to the client as retained counsel, including the obligations of loyalty and confidentiality, and is subject to the same limitations on the client-lawyer relationship, such as the obligation to refrain from assisting the client in violation of the Rules.

Definitional Cross-Reference

"Tribunal" *See* Rule 1.0(m)

Rule 6.3 Membership in Legal Services Organization

A lawyer may serve as a director, officer or member of a legal services organization, apart from the law firm in which the lawyer practices, notwithstanding that the organization serves persons having interests adverse to a client of the

lawyer. The lawyer shall not knowingly participate in a decision or action of the organization:

(a) if participating in the decision or action would be incompatible with the lawyer's obligations to a client under Rule 1.7; or

(b) where the decision or action could have a material adverse effect on the representation of a client of the organization whose interests are adverse to a client of the lawyer.

Comment

[1] Lawyers should be encouraged to support and participate in legal service organizations. A lawyer who is an officer or a member of such an organization does not thereby have a client-lawyer relationship with persons served by the organization. However, there is potential conflict between the interests of such persons and the interests of the lawyer's clients. If the possibility of such conflict disqualified a lawyer from serving on the board of a legal services organization, the profession's involvement in such organizations would be severely curtailed.

[2] It may be necessary in appropriate cases to reassure a client of the organization that the representation will not be affected by conflicting loyalties of a member of the board. Established, written policies in this respect can enhance the credibility of such assurances.

Definitional Cross-References

"Law firm" *See* Rule 1.0(c)
"Knowingly" *See* Rule 1.0(f)

Rule 6.4 Law Reform Activities Affecting Client Interests

A lawyer may serve as a director, officer or member of an organization involved in reform of the law or its administration notwithstanding that the reform may affect the interests of a client of the lawyer. When the lawyer knows that the interests of a client may be materially benefitted by a decision in which the lawyer participates, the lawyer shall disclose that fact but need not identify the client.

Comment

[1] Lawyers involved in organizations seeking law reform generally do not have a client-lawyer relationship with the organization. Otherwise, it might follow that a lawyer could not be involved in a bar association law reform program that might indirectly affect a client. See also Rule 1.2(b). For example, a lawyer specializing in antitrust litigation might be regarded as disqualified from participating in drafting revisions of rules governing that subject. In determining the nature and scope of participation in such activities, a lawyer should be mindful of obligations to clients under other Rules, particularly Rule 1.7. A lawyer is professionally

obligated to protect the integrity of the program by making an appropriate disclosure within the organization when the lawyer knows a private client might be materially benefitted.

Definitional Cross-Reference

"Knows" *See* Rule 1.0(f)

Rule 6.5 Nonprofit and Court-Annexed Limited Legal Services Programs

(a) A lawyer who, under the auspices of a program sponsored by a nonprofit organization or court, provides short-term limited legal services to a client without expectation by either the lawyer or the client that the lawyer will provide continuing representation in the matter:

(1) is subject to Rules 1.7 and 1.9(a) only if the lawyer knows that the representation of the client involves a conflict of interest; and

(2) is subject to Rule 1.10 only if the lawyer knows that another lawyer associated with the lawyer in a law firm is disqualified by Rule 1.7 or 1.9(a) with respect to the matter.

(b) Except as provided in paragraph (a)(2), Rule 1.10 is inapplicable to a representation governed by this Rule.

Comment

[1] Legal services organizations, courts and various nonprofit organizations have established programs through which lawyers provide short-term limited legal services — such as advice or the completion of legal forms — that will assist persons to address their legal problems without further representation by a lawyer. In these programs, such as legal-advice hotlines, advice-only clinics or pro se counseling programs, a client-lawyer relationship is established, but there is no expectation that the lawyer's representation of the client will continue beyond the limited consultation. Such programs are normally operated under circumstances in which it is not feasible for a lawyer to systematically screen for conflicts of interest as is generally required before undertaking a representation. See, e.g., Rules 1.7, 1.9 and 1.10.

[2] A lawyer who provides short-term limited legal services pursuant to this Rule must secure the client's informed consent to the limited scope of the representation. See Rule 1.2(c). If a short-term limited representation would not be reasonable under the circumstances, the lawyer may offer advice to the client but must also advise the client of the need for further assistance of counsel. Except as provided in this Rule, the Rules of Professional Conduct, including Rules 1.6 and 1.9(c), are applicable to the limited representation.

[3] Because a lawyer who is representing a client in the circumstances addressed by this Rule ordinarily is not able to check systematically for conflicts of interest, paragraph (a) requires compliance with Rules 1.7 or 1.9(a) only if the lawyer knows

that the representation presents a conflict of interest for the lawyer, and with Rule 1.10 only if the lawyer knows that another lawyer in the lawyer's firm is disqualified by Rules 1.7 or 1.9(a) in the matter.

[4] Because the limited nature of the services significantly reduces the risk of conflicts of interest with other matters being handled by the lawyer's firm, paragraph (b) provides that Rule 1.10 is inapplicable to a representation governed by this Rule except as provided by paragraph (a)(2). Paragraph (a)(2) requires the participating lawyer to comply with Rule 1.10 when the lawyer knows that the lawyer's firm is disqualified by Rules 1.7 or 1.9(a). By virtue of paragraph (b), however, a lawyer's participation in a short-term limited legal services program will not preclude the lawyer's firm from undertaking or continuing the representation of a client with interests adverse to a client being represented under the program's auspices. Nor will the personal disqualification of a lawyer participating in the program be imputed to other lawyers participating in the program.

[5] If, after commencing a short-term limited representation in accordance with this Rule, a lawyer undertakes to represent the client in the matter on an ongoing basis, Rules 1.7, 1.9(a) and 1.10 become applicable.

Definitional Cross-References

"Law firm" *See* Rule 1.0(c)
"Knows" *See* Rule 1.0(f)

ARTICLE 7. INFORMATION ABOUT LEGAL SERVICES

Rule 7.1 Communications Concerning a Lawyer's Services

A lawyer shall not make a false or misleading communication about the lawyer or the lawyer's services. A communication is false or misleading if it contains a material misrepresentation of fact or law, or omits a fact necessary to make the statement considered as a whole not materially misleading.

Comment

[1] This Rule governs all communications about a lawyer's services, including advertising. Whatever means are used to make known a lawyer's services, statements about them must be truthful.

[2] Misleading truthful statements are prohibited by this Rule. A truthful statement is misleading if it omits a fact necessary to make the lawyer's communication considered as a whole not materially misleading. A truthful statement is misleading if a substantial likelihood exists that it will lead a reasonable person to formulate a specific conclusion about the lawyer or the lawyer's services for which there is no reasonable factual foundation. A truthful statement is also misleading if presented in a way that creates a substantial likelihood that a reasonable person would believe the lawyer's communication requires that person to take further action when, in fact, no action is required.

[3] A communication that truthfully reports a lawyer's achievements on behalf of clients or former clients may be misleading if presented so as to lead a reasonable person to form an unjustified expectation that the same results could be obtained for other clients in similar matters without reference to the specific factual and legal circumstances of each client's case. Similarly, an unsubstantiated claim about a lawyer's or law firm's services or fees, or an unsubstantiated comparison of the lawyer's or law firm's services or fees with those of other lawyers or law firms, may be misleading if presented with such specificity as would lead a reasonable person to conclude that the comparison or claim can be substantiated. The inclusion of an appropriate disclaimer or qualifying language may preclude a finding that a statement is likely to create unjustified expectations or otherwise mislead the public.

[4] It is professional misconduct for a lawyer to engage in conduct involving dishonesty, fraud, deceit or misrepresentation. Rule 8.4(c). See also Rule 8.4(e) for the prohibition against stating or implying an ability to improperly influence a government agency or official or to achieve results by means that violate the Rules of Professional Conduct or other law.

[5] Firm names, letterhead and professional designations are communications concerning a lawyer's services. A firm may be designated by the names of all or some of its current members, by the names of deceased members where there has been a succession in the firm's identity or by a trade name if it is not false or misleading. A lawyer or law firm also may be designated by a distinctive website address, social media username or comparable professional designation that is not misleading. A law firm name or designation is misleading if it implies a connection with a government agency, with a deceased lawyer who was not a former member of the firm, with a lawyer not associated with the firm or a predecessor firm, with a nonlawyer or with a public or charitable legal services organization. If a firm uses a trade name that includes a geographical name such as "Springfield Legal Clinic," an express statement explaining that it is not a public legal aid organization may be required to avoid a misleading implication.

[6] A law firm with offices in more than one jurisdiction may use the same name or other professional designation in each jurisdiction.

[7] Lawyers may not imply or hold themselves out as practicing together in one firm when they are not a firm, as defined in Rule 1.0(c), because to do so would be false and misleading.

[8] It is misleading to use the name of a lawyer holding a public office in the name of a law firm, or in communications on the law firm's behalf, during any substantial period in which the lawyer is not actively and regularly practicing with the firm.

Rule 7.2 Communications Concerning a Lawyer's Services: Specific Rules

(a) A lawyer may communicate information regarding the lawyer's services through any media.

(b) A lawyer shall not compensate, give or promise anything of value to a person for recommending the lawyer's services except that a lawyer may:

(1) pay the reasonable costs of advertisements or communications permitted by this Rule;

(2) pay the usual charges of a legal service plan or a not-for-profit or qualified lawyer referral service;

(3) pay for a law practice in accordance with Rule 1.17;

(4) refer clients to another lawyer or a nonlawyer professional pursuant to an agreement not otherwise prohibited under these Rules that provides for the other person to refer clients or customers to the lawyer, if:

(i) the reciprocal referral agreement is not exclusive; and

(ii) the client is informed of the existence and nature of the agreement; and

(5) give nominal gifts as an expression of appreciation that are neither intended nor reasonably expected to be a form of compensation for recommending a lawyer's services.

(c) A lawyer shall not state or imply that a lawyer is certified as a specialist in a particular field of law, unless:

(1) the lawyer has been certified as a specialist by an organization that has been approved by an appropriate authority of the state or the District of Columbia or a U.S. Territory or that has been accredited by the American Bar Association; and

(2) the name of the certifying organization is clearly identified in the communication.

(d) Any communication made under this Rule must include the name and contact information of at least one lawyer or law firm responsible for its content.

Comment

[1] This Rule permits public dissemination of information concerning a lawyer's or law firm's name, address, email address, website, and telephone number; the kinds of services the lawyer will undertake; the basis on which the lawyer's fees are determined, including prices for specific services and payment and credit arrangements; a lawyer's foreign language ability; names of references and, with their consent, names of clients regularly represented; and other information that might invite the attention of those seeking legal assistance.

Paying Others to Recommend a Lawyer

[2] Except as permitted under paragraphs (b)(1)-(b)(5), lawyers are not permitted to pay others for recommending the lawyer's services. A communication contains a recommendation if it endorses or vouches for a lawyer's credentials, abilities, competence, character, or other professional qualities. Directory listings and group advertisements that list lawyers by practice area, without more, do not constitute impermissible "recommendations."

[3] Paragraph (b)(1) allows a lawyer to pay for advertising and communications permitted by this Rule, including the costs of print directory listings, on-line directory listings, newspaper ads, television and radio airtime, domain-name registrations, sponsorship fees, Internet-based advertisements, and group advertising. A lawyer may compensate employees, agents and vendors who are engaged to provide marketing or client development services, such as publicists, public-relations personnel, business-development staff, television and radio station employees or spokespersons and website designers.

[4] Paragraph (b)(5) permits lawyers to give nominal gifts as an expression of appreciation to a person for recommending the lawyer's services or referring a prospective client. The gift may not be more than a token item as might be given for holidays, or other ordinary social hospitality. A gift is prohibited if offered or given in consideration of any promise, agreement or understanding that such a gift would be forthcoming or that referrals would be made or encouraged in the future.

[5] A lawyer may pay others for generating client leads, such as Internet-based client leads, as long as the lead generator does not recommend the lawyer, any payment to the lead generator is consistent with Rules 1.5(e) (division of fees) and 5.4 (professional independence of the lawyer), and the lead generator's communications are consistent with Rule 7.1 (communications concerning a lawyer's services). To comply with Rule 7.1, a lawyer must not pay a lead generator that states, implies, or creates a reasonable impression that it is recommending the lawyer, is making the referral without payment from the lawyer, or has analyzed a person's legal problems when determining which lawyer should receive the referral. See Comment [2] (definition of "recommendation"). See also Rule 5.3 (duties of lawyers and law firms with respect to the conduct of nonlawyers); Rule 8.4(a) (duty to avoid violating the Rules through the acts of another).

[6] A lawyer may pay the usual charges of a legal service plan or a not-for-profit or qualified lawyer referral service. A legal service plan is a prepaid or group legal service plan or a similar delivery system that assists people who seek to secure legal representation. A lawyer referral service, on the other hand, is any organization that holds itself out to the public as a lawyer referral service. Qualified referral services are consumer-oriented organizations that provide unbiased referrals to lawyers with appropriate experience in the subject matter of the representation and afford other client protections, such as complaint procedures or malpractice insurance requirements. Consequently, this Rule only permits a lawyer to pay the usual charges of a not-for-profit or qualified lawyer referral service. A qualified lawyer referral service is one that is approved by an appropriate regulatory authority as affording adequate protections for the public. See, e.g., the American Bar Association's Model Supreme Court Rules Governing Lawyer Referral Services and Model Lawyer Referral and Information Service Quality Assurance Act.

[7] A lawyer who accepts assignments or referrals from a legal service plan or referrals from a lawyer referral service must act reasonably to assure that the activities of the plan or service are compatible with the lawyer's professional obligations. Legal service plans and lawyer referral services may communicate with the public, but such communication must be in conformity with these Rules. Thus, advertising

must not be false or misleading, as would be the case if the communications of a group advertising program or a group legal services plan would mislead the public to think that it was a lawyer referral service sponsored by a state agency or bar association.

[8] A lawyer also may agree to refer clients to another lawyer or a nonlawyer professional, in return for the undertaking of that person to refer clients or customers to the lawyer. Such reciprocal referral arrangements must not interfere with the lawyer's professional judgment as to making referrals or as to providing substantive legal services. See Rules 2.1 and 5.4(c). Except as provided in Rule 1.5(e), a lawyer who receives referrals from a lawyer or nonlawyer professional must not pay anything solely for the referral, but the lawyer does not violate paragraph (b) of this Rule by agreeing to refer clients to the other lawyer or nonlawyer professional, so long as the reciprocal referral agreement is not exclusive and the client is informed of the referral agreement. Conflicts of interest created by such arrangements are governed by Rule 1.7. Reciprocal referral agreements should not be of indefinite duration and should be reviewed periodically to determine whether they comply with these Rules. This Rule does not restrict referrals or divisions of revenues or net income among lawyers within firms comprised of multiple entities.

Communications about Fields of Practice

[9] Paragraph (c) of this Rule permits a lawyer to communicate that the lawyer does or does not practice in particular areas of law. A lawyer is generally permitted to state that the lawyer "concentrates in" or is a "specialist," practices a "specialty," or "specializes in" particular fields based on the lawyer's experience, specialized training or education, but such communications are subject to the "false and misleading" standard applied in Rule 7.1 to communications concerning a lawyer's services.

[10] The Patent and Trademark Office has a long-established policy of designating lawyers practicing before the Office. The designation of Admiralty practice also has a long historical tradition associated with maritime commerce and the federal courts. A lawyer's communications about these practice areas are not prohibited by this Rule.

[11] This Rule permits a lawyer to state that the lawyer is certified as a specialist in a field of law if such certification is granted by an organization approved by an appropriate authority of a state, the District of Columbia or a U.S. Territory or accredited by the American Bar Association or another organization, such as a state supreme court or a state bar association, that has been approved by the authority of the state, the District of Columbia or a U.S. Territory to accredit organizations that certify lawyers as specialists. Certification signifies that an objective entity has recognized an advanced degree of knowledge and experience in the specialty area greater than is suggested by general licensure to practice law. Certifying organizations may be expected to apply standards of experience, knowledge and proficiency to ensure that a lawyer's recognition as a specialist is meaningful and reliable. To ensure that consumers can obtain access to useful information about an organization granting certification, the name of the certifying organization must be included in any communication regarding the certification.

Required Contact Information

[12] This Rule requires that any communication about a lawyer or law firm's services include the name of, and contact information for, the lawyer or law firm. Contact information includes a website address, a telephone number, an email address or a physical office location.

Rule 7.3 Solicitation of Clients

(a) "Solicitation" or "solicit" denotes a communication initiated by or on behalf of a lawyer or law firm that is directed to a specific person the lawyer knows or reasonably should know needs legal services in a particular matter and that offers to provide, or reasonably can be understood as offering to provide, legal services for that matter.

(b) A lawyer shall not solicit professional employment by live person-to-person contact when a significant motive for the lawyer's doing so is the lawyer's or law firm's pecuniary gain, unless the contact is with a:

(1) lawyer;

(2) person who has a family, close personal, or prior business or professional relationship with the lawyer or law firm; or

(3) person who routinely uses for business purposes the type of legal services offered by the lawyer.

(c) A lawyer shall not solicit professional employment even when not otherwise prohibited by paragraph (b), if:

(1) the target of the solicitation has made known to the lawyer a desire not to be solicited by the lawyer; or

(2) the solicitation involves coercion, duress or harassment.

(d) This Rule does not prohibit communications authorized by law or ordered by a court or other tribunal.

(e) Notwithstanding the prohibitions in this Rule, a lawyer may participate with a prepaid or group legal service plan operated by an organization not owned or directed by the lawyer that uses live person-to-person contact to enroll members or sell subscriptions for the plan from persons who are not known to need legal services in a particular matter covered by the plan.

Comment

[1] Paragraph (b) prohibits a lawyer from soliciting professional employment by live person-to-person contact when a significant motive for the lawyer's doing so is the lawyer's or the law firm's pecuniary gain. A lawyer's communication is not a solicitation if it is directed to the general public, such as through a billboard, an Internet banner advertisement, a website or a television commercial, or if it is in response to a request for information or is automatically generated in response to electronic searches.

[2] "Live person-to-person contact" means in-person, face-to-face, live telephone and other real-time visual or auditory person-to-person communications

where the person is subject to a direct personal encounter without time for reflection. Such person-to-person contact does not include chat rooms, text messages or other written communications that recipients may easily disregard. A potential for overreaching exists when a lawyer, seeking pecuniary gain, solicits a person known to be in need of legal services. This form of contact subjects a person to the private importuning of the trained advocate in a direct interpersonal encounter. The person, who may already feel overwhelmed by the circumstances giving rise to the need for legal services, may find it difficult to fully evaluate all available alternatives with reasoned judgment and appropriate self-interest in the face of the lawyer's presence and insistence upon an immediate response. The situation is fraught with the possibility of undue influence, intimidation, and overreaching.

[3] The potential for overreaching inherent in live person-to-person contact justifies its prohibition, since lawyers have alternative means of conveying necessary information. In particular, communications can be mailed or transmitted by email or other electronic means that do not violate other laws. These forms of communications make it possible for the public to be informed about the need for legal services, and about the qualifications of available lawyers and law firms, without subjecting the public to live person-to-person persuasion that may overwhelm a person's judgment.

[4] The contents of live person-to-person contact can be disputed and may not be subject to third-party scrutiny. Consequently, they are much more likely to approach (and occasionally cross) the dividing line between accurate representations and those that are false and misleading.

[5] There is far less likelihood that a lawyer would engage in overreaching against a former client, or a person with whom the lawyer has a close personal, family, business or professional relationship, or in situations in which the lawyer is motivated by considerations other than the lawyer's pecuniary gain. Nor is there a serious potential for overreaching when the person contacted is a lawyer or is known to routinely use the type of legal services involved for business purposes. Examples include persons who routinely hire outside counsel to represent the entity; entrepreneurs who regularly engage business, employment law or intellectual property lawyers; small business proprietors who routinely hire lawyers for lease or contract issues; and other people who routinely retain lawyers for business transactions or formations. Paragraph (b) is not intended to prohibit a lawyer from participating in constitutionally protected activities of public or charitable legal-service organizations or bona fide political, social, civic, fraternal, employee or trade organizations whose purposes include providing or recommending legal services to their members or beneficiaries.

[6] A solicitation that contains false or misleading information within the meaning of Rule 7.1, that involves coercion, duress or harassment within the meaning of Rule 7.3(c)(2), or that involves contact with someone who has made known to the lawyer a desire not to be solicited by the lawyer within the meaning of Rule 7.3(c)(1) is prohibited. Live, personto-person contact of individuals who may be especially vulnerable to coercion or duress is ordinarily not appropriate, for example, the elderly, those whose first language is not English, or the disabled.

[7] This Rule does not prohibit a lawyer from contacting representatives of organizations or groups that may be interested in establishing a group or prepaid legal plan for their members, insureds, beneficiaries or other third parties for the purpose of informing such entities of the availability of and details concerning the plan or arrangement which the lawyer or lawyer's firm is willing to offer. This form of communication is not directed to people who are seeking legal services for themselves. Rather, it is usually addressed to an individual acting in a fiduciary capacity seeking a supplier of legal services for others who may, if they choose, become prospective clients of the lawyer. Under these circumstances, the activity which the lawyer undertakes in communicating with such representatives and the type of information transmitted to the individual are functionally similar to and serve the same purpose as advertising permitted under Rule 7.2.

[8] Communications authorized by law or ordered by a court or tribunal include a notice to potential members of a class in class action litigation.

[9] Paragraph (e) of this Rule permits a lawyer to participate with an organization which uses personal contact to enroll members for its group or prepaid legal service plan, provided that the personal contact is not undertaken by any lawyer who would be a provider of legal services through the plan. The organization must not be owned by or directed (whether as manager or otherwise) by any lawyer or law firm that participates in the plan. For example, paragraph (e) would not permit a lawyer to create an organization controlled directly or indirectly by the lawyer and use the organization for the person-to-person solicitation of legal employment of the lawyer through memberships in the plan or otherwise. The communication permitted by these organizations must not be directed to a person known to need legal services in a particular matter, but must be designed to inform potential plan members generally of another means of affordable legal services. Lawyers who participate in a legal service plan must reasonably assure that the plan sponsors are in compliance with Rules 7.1, 7.2, and 7.3(c).

Rule 7.4 (Deleted 2018)

Rule 7.5 (Deleted 2018)

Rule 7.6 Political Contributions to Obtain Government Legal Engagements or Appointments by Judges

A lawyer or law firm shall not accept a government legal engagement or an appointment by a judge if the lawyer or law firm makes a political contribution or solicits political contributions for the purpose of obtaining or being considered for that type of legal engagement or appointment.

Comment

[1] Lawyers have a right to participate fully in the political process, which includes making and soliciting political contributions to candidates for judicial and

other public office. Nevertheless, when lawyers make or solicit political contributions in order to obtain an engagement for legal work awarded by a government agency, or to obtain appointment by a judge, the public may legitimately question whether the lawyers engaged to perform the work are selected on the basis of competence and merit. In such a circumstance, the integrity of the profession is undermined.

[2] The term "political contribution" denotes any gift, subscription, loan, advance or deposit of anything of value made directly or indirectly to a candidate, incumbent, political party or campaign committee to influence or provide financial support for election to or retention in judicial or other government office. Political contributions in initiative and referendum elections are not included. For purposes of this Rule, the term "political contribution" does not include uncompensated services.

[3] Subject to the exceptions below, (i) the term "government legal engagement" denotes any engagement to provide legal services that a public official has the direct or indirect power to award; and (ii) the term "appointment by a judge" denotes an appointment to a position such as referee, commissioner, special master, receiver, guardian or other similar position that is made by a judge. Those terms do not, however, include (a) substantially uncompensated services; (b) engagements or appointments made on the basis of experience, expertise, professional qualifications and cost following a request for proposal or other process that is free from influence based upon political contributions; and (c) engagements or appointments made on a rotational basis from a list compiled without regard to political contributions.

[4] The term "lawyer or law firm" includes a political action committee or other entity owned or controlled by a lawyer or law firm.

[5] Political contributions are for the purpose of obtaining or being considered for a government legal engagement or appointment by a judge if, but for the desire to be considered for the legal engagement or appointment, the lawyer or law firm would not have made or solicited the contributions. The purpose may be determined by an examination of the circumstances in which the contributions occur. For example, one or more contributions that in the aggregate are substantial in relation to other contributions by lawyers or law firms, made for the benefit of an official in a position to influence award of a government legal engagement, and followed by an award of the legal engagement to the contributing or soliciting lawyer or the lawyer's firm would support an inference that the purpose of the contributions was to obtain the engagement, absent other factors that weigh against existence of the proscribed purpose. Those factors may include among others that the contribution or solicitation was made to further a political, social, or economic interest or because of an existing personal, family, or professional relationship with a candidate.

[6] If a lawyer makes or solicits a political contribution under circumstances that constitute bribery or another crime, Rule 8.4(b) is implicated.

Definitional Cross-Reference

"Law firm" *See* Rule 1.0(c)

ARTICLE 8. MAINTAINING THE INTEGRITY OF THE PROFESSION

Rule 8.1 Bar Admission and Disciplinary Matters

An applicant for admission to the bar, or a lawyer in connection with a bar admission application or in connection with a disciplinary matter, shall not:

(a) knowingly make a false statement of material fact; or

(b) fail to disclose a fact necessary to correct a misapprehension known by the person to have arisen in the matter, or knowingly fail to respond to a lawful demand for information from an admissions or disciplinary authority, except that this Rule does not require disclosure of information otherwise protected by Rule 1.6.

Comment

[1] The duty imposed by this Rule extends to persons seeking admission to the bar as well as to lawyers. Hence, if a person makes a material false statement in connection with an application for admission, it may be the basis for subsequent disciplinary action if the person is admitted, and in any event may be relevant in a subsequent admission application. The duty imposed by this Rule applies to a lawyer's own admission or discipline as well as that of others. Thus, it is a separate professional offense for a lawyer to knowingly make a misrepresentation or omission in connection with a disciplinary investigation of the lawyer's own conduct. Paragraph (b) of this Rule also requires correction of any prior misstatement in the matter that the applicant or lawyer may have made and affirmative clarification of any misunderstanding on the part of the admissions or disciplinary authority of which the person involved becomes aware.

[2] This Rule is subject to the provisions of the Fifth Amendment of the United States Constitution and corresponding provisions of state constitutions. A person relying on such a provision in response to a question, however, should do so openly and not use the right of nondisclosure as a justification for failure to comply with this Rule.

[3] A lawyer representing an applicant for admission to the bar, or representing a lawyer who is the subject of a disciplinary inquiry or proceeding, is governed by the Rules applicable to the client-lawyer relationship, including Rule 1.6 and, in some cases, Rule 3.3.

Definitional Cross-Reference

"Knowingly" and "Known" *See* Rule 1.0(f)

Rule 8.2 Judicial and Legal Officials

(a) A lawyer shall not make a statement that the lawyer knows to be false or with reckless disregard as to its truth or falsity concerning the qualifications or

integrity of a judge, adjudicatory officer or public legal officer, or of a candidate for election or appointment to judicial or legal office.

(b) **A lawyer who is a candidate for judicial office shall comply with the applicable provisions of the Code of Judicial Conduct.**

Comment

[1] Assessments by lawyers are relied on in evaluating the professional or personal fitness of persons being considered for election or appointment to judicial office and to public legal offices, such as attorney general, prosecuting attorney and public defender. Expressing honest and candid opinions on such matters contributes to improving the administration of justice. Conversely, false statements by a lawyer can unfairly undermine public confidence in the administration of justice.

[2] When a lawyer seeks judicial office, the lawyer should be bound by applicable limitations on political activity.

[3] To maintain the fair and independent administration of justice, lawyers are encouraged to continue traditional efforts to defend judges and courts unjustly criticized.

Definitional Cross-Reference

"Knows" *See* Rule 1.0(f)

Rule 8.3 Reporting Professional Misconduct

(a) **A lawyer who knows that another lawyer has committed a violation of the Rules of Professional Conduct that raises a substantial question as to that lawyer's honesty, trustworthiness or fitness as a lawyer in other respects, shall inform the appropriate professional authority.**

(b) **A lawyer who knows that a judge has committed a violation of applicable rules of judicial conduct that raises a substantial question as to the judge's fitness for office shall inform the appropriate authority.**

(c) **This Rule does not require disclosure of information otherwise protected by Rule 1.6 or information gained by a lawyer or judge while participating in an approved lawyers assistance program.**

Comment

[1] Self-regulation of the legal profession requires that members of the profession initiate disciplinary investigation when they know of a violation of the Rules of Professional Conduct. Lawyers have a similar obligation with respect to judicial misconduct. An apparently isolated violation may indicate a pattern of misconduct that only a disciplinary investigation can uncover. Reporting a violation is especially important where the victim is unlikely to discover the offense.

[2] A report about misconduct is not required where it would involve violation of Rule 1.6. However, a lawyer should encourage a client to consent to disclosure where prosecution would not substantially prejudice the client's interests.

[3] If a lawyer were obliged to report every violation of the Rules, the failure to report any violation would itself be a professional offense. Such a requirement existed in many jurisdictions but proved to be unenforceable. This Rule limits the reporting obligation to those offenses that a self-regulating profession must vigorously endeavor to prevent. A measure of judgment is, therefore, required in complying with the provisions of this Rule. The term "substantial" refers to the seriousness of the possible offense and not the quantum of evidence of which the lawyer is aware. A report should be made to the bar disciplinary agency unless some other agency, such as a peer review agency, is more appropriate in the circumstances. Similar considerations apply to the reporting of judicial misconduct.

[4] The duty to report professional misconduct does not apply to a lawyer retained to represent a lawyer whose professional conduct is in question. Such a situation is governed by the Rules applicable to the client-lawyer relationship.

[5] Information about a lawyer's or judge's misconduct or fitness may be received by a lawyer in the course of that lawyer's participation in an approved lawyers or judges assistance program. In that circumstance, providing for an exception to the reporting requirements of paragraphs (a) and (b) of this Rule encourages lawyers and judges to seek treatment through such a program. Conversely, without such an exception, lawyers and judges may hesitate to seek assistance from these programs, which may then result in additional harm to their professional careers and additional injury to the welfare of clients and the public. These Rules do not otherwise address the confidentiality of information received by a lawyer or judge participating in an approved lawyers assistance program; such an obligation, however, may be imposed by the rules of the program or other law.

Definitional Cross-References

"Knows" *See* Rule 1.0(f)
"Substantial" *See* Rule 1.0(l)

Rule 8.4 Misconduct

It is professional misconduct for a lawyer to:

(a) violate or attempt to violate the Rules of Professional Conduct, knowingly assist or induce another to do so, or do so through the acts of another;

(b) commit a criminal act that reflects adversely on the lawyer's honesty, trustworthiness or fitness as a lawyer in other respects;

(c) engage in conduct involving dishonesty, fraud, deceit or misrepresentation;

(d) engage in conduct that is prejudicial to the administration of justice;

(e) state or imply an ability to influence improperly a government agency or official or to achieve results by means that violate the Rules of Professional Conduct or other law;

(f) knowingly assist a judge or judicial officer in conduct that is a violation of applicable rules of judicial conduct or other law; or

(g) engage in conduct that the lawyer knows or reasonably should know is harassment or discrimination on the basis of race, sex, religion, national origin, ethnicity, disability, age, sexual orientation, gender identity, marital status or socioeconomic status in conduct related to the practice of law. This paragraph does not limit the ability of a lawyer to accept, decline or withdraw from a representation in accordance with Rule 1.16. This paragraph does not preclude legitimate advice or advocacy consistent with these Rules.

Comment

[1] Lawyers are subject to discipline when they violate or attempt to violate the Rules of Professional Conduct, knowingly assist or induce another to do so or do so through the acts of another, as when they request or instruct an agent to do so on the lawyer's behalf. Paragraph (a), however, does not prohibit a lawyer from advising a client concerning action the client is legally entitled to take.

[2] Many kinds of illegal conduct reflect adversely on fitness to practice law, such as offenses involving fraud and the offense of willful failure to file an income tax return. However, some kinds of offenses carry no such implication. Traditionally, the distinction was drawn in terms of offenses involving "moral turpitude." That concept can be construed to include offenses concerning some matters of personal morality, such as adultery and comparable offenses, that have no specific connection to fitness for the practice of law. Although a lawyer is personally answerable to the entire criminal law, a lawyer should be professionally answerable only for offenses that indicate lack of those characteristics relevant to law practice. Offenses involving violence, dishonesty, breach of trust, or serious interference with the administration of justice are in that category. A pattern of repeated offenses, even ones of minor significance when considered separately, can indicate indifference to legal obligation.

[3] Discrimination and harassment by lawyers in violation of paragraph (g) undermine confidence in the legal profession and the legal system. Such discrimination includes harmful verbal or physical conduct that manifests bias or prejudice towards others. Harassment includes sexual harassment and derogatory or demeaning verbal or physical conduct. Sexual harassment includes unwelcome sexual advances, requests for sexual favors, and other unwelcome verbal or physical conduct of a sexual nature. The substantive law of antidiscrimination and antiharassment statutes and case law may guide application of paragraph (g).

[4] Conduct related to the practice of law includes representing clients; interacting with witnesses, coworkers, court personnel, lawyers and others while engaged in the practice of law; operating or managing a law firm or law practice; and participating in bar association, business or social activities in connection with the practice of law. Lawyers may engage in conduct undertaken to promote diversity and inclusion without violating this Rule by, for example, implementing initiatives

aimed at recruiting, hiring, retaining and advancing diverse employees or sponsoring diverse law student organizations.

[5] A trial judge's finding that peremptory challenges were exercised on a discriminatory basis does not alone establish a violation of paragraph (g). A lawyer does not violate paragraph (g) by limiting the scope or subject matter of the lawyer's practice or by limiting the lawyer's practice to members of underserved populations in accordance with these Rules and other law. A lawyer may charge and collect reasonable fees and expenses for a representation. Rule 1.5(a). Lawyers also should be mindful of their professional obligations under Rule 6.1 to provide legal services to those who are unable to pay, and their obligation under Rule 6.2 not to avoid appointments from a tribunal except for good cause. See Rule 6.2(a), (b) and (c). A lawyer's representation of a client does not constitute an endorsement by the lawyer of the client's views or activities. See Rule 1.2(b).

[6] A lawyer may refuse to comply with an obligation imposed by law upon a good faith belief that no valid obligation exists. The provisions of Rule 1.2(d) concerning a good faith challenge to the validity, scope, meaning or application of the law apply to challenges of legal regulation of the practice of law.

[7] Lawyers holding public office assume legal responsibilities going beyond those of other citizens. A lawyer's abuse of public office can suggest an inability to fulfill the professional role of lawyers. The same is true of abuse of positions of private trust such as trustee, executor, administrator, guardian, agent and officer, director or manager of a corporation or other organization.

Definitional Cross-References

"Fraud" *See* Rule 1.0(d)
"Knowingly" and "knows" *See* Rule 1.0(f)
"Reasonably should know" *See* Rule 1.0(j)

Rule 8.5 Disciplinary Authority; Choice of law

(a) Disciplinary Authority. A lawyer admitted to practice in this jurisdiction is subject to the disciplinary authority of this jurisdiction, regardless of where the lawyer's conduct occurs.
A lawyer not admitted in this jurisdiction is also subject to the disciplinary authority of this jurisdiction if the lawyer provides or offers to provide any legal services in this jurisdiction.
A lawyer may be subject to the disciplinary authority of both this jurisdiction and another jurisdiction for the same conduct.

(b) Choice of Law. In any exercise of the disciplinary authority of this jurisdiction, the rules of professional conduct to be applied shall be as follows:

(1) for conduct in connection with a matter pending before a tribunal, the rules of the jurisdiction in which the tribunal sits, unless the rules of the tribunal provide otherwise; and

(2) for any other conduct, the rules of the jurisdiction in which the lawyer's conduct occurred, or, if the predominant effect of the conduct is

in a different jurisdiction, the rules of that jurisdiction shall be applied to the conduct. A lawyer shall not be subject to discipline if the lawyer's conduct conforms to the rules of a jurisdiction in which the lawyer reasonably believes the predominant effect of the lawyer's conduct will occur.

Comment

Disciplinary Authority

[1] It is longstanding law that the conduct of a lawyer admitted to practice in this jurisdiction is subject to the disciplinary authority of this jurisdiction. Extension of the disciplinary authority of this jurisdiction to other lawyers who provide or offer to provide legal services in this jurisdiction is for the protection of the citizens of this jurisdiction. Reciprocal enforcement of a jurisdiction's disciplinary findings and sanctions will further advance the purposes of this Rule. See, Rules 6 and 22, ABA *Model Rules for Lawyer Disciplinary Enforcement*. A lawyer who is subject to the disciplinary authority of this jurisdiction under Rule 8.5(a) appoints an official to be designated by this court to receive service of process in this jurisdiction. The fact that the lawyer is subject to the disciplinary authority of this jurisdiction may be a factor in determining whether personal jurisdiction may be asserted over the lawyer for civil matters.

Choice of Law

[2] A lawyer may be potentially subject to more than one set of rules of professional conduct which impose different obligations. The lawyer may be licensed to practice in more than one jurisdiction with differing rules, or may be admitted to practice before a particular court with rules that differ from those of the jurisdiction or jurisdictions in which the lawyer is licensed to practice. Additionally, the lawyer's conduct may involve significant contacts with more than one jurisdiction.

[3] Paragraph (b) seeks to resolve such potential conflicts. Its premise is that minimizing conflicts between rules, as well as uncertainty about which rules are applicable, is in the best interest of both clients and the profession (as well as the bodies having authority to regulate the profession). Accordingly, it takes the approach of (i) providing that any particular conduct of a lawyer shall be subject to only one set of rules of professional conduct, (ii) making the determination of which set of rules applies to particular conduct as straightforward as possible, consistent with recognition of appropriate regulatory interests of relevant jurisdictions, and (iii) providing protection from discipline for lawyers who act reasonably in the face of uncertainty.

[4] Paragraph (b)(1) provides that as to a lawyer's conduct relating to a proceeding pending before a tribunal, the lawyer shall be subject only to the rules of professional conduct of that tribunal. As to all other conduct, including conduct in anticipation of a proceeding not yet pending before a tribunal, paragraph (b)(2) provides that a lawyer shall be subject to the rules of the jurisdiction in which the lawyer's conduct occurred, or, if the predominant effect of the conduct is in another jurisdiction, the rules of that jurisdiction shall be applied to the conduct. In the case

of conduct in anticipation of a proceeding that is likely to be before a tribunal, the predominant effect of such conduct could be where the conduct occurred, where the tribunal sits or in another jurisdiction.

[5] When a lawyer's conduct involves significant contacts with more than one jurisdiction, it may not be clear whether the predominant effect of the lawyer's conduct will occur in a jurisdiction other than the one in which the conduct occurred. So long as the lawyer's conduct conforms to the rules of a jurisdiction in which the lawyer reasonably believes the predominant effect will occur, the lawyer shall not be subject to discipline under this Rule. With respect to conflicts of interest, in determining a lawyer's reasonable belief under paragraph (b)(2), a written agreement between the lawyer and client that reasonably specifies a particular jurisdiction as within the scope of that paragraph may be considered if the agreement was obtained with the client's informed consent confirmed in the agreement.

[6] If two admitting jurisdictions were to proceed against a lawyer for the same conduct, they should, applying this rule, identify the same governing ethics rules. They should take all appropriate steps to see that they do apply the same rule to the same conduct, and in all events should avoid proceeding against a lawyer on the basis of two inconsistent rules.

[7] The choice of law provision applies to lawyers engaged in transnational practice, unless international law, treaties or other agreements between competent regulatory authorities in the affected jurisdictions provide otherwise.

Definitional Cross-References

"Informed consent" See Rule 1.0(e)
"Reasonably believes" *See* Rule 1.0(i)
"Tribunal" *See* Rule 1.0(m)

Selected Provisions of the State Ethics Codes

Nearly every state has used the ABA Model Rules of Professional Conduct as a starting point in drafting state rules of professional conduct.[1] Most state codes track the Model Rules fairly closely. No state, however, has adopted every rule and comment of the ABA Model Rules. On some issues, the state code drafters have disagreed with policy reflected in the Model Rules and have promulgated rules that impose different boundaries on professional conduct from those articulated in the Model Rules.

We reprint here a limited number of provisions of various state ethics codes whose language differs from the Model Rules. This section of comparative material is far from comprehensive. It is a sampler of some of the more striking variations from the rules that are central in professional responsibility courses. These examples are provided to allow comparison with the Model Rules and exploration of the policy questions reflected in some states' decisions to diverge from the Model Rules.

In reprinting selected provisions of the state rules, we have used italics to highlight the key language that differs from the Model Rule. Often, we have added notes after excerpted rules explaining the divergences. In some instances, where a state rule bears no resemblance to or has no counterpart in the Model Rules — we have italicized the whole excerpt. All of the italics in this section were added by the authors. Bracketed language is used to paraphrase a relevant part of a rule that is not reproduced.

Practicing lawyers and law students working for lawyers or in clinical courses should never rely on the ABA Model Rules to guide their conduct, since there are so many instances in which the states have not adopted the exact language of the Model Rules. One should always consult the ethics code of the relevant state.

This section of the book includes only a small sample of state variations. The full text of every state's ethics code is available online. There also are useful resources

1. All states and the District of Columbia use the format of the Model Rules for their state codes. The Model Rules are a starting point for the drafters, but they were not the first starting point, because all the states had ethics codes long before the Model Rules of Professional Conduct were first adopted by the ABA in 1983. Before then, most of the state codes were based on the ABA Model Code of Professional Responsibility, which was promulgated by the ABA in 1969. And before that, the states had codes based on the ABA Canons of Ethics, promulgated in 1908. Some of the language in the Model Rules and in the state codes is drawn from earlier sources, and, in some cases from other sources such as the Restatement of the Law Governing Lawyers.

that provide more comprehensive information about the relationship between the state ethics codes and the Model Rules. The American Bar Association Center for Professional Responsibility periodically publishes charts with information about the variations in language in each state. ABA, State Rule Comparison Charts, at https://www.americanbar.org/groups/professional_responsibility/policy/rule_charts/ (chart organized by rule) and ABA, Charts Comparing Professional Conduct Rules, at https://www.americanbar.org/groups/professional_responsibility/policy/charts/ (chart organized by state).

KEY FOR STATE VARIATION RULES
Italicized language indicates language in a state rule that diverges from Model Rules.
Language in regular type indicates that this part of the state rule tracks the Model Rules.

RULE 1.0 DEFINITIONS[2]

Florida Rules: Terminology *"Fraud" or "fraudulent" denotes conduct having a purpose to deceive and not merely negligent misrepresentation or failure to apprise another of relevant information.*

Note: Many of the rules predicate a requirement or a prohibition on the commission of a criminal or fraudulent act. Some examples include Rules 1.2(d), 1.6(b)(2) and (3), 1.16(b), 3.3(b), 4.1(b), and 8.4(c). The Model Rules used the above-quoted definition of fraud before the rule was amended in 2002. The Model Rules definition now refers to "conduct that is fraudulent under the substantive or procedural law of the applicable jurisdiction and has a purpose to deceive." The Model Rules retain the language of the previous definition in comment 5. The Tennessee rule, below, takes a different approach.

Tennessee Rule 1.0(d) *"Fraud" or "fraudulent" denotes an intentionally false or misleading statement of material fact, an intentional omission from a statement of fact of such additional information as would be necessary to make the statements made not materially misleading, and such other conduct by a person intended to deceive a person or tribunal with respect to a material issue in a proceeding or other matter.*

District of Columbia Rule 1.0(h) *"Matter" means any litigation, administrative proceeding, lobbying activity, application, claim, investigation, arrest, charge or accusation, the drafting of a contract, a negotiation, estate or family relations practice issue, or any other representation, except as expressly limited in a particular rule.*

Note: The Model Rules include a definition of "matter" in Rule 1.11(e), but only for the purpose of Rule 1.11. The comments following Model Rule 1.9 discuss the scope of a "matter" but do not define the term. DC offers a definition of "matter" in Rule 1.0. That definition is useful because the term "matter" is used in Rules 1.9, 1.10, 1.11, 1.12, 1.18, 3.3, 3.6, 4.2, 4.3, and perhaps others.

2. We have listed as headings those of the Model Rules for which we offer one or more state ethics code provisions for comparison. We include each provision under the rule number used in the Model Rules even where the state ethics code assigns a different number to that rule.

New York Rule 1.0(u) *"Sexual relations" denotes sexual intercourse or the touching of an intimate part of the lawyer or another person for the purpose of sexual arousal, sexual gratification or sexual abuse.* [See New York Rule 1.8(j) and (k) below.]

RULE 1.1 COMPETENCE

New Jersey Rule 1.1 *A lawyer shall not: (a) Handle or neglect a matter entrusted to the lawyer in such manner that the lawyer's conduct constitutes gross negligence. (b) Exhibit a pattern of negligence or neglect in the lawyer's handling of legal matters generally.*

Note: The Model Rules impose a duty to provide competent representation. The 1969 Model Code addressed the same topic in DR 6-101, in part by prohibiting a lawyer from neglecting a matter entrusted to him. The New Jersey rule carries forward the prohibition of neglect in representation, but specifies that discipline may be imposed only if a lawyer is found to have engaged in a single act of gross negligence or in a pattern of negligent conduct.

RULE 1.2 SCOPE OF REPRESENTATION AND ALLOCATION OF AUTHORITY BETWEEN LAWYER AND CLIENT

Colorado Rule 1.2, comment 14 *A lawyer may counsel a client regarding the validity, scope, and meaning of [the new provision of the state constitution permitting possession and sale of marijuana for medical and recreational use], and may assist a client in conduct that the lawyer reasonably believes is permitted by these constitutional provisions and the statutes, regulations, orders, and other state or local provisions implementing them. In these circumstances, the lawyer shall also advise the client regarding related federal law and policy.*

Note: This comment was added after Colorado voters approved the mentioned state constitutional provision. Possession and sale of marijuana remain criminal offenses under federal law, so guidance for lawyers is needed.

RULE 1.5 FEES

Alaska Rule 1.5(b) *If a fee will exceed $1000,* the basis or rate of the fee shall be communicated to the client in a *written fee agreement* before or within a reasonable time after commencing the representation. *This written fee agreement shall describe the scope of the representation and shall include the disclosure [whether the lawyer has the specified amount of malpractice insurance] required under Rule 1.4(c). In a case involving litigation, the lawyer shall notify the client in the written fee agreement that the client may be liable for the opposing party's costs, fees, or expenses if the client is not the prevailing party.*

> **Note:** Alaska, like many other states, requires lawyers to provide clients with written fee agreements in contingent fee cases *and* in other cases. Model Rule 1.5(b), which applies to non-contingent fee cases, uses the words "preferably in writing."

Florida Rule 4-1.5(f)(4)(B)(i) *Without prior court approval as specified below, any contingent fee that exceeds the following standards are presumed, unless rebutted, to be clearly excessive:*

a. Before the filing of an answer or the demand for appointment of arbitrators or, if no answer is filed or no demand for appointment of arbitrators is made, the expiration of the time period provided for such action:

1. *33 1/3% of any recovery up to $1 million; plus*
2. *30% of any portion of the recovery between $1 million and $2 million; plus*
3. *20% of any portion of the recovery exceeding $2 million.*

b. [After the defendant answers, the percentages are increased to 40%, 30%, and 20%.]

c. If all defendants admit liability at the time of filing their answers and request a trial only on damages: [the percentages are limited to 33 1/3%, 20%, and 15%].

> **Note:** While some scholars have criticized contingent fees as sometimes offering excessive compensation to plaintiff's lawyers, very few have undertaken to regulate the percentages charged. This rule has no counterpart in the Model Rules.

New York Rule 1.5(d) *A lawyer shall not enter into an arrangement for, charge or collect: . . .*

(3) *[a] fee based on fraudulent billing (4) a nonrefundable retainer fee; provided that a lawyer may enter into a retainer agreement with a client containing a reasonable minimum fee clause if it defines in plain language and sets forth the circumstances under which such fee may be incurred and how it will be calculated. . . .*

> **Note:** Although quite a few lawyers have been disbarred and/or imprisoned for fraudulent billing, the Model Rules make no mention of the problem nor do they explicitly provide that charging a fee based on false billing is misconduct. Model Rule 1.5 prohibits "unreasonable" fees, but the only guidance in the rule on what is reasonable is a list of eight factors to be considered.

RULE 1.6 CONFIDENTIALITY OF INFORMATION

Alaska Rule 1.6 (a) A lawyer shall not reveal a client's *confidence or secret* unless the client gives informed consent, except for disclosures that are impliedly authorized in order to carry out the representation and disclosures permitted by paragraph (b) below or Rule 3.3. For purposes of this rule, *"confidence" means information protected by the attorney-client privilege under applicable law, and "secret" means other information gained in the professional relationship if the client has requested it be held confidential or if it is reasonably foreseeable that disclosure of the information would be embarrassing or detrimental to the client. In determining whether information relating to representation of a client is protected from disclosure* *under this rule, the lawyer shall resolve any uncertainty about whether such information can be revealed against revealing the information.*

(b) A lawyer may reveal a client's confidence or secret to the extent the lawyer reasonably believes necessary:

(1) to prevent reasonably certain:

(A) death;

(B) substantial bodily harm; or

(C) *wrongful execution or incarceration of another. . . .*

[Alaska Rule 1.6 then replicates Model Rule 1.6(b)(2) – (6).]

Note: The 1969 ABA Code of Professional Responsibility framed the duty of confidentiality as a duty to protect "confidences" and "secrets." These definitions in the Alaska Rules are similar to the language that had been used in the Model Code. The Model Rules allow revelation of confidences to prevent reasonably certain death or substantial bodily harm, like this rule, but they have no provision allowing revelation to prevent the wrongful execution or incarceration of another.

California Rule 1.6 (b) A lawyer may, but is not required to, reveal [certain confidential information] to the extent that the lawyer reasonably believes the disclosure is necessary to prevent a criminal act that the lawyer reasonably believes is likely to result in death of, or substantial bodily harm to, an individual, as provided in paragraph (c).

(c) Before revealing information . . . to prevent a criminal act as provided in paragraph (b), a lawyer shall, if reasonable under the circumstances:

(1) make a good faith effort to persuade the client: (i) not to commit or to continue the criminal act or (ii) to pursue a course of conduct that will prevent the threatened death or substantial bodily harm; or do both (i) and (ii); and

(2) inform the client, at an appropriate time, of the lawyer's ability or decision to reveal information . . . as provided in paragraph (b).

(d) In revealing information . . . as provided in paragraph (b), the lawyer's disclosure must be no more than is necessary to prevent the criminal act, given the information known to the lawyer at the time of the disclosure.

Note: The California rule requires a lawyer, before revealing information about a client's intention to commit a crime that would harm another person, to take steps to try to prevent the crime from occurring. The rule also requires the lawyer to notify the client that the lawyer is permitted to reveal confidential information to prevent such harm.

Illinois Rule 1.6(c) [A lawyer may not reveal information relating to the representation of a client, with certain exceptions, one of which is that] *[A] lawyer shall reveal information relating to the representation of a client to the extent the lawyer reasonably believes necessary to prevent reasonably certain death or substantial bodily harm.*

Note: A substantial number of states *require* a lawyer to reveal confidential information to the extent the lawyer reasonably believes necessary to prevent reasonably certain death or substantial bodily harm.[3] Some of these states, in addition, *require* revelation in the circumstances described in Rule 1.6(b)(2) and (3). Although Model Rule 1.6 uses discretionary language, the Model Rules require revelation of confidential information if necessary to comply with Rules 3.3 and 4.1(a). Illinois adds this provision as 1.6(c). The Model Rules language of 1.6(c) appears as Illinois Rule 1.6(e).

New Jersey Rule 1.6 [A lawyer shall not reveal information relating to the representation of a client, with certain exceptions, including the following:]

(b) A lawyer *shall reveal* such [confidential] information *to the proper authorities, as soon as,* and to the extent the lawyer reasonably believes necessary, to prevent the client or another person:

(1) *from committing a criminal,* illegal *or fraudulent act that the lawyer reasonably believes is* likely *to result in death or substantial bodily harm or substantial injury to the financial interest or property of another;*

(2) *from committing a criminal, illegal or fraudulent act that the lawyer reasonably believes is likely to perpetrate a fraud upon a tribunal.*

(c) *If a lawyer reveals information pursuant to [Rule] 1.6(b), the lawyer also may reveal the information to the person threatened to the extent the lawyer reasonably believes is necessary to protect that person from death, substantial bodily harm, substantial financial injury, or substantial property loss.*

Note: There is much variation in the state rules on lawyer revelation of crime or fraud that causes financial harm, the counterparts to Model Rule 1.6(b)(2) and (3). About a dozen state rules allow revelation in these circumstances even if the lawyer's services were *not* used in the perpetration of the crime or fraud. About five states impose *a mandatory duty* on lawyers to reveal client confidences in these situations rather than allowing lawyers the discretion to make such revelations. About sixteen state rules allow revelation of client crime or fraud causing financial harm even if the harm caused is not "substantial."[4]

Texas Rule 1.05(c)(7) and (8), (e), and (f) (c) A lawyer may reveal confidential information . . . *(7) When the lawyer has reason to believe it is necessary to do so in order to prevent the client from committing a criminal or fraudulent act. (8) To the extent revelation reasonably appears necessary to rectify the consequences of a client's criminal or fraudulent act in the commission of which the lawyer's services had been used. . . .*

(e) *When a lawyer has confidential information clearly establishing that a client is likely to commit a criminal or fraudulent act that is likely to result in death or substantial bodily harm to a person, the lawyer shall reveal confidential information to the extent revelation reasonably appears necessary to prevent the client from committing the criminal or fraudulent act.*

3. See ABA, Variations of the ABA Model Rules of Professional Conduct Rule 1.6, available at https://www.americanbar.org/content/dam/aba/administrative/professional_responsibility/mrpc-1-6.pdf (last visited July 23, 2024).

4. Id. The numbers are approximate and are based on a review of a summary chart. They are intended to provide a general picture of the variation in the state rules on this issue.

(f) *A lawyer shall reveal confidential information when required to do so by [Texas] Rule 3.03(a)(2) [which prohibits a lawyer from knowingly failing "to disclose a fact to a tribunal when disclosure is necessary to avoid assisting a criminal or fraudulent act"].*

Virginia Rule 1.6(b) *To the extent a lawyer reasonably believes necessary, the lawyer may reveal . . . (3) such information which clearly establishes that the client has, in the course of the representation, perpetrated upon a third party a fraud related to the subject matter of the representation . . . [and] (7) such information to prevent reasonably certain death or substantial bodily harm.*

Virginia Rule 1.6(c) *A lawyer shall promptly reveal:*

(1) the intention of a client, as stated by the client, to commit a crime reasonably certain to result in death or substantial bodily harm to another or substantial injury to the financial interests or property of another and the information necessary to prevent the crime, but before revealing such information, the attorney shall, where feasible, advise the client of the possible legal consequences of the action, urge the client not to commit the crime, and advise the client that the attorney must reveal the client's criminal intention unless thereupon abandoned. However, if the crime involves perjury by the client, the attorney shall take appropriate remedial measures as required by Rule 3.3; or

(2) information concerning the misconduct of another attorney to the appropriate professional authority under Rule 8.3. When the information necessary to report the misconduct is protected under this Rule, the attorney, after consultation, must obtain client consent. Consultation should include full disclosure of all reasonably foreseeable consequences of both disclosure and non- disclosure to the client.

RULE 1.7 CONFLICT OF INTEREST: CURRENT CLIENTS

District of Columbia Rule 1.7(d) *If a conflict not reasonably foreseeable at the outset of representation arises under paragraph (b)(1) after the representation commences, and is not waived under paragraph (c), a lawyer need not withdraw from any representation unless the conflict also arises under paragraphs (b)(2), (b)(3), or (b)(4).*

Tennessee Rule 1.7(c) *A lawyer shall not represent more than one client in the same criminal case or juvenile delinquency proceeding, unless: (1) the lawyer demonstrates to the tribunal that good cause exists to believe that no conflict of interest prohibited under this Rule presently exists or is likely to exist; and (2) each affected client gives informed consent.*

RULE 1.8 CONFLICT OF INTEREST: CURRENT CLIENTS: SPECIFIC RULES

Massachusetts Rule 1.8(b) A lawyer shall not use confidential information relating to representation of a client to the disadvantage of the client *or for the lawyer's advantage or the advantage of a third person*, unless the client gives informed consent, except as permitted or required by these Rules.

District of Columbia Rule 1.8(d) *(counterpart of Model Rule 1.8(e))* (d) While representing a client in connection with contemplated or pending litigation or administrative proceedings, a lawyer shall not advance or guarantee financial assistance to the client, except that *a lawyer may pay or otherwise provide:* (1) *The expenses of litigation or administrative proceedings, including court costs, expenses of investigation, expenses or medical examination, costs of obtaining and presenting evidence; and* (2) *Other financial assistance which is reasonably necessary to permit the client to institute or maintain the litigation or administrative proceedings.*

New Jersey Rule 1.8(e)

(e) A lawyer shall not provide financial assistance to a client in connection with pending or contemplated litigation, except that:

(1) a lawyer may advance court costs and expenses of litigation, the repayment of which may be contingent on the outcome of the matter; and

(2) a lawyer representing an indigent client may pay court costs and expenses of litigation on behalf of the client; and

(3) a legal services or public interest organization, a law school clinical or pro bono program, or an attorney providing qualifying pro bono service as defined in R.1:21-11(a), may provide financial assistance to indigent clients whom the organization, program, or attorney is representing without fee.

Note: New Jersey's rule allows lawyers who represent indigent clients to provide financial assistance to their clients as needed without the restriction generally imposed by Rule 1.8(e).

Florida Rule 4-1.8(j)

Note: Florida Rule 1.8(j) requires a lawyer who is representing an insured person other than a government agency and is being compensated for the work by an insurance company, to give the insured person a Statement of the Insured Client's Rights. This statement is included in Rule 1.8(j). We have not reproduced this novel rule here because of its length.

New York Rule 1.8(j) and (k) *(j) (1) A lawyer shall not: (i) as a condition of entering into or continuing any professional representation by the lawyer or the lawyer's firm, require or demand sexual relations with any person; (ii) employ coercion, intimidation or undue influence in entering into sexual relations incident to any professional representation by the lawyer or the lawyer's firm; or (iii) in domestic relations matters, enter into sexual relations with a client during the course of the lawyer's representation of the client.*

(2) Rule 1.8(j)(1) shall not apply to sexual relations between lawyers and their spouses or to ongoing consensual sexual relationships that predate the initiation of the client-lawyer relationship.

(k) Where a lawyer in a firm has sexual relations with a client but does not participate in the representation of that client, the lawyers in the firm shall not be subject to discipline under this Rule solely because of the occurrence of such sexual relations.

Note: New York's rule restricting sexual relationships is considerably broader and more specific than Model Rule 1.8(j).

RULES 1.9 DUTIES TO FORMER CLIENTS

Texas Rule 1.09(a) Without prior consent, a lawyer who personally has formerly represented a client in a matter shall not thereafter represent another person in a matter adverse to the former client:

(1) *in which such other person questions the validity of the lawyer's services or work product for the former client;*

(2) *if the representation in reasonable probability will involve a violation of [the Texas rule on protection of confidences]; or*

(3) *if it is the same or a substantially related matter.*

Note: The Texas rule refers to adversity rather than "material adversity," the term used in the model rule. Subsections 1 and 2 of the Texas rule have no counterpart in the Model Rules.

DC and Illinois Rules

Note: Unlike Model Rule 1.9, The DC and Illinois rules do not require that a client's consent to a conflict under this rule be confirmed in writing.

RULE 1.10 IMPUTATION OF CONFLICTS OF INTEREST: GENERAL RULE

Minnesota Rule 1.10(b) *When a lawyer becomes associated with a firm, and the lawyer is prohibited from representing a client pursuant to Rule 1.9(b), other lawyers in the firm may represent that client if there is no reasonably apparent risk that confidential information of the previously represented client will be used with material adverse effect on that client because:*

(1) any confidential information communicated to the lawyer is unlikely to be significant in the subsequent matter;

(2) the lawyer is subject to screening measures adequate to prevent disclosure of the confidential information and to prevent involvement by that lawyer in the representation; and

(3) timely and adequate notice of the screening has been provided to all affected clients.

Note: Minnesota is one of a number of states that amended their rules to allow screening to avoid imputation of conflicts from an incoming lateral lawyer. Minnesota made this change in its rules in 1999, long before the ABA adopted Rule 1.10(a)(2).[5] The Minnesota rule is drawn from Restatement section 124.

5. See Martin Cole, Law Firm Hiring and Screening, Bench and Bar of Minnesota (October 2008), available at http://lprb.mncourts.gov/articles/Articles/Law%20Firm%20Hiring%20and%20Screening.pdf.

South Carolina Rule 1.10(e) *A lawyer representing a client of a public defender office, legal services association, or similar program serving indigent clients shall not be disqualified under this Rule because of the program's representation of another client in the same or a substantially related matter if: (1) the lawyer is screened in a timely manner from access to confidential information relating to and from any participation in the representation of the other client; and (2) the lawyer retains authority over the objectives of the representation pursuant to Rule 5.4(c).*

Note: The relative laxity of the South Carolina rule on imputation of conflicts in organizations that represent indigent client may be a reaction to the cost to those organizations of imposing the same standard as is afforded to better-heeled clients. In many states, public defender offices prohibit two lawyers in the same office from representing two or more co-defendants in a criminal matter, preferring instead to hire contract lawyers to do this work.

RULE 1.13 ORGANIZATION AS CLIENT

Note: In 2003, in response to Enron and related corporate scandals, the ABA amended Rules 1.6 and 1.13 to allow lawyers to reveal confidential information to prevent or to remedy client fraud and illegal corporate conduct that would cause financial harm. Language was added at the end of Rule 1.13(b), and 1.13(c) and (d) were added. According to the ABA, as of 2018, nineteen states had adopted these changes; seven states had adopted modified versions of the changes. Two states had adopted part of the changes; sixteen states and the District of Columbia had not adopted the changes. Five states had not made any changes to Rule 1.13 since the 2003 amendment.[6]

Minnesota Rule 1.13(c) If, despite the lawyer's efforts in accordance with paragraph (b), the highest authority that can act on behalf of the organization insists upon or fails to address in a timely and appropriate manner an action, or a refusal to act, that is clearly a violation of the law, *the lawyer may resign in accordance with Rule 1.16 and may disclose information in conformance with Rule 1.6.*

Note: This Minnesota rule omits language included in the Model Rules that precludes revelation of confidential information under Rule 1.13(c) unless "the lawyer reasonably believes that the violation is reasonably certain to result in substantial injury to the organization." Where the specified conditions are met, the model rule allows disclosure of confidences "but only if and to the extent the lawyer reasonably believes necessary to prevent substantial injury to the organization." Minnesota instead simply allows the lawyer to resign and to reveal confidences. Also, Minnesota did not adopt Rule 1.13(d).

RULE 1.14 CLIENT WITH DIMINISHED CAPACITY

Massachusetts Rule 1.14(b) and comment 7 (b) When the lawyer reasonably believes that the client has diminished capacity *that prevents the client from*

6. ABA, Variations of the ABA Model Rules of Professional Conduct, available at https://www.americanbar.org/content/dam/aba/administrative/professional_responsibility/mrpc-1-13.pdf (last visited Sept. 20, 2024).

making an adequately considered decision regarding a specific issue that is part of the representation, is at risk of substantial physical, financial or other harm unless action is taken, and cannot adequately act in the client's own interest, the lawyer may take reasonably necessary protective action *in connection with the representation*, including consulting with individuals or entities that have the ability to take action to protect the client and, in appropriate cases, seeking the appointment of a guardian ad litem, conservator or guardian.

Comment 7: . . . *Counsel should follow the client's expressed preference if it does not pose a risk of substantial harm to the client, even if the lawyer reasonably determines that the client has not made an adequately considered decision in the matter.*

Note: Massachusetts Rule 1.14(b) authorizes a lawyer to take "protective action" on behalf of a client only if the client is unable to make an adequately considered decision regarding a specific issue that is part of the representation. The Model Rule authorizes a lawyer to take protective action in a much broader range of circumstances. The comment emphasizes that the lawyer should defer to the client's decision if the decision does not pose a risk of substantial harm to the client.

RULE 1.15 SAFEKEEPING PROPERTY

Note: Pennsylvania Rule 1.15 is much more detailed than the model rule. The rule requires lawyers to keep complete records on every withdrawal from or deposit to their client trust accounts for five years after the termination of the client relationship or the distribution or disposition of property, whichever is later. This rule is not reprinted here because it is lengthy and technical.

RULE 1.16 DECLINING OR TERMINATING REPRESENTATION

Louisiana Rule 1.16(d) Upon termination of representation, a lawyer shall take steps to the extent reasonably practicable to protect a client's interests, such as giving reasonable notice to the client, allowing time for employment of other counsel, surrendering papers and property to which the client is entitled and refunding any advance payment of fee or expense that has not been earned or incurred. *Upon written request by the client, the lawyer shall promptly release to the client or the client's new lawyer the entire file relating to the matter. The lawyer may retain a copy of the file but shall not condition release over issues relating to the expense of copying the file or for any other reason. The responsibility for the cost of copying shall be determined in an appropriate proceeding.*

Note: The italicized language replaces this sentence in Model Rule 1.16(d): "The lawyer may retain papers relating to the client to the extent permitted by other law." This language in Louisiana appears to intend that a lawyer should never prevent a client or a former client from access to the contents of his file based on a dispute over payment of fees or for any other reason.

RULE 1.18 DUTIES TO PROSPECTIVE CLIENT

South Carolina Rule 1.18(a) A person who engages in mutual communication with a lawyer about the possibility of forming a client-lawyer relationship with respect to a matter is a prospective client *only when there is a reasonable expectation that the lawyer is likely to form the relationship.*

> **Note:** This language is much more restrictive than the model rule, which states that consultation with a lawyer about the possibility of forming a lawyer-client relationship makes the person a prospective client of a lawyer.

RULE 3.3 CANDOR TOWARD THE TRIBUNAL

New Jersey RPC 3.3(a) and (b) (a) A lawyer shall not knowingly: (1) make a false statement of material fact or law to a tribunal; (2) fail to disclose a material fact to a tribunal when disclosure is necessary *to avoid assisting an illegal, criminal or fraudulent act by the client;* (3) fail to disclose to the tribunal legal authority in the controlling jurisdiction known to the lawyer to be directly adverse to the position of the client and not disclosed by opposing counsel; (4) offer evidence that the lawyer knows to be false. If a lawyer has offered material evidence and comes to know of its falsity, the lawyer shall take reasonable remedial measures; or (5) *fail to disclose to the tribunal a material fact knowing that the omission is reasonably certain to mislead the tribunal, except that it shall not be a breach of this rule if the disclosure is protected by a recognized privilege or is otherwise prohibited by law.*

(b) The duties stated in paragraph (a) continue to the conclusion of the proceeding, and apply even if compliance requires disclosure of information otherwise protected by RPC 1.6.

> **Note:** New Jersey Rules 3.3(a) and (b) are very similar to the language used in Model Rule 3.3 before its revision in 2002, except that New Jersey added the word "illegal" to Rule 3.3(a) and added Rule 3.3(a)(5).

District of Columbia Rule 3.3(b) *When the witness who intends to give evidence that the lawyer knows to be false is the lawyer's client and is the accused in a criminal case, the lawyer shall first make a good-faith effort to dissuade the client from presenting the false evidence; if the lawyer is unable to dissuade the client, the lawyer shall seek leave of the tribunal to withdraw. If the lawyer is unable to dissuade the client or to withdraw without seriously harming the client, the lawyer may put the client on the stand to testify in a narrative fashion, but the lawyer shall not examine the client in such manner as to elicit testimony which the lawyer knows to be false, and shall not argue the probative value of the client's testimony in closing argument.*

Oregon Rule 3.3(c) The duties stated in paragraphs (a) and (b) continue to the conclusion of the proceeding, *but in no event require disclosure of information otherwise protected by Rule 1.6.*

Note: Oregon 3.3(a) and (b) are similar to the Model Rule, except that Oregon adds two extra provisions to 3.3(a). Model Rule 3.3(c) provides that the duties under 3.3(a) and (b) apply even if they require disclosure of information protected by Rule 1.6. Oregon Rule 3.3(c), on the other hand, requires revelation under Rules 3.3(a) and (b) only if permitted under Rule 1.6.

Florida Rule 3.3(d) Extent of Lawyer's Duties. The duties stated in this rule continue *beyond the conclusion of the proceeding* and apply even if compliance requires disclosure of information otherwise protected by Rule 4-1.6.

Note: Model Rule 3.3(c) provides that the duties listed in Rules 3.3(a) and (b) "continue to the conclusion of the proceeding." The Florida rule imposes no end date on those duties.

RULE 3.4 FAIRNESS TO OPPOSING PARTY AND COUNSEL

Virginia Rule 3.4(a) A lawyer shall not: (a) Obstruct another party's access to evidence or alter, destroy or conceal a document or other material having potential evidentiary value *for the purpose of obstructing a party's access to evidence.* A lawyer shall not counsel or assist another person to do any such act.

Note: Virginia removed the word "unlawfully," which precedes the word "obstruct" and the word "alter" in the Model Rule. Virginia also added the italicized language.

Oregon Rule 3.4(g) *A lawyer shall not . . . threaten to present criminal charges to obtain an advantage in a civil matter unless the lawyer reasonably believes the charge to be true and if the purpose of the lawyer is to compel or induce the person threatened to take reasonable action to make good the wrong which is the subject of the charge.*

Note: The first part of language of the Oregon rule is drawn from the 1969 ABA Code of Professional Responsibility, which stated, at 7-105(a): "A lawyer shall not present, participate in presenting, or threaten to present criminal charges solely to obtain an advantage in a civil matter."

RULE 3.6 TRIAL PUBLICITY

District of Columbia Rule 3.6 *A lawyer engaged in a case being tried to a judge or jury shall not make an extrajudicial statement that the lawyer knows or reasonably should know will be disseminated by means of mass public communication and will create a serious and imminent threat of material prejudice to the proceeding.*

Note: This is the whole of DC Rule 3.6. It is far simpler and imposes a narrower restriction than does Model Rule 3.6.

RULE 3.8 SPECIAL RESPONSIBILITIES OF A PROSECUTOR

Note: In 2008, the ABA amended Rule 3.8 by adopting sections (g) and (h), which impose particular post-conviction duties on prosecutors. Some states have adopted these changes into their rules, but many other states have declined to do so.[7]

Massachusetts Rule 3.8 The prosecutor in a criminal case shall: (a) refrain from prosecuting where the prosecutor lacks a good faith belief that probable cause to support the charge exists, *and refrain from threatening to prosecute a charge where the prosecutor lacks a good faith belief that probable cause to support the charge exists or can be developed through subsequent investigation; . . . (g) not avoid pursuit of evidence because the prosecutor believes it will damage the prosecution's case or aid the accused; and (h) refrain from seeking, as a condition of a disposition agreement in a criminal matter, the defendant's waiver of claims of ineffective assistance of counsel or prosecutorial misconduct.*

Note: Massachusetts adopted a new Rule 3.8 as of 2016. The state largely adopted the ABA's latest version of the rule, and added the italicized language, which is not included in the ABA model rule.

RULE 3.9 ADVOCATE IN NONADJUDICATIVE PROCEEDINGS

Note: The rules in North Carolina and Virginia omit Rule 3.9. In those states, then, the relevant rules on candor to the tribunal may not apply in nonadudicative proceeding such as legislative hearings or agency rulemaking proceedings.

RULE 4.1 TRUTHFULNESS IN STATEMENTS TO OTHERS

Maryland Rule 19-304.1 (a) In the course of representing a client a lawyer shall not knowingly:

(1) make a false statement of material fact or law to a third person; or

(2) fail to disclose a material fact when disclosure is necessary to avoid assisting a criminal or fraudulent act by a client.

(b) The duties stated in this Rule apply even if compliance requires disclosure of information otherwise protected by Rule 1.6.

Note: The Model Rule imposes the requirements listed in Rule 4.1(a) "unless disclosure is prohibited by Rule 1.6." Under Maryland Rule 4.1, disclosure is required even if the information disclosed otherwise would be confidential. The New Jersey rules include language similar to Maryland Rule 4.1(b).

7. For information on which states have adopted these provisions, see https://www.americanbar.org/content/dam/aba/administrative/professional_responsibility/mrpc_3_8.authcheckdam.pdf (last visited Aug. 23, 2018).

RULE 4.3 DEALING WITH UNREPRESENTED PERSON

Wisconsin SCR 20:4.3(a) In dealing on behalf of a client with a person who is not represented by counsel, a lawyer *shall inform such person of the lawyer's role in the matter*. When the lawyer knows or reasonably should know that the unrepresented person misunderstands the lawyer's role in the matter, the lawyer shall make reasonable efforts to correct the misunderstanding. The lawyer shall not give legal advice to an unrepresented person, other than the advice to secure counsel, if the lawyer knows or reasonably should know that the interests of such a person are or have a reasonable possibility of being in conflict with the interests of the client.

Note: Model Rule 4.3 prohibits a lawyer, in talking with an unrepresented person, from stating or implying that the lawyer is disinterested. The Wisconsin rule instead requires such a lawyer to inform the person of the lawyer's role in the matter. Affirmative disclosure would reduce the odds that the other person would misunderstand the lawyer's role.

RULE 5.1 RESPONSIBILITIES OF PARTNERS, MANAGERS, AND SUPERVISORY LAWYERS

New Jersey Rule 5.1(a) *Every law firm, government entity, and organization authorized by the Court Rules to practice law in this jurisdiction* shall make reasonable efforts to ensure that member lawyers or lawyers otherwise participating in the organization's work undertake measures giving reasonable assurance that all lawyers conform to the Rules of Professional Conduct.

Note: This New Jersey rule, and a similar version of Rule 5.1(a) in New York, imposes requirements on organizations that practice law. Model Rule 5.1(a) instead imposes requirements on individual law firm partners and other lawyers who have managerial authority. The New Jersey rule does not explicitly state that law firms, as opposed to individual lawyers, may be disciplined by bar authorities for violations (that is, for failing to make the reasonable efforts that are required). However, it has been so interpreted.[8] New Jersey Rule 5.3 uses similar language regarding the supervision of and responsibility for the conduct of nonlawyer employees.

South Carolina Rule 5.1(d) *Partners and lawyers with comparable managerial authority who reasonably believe that a lawyer in the law firm may be suffering from a significant impairment of that lawyer's cognitive function shall take action to address the concern with the lawyer and may seek assistance by reporting the circumstances of concern pursuant to Rule 428, SCACR.*

Note: This novel rule imposes on every supervisory lawyer a duty to take appropriate action if the lawyer notices a cognitive decline in another lawyer in the law firm.

8. See Julie Rose O'Sullivan, Professional Discipline for Law Firms? A Response to Professor Schneyer's Proposal, 16 Geo. J. Leg. Ethics 1 (2002).

Perhaps the aging of the baby-boomers makes this issue more urgent than it once was. Compare this provision with Texas Rule 8.3(c), below.

RULE 5.3 RESPONSIBILITIES REGARDING NONLAWYER ASSISTANCE

Alaska Rule 5.3 *(b) A lawyer shall advise a nonlawyer who ends an association with the lawyer not to disclose confidences and secrets protected by Rule 1.6 that were learned by the nonlawyer during the association.*

(c) A lawyer who employs, retains, or forms an association with a nonlawyer shall advise the nonlawyer not to disclose confidences and secrets protected by Rule 1.6 learned by the nonlawyer during an association with another lawyer. If the nonlawyer participated in a matter that would create a conflict of interest for a lawyer under Rule 1.7 or Rule 1.9, the nonlawyer shall be screened from any participation in the matter.

(d) A lawyer who learns that any person employed by the lawyer has revealed a confidence or secret protected by these rules shall notify the person whose confidence or secret was revealed.

Note: Alaska Rule 5.3 is similar to the Model Rule except that these three provisions are added to require specific supervision of nonlawyer employees and former employees regarding protection of confidences. It also imposes on lawyers a duty to notify an affected person if the lawyer learns that an employee or former employee has revealed a confidence or secret.

RULE 5.4 PROFESSIONAL INDEPENDENCE OF A LAWYER

Arizona

Note: In 2020, the Arizona Supreme Court repealed Rule 5.4, in order to allow nonlawyers to invest in or own law firms. The Chief Justice stated that "The Court's goal is to improve access to justice and to encourage innovation in the delivery of legal services. . . . [The repeal of this rule will] make it possible for more people to access affordable legal services and for more individuals and families to get legal advice and help. [It] will promote business innovation in providing legal services at affordable prices."

New Hampshire Rule 5.4(a) A lawyer or law firm shall not share legal fees with a nonlawyer, except that: . . . (4) *a lawyer may share legal fees with a nonprofit organization that employed, retained or recommended employment of the lawyer in the matter.*

District of Columbia Rule 5.4(b) *A lawyer may practice law in a partnership or other form of organization in which a financial interest is held or managerial authority is exercised by an individual nonlawyer who performs professional* *services which assist the organization in providing legal services to clients, but only if:*

(1) The partnership or organization has as its sole purpose providing legal services to clients;

(2) All persons having such managerial authority or holding a financial interest undertake to abide by these Rules of Professional Conduct;

(3) The lawyers who have a financial interest or managerial authority in the partnership or organization undertake to be responsible for the nonlawyer participants to the same extent as if nonlawyer participants were lawyers under Rule 5.1;

(4) The foregoing conditions are set forth in writing.

Note: Until 2020, when Arizona repealed its Rule 5.4, the District of Columbia was the only U.S. jurisdiction that allowed lawyers to partner with non-lawyers under certain circumstances. But few lawyers in the District made use of this authority, largely because District lawyers often practiced in other jurisdictions that do not allow such partnerships.

RULE 5.5 UNAUTHORIZED PRACTICE OF LAW; MULTIJURISDICTIONAL PRACTICE OF LAW

Ohio Rule 5.5(c) *A lawyer who is admitted in another United States jurisdiction, is in good standing in the jurisdiction in which the lawyer is admitted, and regularly practices law may provide legal services on a temporary basis in this jurisdiction if one or more of the following apply: . . . (4) the lawyer engages in negotiations, investigations, or other nonlitigation activities that arise out of or are reasonably related to the lawyer's practice in a jurisdiction in which the lawyer is admitted to practice.*

Note: Ohio Rule 5.5(c) is similar to Model Rule 5.5(c) except in two respects. Ohio adds a requirement that, to be eligible for temporary practice, the lawyer must regularly practice law. Also, Ohio adds the quoted subsection 4, which broadens the rule to allow any eligible lawyer to conduct any non-litigation practice activities in Ohio. This rule acknowledges that law practice in the 21st century often requires lawyers to do work in other states than those in which they are admitted to the bar.

RULE 6.1 VOLUNTARY PRO BONO PUBLICO SERVICE

Note: No state requires that lawyers admitted in that state complete pro bono work, but a number of states have implemented requirements that lawyers report the number of hours of pro bono work that they do each year. A number of other states encourage but do not require reporting of pro bono hours. New York has a rule similar to Model Rule 6.1. In addition, it has a bar admission rule requiring completion of at least 50 hours of law-related pro bono service in advance of admission to the bar.[9]

9. NYCOURTS.GOV, Bar Admission Requirements, http://ww2.nycourts.gov/attorneys/probono/baradmissionreqs.shtml.

RULE 7.1 – 7.3 COMMUNICATIONS CONCERNING A LAWYER'S SERVICES, SOLICITATION OF CLIENTS

Note: There is some variation in the content and reach of the rules on advertising and solicitation in the states' ethics codes. The Florida advertising and solicitation rules are far more detailed than those of any other state.

District of Columbia Rule 7.1

(a) A lawyer shall not make a false or misleading communication about the lawyer or the lawyer's services. A communication is false or misleading if it: (1) Contains a material misrepresentation of fact or law, or omits a fact necessary to make the statement considered as a whole not materially misleading; or *(2) Contains an assertion about the lawyer or the lawyer's services that cannot be substantiated.*

(b) A lawyer shall not seek by in-person contact, employment (or employment of a partner or associate) by a nonlawyer who has not sought the lawyer's advice regarding employment of a lawyer, if: (1) The solicitation involves use of a statement or claim that is false or misleading, within the meaning of paragraph (a); (2) The solicitation involves the use of coercion, duress or harassment; or (3) The potential client is apparently in a physical or mental condition which would make it unlikely that the potential client could exercise reasonable, considered judgment as to the selection of a lawyer.

Note: The DC rules do not include Rule 7.3, which imposes restrictions on solicitation of clients, but instead includes Rule 7.1(b) quoted above, which permits lawyers to engage in in-person solicitation of clients so long as they comply with the listed restrictions. The rule goes on to impose other restrictions on the conduct of lawyers seeking new clients.

RULE 8.1 BAR ADMISSION AND DISCIPLINARY MATTERS

New York Rule 8.1 *(a) A lawyer shall be subject to discipline if, in connection with the lawyer's own application for admission to the bar previously filed in this state or in any other jurisdiction or in connection with the application of another person for admission to the bar, the lawyer knowingly:* (1) has made or failed to correct a false statement of material fact; or (2) has failed to disclose a material fact requested in connection with a lawful demand for information from an admissions authority.

Note: Model Rule 8.1 is the only rule that applies to people who are not yet members of the bar; it prohibits deceptive conduct in connection with bar admission matters. New York imposes similar requirements but frames the rule as a basis for discipline of lawyers once they are admitted. Subsection (a) is the whole of New York Rule 8.1.

RULE 8.3 REPORTING PROFESSIONAL MISCONDUCT

Georgia Rule 8.3 (a) A lawyer having knowledge that another lawyer has committed a violation of the Georgia Rules of Professional Conduct that raises a substantial question as to that lawyer's honesty, trustworthiness or fitness as a lawyer in other respects, *should* inform the appropriate professional authority.

(b) A lawyer having knowledge that a judge has committed a violation of applicable rules of judicial conduct that raises a substantial question as to the judge's fitness for office should inform the appropriate authority.

There is *no disciplinary penalty* for a violation of this Rule.

Note: Georgia amended Rule 8.3 to change the word "shall" to "should" in 2011. Also, California has no rule equivalent to Rule 8.3.

Virginia Rule 8.3 (e) *A lawyer shall inform the Virginia State Bar if:*

(1) the lawyer has been disciplined by a state or federal disciplinary authority, agency or court in any state, U.S. territory, or the District of Columbia, for a violation of rules of professional conduct in that jurisdiction;

(2) the lawyer has been convicted of a felony in a state, U.S. territory, District of Columbia, or federal court;

(3) the lawyer has been convicted of either a crime involving theft, fraud, extortion, bribery or perjury, or an attempt, solicitation or conspiracy to commit any of the foregoing offenses, in a state, U.S. territory, District of Columbia, or federal court.

The reporting required by paragraph (e) of this Rule shall be made in writing to the Clerk of the Disciplinary System of the Virginia State Bar not later than 60 days following entry of any final order or judgment of conviction or discipline.

Note: Model Rule 8.3 requires a lawyer to report misconduct by another lawyer, but does not explicitly require a lawyer to report his own misconduct. The Virginia rule imposes a narrower duty of self-reporting than the duty with respect to other lawyers. For other lawyers, Rule 8.3 requires reporting of any violation of a rule that raises a substantial question as to the lawyer's honesty, trustworthiness, or fitness to be a lawyer. Under Virginia Rule 8.3(e), a lawyer must self-report any adjudicated disciplinary violations in other jurisdictions and conviction of felonies and some other criminal offenses.

Texas Rule 8.03(c) *A lawyer having knowledge or suspecting that another lawyer or judge whose conduct the lawyer is required to report pursuant to paragraphs (a) or (b) of this Rule is impaired by chemical dependency on alcohol or drugs or by mental illness may report that person to an approved peer assistance program rather than to an appropriate disciplinary authority. If a lawyer elects that option, the lawyer's report to the approved peer assistance program shall disclose any disciplinary violations that the reporting lawyer would otherwise have to disclose to the authorities referred to in paragraphs (a) and (b).*

Note: Compare this provision with South Carolina Rule 5.1(d), above. While Texas frames the duty to report an impaired lawyer as a variant on the general rule requiring reporting of misconduct, and limits the scope of the rule to problems of addiction or mental illness, South Carolina imposes a duty to take action, possibly including reporting, if one of the lawyer's colleagues seems to be suffering from a cognitive impairment. The South Carolina rule would include the categories listed in Texas, but also would include lawyers suffering a cognitive decline as the result of aging.

RULE 8.4 MISCONDUCT

Oregon Rule 8.4(a)(7) *It is professional misconduct for a lawyer to: . . . (7) in the course of representing a client, knowingly intimidate or harass a person because of that person's race, color, national origin, religion, age, sex, gender identity, gender expression, sexual orientation, marital status, or disability.*

Note: ABA Rule 8.4(g), like the Oregon rule, is directed at prohibiting harassment and discrimination by lawyers, but there are some differences. The ABA covers "conduct related to the practice of law," while Oregon's rule applies "in the course of representing a client." The ABA language is broader. Oregon prohibits discrimination on the basis of gender expression, as well as numerous categories covered in the model rule. The ABA rule lists as prohibited categories of discrimination ethnicity and socioeconomic status, neither of which is listed in the Oregon rule.

New Jersey Rule 8.4 *It is professional misconduct for a lawyer to: . . . (g) engage, in a professional capacity, in conduct involving discrimination (except employment discrimination unless resulting in a final agency or judicial determination) because of race, color, religion, age, sex, sexual orientation, national origin, language, marital status, socioeconomic status, or handicap where the conduct is intended or likely to cause harm.*

Note: Many states have made some discriminatory conduct by lawyers a violation of a disciplinary rule, most often of Rule 8.4. The Model Rules were amended to include such a provision, Rule 8.4(g), in 2016. The Oregon and New Jersey rules provides examples.[10]

Florida Rule 8.4(h) *A lawyer shall not: . . . willfully refuse, as determined by a court of competent jurisdiction, to timely pay a child support obligation; . . .*

Note: A number of states have added various specific prohibitions to Rule 8.4 to make the designated conduct clearly a basis for professional discipline. Above is one example from the Florida rule, and below are two more examples from the Illinois rules. Even in the absence of specific prohibition, some of this conduct might be a basis for discipline under the broad language of Rule 8.4. Nevertheless, the specific

10. ABA, Variations of the ABA Model Rules of Professional Conduct, available at https://www.americanbar.org/content/dam/aba/administrative/professional_responsibility/mrpc_8_4.authcheckdam.pdf (last visited Aug. 23, 2018).

prohibition of particular conduct may serve to put members of the bar on notice that the listed conduct could lead to discipline.

Illinois Rule 8.4 It is professional misconduct for a lawyer to: . . . *(h) enter into an agreement with a client or former client limiting or purporting to limit the right of the client or former client to file or pursue any complaint before the Illinois Attorney Registration and Disciplinary Commission.*

(i) *avoid in bad faith the repayment of an education loan guaranteed by the Illinois Student Assistance Commission or other governmental entity. . . .*

Oregon Rule 8.4(b) *(b) Notwithstanding paragraphs (a)(1), (3) and (4) and Rule 3.3(a)(1), it shall not be professional misconduct for a lawyer to advise clients or others about or to supervise lawful covert activity in the investigation of violations of civil or criminal law or constitutional rights, provided the lawyer's conduct is otherwise in compliance with these Rules of Professional Conduct. "Covert activity," as used in this rule, means an effort to obtain information on unlawful activity through the use of misrepresentations or other subterfuge. "Covert activity" may be commenced by a lawyer or involve a lawyer as an advisor or supervisor only when the lawyer in good faith believes there is a reasonable possibility that unlawful activity has taken place, is taking place or will take place in the foreseeable future.*

Note: This addition to the Oregon rule, which has no counterpart in the Model Rules, is the result of the Oregon Supreme Court's decision in In re Gatti, 8 P. 3d 966 (Or. 2000).

RULE 8.5 DISCIPLINARY AUTHORITY; CHOICE OF LAW

New York Rule 8.5(b) In any exercise of the disciplinary authority of this state, the rules of professional conduct to be applied shall be as follows:

(1) For conduct in connection with a proceeding in a court before which a lawyer has been admitted to practice (either generally or for purposes of that proceeding), the rules to be applied shall be the rules of the jurisdiction in which the court sits, unless the rules of the court provide otherwise; and

(2) For any other conduct: *(i) If the lawyer is licensed to practice only in this state, the rules to be applied shall be the rules of this state, and (ii) If the lawyer is licensed to practice in this state and another jurisdiction, the rules to be applied shall be the rules of the admitting jurisdiction in which the lawyer principally practices;* provided, however, that if particular conduct clearly has its predominant effect in another jurisdiction in which the lawyer is licensed to practice, the rules of that jurisdiction shall be applied to that conduct.

Note: The language of New York Rule 8.5(b) diverges from the Model Rule, especially as to non-litigation matters. While the Model Rules would direct a lawyer to apply the rules of the jurisdiction where the conduct occurred or the rules of the jurisdiction where the predominant effect of the conduct occurred. New York, instead, requires application of the New York rules, except that (a) if the lawyer is admitted also in another jurisdiction, the rules that apply are those of the jurisdiction where the lawyer mainly works, and (b) if the conduct has its main impact in another jurisdiction, the rules of that jurisdiction would apply.

Missouri Rule 4-8.5 [added to the end of 8.5(b)]: *A lawyer shall not be subject to discipline if the lawyer's conduct conforms to the rules of a jurisdiction in which the lawyer reasonably believes the predominant effect of the lawyer's conduct will occur.*

Note: This addition to Rule 8.5 offers protection from discipline to lawyers who have made good faith decisions about which rules apply. The same language is included in the rules of Maryland and Montana.

Practice Questions

In answering these practice questions, assume unless otherwise stated that the highest court of the state in which the lawyer is practicing has adopted the Model Rules of Professional Conduct as the state's ethics code for lawyers, and that it has also adopted the official comments to the ABA rules as the official comments interpreting the state's rule.

The answers, with analysis, are in the last section of this book.

1. THE LEGAL PROFESSION: BAR ADMISSION, HISTORY, AND DIVERSITY

Question 1a.

During his final year of college, Henry got excellent grades and achieved a very high LSAT score. However, during that year, he had two car accidents, ran up $11,500 in credit card debt, and was fired from his part-time restaurant job after he inexplicably failed to show up for work for ten days. Henry was then evaluated and diagnosed by a psychiatrist, who concluded that Henry suffered from bipolar disorder. This condition, if untreated, can cause extreme shifts in mood, energy, and ability to function. Henry's doctor explained that what he went through during his senior year was a manic period. The doctor prescribed medication. Ever since, Henry has been taking his medication as prescribed. Henry's doctor considers his illness "well-managed," and has told Henry that it would not affect his ability to practice law.

Henry started law school three months after he finished college. Now he has completed law school, graduating at the top of his class. He is well-liked by his peers. During his third year, Henry enrolled in a clinical course. He won both of his cases and he received an A in the course.

Henry is applying for admission to the bar. The character and fitness questionnaire asks, among other questions:

> 1) Within the past five years, have you exhibited any conduct or behavior that could call into question your ability to practice law in a competent, ethical, and professional manner?
>
> If you answered "yes," furnish a thorough explanation below.
>
> 2) Do you currently have any condition or impairment (including, but not limited to, substance abuse, alcohol abuse, or a mental or emotional or nervous disorder or condition) that in any way affects your ability to practice law in a competent, ethical and professional manner?
>
> If your answer is "yes," are the limitations caused by your condition or impairment reduced or ameliorated because you receive ongoing treatment?

Henry believes that his disorder does not affect his ability to practice law in a competent, ethical and professional manner, and his physician agrees and has supplied him with a statement.

Which one of the following statements is the most accurate?

☐ **A.** Henry need not disclose his condition, because federal disability law prohibits discrimination on the basis of physical or mental disability.

☐ **B.** Henry need not disclose his condition because he believes that his disorder does not affect his ability to practice law in a competent, ethical, and professional manner.

☐ **C.** Henry need not disclose his condition because his physician has concluded that his illness does not affect his ability to practice law in a competent, ethical, and professional manner.

☐ **D.** Henry must disclose the diagnosis and provide detailed information about it.

Question 1b.

Josh, a third year law student, is planning to apply for admission to the bar. He just looked at the questionnaire of the National Conference of Bar Examiners, which he will have to submit. It asks:

> Have you ever been dropped, suspended, warned, placed on scholastic or disciplinary probation, expelled, requested to resign, or allowed to resign in lieu of discipline from any college or university (including law school), or otherwise subjected to discipline by any institution or requested or advised by any institution to discontinue your studies there?

Four years ago, a residential advisor found alcoholic beverages in Josh's dormitory room in violation of college rules. At a meeting with a dean, Josh agreed to be put on probation for one semester, during which he would be allowed to take classes as usual. If he made it through the semester without any more infractions, the incident would be expunged from his record. He completed the semester without incident, and the matter was therefore expunged from his college record and not recorded on his transcript. His law school asked a similar question on its admission application, and he answered "no" to the question.

Should Josh reveal the above-described incident in his character and fitness questionnaire? Which of the answers below is most accurate?

- ☐ **A.** Yes, because he did not disclose the incident on his law school application.
- ☐ **B.** Yes, because Josh was placed on disciplinary probation by his college, so the question calls for disclosure of the incident, and includes no exemption for "expunged" offenses.
- ☐ **C.** No, because Josh is not yet admitted to the bar, so he is not bound by the ethics code. He has the discretion to make his own best judgment about whether this should be disclosed. This minor incident has no bearing on his fitness to practice law, so there is no reason to reveal it.
- ☐ **D.** No, because it was expunged by his college, reflecting the intention of the college that the minor incident should have no future consequences.

Question 1c.

Leta graduated from law school one year ago and is applying for admission to the bar. While in law school, Leta accumulated $150,000 of debt from law school loans and credit card expenses related to her wedding. Upon graduation, Leta turned down a high-paying job at a prestigious law firm, choosing instead to work for $12 per hour at a public interest organization that represents indigent people in consumer and bankruptcy cases. She plans a career in consumer credit and bankruptcy law. She hopes that her work at the organization will eventually lead to a full-time public service job. Accordingly, she has not been able to begin paying off her debt. One credit card company has obtained a judgment against her for $7,000. The state bar has denied her application for admission to the bar because it finds that her conduct with respect to her finances indicates that she is not fit to practice law. Is the state bar's position legally sustainable?

- ☐ **A.** Yes, because she intends to practice consumer credit and bankruptcy law.
- ☐ **B.** Yes, because a court could conclude that her conduct with respect to her personal finances indicates that she is not fit to practice law.

☐ **C.** No, because the majority of law students have substantial student loan obligations, so it would be unfair to penalize her for having borrowed a large amount of money for law school.

☐ **D.** No, because every lawyer should aspire to provide pro bono service to clients who cannot afford to pay, so a lawyer who does public interest work full-time is not engaged in misconduct but is pursuing a career aiming to help those who are less fortunate.

2. THE LEGAL PROFESSION: REGULATION, DISCIPLINE, AND LIABILITY

Question 2a.

Which one of the following statements is correct?

☐ **A.** Congress and the state legislatures may not adopt binding rules of conduct for lawyers.
☐ **B.** The American Bar Association is the principal regulator of lawyers in the United States.
☐ **C.** State and federal courts adopt ethical rules that govern lawyers admitted to practice before them.
☐ **D.** State supreme courts have the exclusive authority to regulate the lawyers who practice in each state.

Question 2b.

Which of these bodies sometimes exercise functions that are delegated or authorized by governmental institutions?

☐ **A.** State bar associations.
☐ **B.** The Section of Legal Education and Admissions to the Bar of the American Bar Association.
☐ **C.** Both A and B.
☐ **D.** The American Law Institute.

Question 2c.

Membership in a state bar association is required for a person who is being licensed to practice law:

☐ **A.** By some states.
☐ **B.** By no state.
☐ **C.** By every state, unless the person is a member of a bar association in another state.
☐ **D.** By every state, even if the person is member of a bar association in another state.

Question 2d.

Parnik, a licensed attorney and state prosecutor, was arrested for stalking his ex-girlfriend. Parnik did follow his girlfriend on numerous occasions, spied on her through the windows of her house, and called her repeatedly after she had asked him not to do so. Nevertheless, a jury acquitted Parnik of the charges. Is Parnik subject to discipline for stalking his ex-girlfriend if the bar disciplinary authorities determine that he committed a criminal act that reflects adversely on his fitness to practice law?

☐ **A.** Yes, because a lawyer who commits a criminal act can be disciplined for it whether or not the lawyer was convicted of a crime.
☐ **B.** Yes, because Parnik is a prosecutor, so he has a special responsibility beyond that of other lawyers to show respect for the law and the legal system.
☐ **C.** No, because the stalking occurred in Parnik's private life and was not related to the practice of law.
☐ **D.** No, because he was acquitted of the charges, so no criminal act has been proven.

Question 2e.

Attorneys Carrie and Paige are partners in a small law firm. Paige supervises the work of the firm's two associates. Over the last few years, Carrie has noticed that Paige has been intoxicated during the workday. In the last few months, Carrie has been smelling alcohol on Paige's breath during the workday at least two or three days a week. Paige continues to meet with clients and work on cases, but Carrie believes Paige's work is suffering as a result of her drinking. In the past two weeks, she has received calls from three of Paige's clients complaining that Paige either failed to show up for a meeting or failed to return a call. Last Tuesday, she found Paige passed out on the couch in her office at 11 am. There was vomit all over a client file that was on the floor near her head. Today she learned that a case that Paige was handling, to recover damages for a woman who was badly injured in an accident, was postponed for six months after Paige failed to appear for a court hearing. Carrie has tried to talk with Paige about her drinking problem, but Paige refuses to discuss it. Carrie is considering reporting Paige's behavior to the disciplinary authorities. She has not discussed this with other attorneys in the firm or with any clients. Would Carrie be subject to discipline if she fails to report Paige's conduct to the disciplinary authorities?

☐ **A.** Yes, because Paige has supervisory authority over associates.
☐ **B.** Yes, because Paige's alcohol consumption suggests that she is ill and needs medical care, but her conduct also raises a substantial question about her fitness to practice law in her current state.
☐ **C.** No, because Carrie should seek permission from Paige's clients before reporting misconduct, as they could be harmed if Paige is suspended from practice.
☐ **D.** No, because a lawyer is not required to report information relating to the conduct of the lawyer's own partners.

Question 2f.

Grace is an associate in a law firm. Her firm bills clients by the hour. When she began working for the firm, she signed a statement in which she agreed to abide by firm policy. The firm policy stated in part: "All misconduct shall be reported promptly to the managing partner and shall not be revealed to anyone else in the firm or outside the firm." Grace discovers that Arthur, the partner who supervises her work, always alters her time sheets by multiplying the number of hours she reported working by 1.2, thereby claiming to the clients that she spent 20 percent more time on each project than she actually spent, and billing the clients accordingly. Grace reports the misconduct to the managing partner, who tells her that she need not concern herself with the conduct of her superiors. He takes no action. Would Grace be subject to discipline if she failed to report Arthur's conduct to the disciplinary authorities?

☐ **A.** Yes, because otherwise she might be blamed for the over-billing.
☐ **B.** Yes, because Arthur's conduct involves a violation of the rules that raises a substantial question as to his honesty.
☐ **C.** No, because she is contractually bound to report misconduct only to the managing partner in accordance with the firm's policy, and the managing partner has a duty to report the conduct to the bar authorities.
☐ **D.** No, because it is unlikely that she would be disciplined for failure to report Arthur's conduct, and if she does report the matter outside of the firm, the firm will fire her.

Question 2g.

Zarah is a partner at a law firm. She supervises the work of a junior associate, Charlie. They are representing Whitney in her divorce proceedings. The divorce involves a heated battle over the custody of the daughter of Whitney and her husband, Cody. Zarah asks Whitney whether she knows the password for her husband's e-mail. Whitney gives it to her. Then Zarah gives the password to Charlie and instructs him to copy all the e-mails in Cody's account and read them to see whether Cody is having an affair. Charlie objects. Zarah says that this investigative work could win the case for Whitney and threatens to fire Charlie if he does not comply. Charlie complies. They learn that Cody really is having an affair, and Whitney wins custody. When Cody discovers what happened, he files a disciplinary complaint against Zarah and Charlie. Assuming that Charlie's surreptitious review of Cody's e-mail is unlawful and is a rule violation, which one of the following statements is accurate?

- ☐ **A.** Only Charlie is subject to discipline.
- ☐ **B.** Only Zarah is subject to discipline.
- ☐ **C.** Both Charlie and Zarah are subject to discipline.
- ☐ **D.** Neither Charlie nor Zarah is subject to discipline.

Question 2h.

Carson is admitted to practice only in state A. State A has adopted Rule 8.4 of the Model Rules of Professional Conduct. Carson commits a minor fraud in state B against a citizen of state B, and is prosecuted for this misdemeanor offense and punished in state B. Is Carson subject to discipline in state A?

- ☐ **A.** Yes, because Carson's conduct would violate state A's ethics code, regardless of where the conduct occurs.
- ☐ **B.** Yes, because Carson was convicted of the misdemeanor offense in a court of law.
- ☐ **C.** No, because Carson's conduct did not occur in state A and has no impact on the citizens of state A.
- ☐ **D.** No, because the matter has been criminally prosecuted in state B, so a disciplinary proceeding would impose double jeopardy on Carson.

Question 2i.

Eloise is a law professor in state B who maintains active licenses to practice law in states A and B. She has not practiced law in some time and does not plan to practice law in the near future. Eloise wrote and published a law review article in state B criticizing the criminal justice system in state A. The article includes long passages of plagiarized material, and includes some false statements about the law in state A. The disciplinary agency in state B is unable to decide whether the plagiarism and false statements were intentional, but it imposes a six-month suspension for this conduct. Is Eloise subject to discipline in state A?

- ☐ **A.** Yes, because many readers of the article are lawyers in state A, so the article has harmed the administration of justice in state A.
- ☐ **B.** Yes, because a lawyer may be disciplined by more than one state for a single act of misconduct.
- ☐ **C.** No, because a lawyer may be disciplined by only one state for a single act of misconduct.
- ☐ **D.** No, because the article was written and published in state B, so the disciplinary authorities in state A would not have jurisdiction.

Question 2j.

Jabari is an associate at a law firm in state A. He is admitted to practice only in state A. Jabari goes to state B to litigate a matter on behalf of a client. He is admitted pro hac vice in state B. Jabari violates an ethical rule that has been adopted in state B requiring disclosure of client perjury to the judge. State A has not adopted any similar rule. Could Jabari be disciplined in state A even though state A has not adopted the rule that Jabari violated?

☐ **A.** Yes, because the disciplinary authorities in state A would apply the rules adopted in state B in this case.
☐ **B.** Yes, because state A is the only state in which Jabari is a member of the bar, so state A is solely responsible for overseeing his conduct.
☐ **C.** No, because Jabari's conduct did not take place in state A.
☐ **D.** No, because Jabari's conduct does not violate the ethics code in state A.

Question 2k.

Sasha is an associate in the law firm of Garrett & Glass, LLP. Recently, Sasha discovered that Gerry Glass, one of the partners, had stolen large sums of money from Healthwest, a client organization. In one case, for example, Gerry was defending Healthwest in a personal injury suit. Gerry reached a settlement under which Healthwest would pay the plaintiff $100,000, but he told the CEO of Healthwest that the organization was obliged to pay $200,000. Healthwest sent Gerry a check to cover the settlement. Gerry deposited the check in a firm account, paid the plaintiff $100,000, and wrote himself a check for the remainder. Gerry did this secretly. His law firm billed the client for legal fees as usual. Gerry repeated this same pattern in a series of cases over a seven-year period.

The evidence that Gerry has stolen funds from Healthwest is indisputable. Sasha explained the whole situation to the law firm's general counsel. He instructed Sasha to keep the matter to herself. The general counsel, who is an old friend of Gerry's, said that he didn't "want to blow the matter out of proportion and hurt Gerry unnecessarily." He said he would talk with Gerry about it and make sure that the clients were reimbursed and that the situation would not recur.

Which of the following correctly states Sasha's professional duty in this situation?

☐ **A.** She must report the misconduct to the disciplinary authorities if she can do so without disclosing any client confidences.
☐ **B.** She must report the misconduct to the disciplinary authorities even if doing so would reveal client confidences.
☐ **C.** Sasha has reported the matter to a senior supervisory lawyer in the firm and has no further obligations.
☐ **D.** Sasha has no further ethical duties in this case because she has received assurances that the matter will be resolved satisfactorily.

Question 2l.

Mayra, an attorney licensed in Indiana with a law office in Gary, Indiana, had a business office in Illinois. In her Illinois business, she imported maple syrup from Canada and sold it to distributors in California. Her importing work was unconnected with the legal work that she did in Indiana. Two years ago, she deliberately misrepresented the grade of a shipment of syrup and thereby overcharged her U.S. customers. When they discovered the fraud, they confronted Mayra, who settled with them out of court for an undisclosed sum. The matter was reported in the trade press. One of her customers sent a copy of the article to the Indiana bar disciplinary authority. Is Mayra subject to discipline in Indiana based on these events?

☐ **A.** Yes, because Mayra's conduct involved dishonesty.
☐ **B.** Yes, because the matter was not merely reported in the press; a customer made a complaint to the Indiana bar.
☐ **C.** No, because Mayra did not do anything wrong in Indiana.
☐ **D.** No, because Mayra's conduct had nothing to do with her work as a lawyer, and she has settled with her customers.

3. RELATIONSHIPS BETWEEN LAWYERS AND CLIENTS

Question 3a.

Burke is a trusts and estates lawyer. Ida, an acquaintance, asks him to represent her in a negligence lawsuit against a major retail company. She stands to make millions from the lawsuit, and she is happy to hire Burke on a contingent fee basis. Burke has never before handled a negligence action, and he has never handled a trial of any kind. Burke accepts the case. He does not tell Ida that he has no experience in negligence work and has not handled a trial. He wishes that he knew a lawyer who was experienced in handling cases of this sort whom he could consult, but unfortunately, he does not have such a contact. He studies the relevant law and procedure. He performs well but loses the case. Is Burke subject to discipline?

- ☐ **A.** Yes, because he did not tell Ida that he had never handled a negligence claim or a trial.
- ☐ **B.** Yes, because he failed to associate with a lawyer experienced in handling negligence actions.
- ☐ **C.** No, because he studied the relevant law and procedure and performed well.
- ☐ **D.** No, because he is licensed to practice law in the state and may therefore accept any litigated matter in the state.

Question 3b.

Carla, a graduating law student who is in the United States on a student visa, is having lunch with her friend Alice, an environmental lawyer who graduated from the same law school the previous year and who was just admitted to the bar. Carla knows that during law school, Alice did a summer internship at a small immigration law firm, where she helped companies that were seeking employment visas for some of their workers. Carla tells Alice that her student visa is about to expire, but that she has just been offered a job at a law firm. She asks whether the law firm could sponsor her for a visa. Alice responds, "Unfortunately, I don't believe that law firms can sponsor people who are straight out of law school for employment visas. My advice would be to go back to your home country for a year and apply for jobs from there." Carla, who reasonably believes that Alice was providing correct legal advice, turns down the law firm job and returns to her home country. A few months later, she learns that Alice's advice was incorrect. The law firm could have sponsored her for a work visa. She tries to get the job back, but the firm informs her that it hired someone else and can no longer hire her. Alice's advice was negligent and was the cause of Carla's return to her home country and failure to get the job. Alice never signed a retainer, paid a fee, or otherwise agreed to be Carla's lawyer. Carla sues Alice for negligence. May a court grant judgment against Alice for malpractice?

- ☐ **A.** Yes, because Carla reasonably believed that Alice was providing correct legal advice.
- ☐ **B.** Yes, because a person whose only prior experience with a field of law was a summer job should not give legal advice in that field.
- ☐ **C.** No, because no consideration was given in exchange for the advice.
- ☐ **D.** No, because Carla knew that Alice was an environmental lawyer, not an immigration attorney.

Question 3c.

Attorney Priya represents Janice in her suit against a major canned goods company, after she contracted botulism from a can of pickled fish. Priya receives an e-mail from opposing counsel saying that he is ready to meet to discuss settlement. Priya asks Janice if they can meet the next day to talk about what terms Janice wants. When they meet, Priya tells Janice that she thinks she could get at least $4 million dollars in a settlement. Janice is thrilled at that number, and she tells Priya, "I didn't think we could get nearly that much! You have been such an amazing lawyer and friend throughout this process. If they come to us with an amount lower than that, and you think that we can get more by rejecting the offer, I trust your judgment. Do what you think is best." The next day, Priya meets with opposing counsel, who informs her that the company is offering $3.25 million dollars to settle the case. Without conveying the offer to Janice, Priya responds, "That number does not come close to addressing the pain and suffering my client has been through. My client rejects your client's offer." The case goes to trial, and Janice loses and recovers nothing. She complains to the bar. Is Priya subject to discipline for not telling Janice about the offer?

☐ **A.** Yes, because a lawyer must communicate a settlement offer to a client, and Priya did not do so.
☐ **B.** Yes, because a lawyer must promptly inform the client of any decision or circumstance with respect to which the client's informed consent is required, and Priya did not do so.
☐ **C.** No, because Janice authorized Priya to reject the settlement offer.
☐ **D.** No, because the settlement offer was less than the amount that Janice deserved, so Priya made a reasonable judgment in rejecting it.

Question 3d.

In 2009, Anita, a criminal defense lawyer, represented Liam, an immigrant from Australia who was charged with selling cocaine. Under state law, if convicted, Liam could have been sentenced to five years in prison. The district attorney offered a deal providing that if Liam pled guilty, he would be sentenced to serve a term of 14 months. A criminal defense lawyer must give a client accurate advice about the potential adverse legal consequences of entering a guilty plea. Even so, without researching the potential immigration consequences of this guilty plea, Anita recommended that Liam accept the offer, and Liam did so. At the end of the 14 months, the state turned Liam over to federal immigration authorities, who deported him to Australia based on the criminal conviction. Liam cannot show that he would not have been convicted of a deportable offense if he had gone to trial. In 2010, the Supreme Court decided the *Padilla* case, holding that a conviction based on prejudicially incompetent plea-bargaining advice from a lawyer could be reversed. The highest court of the state has held that the *Padilla* decision does not apply to advice given before that decision. May Anita be subject to discipline?

☐ **A.** Yes, because Anita failed to investigate the potential immigration consequences of pleading guilty and failed to advise her client about that.
☐ **B.** No, because Liam cannot show that if he had gone to trial, he would not have been convicted of a deportable offense.
☐ **C.** No, because the state's highest court has held *Padilla* not to be retroactive.
☐ **D.** No, because Liam is not a U.S. citizen, and an American lawyer should not be disciplined for conduct in representing him.

Question 3e.

Jill, an attorney, brings a lawsuit on behalf of her client, Ann, against Grant, after Grant fails to repay Ann's loan to him of $5,000. The retainer provides that Jill's contingent fee will be 30 percent of any recovery. Jill files the complaint one day too late, and the suit is dismissed with prejudice. Jill is chagrinned and embarrassed and wants to make amends for her mistake. She would like to pay Ann out of her own pocket without disclosing her error to Ann or to anyone else. She would simply get Ann a cashier's check for the portion of $5,000 that would have been paid to her if the court had ordered Grant to repay the $5,000. May she do so if she avoids making any false statement about the source of the funds?

☐ **A.** Yes, because this would give Ann the amount she would have expected to obtain as a result of the lawsuit.
☐ **B.** Yes, because she would be doing the right thing without engaging in dishonesty, fraud, deceit, or misrepresentation.
☐ **C.** No, because she is required to report her misconduct to the disciplinary authorities.
☐ **D.** No, because Jill is required to tell Ann that she missed the deadline and that the case was dismissed.

Question 3f.

Client Sylvia hired lawyer Dino to represent her in a personal injury action against Chainmart. In the course of the representation, Sylvia told Dino that she was prepared for the case to go to trial, if necessary, and that she probably would not even consider accepting a settlement offer below $2 million. Dino thought she might be awarded $10 million or more if the claim were decided by a jury.

The evening before trial, opposing counsel called Dino and offered a settlement of $1 million. Dino tried calling Sylvia but could not reach her. Five hours after trying unsuccessfully to reach Sylvia and hoping to be able to get some sleep before the trial, Dino called opposing counsel and rejected the offer. The case went to trial the next morning, and after trial, the jury awarded Sylvia $5 million. Is Dino subject to malpractice liability for his actions?

☐ **A.** Yes, because decisions to accept or reject settlement offers are to be made by the client.
☐ **B.** Yes, because a lawyer has a duty to keep his client informed of all settlement offers.
☐ **C.** No, because Sylvia authorized Dino to reject any offer under $2 million.
☐ **D.** No, because the jury award was greater than the settlement offer.

Question 3g.

Harriet intends to bring an action in small claims court against her landlord. She meets with lawyer Joaquin, who is experienced in landlord-tenant law, to see if he will represent her in the matter. After discussing the case, Joaquin and Harriet agree to a flat fee of $1000 for the representation, a reasonable fee given the time and effort Joaquin will expend on the case. Joaquin knows that Angela, a landlord-tenant lawyer three blocks away, would do the same work for $500. In fact, Joaquin believes that Harriet's case is so strong that she could probably represent herself and win. Joaquin does not inform Harriet of these things, and he accepts the case. Is Joaquin subject to discipline?

☐ **A.** Yes, because Joaquin was required to tell Harriet that she could resolve her problem without the use of Joaquin's services.

☐ **B.** Yes, because Joaquin was required to tell Harriet that she could achieve the same result while paying a lower fee.
☐ **C.** Yes, because Joaquin must make disclosures to the extent reasonably necessary to permit Harriet to make informed decisions regarding the representation.
☐ **D.** No, because attorneys are not required to tell prospective clients that they could resolve their problems at a lower cost or no cost.

Question 3h.

Seymour owns and manages a small dairy farm. Recently, Seymour discovered that his fertilizer supplier had been mislabeling its fertilizers as organic when, in fact, they were not. Seymour has had to recall many of his products that were labeled as organic, at great expense, and his reputation has suffered as a result. He wants to sue the supplier for damages. He meets with attorney Gemma to see whether she will represent him. Gemma's usual fee is $200 per hour. Knowing that Gemma is one of the best lawyers in town, Seymour offers to pay her $250 per hour for her services. Gemma has the time and requisite knowledge and experience in the field to represent Seymour. However, as a vegan, she would find it morally repugnant to represent a dairy farmer. May Gemma refuse to represent Seymour?

☐ **A.** Yes, because a lawyer is not obliged to accept a client whose cause the lawyer regards as repugnant.
☐ **B.** Yes, because Seymour is not indigent.
☐ **C.** No, because lawyers may not refuse to accept clients simply because they disagree with them.
☐ **D.** No, because representing Seymour will not impose an unreasonable financial burden on Gemma.

Question 3i.

Attorney Susan began representing client Taylor five years ago, when Taylor purchased a small sandwich shop. Susan assisted in drawing up the paperwork for the purchase of the business and has since then advised Taylor on various legal matters related to the business. Now, Taylor would like to sell the business, and she has identified a potential buyer. Taylor would like Susan to represent her in negotiations with the buyer. Based on her knowledge of the business over the past five years, Susan suspects that Taylor may have created some fake invoices and overstated the value of the inventory in the shop in order to inflate the value of the business, but she does not know this to be the case. She decides not to investigate further and draws up the paperwork for the sale. Is Susan subject to discipline?

☐ **A.** Yes, because Susan was obligated to withdraw from representing Taylor once she suspected fraud.
☐ **B.** Yes, because Susan was obligated to look into the facts and circumstances of the sale to determine whether she could continue with the representation.
☐ **C.** No, because Susan did not actually know that Taylor was engaging in fraud.
☐ **D.** No, because Susan's representation of Taylor did not involve litigation.

4. THE DUTY TO PROTECT CLIENT CONFIDENCES

Question 4a.

Uma's good friend Wendell is a seasoned litigator. She reasonably believes that he can competently represent Royce at the hearing, so she asks him if he can handle the hearing for her, and he agrees. He agrees to treat the file as confidential and to return it to Uma promptly after the hearing. Uma leaves a phone message for Royce, but he doesn't return her call. She gives Wendell Royce's file so that he can familiarize himself with the case. Assume that Wendell can competently represent the client at the hearing.

Was it proper for Uma to give Wendell the file?

☐ **A.** Yes, because Uma reasonably believes that Wendell can competently represent the client at the hearing.
☐ **B.** Yes, because Wendell agreed to treat the file as confidential and to return it to Uma promptly after the hearing.
☐ **C.** No, because Uma did not obtain Royce's prior consent.
☐ **D.** No, because Uma has not filed a motion to withdraw from representation of Royce.

Question 4b.

Sophia retained Drake as her attorney to sue the city where she lived after she stepped into a deep hole in the sidewalk, fell, and broke her leg. She incurred $4,000 in medical bills and suffered a great deal of pain. State law provides that a city is not liable in suits for personal injury unless the suit is filed within one year after the injury occurs. Drake never filed the suit. Six months after the one-year period was up, Sophia sued Drake for malpractice, based on his failure to file the lawsuit.

In fact, Drake called Sophia five days before the one-year period was up and told her that he was ready to file, and Sophia told him not to go ahead with the case. When he asked why not, she said, "It is because I am a finalist for a job as the city's commissioner of parks, and I probably won't get the job if I sue the city. I'm telling you this in the strictest confidence. If I don't get the job, I don't want anyone, including my husband, to know that I applied for this job and didn't get it." Sophia was not selected for the job. She decided to sue Drake because she needed compensation for her injuries.

Drake asserted, in his answer to Sophia's malpractice complaint, that Sophia told him not to file her suit because she was hoping to get a job as commissioner of parks. He limited the disclosure to the minimum necessary to defend himself against this spurious malpractice claim. Is Drake subject to discipline?

☐ **A.** No, because he revealed no more than necessary to defend himself.
☐ **B.** No, because Sophia provided the information to Drake before she asked for strict confidence about her intention to sue the city.
☐ **C.** Yes, because lawyers must not reveal confidential client information, especially in cases in which the client has expressly told the lawyer that a secret must be kept in strict confidence.
☐ **D.** Yes, because Drake's revelation of information adverse to Sophia is a breach of fiduciary duty.

Question 4c.

A law firm has offices in three major U.S. cities. Once a year, lawyers from all three offices convene for a firm retreat. One of the partners in the firm, Sandler, represents Nigel, a celebrity chef, in several lawsuits (filed both by and against Nigel). Sandler prepares a complex counseling exercise for the retreat, based on his relationship with Nigel, called "Dealing with a Difficult Client." Sandler does not change Nigel's name or any of the facts in any of the training materials. The materials provide detailed descriptions of cases in which Nigel was a party, and included stories about difficult interactions between the chef and his lawyers. The materials are distributed in loose leaf notebooks clearly marked "confidential training materials." Nigel learns about the training program from Tommy, one of the firm's junior lawyers, whom Nigel is dating casually (unbeknownst to Sandler). Nigel is furious. Is Sandler subject to discipline for violation of Rule 1.6?

- ☐ **A.** Yes, because that information was obtained in the course of representation, and the disclosure was not impliedly authorized to carry out the representation.
- ☐ **B.** Yes, because Sandler did not obtain Nigel's consent to the use of this information in the training.
- ☐ **C.** Yes, because Sandler disclosed confidences to lawyers who work in offices of the law firm that are located in other cities.
- ☐ **D.** No.

Question 4d.

On a dark night in a bad part of town, a young man named Alan is found dead. Chad is arrested and put in jail, accused of murdering Alan. Chad tells Alberto, his lawyer, that he could not have murdered Alan, because at the time of the murder, he was burying the body of another man, Ethan, whom he *had* killed. Ethan has been declared missing, and the police are investigating whether foul play has occurred. Chad tells Alberto where he buried Ethan. Obviously, Chad does not want anyone to know his alibi because then he would be charged with another murder. In exchange for the alibi information, Alberto could obtain a desirable plea bargain for Chad on the current and prospective charges. May Alberto reveal this information to the prosecutor without consulting Chad?

- ☐ **A.** Yes, because he can use the information to obtain a desirable plea bargain for Chad on the current and prospective charges.
- ☐ **B.** Yes, because unless he reveals the information, he is impeding the state's investigation of Ethan's disappearance.
- ☐ **C.** No, because Alberto obtained this information in the course of representing Chad.
- ☐ **D.** No, because Alberto does not have objective evidence indicating that Chad killed or buried Ethan.

Question 4e.

Jennifer is a partner at a small law firm, and she has been practicing law for eight years. During that time, she has handled primarily trusts and estates cases. Recently, however, she has taken on a domestic relations case representing a woman named Eunice, who is seeking a divorce from her husband, Rudy. During this representation, Jennifer discovered some evidence that indicated that Rudy was sexually abusing Eunice's daughter. Eunice does not want Jennifer to report this to authorities, because she doesn't believe that it is true. Jennifer is not sure whether she has a duty to report the apparent child abuse to the state authorities pursuant to a state reporting statute. Nobody else in Jennifer's firm has any experience with family law. A friend of Jennifer, Isai, is an experienced domestic relations lawyer in a different law firm but is not her firm's ethics counsel. Jennifer has not talked with Eunice about consulting another lawyer. May Jennifer consult Isai about whether she has a duty to report the sexual abuse?

- ☐ **A.** Yes, because there is nobody in Jennifer's firm who is qualified to advise her.
- ☐ **B.** Yes, because the purpose of the disclosure is to obtain advice about whether Jennifer must report the child abuse.
- ☐ **C.** No, because she has not obtained her client's informed consent.
- ☐ **D.** No, because Isai has not been designated as her firm's ethics counsel.

Question 4f.

Attorney Moira represents defendant Oleg in a murder trial. The police discovered the victim's body in a ditch and found Oleg's fingerprints on a kitchen knife that was under the body. Before the trial commences, Oleg tells Moira that he did not murder the victim, but he knows that his son did, because his son confessed to him. He tells her that under no circumstances will he turn his son in, and he does not want his son to know that he told Moira of his son's confession. He refuses to testify at his trial. What is Moira's best course of action?

- ☐ **A.** Reveal the information to the prosecutor to avoid a miscarriage of justice but remain as Oleg's attorney if he wants her to do so.
- ☐ **B.** Reveal the information to the prosecutor to avoid a miscarriage of justice but move to withdraw from representing Oleg.
- ☐ **C.** Tell Oleg's son that she has learned of his confession to his father and urge Oleg's son to retain her as his lawyer so that she will have an obligation not to reveal the information.
- ☐ **D.** Do not reveal the information and do not tell Oleg's son that she is aware of his confession to his father.

Question 4g.

Attorney Mosi is representing Blake, a naturopathic doctor accused of malpractice. Blake is accused of having prescribed Amaronset, a homeopathic compound to Eloise, a patient suffering from migraine headaches. Amaronset is not regulated by the FDA and it has not been widely used to treat migraines. Blake did not tell Eloise that the use of this substance was experimental. Three years after her treatment ended, Eloise died from a brain tumor. Her family is suing Blake, who is no longer prescribing Amaronset.

A study recently published in Germany found that 1 in 20 of the people who took Amaronset for more than two years developed malignant tumors. During the course of his representation, Blake tells Mosi that he prescribed Amaronset to two other individuals who suffered from migraines. They both took this compound for three years, and in both cases stopped taking it four years ago. These two patients do not know about the recent research on Amaronset or that Eloise died from a brain tumor. Blake refuses to inform these patients about the research or the demise of Eloise, because he does not want to open himself up to further liability. Mosi reasonably believes that it is not reasonably certain that Blake's two other patients are at risk of death or substantial bodily harm.

Does Mosi have the discretion to reveal this information to Blake's other patients?

- ☐ **A.** Yes, because failure to do so would involve dishonesty, fraud, deceit, or misrepresentation.
- ☐ **B.** Yes, because Mosi may disclose to avoid assisting a criminal or fraudulent act by Blake.
- ☐ **C.** No, because Mosi is required to disclose the information to Blake's other affected patients.
- ☐ **D.** No, because even if the two patients might have tumors, Mosi must keep this information confidential.

Question 4h.

Attorney Dahlia represents restaurant owner Stefan in a negligence suit. During the course of her representation, Dahlia learns that Stefan uses PestOFF, a rat poison, in his kitchen. PestOFF has recently been shown to cause birth defects if consumed, even in tiny amounts, by pregnant women, and its use within the state has been banned. Its use is a misdemeanor punishable by imprisonment for up to six months. The product was applied only once, and only to the floor of a closet where cleaning supplies were kept. It was never used near food. There is nothing to suggest any ingestion or injury to a person. A city ordinance requires anyone, including lawyers and doctors, who learns of the use of PestOFF to report it to local police immediately. Failure to report is a violation punishable by a $50 fine. Dahlia confronts Stefan and insists that he stop using this product and that they report his past use to the police. Stefan agrees to stop using the product but refuses to report his past use to the police. Dahlia then withdraws from representation of Stefan and reports Stefan's use of PestOFF to the police. Is Dahlia subject to discipline for reporting Stefan's use of PestOFF to the police?

- ☐ **A.** Yes, because she did not reasonably believe that revelation would be necessary to prevent reasonably certain death or substantial bodily harm to any individual.
- ☐ **B.** Yes, because her duty to protect Stefan's confidences continued even after she terminated her representation.
- ☐ **C.** No, because Dahlia's disclosure is permitted under these circumstances.
- ☐ **D.** No, because by using PestOFF, Stefan had committed a crime.

Question 4i.

Attorney Seamus represents Rona in her purchase of an apartment in a major metropolitan city. The apartment is priced well below market value, and it seems to both Seamus and Rona that it is a very good deal. Seamus learns that the apartment is priced so low because one of the bedrooms was constructed below ground level in violation of the city's housing code. When Seamus relays this information to Rona, she gets cold feet and decides not to sign the contract. She finds another apartment and closes a purchase agreement. As it happens, Seamus is also looking to buy an apartment. The apartment that Rona declined to buy would work well for him and his family. He is also willing to buy the apartment knowing that it has a bedroom that does not meet the code requirements. He talked with Rona about his interest in the apartment. She says it would not concern her at all if he bought it. May Seamus purchase the apartment?

- ☐ **A.** Yes, because Rona consented to allow him to purchase it.
- ☐ **B.** Yes, because Rona no longer wants to buy the apartment.
- ☐ **C.** No, because he learned about the apartment in the course of his representation of Rona.
- ☐ **D.** No, because it is impermissible to use confidential information for the attorney's benefit.

Question 4j.

Salima represents Anthony, a man accused of stealing money from his company. Anthony was a bookkeeper at a small bakery. His duties included administering the payroll system. Anthony altered a computer program so that he would be paid an extra few hundred dollars a month by the company. He got this higher pay every month for several years. Anthony's theft from the company was noticed during an accounting audit and he is facing criminal charges.

During a meeting to discuss the criminal charges, Anthony tells Salima that he also rigged the program so that he would also receive approximately $200/month that should have been paid to Jason, a custodian with six children. He says that after he was caught stealing, Anthony re-programmed the system so that the checks would be properly paid going forward. Neither Jason nor the company are aware that Anthony stole from Jason. Salima asked Anthony if he plans to fess up and repay Jason. He says "No way. I'm in enough trouble already." Salima disapproves but says nothing.

Salima meets with the company's general counsel to discuss restitution to the company. The general counsel tells Salima that the audit is complete and presents an accounting that lists only the money that Anthony stole from the company.

Salima reasonably believes that unless she reveals the theft, there will be no restitution to Jason. May Salima reveal this information without Anthony's consent?

☐ **A.** Yes, because revelation is necessary to ensure that Anthony will be asked to repay Jason.
☐ **B.** Yes, because in stealing Jason's money, Anthony committed a crime.
☐ **C.** No, because Anthony did not use Salima's services to steal Jason's money.
☐ **D.** No, because the company's general counsel has stated that the audit is complete.

Question 4k.

Attorney Yoshi represented client Cyrus in his divorce. During the course of the representation, Cyrus told Yoshi that if his ex-wife, Tisha, was awarded their beachfront vacation home in Florida, he would burn it down when it is vacant, because he could not stand the thought of his ex-wife using the vacation home without him. Yoshi advises Cyrus that this is a terrible idea. He points out that deliberate arson could lead to criminal charges and civil liability, not to mention termination of visitation rights. He also cautions that Cyrus could injure or kill a member of his family if he burns down that house. Cyrus repeats to Yoshi that he would not do this if anyone was in the house, but he does not assure Yoshi that he won't torch the building. The divorce was finalized, and Tisha was awarded the vacation home. Yoshi has terminated his lawyer-client relationship with Cyrus. Yoshi reasonably believes that revelation is necessary to prevent Cyrus from committing a crime that is reasonably certain to result in substantial injury to Tisha's house. May Yoshi warn Tisha or her attorney that Cyrus is planning to burn down the vacation home?

☐ **A.** Yes, because Cyrus is no longer Yoshi's client.
☐ **B.** Yes, because Yoshi reasonably believes that revelation is necessary to stop Cyrus from burning down the house and committing the crime of arson.
☐ **C.** No, because Yoshi learned this information during the course of the representation.
☐ **D.** No, because the rules bar lawyers from revealing their clients' stated intentions to destroy the property of others.

Question 4I.

Ella, a public defender, represented a college student named Kenneth. Kenneth was driving his brother Thomas' car and was stopped for going through a red light. The officer spotted what looked like cocaine and drug paraphernalia on the front seat and arrested Kenneth. When the substance was tested, it turned out to be cocaine. Against Ella's advice, Kenneth told Ella that he planned to plead guilty. Ella writes a blog in which she regularly recounts her experiences as a public defender. After Kenneth was released pursuant to a negotiated deal for deferred prosecution, she wrote on her blog: "#126409 (the client's jail identification number): This stupid kid is taking the rap for his drug-dealing dirtbag of an older brother because 'he's no snitch.' I managed to talk the prosecutor into treatment and deferred prosecution, since we both know the older brother from prior dealings involving drugs and guns. My client is in college. Just goes to show you that higher education does not imply that you have any sense." Jail identification numbers are not available to the general public. Is Ella subject to discipline?

- ☐ **A.** Yes, because Ella's comment about the case did not reveal any confidential information, but it disparaged her unnamed client.
- ☐ **B.** Yes, because Ella revealed confidential information.
- ☐ **C.** No, because Ella did not name her client.
- ☐ **D.** No, because the only identifying information in Ella's disclosure was the non-public jail identification number.

5. THE ATTORNEY-CLIENT PRIVILEGE AND THE WORK PRODUCT DOCTRINE

Question 5a.

Which one of the following statements would be protected by the attorney-client privilege if an adverse party sought to compel the lawyer to disclose the information?

☐ **A.** At a firm holiday party, a client with a products liability claim tells his lawyer's partner (who is not working on that case) that he plans to divorce his wife because she just wants his money. The partner informs the lawyer of that revelation. The wife's divorce lawyer later seeks disclosure of this conversation.

☐ **B.** A lawyer represents a doctor in a medical malpractice suit. The plaintiff is still in the hospital. To obtain facts about how much his client has been suffering, the lawyer interviews a patient in the bed adjacent to the plaintiff's bed.

☐ **C.** A paralegal interviews a client about his case, and she gives her notes to her supervising attorney.

☐ **D.** A lawyer advises several clients to buy certain securities that will minimize the clients' tax liabilities. The government believes that the securities are unlawful tax shelters and issues a subpoena to the lawyer, seeking the names of the clients.

Question 5b.

Attorney Leticia represents client Benjamin, a pharmacist, in an employment discrimination suit. With the help of his best friend Rocky, who happens to be sleeping on his couch that month, Benjamin writes a summary of the case, which Benjamin then emails to Leticia. Which one of the following statements is correct?

☐ **A.** Only Benjamin can be compelled to testify about the communication.

☐ **B.** Only Rocky can be compelled to testify about the communication.

☐ **C.** Benjamin or Rocky can be compelled to testify about the communication.

☐ **D.** Neither Benjamin nor Rocky can be compelled to testify about the communication.

Question 5c.

Attorney Damon represents his friend George in a civil case in which George is a defendant. George is alleged to have driven into the plaintiff's fence negligently. George and Damon meet in Damon's office to discuss the case. After some discussion about their children, who play together, George tells Damon that he was driving under the influence of PCP at the time of the incident. Several months later, George's wife files for divorce, and her lawyer subpoenas Damon to testify. The wife's attorney wants Damon to testify that George told Damon that he drove under the influence of drugs. May Damon be required to testify about George's use of PCP?

☐ **A.** Yes, because a subpoena has been issued.

☐ **B.** Yes, because the litigation in which Damon represented George was unrelated to the present litigation in which Damon will testify.

☐ **C.** No, because the information is privileged.

☐ **D.** No, because George shared this information with Damon before George's wife filed for divorce.

Question 5d.

Attorney Salim represents Roland, a doctor, in a medical malpractice case. In an e-mail, Roland reveals to Salim that on the day in question, he had had a couple of drinks before he performed the surgery at issue. He asks Salim whether that would expose him to punitive damages. Salim replies that it would not, under the law of the state. Roland is to testify at the trial. In preparing for his testimony, Roland asks Salim whether, if the opposing counsel asks Roland whether he had anything to drink on the day in question, he can successfully invoke attorney-client privilege to avoid answering the question. Salim's answer should be:

☐ **A.** Yes, because the information is protected by attorney-client privilege.
☐ **B.** Yes, because the e-mail exchange is protected by attorney-client privilege.
☐ **C.** No, because the attorney-client privilege does not shield him from having to answer the question.
☐ **D.** No, because although Roland's statement to Salim that he was drinking would have been privileged if it had been made orally, it is not covered by attorney-client privilege because it was transmitted via e-mail.

Question 5e.

Which one of the following communications would be protected by the attorney-client privilege?

☐ **A.** A prospective client tells an attorney the facts of her case, but the attorney decides not to take the case.
☐ **B.** An attorney and client meet in a crowded restaurant to discuss the client's case. They do not know anyone sitting around them, but they are sitting near enough to other diners that others could hear their conversation. In fact, no one hears the conversation.
☐ **C.** A lawyer represents a client in a dispute about a real estate contract. The client gives the attorney a copy of the contract at issue. The contract includes statements about the obligations of both parties and statements about their reasons for entering into the contract.
☐ **D.** A lawyer and a client go out to celebrate after obtaining a favorable settlement. While they are out to dinner, they talk at length about the personalities of the opposing party in the case, that person's lawyer, and the judge.

Question 5f.

Tax attorney Tammy represents client Lilian, who plans to buy several tickets to upcoming concerts using her student ID and sell them to non-students for a significant profit. Lilian seeks Tammy's advice as to whether she must pay income tax on the money she expects to make. Lilian does not know that reselling student tickets for profit is illegal in her state, and when Tammy informs her that it is, she does not go forward with the plan. Is Lilian's conversation with Tammy privileged?

☐ **A.** Yes, because all confidential communications between lawyers and clients for the purpose of obtaining legal advice are privileged.
☐ **B.** Yes, because Lilian did not go through with her plan.
☐ **C.** No, because Lilian did not know that reselling the tickets was a crime when she asked Tammy for advice.
☐ **D.** No, because the crime-fraud exception to the attorney-client privilege applies.

Question 5g.

Attorney Aria represents Jaya, who is a defendant in a securities fraud prosecution. One day, Aria is interviewing Jaya about the allegations that she engaged in insider trading. Jaya, who is married, brings a man named Josh to the interview, and she reveals to Aria that she is having an affair with him. She further reveals that the Josh provided her with some inside information. Josh is not a defendant in the case and is not represented by Aria. Jaya's statements about Josh are:

☐ **A.** Confidential and privileged.
☐ **B.** Confidential, but not privileged.
☐ **C.** Not confidential, but privileged.
☐ **D.** Neither confidential nor privileged.

Question 5h.

The police arrested a middle school band teacher for repeatedly sexually abusing numerous female students aged 9 to 12. The molestation occurred during private music lessons and took place over a seven-year period before the teacher was arrested. Some of the victims told the police that they had reported the abuse to the school principal after it occurred, but the principal had failed to take action against the teacher. After the teacher was arrested, some of the victims and their families filed suit against the principal and the school board. The school board hired the firm of Schoenholtz & Koplow "to investigate the response of the school administration to allegations of sexual abuse of students." The board explained that it would need a full report so that it could decide whether to settle or litigate the claims against it. Meanwhile, the school board also hired a respected trial lawyer, Lindsay, at another firm, to represent the board in the lawsuit. Schoenholtz & Koplow interviewed all the officers of the school board to find out what they knew about the molestation, when they learned what they knew, and what they did after they received the information. Their notes and report were turned over to the school board, which gave them to Lindsay. The plaintiffs in the lawsuit requested, during discovery, the notes made by Schoenholtz & Koplow during their interviews. Lindsay must:

☐ **A.** Turn over the notes to the plaintiffs because while the communication may be protected, the underlying facts are not protected from disclosure.
☐ **B.** Turn over the notes to the plaintiffs because Schoenholtz & Koplow was hired to do the investigation, not to defend the school board against the lawsuit.
☐ **C.** Refuse to turn over the notes to the plaintiffs because they are protected by attorney-client privilege.
☐ **D.** Refuse to turn over the notes to the plaintiffs, based on attorney-client privilege, because the crimes discussed in those documents could result in liability for the school board.

Question 5i.

Attorney Alton recently filed a medical malpractice action on behalf of Juan against Metropolitan Hospital, where Juan was sexually assaulted by a staff member while he was being treated for a psychotic episode in the psychiatric ward. Juan was traumatized by his experience at the hospital. In a telephone call before their first meeting, Alton learned that Juan suffers from post-traumatic stress disorder and needs a social worker to be present in all stressful situations. Alton therefore asked Juan to bring his social worker, Pierre, to all of their meetings. Juan pays Pierre to assist him, and he brought Pierre to all of his meetings with Alton. The lawyers for Metropolitan Hospital have learned about Pierre's presence during the meetings between Juan and Alton. The hospital is seeking discovery of the conversations that took place during those meetings. Which one of the following statements is correct?

- ☐ **A.** The attorney-client privilege is likely to protect the conversations from discovery because Alton, rather than Juan, suggested that Pierre should participate in the meetings.
- ☐ **B.** The attorney-client privilege would have protected the conversations between Alton and Juan from discovery despite Pierre's presence even if Juan had brought him to the meetings without any suggestion from Alton.
- ☐ **C.** The conversations are unlikely to be protected from discovery by the attorney-client privilege because Pierre was hired by Juan rather than Alton.
- ☐ **D.** The attorney-client privilege is unlikely to protect from discovery any conversation between Alton and Juan because Pierre was present at their meetings.

Question 5j.

Paula, a lawyer, drafted a will for Viet. The will stated that in the event of his death, his property should go to "my children." Viet and his wife Jenny had two sons. After his death, Edith, a woman with whom he had had an affair, proved through DNA evidence that he also had fathered her son Michael. She claimed that her son was entitled to one third of the estate. During probate of the will, Paula plans to testify that Viet had told her that what he meant was that his property should go to his children Gabriel and Veronique, and any children that he and Jenny later produced. Since Jenny is next of kin, Paula has obtained her informed consent to this plan. Paula would assert that she was waiving the privilege on behalf of her deceased client.

Edith's lawyer objects on the ground that Paula's testimony would violate the attorney-client privilege. Should the probate judge allow Paula to testify about Viet's intent?

- ☐ **A.** Yes, because Jenny as next of kin has given informed consent.
- ☐ **B.** Yes, because Paula's testimony would fall under an exception to the privilege.
- ☐ **C.** No, because the information is privileged.
- ☐ **D.** No, because Paula's testimony would result in an injustice to Michael.

Question 5k.

Attorney Khalid represents Martin, who is in jail awaiting trial. Martin has been charged with robbing a bank. The evidence against him, including potential testimony from Terence, the getaway driver who has been given immunity from prosecution, is strong. Khalid receives a letter from Martin, written from jail. The envelope is marked "legal mail," meaning that it would not be opened or read by the jail's corrections officers. The letter instructs Khalid to forward to Martin's cousin Jasper the sealed envelope, addressed to Jasper, that is enclosed with the letter. Instead of contacting Jasper or forwarding the letter, Khalid opens the envelope that is addressed to Jasper. It says that Jasper should supply a false alibi to Martin by testifying that Martin and Jasper had been together all day on the day of the robbery, packaging marijuana that they planned to sell. Khalid does not forward the letter to Jasper. Instead, he keeps it in his office. Before the trial, the prosecutor issues a subpoena to Khalid, directing him to produce at the trial any non-privileged correspondence from Martin. Must Khalid produce the letter to Jasper?

☐ **A.** Yes, because it is not privileged.
☐ **B.** Yes, because even if it is privileged, withholding it would be prejudicial to the administration of justice.
☐ **C.** No, because it is protected by the attorney-client privilege.
☐ **D.** No because lawyers do not have to comply with subpoenas for their office records.

6. CONFLICTS OF INTEREST: CURRENT CLIENTS

Question 6a.

Tandy is a practicing lawyer and adjunct law professor at Frostburg Law School, which is part of Frostburg University. Two Caucasian high school seniors have asked her to represent them in their lawsuit against Frostburg University. They allege that Frostburg University did not admit them to the undergraduate program because of race discrimination. Specifically, they allege that students of color with similar test scores and grades were admitted to Frostburg University, while they were not. Tandy reasonably believes that she can competently and diligently represent the students in their lawsuit. She obtains informed consent, confirmed in writing, from both the students and the university. May Tandy represent the two students in their lawsuit?

- ☐ **A.** Yes, because the university gave informed consent, confirmed in writing.
- ☐ **B.** Yes, because the students gave informed consent, confirmed in writing.
- ☐ **C.** No, because the interests of the students are directly adverse to the interests of the university.
- ☐ **D.** No, because the university employs Tandy, so this representation would present a nonconsentable conflict of interest for Tandy.

Question 6b.

Attorney Charlie works at a law firm of 30 lawyers in a large city. He represents his friend Suma in a wrongful discharge suit against her former employer, an architecture firm. Suma and her husband, Todd, are in the process of divorcing. Suma has retained a family lawyer associated with another firm to represent her in the divorce case. Charlie just learned that one of his law partners, Angus, is representing Todd in the divorce. Charlie and Angus agreed not to communicate with one another about either of the matters. They did not speak to Suma and Todd about the conflict. May Charlie continue to represent Suma in her civil suit against her former employer?

- ☐ **A.** Yes, because Charlie and Angus agreed not to communicate with one another about either of the matters.
- ☐ **B.** Yes, because the conflict involves only Charlie's personal interests and does not present a significant risk of materially limiting Angus's representation of Todd.
- ☐ **C.** No, because the firm did not obtain both clients' informed consent, confirmed in writing.
- ☐ **D.** No, because law firms are not permitted to sue current clients.

Question 6c.

Attorney Pavel is a criminal defense lawyer representing Denny, who is charged with larceny. Denny, a pro bono client, is alleged to have stolen a piece of jewelry from a jewelry box during a house party. In an unrelated matter, Pavel is defending Betty, for a fee, against a criminal charge of arson. Both cases are assigned to be heard by a single judge. During Denny's trial, the prosecutor calls Betty to the stand. She testifies that she was at the party in question and saw Denny go in and out of the room where the alleged theft occurred. She further testifies that she never went into that room. Earlier, Denny had told Pavel that he saw Betty go into the room, and he suggested that she may be the thief. Pavel intends to cross-examine Betty on this point. Is there a conflict of interest?

- ☐ **A.** Yes, because Denny's interests are directly adverse to Betty's.
- ☐ **B.** Yes, because Betty is a paying client.
- ☐ **C.** No, because the representation does not involve the assertion of a claim by Denny against Betty or vice-versa.
- ☐ **D.** No, because Pavel's cross-examination of Betty is impliedly authorized to carry out the representation.

Question 6d.

Attorney Meghan represents Walter, a used-car salesman who has been criminally charged with driving while intoxicated. Before Walter's trial, a friend of Meghan's, Laurel, asks Meghan to represent her in her breach of contract suit against Walter and his company. If Meghan were to sue Walter on behalf of Laurel, another lawyer would defend Walter in that matter. Meghan has formed a close bond with Walter as a result of her work on his criminal case, and she reasonably believes that she could not represent Laurel very vigorously, because of her friendship with Walter. She explains her concern to Laurel, and Laurel states that she understands the risks and agrees to the representation anyway. She confirms her understanding in writing. Walter also gives informed consent in writing. May Meghan represent Laurel?

- ☐ **A.** Yes, because the representation is not prohibited by law.
- ☐ **B.** Yes, because Walter's case is criminal and Laurel's case is civil.
- ☐ **C.** No, because the representation would involve the assertion of a claim by one client against another client represented by the lawyer in the same litigation.
- ☐ **D.** No, because Meghan does not reasonably believe that she can competently and diligently represent Walter and Laurel, even though both clients gave informed consent, confirmed in writing.

Question 6e.

The state in which Stella practices recently enacted an animal cruelty law. Stella represents Chix, Inc., a poultry company, in a suit brought by a local animal rights group. The suit alleges that the poultry company has violated the new state law by failing to provide adequate ventilation in the chicken coops. The suit seeks punitive damages. Stella files a motion to strike the punitive damages request, urging that the new law does not allow recovery of punitive damages.

In an unrelated matter, Stella represents a group of students at a small Christian college, seeking to recover punitive damages against the school for allowing dissection of live animals in their school's biology classes in violation of the statute. When Stella agreed to represent the students, she explained to them that she was arguing against the availability of punitive damages in the Chix case. Stella is representing the students pro bono, so even if punitive damages were granted, she would not receive a portion of the award as a legal fee.

Which of the following factors is least relevant to determining the risk that Stella's actions on behalf of one client would materially limit Stella's effectiveness in representing the other?

- ☐ **A.** The fact that she will represent both clients in lawsuits at the trial court level.
- ☐ **B.** The fact that the lawsuits will be litigated during the same period of time.
- ☐ **C.** The fact that Stella would not benefit financially if the statute were interpreted to allow punitive damages.
- ☐ **D.** The fact that, when Stella agreed to represent the students, she explained to them that she was arguing against the availability of punitive damages in the Chix case.

Question 6f.

Chloe and Matilda are partners in a small law firm. Chloe has represented Speisler Motors, an auto manufacturer, for years. She represents Speisler in all litigation in which it is a party. At present she is defending the company in a lawsuit brought by Tom, a driver of a Speisler car who was blinded when an airbag spontaneously exploded while he was driving. When the bag exploded, Tom's car hit Anton, a pedestrian, who died some days after the accident. The executor of Anton's estate has asked Matilda to represent the estate in a lawsuit against Tom and Speisler Motors. Matilda believes that she would be able to provide competent and diligent representation to Anton's estate, and Chloe believes that she would be able to provide competent and diligent representation to Speisler Motors. They have agreed not to talk with each other or to share documents relating to the matter. Speisler, Tom, and Anton's executor all give verbal consent to the representation after full disclosure of all material risks. Is it proper for Matilda to accept representation of Anton's estate?

- ☐ **A.** Yes, because Matilda could reasonably believe that she would be able to provide competent and diligent representation to Anton's estate, and Chloe could reasonably believe that she would be able to provide competent and diligent representation to Speisler Motors.
- ☐ **B.** Yes, because Matilda and Chloe have agreed not to talk with each other or to share documents relating to the matter.
- ☐ **C.** No, because although the conflict is consentable, neither Matilda nor Chloe confirmed her client's informed consent in writing.
- ☐ **D.** No, because there is a conflict of interest and the conflict is not consentable.

Question 6g.

Valladia, Inc., is a small, closely held corporation. Valladia and its president, Alan, are defendants in a civil action brought by a state attorney general who accuses both of them of fraud, based on the same facts and the same law. Both of them desire to be represented by Martha, an attorney. Martha will bill each defendant for services provided on behalf of that defendant. Martha reasonably believes that she could provide competent and diligent representation to both of them. Martha advises the board of directors of Valladia of all the foreseeable risks of the corporation being represented by the same attorney who is representing Alan, and she advises Alan of all of the foreseeable risks of being represented by the lawyer who is representing the board. Valladia's board of directors votes to approve the representation, and Alan approves as well. Martha writes a letter to the corporation and to Alan noting that both have given their informed consent to her representation of both parties. May Martha represent both of them?

☐ **A.** Yes, because the corporation gave informed consent to the joint representation.
☐ **B.** Yes, because both defendants gave informed consent to the joint representation.
☐ **C.** No, because a single lawyer may not represent two co-defendants in civil litigation.
☐ **D.** No, because even though conflicts are not foreseeable at present, they could arise in the future.

7. CONFLICTS INVOLVING FORMER AND PROSPECTIVE CLIENTS

Question 7a.

Carlos, a sole practitioner, represents Sharky Products, Inc., a property owner that disputes an adjoining owner's right of access to an alleyway between their buildings. Carlos sent a letter to the other property owner, Berry's Beauty Supply Co., to explain the problem. He received a reply from Berry's lawyer, Eleanor, requesting that Carlos withdraw from representation of Sharky. Eleanor claimed that Carlos was prohibited from handling this matter because five years ago, Carlos represented Matthew, the president and sole owner of Berry's, in a claim against the manufacturer of a lawn care product that he used at his home. The matter took three hours of Carlos' time and Matthew was satisfied with the resulting settlement. Carlos has had no contact with Matthew since then.

May Carlos continue to represent Sharky Products, Inc.?

☐ **A.** Yes, because there is no substantial relationship between the two matters.
☐ **B.** Yes, because he only worked on Matthew's case for three hours.
☐ **C.** No, because his representation of Sharky is materially adverse to his former client.
☐ **D.** No, because Matthew is the president and sole owner of Berry's.

Question 7b.

Last year, attorney Mira represented Sally, the owner of a small pizza restaurant, in a suit against Rome's Own, Inc., a supplier of shredded cheese, based on breach of contract. The parties settled the claim for $15,000. Mira and Sally remained friendly after the matter was settled, and they have gone to the movies and to dinner a few times in the last year. Earlier today, Sally's next door neighbor, Jose, came into Mira's office for a consultation and asked Mira to represent him in a civil suit against Sally. Jose alleges that Sally's pet macaw bit him, causing an infection and permanent scarring. Jose wants to get a court order against Sally requiring that the bird be euthanized pursuant to a state law. Sally already paid for his medical care. Jose does not want further damages. Must Mira obtain Sally's informed consent before she can agree to represent Jose?

☐ **A.** Yes, because Jose's interests are directly adverse to Sally's.
☐ **B.** Yes, because there is a significant risk that Mira's representation of Jose will be materially limited by her loyalty to Sally.
☐ **C.** No, because Jose's lawsuit is not substantially related to the breach of contract lawsuit against Rome's Own, Inc.
☐ **D.** No, because Jose's interests are not materially adverse to Sally's.

Question 7c.

Use the facts from the previous question. Must Mira obtain Jose's informed consent before she can agree to represent Jose?

☐ **A.** Yes, because Jose's interests are directly adverse to Sally's.
☐ **B.** Yes, because there is a significant risk that Mira's representation of Jose will be materially limited by her loyalty to Sally.
☐ **C.** No, because Jose's lawsuit is not substantially related to the breach of contract lawsuit against Rome's Own, Inc.
☐ **D.** No, because Jose's interests are not materially adverse to Sally's.

Question 7d.

Lawyer Shawn has handled various property and business transactions for Evelyn, her adult daughter Adelaide, and Evelyn's business partner, Oliver, during the last decade. Those matters are all completed. Five years ago, Shawn wrote a will for Evelyn in which she left all of her property to Adelaide. In that work, Shawn represented and gave advice to both Evelyn and Adelaide. Adelaide, who lives with her mother, suffers from disabling epilepsy and has not been able to support herself. After Shawn finished drafting the will, he drafted a letter to Evelyn and Adelaide informing them that his office was closing their file and confirming the termination of their lawyer-client relationship. However, he failed to mail them the letter.

Last week, Evelyn came to Shawn to tell him that it's time for Adelaide to stand on her own two feet. She mentioned that Adelaide has become involved with a boyfriend, Felix, and has been staying out nights. She would like Shawn to write a new will for her in which she would leave all of her property to Oliver. She further asks Shawn not to reveal to Adelaide the contents of the new will.

May Shawn write the new will for Evelyn?

☐ **A.** Yes, because his prior representation of Adelaide was incidental to his representation of Evelyn.

☐ **B.** Yes, because he will not reveal the contents of the new will to Adelaide without authorization by Evelyn.

☐ **C.** No, because he failed to inform Adelaide that he no longer represents her.

☐ **D.** No, because he did not obtain Adelaide's informed consent to his representation of Evelyn with respect to the new will.

Question 7e.

Kieran, five years out of law school, accepted a job with Sato & Perlmutter, LLP. A couple of months after he started work, Miranda Perlmutter was asked to take over representation of Kasho Natural Foods in an ongoing lawsuit against the Roxbury Box Company. Kasho had fired its previous counsel after a dispute over legal fees. Miranda wants to accept Kasho as a client. However, there may be a problem.

Kieran came to Sato & Perlmutter from another firm, Podkrash and Associates, LLP, where he had worked for three years. The Podkrash firm has been representing the Roxbury Box Company in the Kasho litigation for the last two years. Kieran did not work on the Roxbury matter while he worked at Podkrash. While Kieran was working at Podkrash, he dated Lance, the senior paralegal at the firm. Lance oversaw all the staff work on the Roxbury matter and talked at length about the factual and strategic issues in the case with Kieran on many occasions. For example, the two men talked about a decision of the partner in charge of the litigation that a key document that might impact Roxbury's liability was not covered by the plaintiffs' discovery request. Lance disagreed with the partner's decision, but ultimately decided to keep his mouth shut.

After consultation with her firm's ethics counsel, Miranda decides to undertake representation of Kasho. However, she does not wish to terminate Kieran's employment as a way to solve any conflicts problem. Instead, she timely screens Kieran from the lawyers working on the matter, sees to it that he receives no part of the fee from the Kasho matter, and provides appropriate written notices to Roxbury about the screening procedures.

Was Sato & Perlmutter permitted to undertake representation of Kasho in this manner?

- ☐ **A.** Yes, because Lance and Kieran's relationship was personal in nature.
- ☐ **B.** Yes, because Kieran was properly screened from the Kasho representation.
- ☐ **C.** No, because there is a substantial risk that confidential information that Kieran would have learned at the Podkrash firm would materially advance Kasho's position in the litigation.
- ☐ **D.** No, because this is a situation in which screening is insufficient to avoid the possibility of a conflict of interest so long as Kieran remains at the firm.

Question 7f.

Spencer, a businessman, calls Kai, an attorney. He says he is looking for a lawyer so that he can sue his former business partner, Max, with whom he has had a falling out. Kai says that he is accepting new clients and would be happy to meet with Spencer the following week if the type of case is one with which he is familiar. Spencer asserts that he has proof that Max was stealing money from his company and covering it up by keeping two sets of books. Spencer says he has photos of several pages from both sets of books, which he obtained by sneaking into Max's house, where he found the books in the study and photographed them with his cell phone. Kai says he could handle that type of matter but before Kai can agree to represent Spencer, the two of them should meet in person, next week, to discuss fees and the other terms of representation.

The day after the phone call, Max calls Kai to ask for representation because he thinks Spencer is going to sue him. Max offers Kai a generous flat fee for the work. Kai would like to represent Max.

May Kai represent Max without Spencer's consent?

- ☐ **A.** No, because an attorney may not accept representation of a person when the attorney's representation has first been requested by a potential adversary of that person.
- ☐ **B.** No, because Spencer has given Kai information that could be used adversely to Spencer if Kai represents Max.
- ☐ **C.** Yes, because there is no conflict of interest, since Kai has not yet agreed to represent Spencer.
- ☐ **D.** Yes, because Spencer's actions were not lawful.

Question 7g.

Five years ago, attorney Barry worked at a large law firm with offices across the country. One of the firm's partners defended Panko, Inc., an appliance manufacturer, against allegations that its toasters had a defect that would cause many of them to catch fire. Barry was not involved in that litigation and did not learn anything about it during his time at the firm. Barry has since opened up a private practice of his own. Ted comes to Barry's new office seeking legal help. Ted tells Barry that his Panko toaster recently overheated and caused a house fire. He would like to sue Panko for damages. May Barry represent him a suit against Panko without Panko's informed consent?

- ☐ **A.** Yes, because there was not a substantial risk that confidential factual information as would normally have been obtained in the prior representation of Panko would materially advance Ted's position in the subsequent matter.
- ☐ **B.** Yes, because Barry did not actually acquire confidential information that is material to Ted's lawsuit while he was working at his old law firm.

☐ **C.** No, because the matters are the same or substantially related.
☐ **D.** No, because Ted's interests are materially adverse to those of Panko.

Question 7h.

Armand, a lawyer, represented Walter, a plastic surgeon, during Walter's contested divorce from his wife five years ago. Armand no longer has any contact with Walter, and he does not remember anything about Walter's case. Recently, one of Walter's patients, Celia, developed serious complications and nearly died as the result of the extensive cosmetic surgery that Walter performed on her. She wants to sue him for punitive damages based on gross negligence. She has asked Armand to represent her. May he do so without Walter's consent?

☐ **A.** Yes, because he no longer represents Walter and the medical malpractice matter is unrelated to the divorce.
☐ **B.** Yes, because he does not remember anything about Walter's case.
☐ **C.** No, because a lawyer may not sue a former client without the former client's consent.
☐ **D.** No, because Armand would normally have obtained information in the divorce case that could be helpful to Celia.

Question 7i.

Attorney Ash is a solo practitioner specializing in serving small businesses. Ten years ago, Ash handled a routine health department license application for Sprinkles, a newly founded small family-owned bakery. Sprinkles is now known for its cupcakes. Death by Cupcake (DBC) is a bakery across town from Sprinkles that also specializes in cupcakes. DBC would like to hire Ash to represent them in negotiating a commercial lease to open a new bakery. As it happens, the property it wants to lease is across across the street from Sprinkles. The increased competition would significantly hurt Sprinkles' business. May Ash accept the representation without obtaining Sprinkles' informed consent?

☐ **A.** Yes, because informed consent is not required when a prospective client and a former client are merely economic competitors.
☐ **B.** Yes, because the two matters are not substantially related.
☐ **C.** No, because DBC and Sprinkles are economic competitors.
☐ **D.** No, because DBC's interests are materially adverse to Sprinkles'.

Question 7j.

Attorney Roger is a solo practitioner in a small town. There are only about 70 lawyers in the town, and of those, only 20 (including Roger) handle divorce cases. One day, Roger does an intake interview with Leon, who is seeking a divorce. Leon reveals to Roger that he had several affairs during his marriage and that his wife, Reva, does not know about them. At the end of the interview, Roger tells Leon that he will let Leon know within a week whether he can accept his case.

The next day, Leon calls Roger to say that he has decided to retain another lawyer. A week later, Reva comes to Roger's office seeking representation in the divorce. Recognizing her name, and before she says anything else, he asks her if Leon is her spouse. She confirms that he is. Roger immediately tells Reva that he may not be able to represent her. Before he can finish his sentence, Reva interrupts, "Is this because he came to see you already? I have already been told by five different lawyers that they cannot represent me because of a conflict of interest! I think Leon is just trying to prevent me from hiring a lawyer in this town." A few days later, Roger is able to confirm that over the course of three days, Leon did a one-hour intake interview with every divorce lawyer in town.

May Roger represent Reva in the divorce?

☐ **A.** Yes, because Leon is only a prospective client; therefore Roger owes no duty to him.
☐ **B.** Yes, because Leon met with every divorce lawyer in town.
☐ **C.** No, because Roger received information from Leon that could be used against Leon.
☐ **D.** No, unless he gets Leon's informed consent, confirmed in writing.

8. CONFLICTS ISSUES IN PARTICULAR PRACTICE SETTINGS

Question 8a.

Attorney Darla represents the plaintiffs in a class action lawsuit against Nutrisnax, a granola bar company, alleging false advertising. The plaintiffs allege that Nutrisnax falsely advertised its granola bars as a healthy alternative to candy bars when, in fact, the granola bars contained just as much fat, sugar, and sodium as the average candy bar. The class includes anyone who purchased a Nutrisnax granola bar in the last three years. Last week, a potential client named Samuel came into Darla's office and asked her to represent him in his claim for child support against his former husband, Franklin. Darla learned that Franklin purchased hundreds of Nutrisnax granola bars during the relevant period, making him one of the unnamed members of the class in the granola bar suit. Must Darla obtain Franklin's informed consent before agreeing to represent Samuel?

☐ **A.** Yes, because Samuel's interests are directly adverse to Franklin's.
☐ **B.** Yes, because Darla cannot reasonably believe that she can competently and diligently represent both Franklin and Samuel.
☐ **C.** No, because the child support claim is unrelated to the class action lawsuit.
☐ **D.** No, because unnamed members of a class are ordinarily not considered to be clients of the lawyer for conflicts purposes.

Question 8b.

Chris and Bobby are accused of burglarizing a house. They want Meyer to represent both of them in the criminal matter because they prefer not to have to pay two lawyers. Also, they believe that if they coordinate their stories and refuse to cooperate with the police, the state won't have enough evidence to convict either of them. No state statute prohibits lawyers from representing criminal co-defendants. Meyer obtains the police reports and charging documents. He also obtains the criminal records of both Chris and Bobby. From his investigation, Meyer learns that Chris may have been the instigator. Chris is 26 years old and Bobby is 19. Chris has three prior felony convictions, while Bobby has a prior conviction for possession of a small amount of marijuana, for which he received a suspended sentence that could be revoked if he is again convicted. Meyer's law clerk recommends that Meyer obtain a court order permitting the joint representation, but Meyer declines to seek such an order because he believes that he can provide competent and diligent representation to both defendants. May Meyer represent both defendants if each gives informed consent to the joint representation, confirmed in writing?

☐ **A.** Yes, because both clients have provided consent confirmed in writing.
☐ **B.** Yes, because the charges arise out of a single incident.
☐ **C.** No, because Meyer did not seek an order from the judge allowing the joint representation.
☐ **D.** No, because the joint representation presents a non-consentable conflict.

Question 8c.

Larry, the father of Linda, Abby, and Carl, died at age 87. His property was to be divided equally among his children. Louise, Larry's partner, is executor of the estate. Most of his property is in cash and stocks, but Larry also left his children a lakeside cabin. The three adult children decide that Carl should take the cabin and should pay his sisters one-third of its value each out of his share of the cash and stocks. The appraised value of the cabin is $225,000, but Carl urges that, for the purpose of the transfer, the cabin should be valued at $150,000, because he believes the appraised value is unrealistic and that he will soon have to replace the water and septic systems for the cabin, at considerable cost. After some discussion, Linda and Abby are willing to go along with their brother's suggestion as to the valuation of the cabin because they care more about their brother than they do about the money. The three siblings need to hire legal assistance to prepare and file the documents relating to the transfer of the cabin. Carl proposes that they hire Morton, a lawyer he has used for other legal matters over the last ten years. Morton reasonably believes that he could competently represent all three siblings. He explains the potential problems and the advantages and risks of joint representation and obtains their consent to the joint representation. None of the siblings has any questions or new proposals, and he does not provide any legal advice to them. Morton then prepares a document valuing the cabin at $150,000 for purposes of the transfer, just as the siblings agreed. Each sibling confirms that all of them still want him to be their attorney. May he represent all three siblings in the transaction?

- ☐ **A.** Yes, because Morton merely prepared documents per their joint instructions, so he did not even need their informed consent.
- ☐ **B.** Yes, because there is no apparent conflict between the interests of the three siblings and he obtained their informed consent.
- ☐ **C.** No, because Carl would benefit by the cabin being assigned a lesser value, while Abby and Linda would be paid more if the assigned value is higher, so the conflict is non-consentable.
- ☐ **D.** No, because Morton's prior representation of Carl creates a significant risk that his representation of Linda and Abby would be materially limited by his felt loyalty to Carl.

Question 8d.

In answering this question, use the facts of the previous question and assume that Morton has properly undertaken the representation of the three siblings.

In the course of his research before preparing the property transfer documents for Larry's summer cabin, Morton discovers that Carl could obtain a reduction in tax liability for the cabin if the transfer of the cabin is postponed until next year. Morton knows that Linda and Abby are eager to conclude the transaction and that they will be able to earn more interest on funds paid to them by Carl if the payment is made this year instead of next year. Carl asks Morton whether he could postpone the transfer of the cabin until next year, slowing things down without revealing any reasons for the delay.

May Morton delay the transaction without disclosing the reasons to Carl's sisters?

- ☐ **A.** Yes, because the adverse consequence to them from the delay will not be as significant as the resulting benefit to Carl.
- ☐ **B.** Yes, because this will allow him to avoid the clients' potentially adverse interests and to focus on their common interests.

☐ **C.** No, because each client is entitled to be told information relating to the representation that might affect the client's interests.

☐ **D.** No, because Carl's suggestion would involve Morton in a fraud against Linda and Abby, requiring Morton's immediate withdrawal from representation of Carl.

Question 8e.

Jaiden, an assistant general counsel of Plenum, Inc., a pharmaceutical manufacturer, was asked to investigate whether the research division of Plenum was concealing reports of adverse reactions to the company's best-selling product, Somalox, an anti-depressant. Two users of Somalox had contacted the general counsel's office, reporting that they had submitted adverse reaction reports to the research division, as directed on the package insert, but that they had received no response from the company. One of these two users alleged that he had suffered hallucinations and suicidal ideation after taking Somalox, and that he had described these reactions in his earlier report. The other user reported that she was hospitalized for depression after having taken Somalox for several weeks. She also had reported this to the research division. The non-response is worrisome. The company policy is to acknowledge receipt of any adverse reaction reports and to assure users that the company will report adverse reactions to the Food and Drug Administration as required by law. The research division would route any adverse reaction reports through the general counsel's office to the FDA, but none have been received or sent for Somalox.

Jaiden schedules a meeting with Bertha, the chief of the research division. Jaiden shows her the correspondence sent to the general counsel's office by the two users and asks her to show him these and any other adverse reaction reports that the company has received. Bertha flushes and stammers in response to Jaiden's query. "I am afraid that I have let a few of these slip through the cracks. Since you are the company's lawyer, I can speak to you in confidence, right? Am I in trouble here?"

In answering Bertha's questions, which of the following statements would Jaiden be best advised to make?

☐ **A.** "Our conversation is protected by attorney-client privilege, so you can talk with me in confidence."

☐ **B.** "You can speak to me in confidence, because you are an employee of Plenum, and therefore your interests are aligned with those of the company."

☐ **C.** "I represent Plenum, so I cannot give you any legal advice except the advice to get a lawyer."

☐ **D.** "I have to report anything that you tell me to the company's leadership, because I represent the company, but I can assure you that the information won't be shared outside of the company— for example, with law enforcement agencies."

Question 8f.

Nathan is a partner in the law firm of Pace and Gillespie, which represents Bostwick Corp., which is not publicly traded. The corporation manufactures boots. Nathan is a friend of David Bostwick, the chairman of his client's board of directors, who owns 12 percent of the stock of the company. Nathan himself owns 3 percent of the stock, which he acquired long before Pace and Gillespie began representing Bostwick. Whenever there is a vacancy on the board, the board selects a replacement director. No directors are elected by the shareholders.

On David's recommendation, the board takes a formal vote and offers Nathan the opportunity to join the board. Nathan would like to accept, and neither he nor anyone on the board knows of any actual or apparent conflict of interest. Nathan is not willing to divest himself of his stock in the company. May Nathan accept the offer to join the board?

☐ **A.** Yes, because there is no law or ethical rule barring his joining the board.
☐ **B.** Yes, because although Nathan is a friend of David, the board took a formal vote to appoint him.
☐ **C.** No, because he is a friend of David and therefore there is at least the appearance of a conflict of interest, regardless of the opinion of Nathan or board members.
☐ **D.** No, because Nathan refuses to divest himself of stock in the company.

Question 8g.

Eleanor represents Carmichael Inc., an energy company that sells electricity to residential and commercial customers. The corporation has five stockholders; four are Carmichael family members, and the fifth is an outside investor who provided start-up funds five years ago. In the course of her review of corporate documents, including e-mails exchanged among company personnel, Eleanor discovers that Marcus, the company's Director of Information Technology, has been harvesting cell phone numbers from employees' and customers' e-mail messages that went through the company's server and selling them to telemarketing companies. This information about Marcus's activities, if it became public, would be very damaging to Carmichael Inc.'s reputation. She consults Carmichael's president, Joseph Carmichael, who says that he has suspected that something like this might be happening, but that Eleanor should just leave it alone. Eleanor suspects that Joseph may be collaborating with Marcus and sharing the revenue from the telemarketing companies. Eleanor goes to a meeting of the board of directors that is attended only by Joseph and his wife and son, who are also members of the board, and Joseph again tells her to leave it alone. His wife and son concur. The company is regulated by the Public Service Commission. Eleanor continues to believe that exposure would hurt the company's reputation and therefore its future profits.

Do the Rules require Eleanor to reveal the misconduct to the commission?

☐ **A.** Yes, because what Marcus has been doing is harmful to members of the public.
☐ **B.** Yes, because Rule 1.13 requires such disclosure.
☐ **C.** No, because Rule 1.13 does not require such disclosure, and the disclosure would violate Rule 1.6.
☐ **D.** No, because although Rule 1.13 would require such disclosure, Rule 1.6 prohibits it.

Question 8h.

In answering this question, use the facts of the previous question. Must Eleanor withdraw from representation of Carmichael?

☐ **A.** Yes, because a lawyer must withdraw from representation of an organizational client when she discovers that an employee of the client corporation has committed misconduct.
☐ **B.** Yes, because the board of directors failed to address the misconduct after Eleanor called it to the board's attention.
☐ **C.** No, because nothing in Rule 1.16 requires withdrawal.
☐ **D.** No, because she represents the corporation, not Marcus.

9. CONFLICTS OF INTEREST BETWEEN LAWYERS AND CLIENTS

Question 9a.

Lucille, a criminal defense lawyer, receives a frantic call from Sylvia, who states that her sister, Basia, who recently immigrated from Poland, has been arrested by state police for a drug violation, and that the bail hearing will be held in less than two hours. She asks Lucille to represent Basia at the bail hearing and in her criminal case. Lucille hires Magda, a Polish-speaking interpreter, and rushes to the courthouse, where she is able to briefly meet with Basia and represent her at the bail hearing. The judge sets the bail at $2,000. Sylvia is able to pay the bail amount, and Basia is released from prison that night. The next day, Lucille meets with Basia, with Magda interpreting, and informs her that her rate for legal services is $300 per hour. She states that that rate will be used to calculate the bill for the work that Lucille did on the bail hearing, and for future work that she will do on the criminal case. Basia agrees to the rate and Lucille begins work on her case. There is no other discussion of how much Basia will have to pay. At Basia's hearing five months later, the arresting officer fails to appear, and the charges against Basia are dropped. The next month, Lucille sends Basia a bill for $1,800, including five hours of her work, plus $300 for Magda's services. Is Lucille subject to discipline?

- ☐ **A.** Yes, because she did not communicate the rate in writing or give Basia an estimate of the total fee.
- ☐ **B.** Yes, because she did not communicate the expenses for which Basia will be responsible within a reasonable time after commencing the representation.
- ☐ **C.** No, because a lawyer's rate need not be communicated in writing.
- ☐ **D.** No, because Lucille was hired on such short notice that she could not discuss compensation in advance.

Question 9b.

Spencer desires to represent his golfing partner Craig, who was injured on a ski slope that was apparently negligently maintained. Spencer tells Craig on the phone that he is willing to work on a contingent fee basis, under which Craig will be charged nothing unless Spencer obtains a settlement or wins a judgment. In either case, Spencer would charge 33 percent of any recovery after the deduction of the expenses of litigation. Spencer explains that Craig will not be responsible for any litigation expenses unless there is a recovery that exceeds the amount of the expenses. They discuss these points, and Craig agrees to the fee arrangement. Spencer contacts the ski slope's insurer, and within three weeks, with Craig's approval, the case is settled for $21,000. Spencer transmits $14,000 of that settlement to Craig. Spencer spent only four hours on the case. Was Spencer's conduct proper?

- ☐ **A.** Yes, because he disclosed all the details of the fee arrangement.
- ☐ **B.** Yes, because a lawyer's rate need not be disclosed in writing.
- ☐ **C.** No, because he did not disclose all the details of the fee arrangement in a writing signed by Craig.
- ☐ **D.** No, because a rate of 33 percent is unreasonable for a matter that required so little of the lawyer's time and attention.

Question 9c.

Joseph is an immigrant who was recently denied asylum by the administrative appeals body that handles immigration cases. He hires Cyrus to appeal the decision to the U.S. Court of Appeals. Joseph knows that there is a $500 filing fee that he will have to pay. The appeal and fee are due tomorrow. Cyrus called Joseph and left a message, but Joseph did not call him back. He knows from prior conversations, however, that Joseph wants to appeal the decision. If he misses the filing deadline, Joseph will be barred from appealing. May Cyrus go ahead and file the appeal, paying the filing fee, with the expectation that Joseph would reimburse him?

☐ **A.** Yes, because lawyers are permitted to advance court costs.
☐ **B.** Yes, because $500 is not excessive.
☐ **C.** No, because lawyers are not permitted to provide financial assistance to clients.
☐ **D.** No, because Joseph did not exercise reasonable diligence in communicating with Cyrus before advancing the fee.

Question 9d.

Attorney Cherie represents Patience in a suit against her landlord for failure to do adequate remediation after a flood caused mold growth in the attic. Patience is an anthropologist who is writing a novel about a forensic anthropologist who solves murder mysteries. Patience is low on cash, but her upcoming book is expected to be a bestseller. Cherie proposes a fee arrangement in which Patience will pay Cherie a percentage of the royalties from her book as the fee for the landlord-tenant dispute. She discusses the advantages and disadvantages of this arrangement. Patience agrees to pay the legal fee in this manner. Cherie then sends Patience a letter that includes a clear explanation of the terms of the arrangement, which are fair and reasonable. The letter also advises Patience that it is desirable for her to seek independent legal advice before signing this agreement. A few weeks later, Patience signs the letter to indicate her consent.

May Cherie and Patience agree that the legal fee will consist of a percentage of Patience's royalties from the book?

☐ **A.** Yes, because Cherie complied with the disclosure and other requirements that govern business transactions between lawyers and clients.
☐ **B.** Yes, because Patience's payment of the royalties to Cherie is not contingent upon her winning the case.
☐ **C.** No, because a lawyer may not enter into a fee agreement with a client that gives the lawyer media or literary rights.
☐ **D.** No, because the litigation is ongoing. Once the litigation has ended, Cherie and Patience may make an agreement to give Patience a share of the royalties.

Question 9e.

Barbara approaches attorney Morgan to ask for representation in a landlord/tenant suit. Morgan has not handled this type of case before. She is willing to take it on and will charge a much lower hourly rate than her normal rate, but only if Barbara agrees not to sue her for any mistake she might make. Morgan has accordingly drafted a retainer agreement with Barbara that Barbara waives any potential claims for malpractice against Morgan. Morgan has read Barbara this provision and explained it to her, and she has encouraged her orally to seek the advice of another lawyer about whether to hire Morgan on these terms. Barbara says that she fully understands the provision, that she does not need to consult another lawyer, and that she wants to sign the retainer agreement. May Morgan represent Barbara pursuant to this agreement?

☐ **A.** Yes, because Morgan obtained Barbara's informed consent.
☐ **B.** Yes, because Morgan advised Barbara of the desirability to seek the advice of an independent lawyer.
☐ **C.** No, because Morgan did not advise Barbara in writing of the desirability to seek the advice of an independent lawyer.
☐ **D.** No, because Barbara was not independently represented in making this agreement.

Question 9f.

Use the facts from the previous question. Suppose Morgan decides not to include the malpractice language in the retainer agreement, and both she and Barbara sign the agreement. Suppose further that Morgan indeed makes a serious mistake in the course of representation. Morgan and Barbara estimate that the mistake cost Barbara $9,500. Morgan would like to settle any malpractice claim that Barbara may have against her for $12,000 without litigation. Morgan does not wish to notify her malpractice insurer of the mistake, because then her rates would go up. She advises Barbara in writing to seek independent counsel, and she tells her she can take her time finding another lawyer. Barbara declines, saying she does not need another lawyer and that she agrees with the $12,000 settlement. May Morgan go forward with the settlement?

☐ **A.** Yes, because Morgan's mistake cost Barbara less than $12,000.
☐ **B.** Yes, because Morgan advised Barbara in writing regarding the desirability of seeking independent counsel.
☐ **C.** No, because Barbara was not represented by another lawyer in the settlement negotiations.
☐ **D.** No, because the ethics code requires lawyers to report professional errors to their malpractice insurers before settling malpractice claims based on those errors.

Question 9g.

Attorney Eli has represented Jacques, an elderly but lucid man, in his legal matters for the past eight years. He continues to do so from time to time. The legal matters with which Eli has assisted Jacques have been minor; the most Jacques ever paid Eli was $1,500. One day, Jacques tells Eli that as a token of his appreciation for his years of service and friendship, he would like to give Eli his mint condition 1970 Chevrolet Chevelle, a car Eli knows to be worth over $70,000. Eli refers Jacques to another lawyer who can prepare the documents transferring the title to the vehicle to Eli. May Eli accept the gift?

☐ **A.** Yes, because there are no restrictions with respect to receiving unsolicited gifts from clients.
☐ **B.** Yes, because Eli referred Jacques to another lawyer who will prepare the documentation to effectuate the transfer of the title to the vehicle.

☐ **C.** No, because Eli did not first arrange for a guardian ad litem to be appointed for Jacques.
☐ **D.** No, because a lawyer may not accept a substantial gift from a current client, and the car would be considered a "substantial" gift.

Question 9h.
Attorney Sebastian graduates from law school and starts his own criminal defense practice. He establishes an LLC for his practice and sets up a bank account for the office expenses. He also has a personal bank account. He decides to charge the relatively low fee of $200 per hour for his work. Within the first month of opening his practice, five different clients retain him in connection with their criminal matters. Pursuant to the retainer agreements, each client gives Sebastian a check for $4,000. Sebastian will earn $200 for each hour that he works. After 20 hours, he will bill each client for additional sums. At a minimum, how many additional bank accounts must Sebastian open?

☐ **A.** 0
☐ **B.** 1
☐ **C.** 4
☐ **D.** 5

Question 9i.
Attorney Maria is a divorce lawyer. Several months ago, Maria represented Jillian in her divorce from her husband, Jack. At that time, Maria charged her an hourly fee of $400 per hour. The judge granted the divorce and ordered Jack to pay her $1,000 per month child support. Recently, Jillian came to Maria seeking help, because Jack has not been paying the child support for the past 6 months. She would like Maria to help her get the $6,000 that Jack owes her. Maria wishes to charge Jillian a contingent fee of 30 percent of the recovery. She discloses the fee and expense terms and receives Jillian's informed consent in writing.

May Maria charge the contingent fee?

☐ **A.** Yes, because Jillian is Maria's former client.
☐ **B.** Yes, because she obtained Jillian's consent in writing.
☐ **C.** No, because contingent fees are not permitted in domestic relations cases.
☐ **D.** No, because 30 percent is excessive because it will drain resources needed to support the couple's children.

Question 9j.
Ellen wants to hire Donna, an attorney, to handle her divorce case. Ellen works as a saleswoman in a department store, earning $26,000 a year. Donna proposes to charge a fee of $300 per hour, which is not an unusual hourly rate for divorce work in Ellen's community, although some lawyers charge less. Donna discloses her fee and all expenses for which Ellen will be responsible in writing, and Ellen signs the writing. May Donna charge this fee?

☐ **A.** Yes, because Donna informed Ellen, before starting to work, that her fee will be $300 per hour and listed the expenses for which Donna will be responsible.
☐ **B.** Yes, because the notice of the fee arrangement was in writing.

- ☐ **C.** No, because Donna did not give Ellen a good faith estimate of the likely total fee.
- ☐ **D.** No, because some other lawyers in the community charge less than $300 per hour for divorce work.

Question 9k.

Laila was a pedestrian who was hit by a car. Her best friend Joan, who is a nurse, visited her in the hospital. Neither Joan nor Laila knew the driver of the car. Joan later discussed the accident with her friend Craig, who is an attorney. Craig would like to represent Laila, on a contingent fee basis, in a claim against the driver of the car. Craig tells Joan that if she recommends him to Laila, and Laila retains him, Craig will pay Joan 10 percent of his share of any recovery that Laila collects. He does not tell Laila about this part of the arrangement. Is Craig subject to discipline?

- ☐ **A.** Yes, because he did not disclose the arrangement to Laila.
- ☐ **B.** Yes, because Joan is not a lawyer.
- ☐ **C.** No, because Joan has no connection with the driver of the car and there is therefore no conflict of interest.
- ☐ **D.** No, because he offered Joan 10 percent of his own fee, rather than 10 percent of the recovery.

Question 9l.

Cindy, an indigent single mother of four, sought the help of Rona, an attorney, in filing an application for emergency food stamps. Rona agreed to help Cindy for a very low, fixed fee, which Cindy paid immediately. While the application is pending, Rona realizes that even if the application is approved, Cindy's family will go hungry, because the state's welfare benefits are so low. She wants to help Cindy by giving her $100 a month, for six months, out of her own funds. May she do so?

- ☐ **A.** Yes, because Cindy is indigent.
- ☐ **B.** Yes, because the financial assistance is not being offered in connection with litigation.
- ☐ **C.** No, because Cindy did not waive any potential conflict of interest in writing.
- ☐ **D.** No, because she did not terminate the representation before providing the assistance.

Question 9m.

Geraldine, an attorney in a legal aid program, provides pro bono representation to Amber, who is indigent, disabled, and homeless, in litigation against Mike's Job Counseling Service. Amber had paid $300 to Mike's, which did not give her any job leads or help. Mike's has recently been exposed in the local paper for not actually having helped anyone to get a job. Winter is approaching, and it has become increasingly difficult for Amber to live on the streets. She is in danger of freezing to death. All of the homeless shelters in the area are full. Geraldine cares about Amber and wants to keep her from freezing. Which of the following statements is correct?

- ☐ **A.** Geraldine may loan Amber $500 so that she can rent a modest room.
- ☐ **B.** Geraldine may give Amber $500 so that she can rent a modest room.
- ☐ **C.** Both A and B are correct.
- ☐ **D.** Neither A nor B is correct.

Question 9n.

Eduardo is a sole practitioner. He wants to handle the following matters and to make agreements with clients under which he would receive 20 percent of any recovery awarded to the client. In which of these cases would Eduardo be subject to discipline if he undertook the representation under those terms?

- ☐ **A.** Eduardo previously represented Atticus in a criminal matter. Atticus pleaded guilty and was incarcerated for a year. During that year, he reports, prison officials deprived him of medication that he needed, resulting in his having a mild stroke. Atticus wants to sue the prison for damages.
- ☐ **B.** Byron and his ex-wife are each half-owners of a mini-golf business. Byron has asked Eduardo to seek a partition (court-ordered division) of the property.
- ☐ **C.** Celeste has asked Eduardo to file an action seeking an order requiring her ex-boyfriend, who is the father of her daughter, to pay child support.
- ☐ **D.** In a fit of rage, Dana's former husband smashed her new sports car, requiring $12,000 worth of repairs. She wants to sue him for damages.

Question 9o.

Sol practices tax law, but his expertise is in giving tax advice rather than handling litigation. Recently, Sol provided personal tax advice to businessman Bill. Bill then asked Sol to look at another tax matter involving a deduction denied by the Internal Revenue Service. Bill wants Sol to litigate the matter in the tax court. Sol mentioned to his friend Al, a litigator in a different firm, that one of his clients wants him to take on a litigation matter. Al responded, "Great! Just tell your client that you will do it with co-counsel. I will charge Bill 33 percent of the recovery, and I'll give you half of what he pays us. We'll both enter appearances and sign the papers, but you can leave everything to me. It will be as if we were in a law partnership together!" Sol believes that Al is an excellent litigator capable of doing a good job for Bill. Sol and Al agree to accept any liability for mistakes. The overall fee they intend to charge is reasonable. Bill gives his informed consent to Al's association with Sol and to the proposed fee and to how Sol and Al will split it, and he signs a writing to that effect.

May Sol and Al enter into this split-fee arrangement?

- ☐ **A.** Yes, because the arrangement complies with all of the relevant rules.
- ☐ **B.** Yes, because there are no restrictions on lawyers sharing fees.
- ☐ **C.** No, because Sol is not competent to litigate the matter.
- ☐ **D.** No, because the division is not in proportion to the actual work performed by each lawyer.

Question 9p.

Johann, a lawyer, is has recently taken Carly's products liability case. They have agreed to a fee of $250/hour. Because he has only handled a few such cases, he wants to avoid being sued for malpractice. He would like Carly to sign a retainer agreement that provides that any malpractice claim that she wants to make against him has to be resolved by an arbitration rather than in a court. He drafts the retainer agreement and explains it to her but does not tell her that she may have a different lawyer advise her about the desirability of agreeing to the arbitration. Arbitration agreements between professional persons and their patients or clients are not prohibited by state law. She signs the agreement. Is Johann subject to discipline?

☐ **A.** Yes, because Carly was not independently represented in signing the agreement.
☐ **B.** Yes, because Johann did not advise Carly of the desirability of seeking independent counsel before she signed the agreement.
☐ **C.** No, because the matter is not a contingent fee case.
☐ **D.** No, because Johann explained the effect of the arbitration term to Carly.

Question 9q.

Milan graduated from law school, took the bar exam in state A, passed the exam, and was admitted to the bar in state A. He maintains active membership even though he is neither practicing law, nor living in state A. Milan bought a small computer consulting firm in neighboring state B and ran it successfully for a few years, earning a good living. Then Milan decided to sell the business. He found a buyer who purchased the business. In the course of their discussions about the business, Milan represented that the business had been twice as profitable as it actually was. After a few months of operating the business, the buyer sued Milan for damages for fraud and to rescind the contract. That lawsuit is pending. Is Milan subject to discipline in state A?

☐ **A.** Yes, because Milan lied to the buyer about the value of the business, even though his dishonesty took place in state B.
☐ **B.** Yes, because the terms of the agreement (including the value of the business) were not fair and fully disclosed to the buyer, as required by Rule 1.8(a), nor did the buyer give informed consent.
☐ **C.** No, because Milan was not practicing law and this deal was not related to law practice.
☐ **D.** No, because Milan's acts have not yet been found to be fraudulent by a court.

Question 9r.

Danielle is a lawyer. Ted, the son of her brother Matthew, is very ill with a life-threatening condition. Ted must get a certain medication that costs $1,400 in the next 24 hours or else he will go into kidney failure. Matthew has no cash, but he will receive a large sum from the sale of his home in one week. Matthew has no other possible source of funds until then unless Danielle gives him a short-term loan. Danielle is flat broke (in fact, she is deeply in debt), but there is $120,000 in Danielle's trust account. This amount is the proceeds of a personal injury settlement that Danielle will distribute to her client Van. She represented him on a pro bono basis, so she is not owed a fee from the settlement. Van is in prison for the next few years. Danielle has agreed to hold the funds for Van in the interim and to make mortgage payments on his house as they become due. Danielle lends Matthew $1,400 from this account for Ted's medication. She is unable to ask for Van's approval because he is in solitary confinement because he talked back to a prison guard and is not allowed to receive phone calls. Danielle, confident that Van would approve, sends him a letter explaining her intention to make the loan to her brother. A week later, Matthew receives the proceeds from the sale of his house. He repays Danielle, who replenishes the client trust account. Van later writes Danielle that he is glad that she was able to make the loan to her brother. There is no resulting delay in the distribution of the settlement funds to Van or in the making of mortgage payments. Is Danielle subject to discipline?

☐ **A.** Yes, even though she promptly informed Van that she borrowed the money and he ratified her prior action.
☐ **B.** No, because she promptly informed Van that she loaned out a chunk of his money and he ratified her prior action.
☐ **C.** No, because there was no delay either in making the payments on Van's mortgage or in the distribution of the settlement funds to Van.
☐ **D.** No, because she did this to prevent reasonably certain death or substantial bodily harm to a child.

10. CONFLICTS ISSUES FOR GOVERNMENT LAWYERS AND JUDGES

Question 10a.

Pablo, a lawyer who used to work at the U.S. Department of Justice, now works at a private law firm. Which of the following rules does NOT apply to potential conflicts between Pablo's duties to the U.S. government and his duties to any current clients?

- ☐ **A.** 1.7
- ☐ **B.** 1.9(a)
- ☐ **C.** 1.9(c)
- ☐ **D.** 1.11

Question 10b.

Abdul, a lawyer, is employed by the United States Department of Labor and works in its Office of Civil Rights. He is also an experienced litigator. His neighbor, Blaine, has been having a dispute with the Internal Revenue Service, which claims that Blaine's deduction for home office expenses is not valid and has withheld part of his claimed tax refund. Abdul wants to represent Blaine in a suit against the United States in the federal Tax Court to try to obtain the withheld portion of Blaine's refund. He would not charge Blaine any fee. Also, Abdul has spoken to his supervisor in the Department of Labor, who has confirmed that the Department would have no objection to Abdul providing legal assistance to Blaine in his dispute with the Internal Revenue Service and will confirm this in writing. As a result, Abdul is confident that there is no conflict of interest, and he does not intend to advise Blaine that he should get a different lawyer, because any other lawyer would charge a substantial fee to Blaine. May Abdul represent Blaine in this litigation?

- ☐ **A.** Yes, because he is not going to charge a fee.
- ☐ **B.** Yes, because he is obtaining written approval from the Department of Labor.
- ☐ **C.** No, because he does not plan to advise Blaine about the possibility of obtaining a different lawyer.
- ☐ **D.** No, because a federal employee may not represent an unrelated client in a claim against the United States.

Question 10c.

After she graduated from law school, Dania worked for the Securities and Exchange Commission (SEC) for three years. During that time, she worked on securing an indictment in a large securities case involving seven defendants who collaborated on an insider trading scheme. At the end of three years, she moved on to a position at one office of a large private law firm whose practice includes defense of securities fraud cases. A month after she started work at the firm, Dania learned that a partner in the firm was representing one of the defendants in the securities case that Dania had worked on while she was at the SEC. This did not emerge in the preliminary conflicts screening before she was hired because Dania's work focused on three of the other defendants in the suit. The basic facts were the same, but the targets were different. What should the firm do to enable it to represent the defendant in the securities fraud case?

- ☐ **A.** Instruct Dania not to reveal to anyone in the law firm anything she learned about the case while she was at the SEC.
- ☐ **B.** Screen Dania from any participation in the matter, prevent her from receiving any extra pay related to the matter, and give written notice of the potential conflict to the SEC.
- ☐ **C.** Transfer Dania, while the litigation is pending, to a different office of the firm, in another city.
- ☐ **D.** Discharge Dania, because that is the only way in which the firm could both comply with the ethics rules and continue to represent its client.

Question 10d.

Paul, an associate justice of the United States Supreme Court owns a substantial amount of stock in a publicly traded corporation called Exrix, LLC. The Court grants certiorari to decide a class action suit brought by shareholders of Exrix. Paul has disclosed his stock ownership but is not planning to sell his stock. No party has made a recusal motion. Must Paul recuse himself pursuant to a code of judicial conduct?

- ☐ **A.** Yes, because he owns some stock in a corporation whose case he must decide.
- ☐ **B.** Yes, because the amount of stock that he owns is substantial.
- ☐ **C.** No, because no party has made a recusal motion.
- ☐ **D.** No, because no ethics rule requires him to recuse himself.

Question 10e.

In a state in which judges are elected, Damian Garner, the President of Garner Industries, a manufacturer of firearms, has donated $3,000 to the successful campaign of Ambrose Zoltan, who was elected as a judge of the state's highest court. That contribution represented 2 percent of the campaign contributions that the judge received. All contributions were disclosed pursuant to the state's campaign finance disclosure law.

A gun control group sued Garner Industries for violating the state's gun control laws by manufacturing and selling guns with built-in silencers. The court ruled against Garner and it has appealed to the state supreme court, arguing that the gun control law is inconsistent with the Second Amendment. The gun control group filed a motion asking Judge Zoltan to recuse himself, but he denied the motion. Would Judge Zoltan's participation in the adjudication of this case be unconstitutional?

- ☐ **A.** Yes, because Garner made a substantial contribution to his campaign.
- ☐ **B.** Yes, because not all parties have consented to his participation.
- ☐ **C.** No, because the contribution was only a small part of his campaign treasury.
- ☐ **D.** No, because the contribution was disclosed.

Question 10f.

Evelyn, a recently admitted attorney, is serving as a law clerk to Judge Leopold Osterman on the state court of appeals. The judge has heard the appeal in a contract dispute in which IGL Corp. has sued Mountain Hardware, Inc., for damages. Mountain Hardware was represented by the law firm of Westerfield & Pilson, which Evelyn worked for during her second summer in law school. She did not work on that dispute while she was at the firm, because the firm accepted it after she left the job, but Judge Osterman has asked her to write the opinion in the case. While she was working on the opinion, Margaret Pilson from Westerfield & Pilson emailed Evelyn, on her private email account, asking whether she would like to discuss joining the firm as an associate after she finished her clerkship. Evelyn wanted to take that job, so she told Judge Osterman about the email, and he said that it was fine to discuss a possible job with the firm. Evelyn and the firm then agreed on a starting salary of $95,000, and that she would begin work two weeks after her clerkship ended. A week later, Evelyn completed the opinion, which the judge adopted. It dismissed the case against Mountain Hardware. Is Evelyn subject to discipline?

- ☐ **A.** Yes, because she entered into negotiations and a future employment agreement with a firm while participating personally and substantially as a judicial law clerk writing an opinion that would affect a present client of that firm.
- ☐ **B.** Yes, because her opinion favored the firm that was offering her a job.
- ☐ **C.** No, because she notified her employer of the overture from the law firm and her intent to pursue it.
- ☐ **D.** No, because she did not submit the opinion to the judge until after she had accepted the firm's offer, so she could not have been helping a client of the firm in order to procure a job offer.

Question 10g.

Armand DuBois was elected as a state court judge seven years ago. This year, he is up for re-election. His state has adopted the Model Code of Judicial Conduct, which bars a candidate for judicial office from personally soliciting or accepting campaign contributions. A rule of the state supreme court provides that violation of the Code may be punished by that court's judicial conduct committee, which may impose sanctions ranging from a reprimand to suspension of judicial duties. Judge DuBois personally accepted a $500 contribution from his close friend and tennis partner, Stanley Baskin. Is he subject to discipline by the judicial conduct committee?

- ☐ **A.** Yes, because the Supreme Court's Citizens United decision does not apply to judicial campaigns.
- ☐ **B.** No, because under the Citizens United case, Judge DuBois has a First Amendment right to accept campaign contributions.
- ☐ **C.** No, because a judge may be punished only by impeachment and conviction by the legislature.
- ☐ **D.** No, because contributions from close friends and relatives to judicial candidates are permitted.

Question 10h.

Erin, a lawyer, had a motion that was scheduled to be argued on November 5. Another attorney, Manfred, represented her adversary. On October 31, Erin learned that her son's surgery had been scheduled for November 5, and she wanted to be with her son on the day of the surgery. She tried to call Manfred to discuss rescheduling, but he was out of town and could not be reached that day. So without first notifying Manfred, she telephoned the judge's clerk to find out whether the argument on the motion could be heard the following week. To her surprise, the judge picked up the phone and explained that he had answered because his clerk was at lunch. Erin explained the situation and asked the judge whether the argument could be scheduled for November 12. The judge checked his computer and advised that he could fit in the argument on that date, and he advised Erin to notify Manfred of her request and if Manfred had no objection, to telephone his clerk in a few hours. He said that his clerk would also send a notice to her and to Manfred, describing his conversation with Erin and notifying that in the absence of any objection, the hearing would be rescheduled as requested. Is Erin subject to discipline?

☐ **A.** Yes, because she didn't notify Manfred that she was going to telephone the judge's chambers about rescheduling the hearing.
☐ **B.** Yes, because she spoke directly to the judge rather than to his clerk.
☐ **C.** No, because it was not her fault that the judge picked up the telephone.
☐ **D.** No, because she only discussed a procedural issue with the judge.

Question 10i.
Winthrop, a judge, and his brother Leonard, a lawyer, have both been members, for many years, of the exclusive and private Antelope Club, one of the most prestigious clubs in their city. The club includes some lawyers and judges but it is not a club only for lawyers; its membership also includes business leaders, journalists, educators and others. The club has no openly gay members, and it recently voted that openly gay individuals are not eligible for membership. The club provides a social setting for meals, relaxation, golf and tennis. Neither Winthrop nor Leonard engage in any judicial or legal activities at the club. Who, if anyone, must resign from membership?

☐ **A.** Only Winthrop
☐ **B.** Only Leonard
☐ **C.** Both Winthrop and Leonard
☐ **D.** Neither Winthrop nor Leonard

11. LAWYERS' DUTIES TO COURTS

Question 11a.

Attorney Ria represents criminal defendant Carl, who is charged with armed robbery. Carl is in jail pending his trial. During a meeting at the prison, Carl tells Ria that on the night of the alleged robbery, he was at a hockey game with his girlfriend. When Ria returns to her office, she does an Internet search and finds out that the hockey game actually took place on the night before the robbery, not the night of the robbery. Ria tells Carl this information during their next meeting, and Carl tells her he was mistaken. He says he went to the hockey game the night before the robbery, and on the night of the robbery, he was having dinner with his mother an hour away from where the robbery took place. Ria reasonably thinks that Carl probably is lying about the dinner with his mother. Without first counseling Carl to tell the truth, she refuses to allow Carl to testify about the dinner at his trial. Is her refusal proper?

☐ **A.** Yes, because her belief that Carl is lying is reasonable.
☐ **B.** Yes, because she believes that Carl is lying, and the reasonableness of her belief is not relevant.
☐ **C.** No, because she was required first to counsel Carl that he should tell the truth in court, and she could only refuse to allow him to testify that he was at dinner with his mother if he persisted in doing so after this caution.
☐ **D.** No, because she does not know for sure that Carl is lying.

Question 11b.

Attorney Kristin is a state prosecutor, and she is prosecuting Oliver Burson for the murder of his ex-wife. Before the trial begins, a reporter asks to interview Kristin for a television report. Which of the following statements would Kristin be well-advised NOT to make during the interview?

☐ **A.** "We are investigating the murder of Oliver Burson's ex-wife, Nina Richards."
☐ **B.** "Oliver Burson, who murdered his ex-wife, will be prosecuted to the fullest extent of the law."
☐ **C.** "Oliver Burson lives at 530 Orange Street."
☐ **D.** "Oliver Burson was arrested on January 22nd."

Question 11c.

Attorney Tito is a sole practitioner. He represents Laura, a criminal defendant charged with stealing a diamond necklace from Matteo. Matteo and Laura went on a few dates and then the relationship went sour. Laura claims that Matteo gave her the necklace on their second date. On the day of the jury trial, in the elevator on the way to the courtroom, Tito overhears Matteo telling his friend that he gave Laura the necklace, and that the only way he could get it back was to claim that she stole it. Tito has been preparing for the trial for weeks. Tito plans to continue to represent Laura and testify in the trial as to what he heard. He has a co-counsel who could take over the trial while Tito is testifying, but Tito is much better prepared and more experienced. The transfer of primary responsibility for the trial to another lawyer would work substantial hardship on Laura. May Tito continue to represent Laura and testify in the trial?

- ☐ **A.** Yes, because Tito's testimony relates to an uncontested issue.
- ☐ **B.** Yes, because his disqualification would impose a substantial hardship on Laura.
- ☐ **C.** No, because a lawyer may not serve in the same trial as both advocate and witness.
- ☐ **D.** No, because a lawyer may not act in a trial as both an advocate and a witness unless a judge rules that such testimony is necessary to avoid a substantial hardship on a party.

Question 11d.

Angus hired Vojtech to file a lawsuit against Linkbook, a major social media outlet. He claimed that when Byron, the founder of the company, was just starting Linkbook, Angus made a small personal investment in the company ($1,000) and that in exchange for his investment, Byron promised that would receive 20 percent of the earnings of Linkbook. After Vojtech did some investigation, he obtained indisputable factual evidence that Angus' claim was entirely fraudulent. Angus then admitted to Vojtech that his claim was baseless but asked Vojtech to press the claim anyway, because he thought that Linkbook would pay him something just to end the lawsuit. Vojtech declined to file the lawsuit and withdrew from representing Angus. Angus then hired a new lawyer, who filed a lawsuit against Byron and Linkbook. Vojtech has not informed either the lawyer who is now handling the suit or the judge who will try the case about Angus's fraudulent claim, and he will not do so even if Angus gets a handsome settlement. Is he subject to discipline?

- ☐ **A.** Yes, because a lawyer may not assist a client or a former client to commit a crime or fraud.
- ☐ **B.** Yes, because Angus's fraudulent conduct is related to a judicial proceeding.
- ☐ **C.** No, because Vojtech is obliged to protect Angus's confidences.
- ☐ **D.** No, because Angus' fraud is not reasonably certain to cause substantial injury to the defendants' property.

Question 11e.

Athena practices law in a city of medium size. She specializes in trusts and estates and in elder law. For many years, Athena lived next door to Meredith, an elderly widow. Meredith lived with her middle-aged daughter Dora, but spent most of her time with her boyfriend, Sven. Athena did not do any legal work for Meredith, though she got to know her well. At Meredith's request, a year ago Athena acted as one of two subscribing witnesses to Meredith's most recent will. This new will replaced an earlier will which had left everything to Dora. The new will left $500,000 to Dora, $1,000,000 to Sven, and the rest of Meredith's multi-million-dollar estate to charity. Meredith named her cousin Ernest as her executor. The other witness to the new will died in February.

Meredith died last week. Dora has announced that she plans to contest the will on the ground that Meredith was incompetent when she executed the will. Athena probably will be required to testify in the probate proceeding on the subject of Meredith's competency at the time she signed the will. Ernest, the executor, has asked Athena to represent him and defend the will in the probate proceeding. Athena has never before represented Dora, Sven, or Ernest.

Athena wants to represent Ernest in probating the will, and also to testify truthfully that she knew Meredith well and that Meredith appeared to her to be competent. Is her proposed conduct proper?

- ☐ **A.** Yes, because she plans to tell the truth.
- ☐ **B.** Yes, because she does not represent and has never represented any of the heirs.
- ☐ **C.** Yes, because her testimony would support her client's position, so she would not have a conflict with her own client.
- ☐ **D.** No, because she is a necessary witness on a contested issue.

Question 11f.

Attorney Mort represents Julio, who was injured in an automobile accident caused by Yvonne. Julio has back pain and frequent, severe headaches. Julio is suing Yvonne and will soon have his deposition taken. When Mort interviewed Julio and asked him how frequently he had severe headaches, Julio said, "I don't have them every day, and sometimes they aren't so bad. But about four days a week, I wake up with a severe headache." Mort told Julio that minimizing the frequency of his head pain would weaken his case. Julio asked Mort what he should say. Mort said, "Well you don't have to say, unless you are asked, that you don't have headaches every day, or that they aren't so bad." Julio said, "So, what should I say?" Mort said, "I understand that you wake up most mornings with severe headaches? Isn't that right?" Julio said, "That's right." Mort said, "When I ask you about your headaches, you can say: 'Most mornings, I wake up with severe headaches.' "

Julio testified in the deposition that he woke up most days with severe headaches, and he was not asked more questions about this subject. The case was settled shortly thereafter. However, Julio got into a dispute with Mort about the calculations of Mort's fee, and Julio filed a bar complaint against Mort. During the investigation by the bar counsel's office, Julio described how Mort had coached him to testify regarding his headaches. Is Mort subject to discipline for his conduct regarding Julio's testimony?

- ☐ **A.** Yes, because he advised Julio not to use words that would minimize the frequency of his head pain.
- ☐ **B.** Yes, because he told Julio exactly what to say, which was different from what Julio would have said if he had not been coached.
- ☐ **C.** No, because Mort's coaching was only in connection with a deposition, not a trial.
- ☐ **D.** No, because he did not tell Julio to lie.

Question 11g.

Libby, a lawyer, represents Lawncare Enterprises, the defendant in a negligence case. Lawncare Enterprises manufactures power lawn mowers. Pierre, the plaintiff, had purchased a Model LC-15 Lawncare mower. One day when Pierre was operating the mower, the mower hit a small stone, which flew up and hit Pierre's left eye, blinding that eye permanently. Pierre claims that Lawncare knew or should have known that the protective shield on the mower he used was too short to prevent an accident of this type. During preparation for trial, Libby asked Ira, Lawncare's chief of customer relations, whether his department had received other complaints of stones or other small objects being thrown up during use of the Model LC-15. Ira said that the department had received more than two dozen such complaints, about half of which had involved minor injuries, but no serious injuries.

During the trial, Ira was asked on cross-examination whether his department had received any prior complaints of injuries resulting from the use of the Model LC-15. Ira replied that there had been two or three complaints of scratches from debris kicked up by the mower, but none of those were serious, and none of those incidents had resulted in litigation. Libby observed this testimony by Ira without betraying, through her expressions or otherwise, that it was inconsistent with what Ira had told her earlier about the number of injuries that had been reported.

A jury ruled in favor of Lawncare, and Pierre appealed. While she is working on the appeal, Libby visits the Lawncare factory and runs into Ira. She asks him why he had told her that about half of the two dozen complaints about the LC-15 resulted in injuries but then testified that there had been only two or three complaints of scratches. Ira replies that Lawncare's general counsel had advised him to testify truthfully but to try to minimize how much Lawncare knew about prior injuries caused by the product. He added that he had been careful to say that there had been two or three complaints of scratches, without saying that those had been the *only* complaints of injuries.

What if anything should Libby do as a result of this disclosure?

☐ **A.** Nothing, because misleading testimony by a witness is not perjury unless that witness has made a literally false statement.

☐ **B.** Nothing, because the trial is over.

☐ **C.** Contact senior management officials at Lawncare and advise them to inform the trial judge that Ira's statement at the trial was not true – but do nothing further if they choose not to so inform the judge.

☐ **D.** Contact senior management officials at Lawncare and advise them that if they do not inform the trial judge that Ira's statement at the trial was not true, she will be obligated to do so.

Question 11h.

Percy is a lawyer who is the Attorney General of a state in which abortion is legal. He is well known for his opposition to abortion and his advocacy for outlawing it. Dr. Amanda Belknap performed an abortion on a 10-year-old girl who had become pregnant. As she always did after performing an abortion, and as required by law, she reported the abortion to the State Medical Board. When the case attracted publicity, including angry protests from anti-abortion activists who wanted to make abortion illegal, Percy opened an investigation into Dr. Belknap's conduct, sent a letter to the Medical Board asking it to find out whether Dr. Belknap had reported every abortion she had conducted, and immediately went on television to discuss the matter. The host of the show said that "Dr. Belknap has a history of failing to report abortions." Percy said that he was disgusted by people like Dr. Belknap, "an abortion activist acting as a doctor, with a history of failing to report." He said that his office was investigating her medical license and that he would be filing a formal complaint with the Medical Board. He filed such a complaint a few days later. Is Percy subject to discipline?

- ☐ **A.** Yes, because he violated a Rule of Professional Conduct.
- ☐ **B.** Yes, because although he did not violate a Rule of Professional Conduct, he committed defamation of Dr. Belknap.
- ☐ **C.** No, because as the Attorney General of his state, he is immune from being charged with ethical misconduct.
- ☐ **D.** No, because he had a First Amendment right to discuss the Belknap case on television.

12. LAWYERS' DUTIES TO ADVERSARIES AND THIRD PARTIES

Question 12a.

Maude, a lawyer, was retained by Anya, who lives in an assisted-living building for elderly persons. Anya noticed that many residents of the building were contracting respiratory infections. Anya has noticed that the ceiling tiles by some of the air vents in her apartment have turned black, an indicator of mold in the HVAC system. She suspected that Warner Management, Inc., which was running the building, was cutting costs, and had not been servicing the air conditioning and heating systems often enough. Regular servicing and changing the filters quarterly is necessary to maintain clean indoor air.

Maude wants to question Xavier, the Warner employee who services the heating and air conditioning systems and changes the filters at Anya's building. Under the substantive law of the jurisdiction, if Xavier reveals that he failed to service the system or change the filters regularly, Warner Management could be liable for his negligence on the theory of *respondeat superior*. Maude knows that Warner is represented by attorney Peter in all matters related to Anya's building. Maude is planning to tell Xavier that she represents Anya but is not planning to tell him that he has a right to consult with counsel of his choice. Also, she does not plan to ask Peter's permission to question Xavier, or even to notify Peter that she is interviewing him. May she question Xavier without getting Peter's permission?

- ☐ **A.** Yes, because a lawyer may always interview the employee of a corporation that is an adversary of her client.
- ☐ **B.** Yes, because Xavier is not an officer or director of Warner or a member of Warner's management group.
- ☐ **C.** No, because while Anya should notify Peter before interviewing Xavier, she does not need his permission to conduct the interview.
- ☐ **D.** No, because his failure to change the filters often enough could be imputed to the organization for the purpose of civil liability.

Question 12b.

The Packard Management Company manages an apartment building in which Manuel is a tenant. Tom, a lawyer, handles all legal matters for Packard. Manuel has not paid his rent for three months. Packard wants to evict him. Manuel has called Packard several times to complain about minor deficiencies in the building's services but has never asserted that he was declining to pay rent because of the inadequate services. Packard's policy directs Tom to make one effort to negotiate with a non-paying tenant for full payment within 30 days before commencing eviction proceedings.

Tom's friend Ivan is Manuel's boss at Ecosystem, Inc. Ivan told Tom last week that Manuel has hired a lawyer named Serena to sue Ecosystem for race discrimination. Ecosystem has no connection to Packard.

When Tom calls Manuel, he is planning to identify himself as a lawyer for Packard at the beginning of the call, but he is not planning to ask Manuel whether he is being represented by counsel with respect to his tenancy, or to advise Manuel that he has a right not to speak to Tom or to be represented by a lawyer in connection with the threatened eviction. After identifying himself, Tom is planning to ask why Manuel hasn't paid his rent and then to negotiate for prompt payment. May Tom have this conversation with Manuel?

☐ **A.** Yes, because no rule of professional conduct imposes restrictions on conversations between lawyers and unrepresented persons before proceedings have been initiated.
☐ **B.** Yes, because Tom does not know that Serena is representing Manuel in his dealings with Packard.
☐ **C.** No, because Tom knows that Manuel has a lawyer, Serena.
☐ **D.** No, because Tom is not planning to ask Manuel whether he has a lawyer with respect to his tenancy, or to advise Manuel that he has a right not to speak to Tom or to be represented by a lawyer.

Question 12c.

Sam, a lawyer, represents Alan Pauly, a tall man who is in jail facing assault charges stemming from a fight in a bar with a short man, Don. Sam is investigating the facts. The police report mentions no witnesses other than the victim. The bartender did not see the fight but tells Sam that Toby was in the bar that Saturday night. Sam goes to Toby's house. He knocks on the door. Toby answers. After Sam confirms that the man who answered the door is Toby, the conversation goes like this:

Sam: I am a lawyer for Alan Pauly, and I am investigating the fight at Harry's Bar two weeks ago this Saturday. I understand that you were there that night.
Toby: That's right. It was really awful.
Sam: Is a lawyer representing you in connection with this matter?
Toby: No, I was not involved in the fight.
Sam: Could you tell me what happened?
Toby: There were these two guys. They had been drinking a lot. Then they started arguing. One was tall and the other was short.
Sam: Where were they and where were you?
Toby: They were at a table. I was on the barstool nearest to them.
Sam: Could you hear what they were saying?
Toby: I might have, but I can't remember. But I remember the fistfight well enough. I saw that pretty clearly.
Sam: Have you talked to anyone else about this?
Toby: No, I thought about going down to your station, but I didn't want to get involved with police.

Sam wants to ask Toby who threw the first punch, the tall man or the short one. Would he be subject to discipline if that is the next thing he does?

☐ **A.** Yes, because he must first advise Toby that he may seek independent legal advice.
☐ **B.** Yes, because he must first make a reasonable effort to correct Toby's confusion about his role.
☐ **C.** No, because Toby is a witness, not a potential party, and does not have interests that are adverse to those of Alan.
☐ **D.** No, because Sam has identified himself as a lawyer for Alan.

Question 12d.

Tomas, an attorney, represented the IWT Corporation, which fired a woman named Celinda. IWT claims that Celinda's written work was sloppy; Celinda claimed that IWT simply wanted to give the job to a younger person. She wanted her job back or a substantial cash settlement. Pursuant to a clause in Celinda's employment contract, her dispute had to be resolved through arbitration. While the arbitration proceeding was pending, IWT's general counsel read the emails that Celinda had sent to her lawyer through the company's email system, from the time that Celinda received notice that she was being fired until a month later, when she actually departed. IWT's 250-page office handbook, a copy of which was given to Celinda two years ago, says on page 138 that the e-mail system belongs to the company and that information sent over the system may be read or disclosed by company officials. One of Celinda's e-mails said, "I know that my work isn't as good as it used to be, and that I have been making a lot of mistakes this year. So maybe they do have good reason to fire me after all." IWT's general counsel sent a copy of this e-mail to Tomas. Tomas did not tell Celinda's lawyer that he had a copy of the email, planning to use it to surprise her during the arbitration proceeding. Is Tomas subject to discipline?

☐ **A.** Yes, because this document consisted of electronically stored information relating to the representation and he therefore had a duty to notify Celinda, the sender, or her attorney.
☐ **B.** Yes, because Celinda's communications with her lawyer were privileged.
☐ **C.** No, because no ethics rule requires this disclosure, even if litigation or arbitration is pending.
☐ **D.** No, because the matter is in arbitration, and the disclosure would be required if litigation were pending.

Question 12e.

Bobby, a former employee of Talmart, Inc., has retained Ashley to bring an employment discrimination action against Talmart, claiming that his firing last year was unlawful discrimination on the basis of religion. Ashley is investigating the matter but has not yet initiated a suit. Ashley wants to interview Chi, a former Talmart employee who left the company two years ago. Chi was Talmart's Vice President for Human Resources; she was responsible for hiring, promotion, and discharge of employees.

Bobby told Ashley that he was fired after he complained about Talmart's policy prohibiting employees from wearing turbans while at work. Bobby says his Sikh faith requires him to wear a turban.

Ashley wants to contact Chi, and ask questions about Talmart's turban policy, without first informing Ned, the lawyer who Ashley knows represents Talmart in all employment-related litigation. Assuming that Ashley would identify herself to Chi as Bobby's lawyer, may she interview Chi without seeking permission from Talmart's lawyer?

☐ **A.** Yes, because Chi no longer works for Talmart.
☐ **B.** Yes, because Ashley has not yet initiated litigation, so Talmart is not a party to a suit by Bobby.
☐ **C.** No, because Ashley knows that Ned represents Talmart in all of its legal employment matters.
☐ **D.** No, because Chi was responsible for hiring and promotion at Talmart and therefore is a person whose admissions may be imputed to Talmart for purposes of civil liability.

Question 12f.

Donald was suspected of having robbed a liquor store. Shortly after he was arrested, he demanded to see his lawyer, Craig. The police did not attempt to question Donald, and Craig arranged for him to be released on bail at his arraignment, after Donald was read the charges filed against him and given a court date. Craig filed papers informing the court and the prosecutor's office that he would be representing Donald in the matter. Brenda, a prosecutor, was assigned responsibility for Donald's case. A state statute authorizes prosecutors to investigate criminal cases by questioning witnesses or authorizing police officials to do so up to the point at which charges are filed. Brenda visited Donald's home a week after he was released, identified herself as the prosecutor in the case, and asked if she might ask him some questions. Donald said he would answer her questions because he was innocent of the charges and therefore had nothing to hide. Brenda did not make any false or misleading statements to Donald. On the basis of information from his answers, Brenda was able to contact and interview other witnesses. She did not offer into evidence any information that she received from Donald. Is Brenda subject to discipline?

- ☐ **A.** Yes, because she did not first obtain Craig's consent to talk to Donald.
- ☐ **B.** Yes, because she did not first notify Donald of his right to have counsel present at the interview.
- ☐ **C.** No, because she did not make any misleading statements to Donald.
- ☐ **D.** No, because prosecutors are authorized by law to interview defendants.

Question 12g.

Five years ago, Tammy was murdered at night while alone in her home. Her boyfriend Ray, with whom she had been quarreling, was accused of the crime. At first he claimed innocence and said she must have been killed by an intruding stranger. Initially, he declined the opportunity to consult a lawyer. After 12 hours of police questioning, he confessed to the crime. Subsequently, he retained Ming, a lawyer. Ray was convicted, largely on the basis of his confession, and was sentenced to 40 years in prison. Ray is now in prison.

Daniel, a prosecutor in the county where Ray was tried, recently negotiated a plea bargain with the attorney for Burt, another man who was alleged to have committed several murders. Burt agreed to plead guilty to manslaughter and to receive a life sentence to avoid being charged with a capital offense. Part of the deal is that he would provide Daniel with details on his other crimes. During those discussions, Burt revealed that he had robbed and killed Tammy. He had dated her a year earlier, but she had rejected him in favor of Ray. Burt consents to provide a sample of his blood, which matches the blood that was found in Tammy's house the day after the murder. Ray's blood had not been found in the house. What if anything must Daniel do?

- ☐ **A.** Nothing, because Ray confessed, so he would have been convicted anyway.
- ☐ **B.** Promptly disclose this new evidence of Ray's innocence to Ming (unless a judge orders a delay in disclosure), but not to the court or chief prosecutor.
- ☐ **C.** Promptly disclose this evidence to Ming (unless a judge orders a delay in disclosure), and also disclose the new evidence to a court or to the chief prosecutor.
- ☐ **D.** Make a motion to the court to reopen Ray's case.

Question 12h.

Herman was mugged in a dark alley, and his wallet, which contained $200 in $20 bills, was stolen. Moments after the assailant fled with his money, Herman spotted a police officer and reported the crime. Herman described the assailant as a male who had dark hair, was of medium height, and wore a dark colored shirt and white sneakers. He said the assailant had showed him a knife. The officer alerted other officers in the vicinity by radio. An officer arrested John three blocks away. John has dark hair and is of medium height. He was wearing a dark blue shirt and white sneakers. When searched, he was found to have $454 in cash in his pocket, including eight twenty dollar bills. He was not in possession of a knife. When arrested, John acted suspiciously and refused to answer any questions. He has not confessed. Herman's wallet was never found, and no knife was found in the vicinity. The case was assigned to Marcella, a prosecutor. Marcella investigates but discovers no additional facts. She believes that John is guilty, though she doubts that a jury would find him guilty beyond a reasonable doubt. In fact, she is uncertain whether the charge is even supported by probable cause. Is it proper for Marcella to charge John with robbery?

☐ **A.** Yes, because she believes that John is guilty.
☐ **B.** Yes, because she does not know that the charge is not supported by probable cause.
☐ **C.** No, because she doubts that a jury would convict him.
☐ **D.** No, if she thinks that he is not guilty beyond a reasonable doubt.

Question 12i.

Attorney Lilith represents Opal in a custody case against Opal's ex-husband, Claude. Lilith knows that Claude is represented by another lawyer, Oscar. Claude enters Lilith's office one day and tells her that he wants to speak with her about Opal's treatment of their children. Lilith says, "As you know, Oscar represents you in this matter." Claude says, "I know that, but I want to talk to you anyway." May Lilith allow Claude to continue?

☐ **A.** Yes, because she did not initiate the conversation; Claude did.
☐ **B.** Yes, because she has obtained Claude's oral consent after reminding him that he was represented by Oscar.
☐ **C.** No, because she did not obtain Claude's written consent.
☐ **D.** No, because she does not have consent from Claude's lawyer.

Question 12j.

Yvonne was seriously injured in a parking lot accident at the Woodbridge Supermarket, when a Woodbridge delivery truck, driven by a Woodbridge employee, rammed her car. The Woodbridge driver claimed, at the time, that Yvonne drove right in front of him and that the accident was her fault. Yvonne hired Kate, a lawyer, to sue the Supermarket. Kate has learned that Nora, a cashier employed by Woodbridge, witnessed the accident because she was standing outside the store during a ten-minute work break. Nora has no responsibility for driving delivery trucks or maintaining the parking lot. Kate wants to interview Nora, but she suspects that Woodbridge's lawyers (if asked) would decline permission for her to conduct this interview and would insist that she initiate formal discovery. Kate does not want to incur the expense of discovery without having an idea of what Nora would say. Kate is not planning to give Woodbridge's lawyers any prior notice that she is interviewing Nora, much less ask their permission, and she is not planning to advise Nora that she has a right to consult either Woodbridge's lawyers or a lawyer of her own choosing before talking to Kate. May Kate interview Nora, away from Woodbridge's premises, under these conditions?

☐ **A.** Yes, because Nora is not a managerial employee of Woodbridge and has no responsibility for driving delivery trucks or maintaining the parking lot.

- ☐ **B.** No, because she must first give Woodbridge's lawyers enough advance notice that they could seek a court order preventing the interview.
- ☐ **C.** No, because before interviewing Nora she must advise Nora that she has a right to consult Woodbridge's lawyers.
- ☐ **D.** No, because before interviewing Nora, she must advise Nora that she has a right to consult with a lawyer of her own choosing.

Question 12k.

Which one of the following statements is correct?

- ☐ **A.** American lawyers must comply with ABA Model Rules of Professional Conduct or face discipline.
- ☐ **B.** No judicial conduct code binds the justices of the United States Supreme Court.
- ☐ **C.** The Restatement of the Law Governing Lawyers provides a synthesis only of the state ethics codes and the case law interpreting those rules.
- ☐ **D.** A state ethics code may not impose requirements on lawyers employed by the federal government that conflict with duties imposed by federal agency regulations.

Question 12l.

Hussain, a lawyer, represents Surety, Inc., an automobile insurance company that insures rental car companies. Lee was seriously injured when the brakes on his rental car failed. Through his lawyer, Esther, Lee sued the rental car company, and pursuant to his agreement with Surety, Hussain represented the defendant in the lawsuit. Surety's investigation revealed that the brakes were faulty and the rental car company is therefore liable. Hussain knew that Esther had not done her own forensic investigation of the brakes. Surety authorized Hussain to offer Lee up to $500,000 to settle the suit. When Esther and Hussain met to explore whether a negotiated settlement was possible, Esther said her client was willing to accept a settlement of $400,000. Hussain said, "I know that my client won't pay a penny more than $300,000." Is Hussain subject to discipline for lying to Esther?

- ☐ **A.** Yes, because a lawyer may not make a false statement of material fact to a third person.
- ☐ **B.** Yes, because lawyers may not make false statements about how much a client is willing to offer in settlement.
- ☐ **C.** No, because lawyers are permitted to make false statements to other lawyers, provided that the statements are not made under oath or in the course of a proceeding.
- ☐ **D.** No, because lawyers are allowed to make false statements about a client's intentions regarding an acceptable settlement.

13. THE CHANGING LANDSCAPE OF LAW PRACTICE

Question 13a.

Assume that the lawyer's primary motive for each of the following is to earn money. Which one is prohibited by the Model Rules?

☐ **A.** A lawyer sees a post on Facebook from Pauline, whom he has never met, complaining that she had just discovered that she was a victim of identity theft. In a reply on Facebook to her post, the lawyer offers to represent Pauline in a civil suit for $150 per hour.

☐ **B.** After a lawyer learns that one of her former clients was the victim of medical malpractice, the lawyer visits the former client's home to tell him that she will represent him in a civil suit against the hospital and doctor for a one-third contingent fee.

☐ **C.** A lawyer is walking on the beach during a summer evening. He sees a drunk man throw his girlfriend against the wall, causing her to lose consciousness briefly. The boyfriend leaves the scene. When the woman comes to, the lawyer gives her his card and offers to represent her in a suit against the man on a contingent fee basis.

☐ **D.** Two days after a major gasoline company negligently causes an oil spill that results in severe property damage to several beachfront homes, a lawyer sends the owners of those homes a letter offering to represent them in a suit against the gas company. The letter states that he would charge them $250 per hour for his services.

Question 13b.

Attorney Betsy has more clients than she can handle and wants to expand her law firm. She would like to hire two associates but does not have enough capital to do so. Banks will not loan her enough money to pay the associates for the year or so until their fees would cover their own costs. But Betsy's father Roberto, who is a successful investment banker and not a lawyer, would like to provide Betsy with one million dollars to help her expand her business. In return, Roberto would become a limited partner of Betsy, entitled to receive two percent of all of the gross profits of the firm for as long as it exists. Betsy would like to enter into this agreement with Roberto. She and Roberto agree that Roberto will never try to influence Betsy's judgment in rendering legal services. May Betsy enter into this agreement?

☐ **A.** Yes, because Roberto is a member of Betsy's nuclear family.

☐ **B.** Yes, because Betsy will not permit Roberto to influence her professional judgment in providing legal services.

☐ **C.** No, because Roberto will be only a limited partner, rather than a general partner, and therefore not fully responsible for any liabilities of the partnership.

☐ **D.** No, because Betsy may not enter into this arrangement even though Roberto would never try to influence Betsy's professional judgment.

Question 13c.

Esteban, a lawyer in State A with a general practice, regularly represents and advises Patrick who lives just a few miles away in State B. Patrick owns and operates a hunting supply store in State A. For years, Esteban has advised him about employment and tax issues related to his business. Patrick has amassed enough capital to start a second business, a wilderness tour company, and he decided to locate this enterprise near his home in State B. He asked Esteban if he would meet with him once at the new office to advise him on State B tax and real estate law to assist him in launching the new business. Esteban has the knowledge to provide competent legal advice to Patrick on these issues even though he is not a member of the bar of State B. He would not charge Patrick fees that were higher than those permitted by State B. Esteban has not mentioned to Patrick that he is not licensed in State B; it did not cross his mind. Would Esteban be subject to discipline if he provides legal advice to Patrick as Patrick requests?

☐ **A.** Yes, because he has not disclosed to Patrick that he is not licensed to practice law in State B.
☐ **B.** Yes, because he is not licensed to practice law in State B.
☐ **C.** No, because the advice arises out of Esteban's practice in State A.
☐ **D.** No, because Esteban is licensed to practice law and could competently provide the advice.

Question 13d.
Ian, a lawyer, is trying to build up his client base. He frequently reads in his local newspaper about automobile accidents in which pedestrians are injured. He would like to visit the victims, either at hospitals or their homes, within a few days after the accidents, before insurance adjusters contact those potential plaintiffs and persuade them to sign settlements in which they receive only small amounts of compensation. He would represent these clients on a contingent-fee basis. Ian knows that the ethics code imposes some restrictions on solicitation, but he thinks he has a right to reach out to these victims before the insurance adjusters get to them. Assuming that none of the victims are people known to Ian or his partners, and that none of them are lawyers, may Ian visit the victims as he desires?

☐ **A.** Yes, because the U.S. Constitution protects his right to free speech and association.
☐ **B.** Yes, because the insurance adjusters are allowed to contact the victims.
☐ **C.** No, because Ian is pursuing this work to acquire fee-generating cases.
☐ **D.** No, because if he wants to challenge the validity of any ethics rule, he may only petition the court that issued it or bring an affirmative lawsuit to challenge the rule.

Question 13e.
Margery owns and manages a successful law practice. Her specialty is representing plaintiffs in employment discrimination cases alleging gender discrimination. Recently, she has gotten referrals of a substantial number of cases involving people who have suffered sexual harassment or sexual assault in the workplace. At the end of every calendar year, Margery directs her office manager to send a $50 bottle of champagne to every individual who referred a new client to her practice that year to thank them for sending clients her way. The recipients include other lawyers, clients, former clients, and friends, relatives, or any others who have referred matters to her.

Giles, an estate planning lawyer, referred a prospective client to Margery whom she represented in an administrative matter. Giles, who does not drink alcohol, received a bottle of champagne from Margery. Giles files a complaint against Margery with the local bar counsel for giving gifts to get business. Is Margery subject to discipline?

☐ **A.** Yes, because a lawyer may not give an inducement to another person to refer a case to the lawyer.

☐ **B.** Yes, because the recipient of a bottle of champagne might perceive it as compensation for the referral.
☐ **C.** No, because a $50 bottle of champagne is not greater in value than a token item that might be given for the holidays or for other ordinary social hospitality.
☐ D. No, because a lawyer may give any tangible thank-you gift to another lawyer who refers a matter as a professional courtesy.

Question 13f.
Attorney Suzette is a solo practitioner in a small town. She specializes in medical malpractice cases and has handled hundreds of such cases over the past two decades. Suzette's friend Gunter hosts a local radio program, and he offers Suzette a 15-second advertising spot in his program. Suzette's ad reads, in its entirety: "Have you or has someone you know been hurt by a doctor's negligence? Attorney Suzette Bellows can help. Bellows specializes in medical malpractice cases. Call (555) DOC-HELP now for a free consultation." Gunter plays a recording of the ad on the radio. Is Suzette subject to discipline?

☐ **A.** Yes, because the ad states that she specializes in medical malpractice claims.
☐ **B.** Yes, because the ad did not contain her office address.
☐ **C.** No, because any regulation of lawyer advertising violates the First Amendment.
☐ **D.** No, because everything in the ad is truthful.

Question 13g.
Samir practices family law. His clients often have problems that might better be addressed by a marital counselor, who might be able to help a divorcing couple to reconcile or to separate more amicably. He wants to form a partnership with his cousin Veena, a licensed social worker. They would share a suite of offices, and a client could receive services from either or both of them, as the client preferred. Samir and Veena want to share the fees earned by either of them, in proportion to the work done by each. Samir will take steps to ensure that Veena complies with the Rules of Professional Conduct. Veena will not direct or regulate Samir's professional judgment in rendering legal services, and all clients will be informed that only Samir is licensed to practice law. However, Samir does not plan to seek each client's written consent to receive legal services from a partnership that includes a social worker who is not also a lawyer. May they create this partnership?

☐ **A.** Yes, because Samir will take steps to ensure that Veena complies with the Rules of Professional Conduct.
☐ **B.** Yes, because the fees will be shared in proportion to the work done by each.
☐ **C.** No, because Samir does not plan to seek written consent from his clients to be served by a partnership that includes a non-lawyer.
☐ **D.** No, because the partnership would be prohibited in any event.

14. ACCESS TO JUSTICE: THE LAWYER'S ROLE

Question 14a.

Duncan, an attorney, would like to meet the pro bono standard in the rules. However, he is extremely busy and barely earning enough in fees from his paying clients to pay his bills and feed his family. Some of his clients earn only the minimum wage and their family incomes put them below the federal poverty level. If all Duncan does to provide pro bono services is to devote 40 hours of legal services per year to such clients at a 50 percent discount from his usual fee, would he be subject to discipline?

☐ **A.** Yes, because he should provide most of his hours of "pro bono" service without charging any fee.
☐ **B.** Yes, because clients who are employed at the minimum wage are not indigent.
☐ **C.** No, because despite earning barely enough to pay his bills, he discounts his bills for clients whose family incomes are below the poverty level.
☐ **D.** No, because lawyers are not disciplined for providing few pro bono services, or even no such services.

Question 14b.

Troy goes to see Samantha, an attorney, to see if she can help him with a legal problem. Troy worked as a salesperson for three years for Glory Vacations, Inc., which sells vacation timeshares. Heidi, one of Glory's customers, has sued both Glory and Troy for $50,000, alleging that Troy made fraudulent statements while selling her some timeshare property. Upon receiving the summons, Glory fired Troy and cross-claimed against Troy, claiming that any fraud was unauthorized and is Troy's fault. Troy says he is being scapegoated and never made any false statements.

Troy wants Samantha to represent him. He is now unemployed and has very little money. Samantha cannot afford to accept him as a pro bono client. Troy says that he has been turned down by several other lawyers because of his financial situation. He owns a house, so the local legal services office will not represent him. Without representation, Troy, whose formal education ended after high school, will be unable to defend himself effectively. He asks Samantha whether he has a due process right to have the court appoint a lawyer to represent him without charge.

What should Samantha say?

☐ **A.** "Yes, because you are an indigent defendant."
☐ **B.** "Yes, because you can't afford a lawyer."
☐ **C.** "No, unless you sell your house and invest the proceeds, and your income remains below the federal poverty level."
☐ **D.** "No, even if your house is repossessed and you become totally indigent."

Question 14c.

Julie works for a federal government agency. Agency regulations prohibit lawyers employed by the agency from representing individual clients. Julie wants to fulfill the aspirational requirements of pro bono service as stated in Rule 6.1. May she fulfill the Rule's aspirational requirements without quitting her job?

☐ **A.** Yes, by contributing a significant amount of money to the Environmental Law Awareness Council, a statewide organization that publishes newspaper columns and podcasts to explain the rights of members of the public to clean water and clean air, as well as how to sue polluters.

☐ **B.** Yes, by serving on a bar association committee that makes recommendations for law reform.

☐ **C.** No, because in order to fulfill the aspirational requirements of Rule 6.1, lawyers must represent low-income clients without charging fees.

☐ **D.** No, because she cannot satisfy the aspirational requirements of Rule 6.1 without violating the agency's prohibition on representing individual clients.

Question 14d.

Mindy represents RenTV, which leases television sets by the month to people who do not have enough money to buy televisions. Some of its customers, represented by Ross, brought a class action against it for failure to comply with the federal Truth-in-Lending Act. That law provides that the lawyer for a prevailing plaintiff may recover attorney's fees from the defendant in addition to the judgment. RenTV is willing to pay $120,000 to the members of the class to settle the suit. But it does not want any of the settlement money to be paid to Ross, the plaintiff's attorney, because Mindy and RenTV believe that he will just use the money to bring more troublesome litigation against RenTV or other companies owned by RenTV's parent company. May Mindy condition the settlement offer on Ross's waiver of attorney fees?

☐ **A.** Yes, because if the plaintiff class accepts the offer and Ross receives no fee, that's Ross's problem, not Mindy's.

☐ **B.** No, because Mindy is receiving a fee from her client, RenTV.

☐ **C.** No, because the offer would create a conflict of interest between Ross and his clients.

☐ **D.** No, because the federal policy of encouraging enforcement of the Truth-in-Lending Act overrides the policy of allowing parties to settle on any terms on which they agree.

Question 14e.

Warren, a lawyer, represented Carrie, a state university student, in a lawsuit challenging her state's restrictive voter identification law. The retainer agreement specifies that Warren would not charge Carrie a fee but may keep, as his fee, any counsel fees that the court requires the state to pay.

A state law allows out-of-state students to vote, but it requires voters to supply photo identification. Pursuant to regulation, the state accepts many forms of picture identification, including passports, in-state driver's licenses, and gun licenses, but it does not accept out-of-state driver's licenses. Carrie only has an out-of-state driver's license. After Warren filed a civil rights suit in federal court on her behalf, the state changed its regulation to allow out-of-state driver's licenses to qualify as identification. The state attorney general explained to the press, "We didn't think that the court would sustain our regulation." Warren has signed an agreement with the state attorney general in which he agreed to withdraw the lawsuit and the attorney general agreed, on behalf of the state, to accept out-of-state driver's licenses as photo identification for purposes of voting for at least 25 years. Now Warren plans to request the court to award him counsel fees based on the time he spent researching the law and filing the suit.

Should he expect to obtain court-awarded fees?

☐ **A.** Yes, because the Civil Rights Attorney's Fees Act of 1976 (the Fees Act) permits federal judges to shift fees to prevailing parties in civil rights cases against state actors, and judges usually do so.

☐ **B.** No, because the settlement was not embodied in a court judgment.
☐ **C.** No, because the Supreme Court has held the Fees Act to be unconstitutional.
☐ **D.** No, because under the American Rule, each party pays his own attorney's fee.

Question 14f.

Amar, a lawyer, has earned an undergraduate degree, a social work degree, a law degree, and an LL.M. degree. He now owes $260,000 in federal student loans, the last of which he obtained in 2016. He takes a job at his county's legal aid office. He enjoys the work there and can imagine working there, or in similar public service employment, indefinitely. But his salary is only $42,000 a year before taxes. He can't afford to make his monthly student loan payments on a standard ten-year repayment plan, or even on an extended 30-year repayment plan. He has an offer from a small law firm that would pay $54,000 a year, but the work would involve a lot of drudgery and be much less interesting than his legal aid job. What is his best option?

☐ **A.** Default on his loans and hope that the federal government does not sue him.
☐ **B.** Declare bankruptcy and hope that his loans will be discharged through that process.
☐ **C.** Elect to make monthly payments through the federal income-based repayment plan, even though this option will cause the amount he owes to rise rapidly, because he won't be paying all the interest that accrues each month.
☐ **D.** Quit his job and accept employment at the small law firm.

Question 14g.

Pablo is a "notario," a non-lawyer who helps Spanish-speaking low-income undocumented immigrants with their immigration problems. He charges much less for legal advice than a lawyer would charge; in fact, his clients are so poor that they could not afford to pay any lawyer for the help that Pablo provides. He is committed to serving his community. One day, Pablo telephones Ann, an immigration lawyer he met at a party. Ann and Pablo are friendly because both of them serve truly indigent clients for no charge at all. Pablo says, "I've got a guy in my office, from Honduras, who wants to apply for asylum, but he has two misdemeanor convictions for possession of drug paraphernalia, for which he was sentenced, in each case, to a month in jail. He wants to know whether that is an absolute bar to getting asylum, in which case he would decide not to apply. What's the answer?" Ann has all the clients she wants at present and does not want to suggest that the man become her client. Which of the following responses is best?

☐ **A.** "It would not be an absolute bar, but it could affect an adjudicator's exercise of discretion, especially if he has been involved in any other misdeeds, such as domestic violence." (That answer would be a correct statement of the law.)
☐ **B.** "I would like to help you, but I can't, because it is improper to give legal advice to an undocumented foreign national."
☐ **C.** "I would like to help you, but I can't, because it is improper for me to assist a notario in providing legal advice."
☐ **D.** "It's really important that you serve this man competently, so I'll give you the answer, provided that you call me with any other legal questions that may arise. But let's be clear about this: I am not going to be his lawyer; he's your responsibility, not mine."

Answers to Multiple-Choice Practice Questions, With Explanations

1. The Legal Profession: Bar Admission, History and Diversity

Question 1a.

D is correct. Applicants must answer bar application questions fully and truthfully. Question 1 of the character and fitness questionnaire asks for information about conduct within the last five years that would call into question an applicant's fitness to practice. Henry's sudden run-up of debt and his absence from work, apparently caused by his disorder, could reflect on his fitness to practice law. The "thorough explanation" of the conduct required by question 1 would require disclosure of the diagnosis.

A is incorrect. Federal law does prohibit discrimination based on disability, but these questions are limited to asking whether the applicant has an impairment that would restrict his ability to practice or has engaged in conduct that raises a question about his ability to practice. The Department of Justice concluded in 2014 that some mental health questions previously used by bar examiners violate disability laws. But the National Conference of Bar Examiners (NCBE), which handles the character and fitness review for a majority of states, and the Department of Justice have agreed that the character and fitness questions stated above, which are currently used by the NCBE, do not violate the law.[1]

B and C are incorrect because the first of the two bar application questions asks about behavior within the last five years, not about a doctor's or patient's subjective beliefs regarding their impact. Therefore Henry must report the condition, even if he or his doctor believes that it will not impact his ability to practice.

Question 1b.

B is correct. Josh must reveal the incident and provide any requested details. Minor transgressions in the past are unlikely to derail a bar application but answering a question falsely on a bar application would violate Rule 8.1(a) and could lead to denial of admission or to discipline if the false statement is ever discovered.

A is incorrect. Although Josh must disclose the incident on his bar application, his obligation is not triggered by his prior dishonesty. He is obliged to disclose because the questionnaire asks for this information. The bar examiners do send a questionnaire to the law school each applicant attended, and this questionnaire might lead the law school to report that Josh reported no disciplinary infractions during college. Josh would be well-advised to reveal the incident to the law school, explaining that he now realized it should have been reported to the school when he applied.

C is incorrect. As is explained above, Rule 8.1 imposes a mandatory duty of candor on applicants for admission to the bar. While the other rules in the ethics codes are not binding on law students or on applicants for admission to the bar, Rule 8.1 is binding on applicants. Therefore, Josh does not have the discretion to decide not to disclose. His subjective judgment that the incident is not relevant to his fitness to practice provides no legitimate basis for non-disclosure. The character and fitness authorities have the responsibility to decide what information might be relevant to determine fitness to practice.

1. See Press Release, Settlement Agreement Between the United States and the Louisiana Supreme Court, https://www.justice.gov/opa/pr/department-justice-reaches-agreement-louisiana-supreme-court-protect-bar-candidates (accessed May 25, 2016) and National Conference of Bar Examiners, Request for Preparation of a Character Report, http://www.ncbex.org/dmsdocument/134 (accessed May 25, 2016).

D is incorrect. The intention of the college as expressed in the expungement of the record is not relevant here. The character and fitness review authorities often ask for criminal and other records that have been expunged. Expungement does not protect applicants from the obligation to answer questions fully and honestly.

Question 1c.

B is correct. Each state conducts a character and fitness evaluation as part of the bar application process, and the states have broad discretion to deny admission. There have been instances in which individuals were denied bar admission based on failure to pay loans.[2] These decisions are arguably misguided or unfair, but they are within the states' discretion.

A is incorrect. All lawyers must be financially responsible enough to be trusted with client matters, so Leta could be denied admission even if her intended area of practice was not directly related to finances.

C is incorrect. It is true that most law students take out loans to pay tuition, and it is arguably true that it is unfair to penalize them for doing so. Even so, a state *may* deny admission to Leta if it finds, based on these or other facts, that she is unfit to practice law, and an appellate court may sustain that decision.

D is incorrect for reasons similar to those articulated for C. It is true that every lawyer should aspire to provide pro bono service to clients who cannot afford to pay, and it is true that the profession generally applauds the efforts of those who do full-time service to indigents. Even so, these facts do not preclude a state from denying admission to Leta.

2. The Legal Profession: Regulation, Discipline, and Liability

Question 2a.

C is correct. The ethics codes in most states attain the force of law after they are adopted by the supreme court in each state. Federal courts also adopt ethics codes for lawyers admitted to practice before them. While most legislative rules are adopted by legislative bodies, the courts have traditionally had the principal responsibility for regulation of lawyers, so the ethics codes are adopted by courts.

A and D are incorrect. The "negative inherent powers" doctrine once asserted that the courts are the exclusive regulators of lawyers and that legislative bodies have no such authority. This doctrine has been used to strike down some legislation that sought to impose rules on American lawyers. However, this doctrine has long since been rendered obsolete. American lawyers are subject to all sorts of regulatory rules and statutes enacted or adopted by state and federal legislative and administrative bodies. While the courts retain the authority to regulate lawyers, it is incorrect to assert that they have the exclusive authority to do so.

B is incorrect. The ABA has enormous influence over the regulation of American lawyers, but it is a non-profit organization and has limited regulatory governmental authority. The ABA Model Rules of Professional Conduct do not have the force of law and are therefore not binding. Instead, they provide a model used in most states for guidance in drafting ethics codes.

2. *See In re Application of Griffin*, 942 N.E. 2d 1008 (Ohio 2010); see also Matter of Anonymous (New York 2009) (available at http://decisions.courts.state.ny.us/ad3/Decisions/2009/D-11-09Anonymous.pdf).

Question 2b.

C is correct. State bar associations draft and interpret ethical rules, investigate and prosecute lawyer misconduct and carry out other functions delegated by the highest courts of their states. The Section of Legal Education accredits law schools by virtue of authorization from the U.S. Department of Education.

D is incorrect because the American Law Institute is a non-profit organization that publishes restatements but has no legal authority.

Question 2c.

A is correct. Some states have an "integrated bar" in which, to be licensed, a lawyer must belong to the state bar association. Other states have voluntary state bar associations, and a lawyer may be licensed even if he or she does not join the state bar association.

B, C, and D are therefore incorrect.

Question 2d.

A is correct. Under Rule 8.4(b), Parnik can be disciplined if the bar authorities find that the stalking raises a question as to his fitness to practice law. Conviction on charges that he committed the act is not a prerequisite to discipline.

B is incorrect because any lawyer could be disciplined for stalking whether or not the lawyer served as a prosecutor.

C is incorrect because a lawyer can be disciplined for conduct that occurs outside the practice of law.

D is incorrect because a lawyer may be disciplined for conduct even if he was acquitted of charges related to the conduct. The acquittal just means that the charge was not proven beyond a reasonable doubt.

Question 2e.

B is correct. The pattern of neglect of and damage to client matters probably raises a substantial question as to Paige's fitness. When a lawyer knows of conduct that raises such a question, reporting the matter to the disciplinary authorities is mandatory.

A is incorrect, because Carrie would have a duty to report Paige's conduct even if Paige had no supervisory authority.

C is incorrect because Rule 8.3 does not condition the duty to report misconduct on the consent of the clients affected by the misconduct.

D is incorrect because lawyers are required to report misconduct of their partners that raises a substantial question as to those partners' fitness, and Paige's conduct can be reported without revealing client confidences.

Question 2f.

B is correct. Arthur is committing fraud, which violates Rule 8.4(c). The repeated dishonesty would raise a substantial question as to Arthur's honesty. Therefore, Rule 8.3(a) requires Grace to report Arthur's conduct to the appropriate professional authority. Comment 3 identifies the professional authority as the bar disciplinary agency.

The other answers are incorrect because reporting to the disciplinary authority is mandatory.

C is incorrect because the law firm may not exempt its lawyers from compliance with the duties imposed on each individual lawyer by the ethics code.

The statements in D may well be accurate, but the question asked about Grace's obligation under the rules.

Question 2g.

C is correct. Zarah is subject to discipline because Rule 5.1(c)(1) states that a lawyer shall be responsible for another lawyer's misconduct if the lawyer orders the actions. Charlie also is subject to discipline. Under Rule 5.2(b), a subordinate lawyer does not violate a rule if he acts in accordance with a supervisor's reasonable resolution of an arguable question of professional duty, but Zarah told Charlie to engage in unambiguously illegal conduct.

The other answers are therefore not correct.

Question 2h.

A is correct. Carson is subject to discipline in state A because Rule 8.5 (a) provides that "A lawyer admitted to practice in this jurisdiction is subject to the disciplinary authority of this jurisdiction, regardless of where the lawyer's conduct occurs."

This is the reason why C is incorrect.

B is incorrect because dishonest conduct renders a lawyer subject to discipline whether or not there is a criminal conviction.

D is incorrect because a disciplinary proceeding based on a criminal offense is not double jeopardy. Instead, its purpose is to protect the state's interest in ensuring that those practicing law are fit and trustworthy.

Question 2i.

B is correct. Each state's disciplinary system is responsible for policing its membership, and it is proper and common for a lawyer to face discipline in multiple jurisdictions for a single act of misconduct.

Therefore, C is incorrect.

A and D are incorrect because the connection of the conduct to the state is not relevant to the propriety of a disciplinary action. Rule 8.5(a) states: "A lawyer may be subject to the disciplinary authority of both this jurisdiction and another jurisdiction for the same conduct." Every state allows discipline for dishonesty, so it does not matter which state's rules apply.

Question 2j.

A is correct. Jabari is subject to discipline in state A for the conduct in state B. Rule 8.5(b)(1) states that in cases involving litigation before a tribunal, the ethical rules that apply are those of the jurisdiction in which the tribunal sits. Therefore, the disciplinary agency in state A would apply the rules in state B in this matter.

B is incorrect because Jabari's pro hac vice admission in State B makes him subject to discipline in State B for misconduct there, even though he is also subject to the jurisdiction of the disciplinary authority in State A.

C and D are incorrect because Rule 8.5 makes the violation in State B a disciplinary violation in State A.

Question 2k.

A is correct. Rule 8.3 requires reporting the misconduct of a lawyer that raises a substantial question of that lawyer's honesty, which is clearly the case here. The only exception, contained in Comment 2, is that the report is not required if it would require a violation of Rule 1.6, which governs protecting client confidences.

B is incorrect because misconduct is not required to be reported if a report would reveal client confidential information.

C and D are incorrect because no exception to the reporting requirement exists for a subordinate lawyer who has reported the matter within her firm.

Question 2l.
A is correct. An attorney may be disciplined for dishonest conduct even if it occurred out of state and even if it was unconnected with the attorney's legal work.

B is incorrect because the disciplinary system need not wait for a complaint to punish a lawyer for misconduct. It could have investigated and punished Mayra without a complaint, if it had read about the misconduct in the press.

C is incorrect because a state may discipline its licensees for misconduct committed elsewhere.

D is incorrect because the settlement did not, and could not, foreclose disciplinary action.

3. Relationships Between Lawyers and Clients

Question 3a.
C is correct. Burke may acquire the knowledge he needs to represent a client in an unfamiliar area through necessary study. See Rule 1.1, Comment 2.

A is incorrect, because although informing clients about one's prior lack of experience in handling certain types of cases might be a good practice, no rule requires lawyers to disclose this information to clients.

B is incorrect, because although co-counseling with an experienced lawyer is one way of providing competent representation, it is not the only acceptable method.

D is incorrect, because a lawyer might be subject to discipline if he accepted a matter in an unfamiliar area of law and did not "study up" to compensate for his inexperience.

Question 3b.
A is correct. Under *Togstad v. Vesely, Otto, Miller & Keefe*, 291 N.W.2d 686 (Minn. 1980) an attorney-client relationship is formed when an individual seeks and receives legal advice, and a reasonable person would rely on that advice. If an attorney-client relationship existed, the plaintiff need only show that the attorney acted negligently, that such acts were the cause of plaintiff's damages, and that but for the negligent advice, she would not have suffered damage.

B is accordingly incorrect.

C is incorrect because consideration is not required for malpractice liability, which could be grounded either in tort or contract.

D is incorrect because the question posits that Carla reasonably believed that Alice was giving legal advice and that the advice was correct. American lawyers are not licensed to provide services only in particular specialties.

Question 3c.
C is correct. Even though lawyers are generally required to communicate settlement offers to clients, and clients generally have the authority to accept or reject them under Rule 1.2(a), a client can expressly delegate this authority to her lawyer. Comment 3 after Rule 1.2 says that a "client may authorize the lawyer to take specific action on the client's behalf without further consultation. Absent a material change in circumstances and subject to Rule 1.4, a lawyer may rely on such an advance authorization." Comment 2 following Rule

1.4 explains that "a lawyer who receives from opposing counsel an offer of settlement in a civil controversy . . . must promptly inform the client of its substance unless the client . . . has authorized the lawyer to accept or to reject the offer."

The other answers are accordingly incorrect.

Question 3d.

A is correct. Anita's failure to investigate and advise her client about the immigration consequences of a conviction for her immigrant client is arguably incompetent and therefore Anita could be subject to discipline for violation of Rule 1.1. Although Liam would have to prove that the advice was prejudicial to have his conviction reversed (in a state in which *Padilla* was retroactive), the lack of prejudice to a client is not a defense to a disciplinary charge.

B is accordingly incorrect.

C is incorrect because Anita could be disciplined for incompetence even if no Sixth Amendment remedy is available to Liam.

D is incorrect because a disciplinary body can punish a lawyer for violating the ethical rules whether or not the client is an American citizen.

Question 3e.

D is correct. Under Rule 1.4, a lawyer must keep a client informed about the status of a matter. The fact that the client's case was dismissed is a significant event in the litigation. A lawyer who makes a serious mistake must inform the client (and should inform her malpractice insurer) of her mistake.

A and B are incorrect for this reason.

C is incorrect. Rule 8.3 requires reporting of misconduct by another lawyer but does not require reporting one's own misconduct.

Question 3f.

D is correct. Sylvia will be unable to demonstrate that she suffered any damages. Dino violated Rule 1.2 because he rejected a settlement offer without communicating it to his client. However, he would not be subject to malpractice liability for his failure to communicate the settlement offer because there are no damages.

The other answers are accordingly incorrect.

Question 3g.

D is correct. The Model Rules do not require a lawyer to reveal to a prospective client that the client might obtain similar services elsewhere for a lower price or the lawyer's belief that the client might be able to resolve the problem without using legal services at all.

A and B are accordingly incorrect.

C is incorrect because although Rule 1.4(b) requires a lawyer to explain a matter to the extent reasonably necessary to permit the client to make informed decisions regarding the representation, it does not apply to prospective clients. In addition, a lawyer's duties toward a prospective client are specified in Rules 1.5 and 1.18, but they do not require disclosure of less expensive options for legal services.

Question 3h.

A is correct. "A lawyer ordinarily is not obliged to accept a client whose character or cause the lawyer regards as repugnant." Rule 6.2, Comment 1.

C is incorrect for that reason.

B is incorrect because although Rule 6.1 strongly encourages lawyers to represent indigent clients, a lawyer is not required to represent an indigent client unless appointed by a judge to represent a criminal defendant, and even then, Rule 6.2(c) allows a lawyer to decline such an appointment if the client or the cause is repugnant to the lawyer, among other reasons.

D is incorrect, because except for certain court appointments, a lawyer may decline to represent any client the lawyer does not wish to represent. The rules impose no duty to accept representation of a client just because he can pay the lawyer's full fee.

Question 3i.

B is correct. Rule 1.16 requires attorneys to "inquire into and assess the facts and circumstances of each representation to determine whether the lawyer may accept *or continue* the representation" (emphasis added). Comment 1 adds that a change in the facts or circumstances of the representation requires the lawyer to "make further inquiry and assessment" to determine whether the lawyer is permitted to continue the representation. Taylor's asking Susan to represent her in the sale of the business would be such a change in the circumstances of the representation. Moreover, if Susan's inquiry revealed that Taylor was in fact engaging in fraud, Susan would be required by Rule 1.16(a)(4) to advise Taylor that she could not assist her with the sale, because the rules of legal ethics (in this case Rule 1.2(d)), prohibit a lawyer from assisting a client to commit fraud. If Taylor then insisted that Susan help her with the sale, Rule 1.16(a)(4) would require Susan to withdraw from the representation.

C is incorrect for those reasons.

D is incorrect because Rule 1.16 applies to transactional representation as well as to litigation.

A is incorrect because Rule 1.16 does not require attorneys to withdraw from representation based upon mere suspicion of fraud. But it does require the lawyer to make an inquiry, and if the inquiry were to confirm Susan's suspicions, she could not represent Taylor in selling the business.

4. The Duty to Protect Client Confidences

Question 4a.

C is correct. Rule 1.6(a) prohibits a lawyer from revealing information relating to the representation of a client without client consent. Comment 5 explains that a lawyer practicing in a law firm is impliedly authorized to disclose client confidences to other lawyers within the law firm, but not to lawyers outside the firm.

A and B are accordingly incorrect. In truly exigent circumstances, a lawyer might be impliedly authorized to enlist the assistance of another lawyer without express client consent. However, in this case, the lawyer has made only a single casual attempt to contact the client.

D is incorrect because, with the permission of Royce, Uma could enlist substitute counsel for the hearing without withdrawing from representation of Royce.

Question 4b.

A is correct. Rule 1.6(b)(5) allows lawyers to reveal confidential information to respond to allegations in a lawsuit by a client concerning the lawyer's representation of the client. In addition, Comment 16 provides that a lawyer should make efforts to limit disclosure to the parties and the tribunal.

B is incorrect because under Rule 1.6(a), all information relating to the representation of a client is confidential, regardless of whether the client specifically asks that the information be kept confidential or when the client makes such a request.

C is incorrect because Rule 1.6(b)(5) allows revelations necessary for a lawyer's self-defense. A lawyer may reveal confidential information in the circumstances listed in 1.6(b) regardless of a special request for secrecy.

D is incorrect because the ethics code explicitly protects a lawyer's right to make limited revelations in this situation.

Question 4c.

D is correct. Under Rule 1.6, Comment 5, "[l]awyers in a firm may, in the course of the firm's practice, disclose to each other information relating to a client of the firm, unless the client has instructed that particular information be confined to specified lawyers." Sandler's preparation of materials using client information without changing the client's name, for wide dissemination within the firm, may have been unwise. However, because the rules allow sharing of confidences within a firm, irrespective of the size of the firm, this conduct would not be a basis for discipline. Sandler's notation on the cover of the materials, stating that they were confidential, took account of Rule 1.6(c), which requires reasonable efforts to prevent improper disclosure of confidences.

A is incorrect because sharing information within a firm is not regarded as a "disclosure."

B is incorrect; Nigel's consent is not required to share information within a law firm.

C is incorrect because a firm is regarded as a single entity even if it has offices in several cities. Nevertheless, the use of Nigel's name in the training materials might possibly violate Rule 1.8(b), which prohibits using confidential information to the disadvantage of a client. Since Nigel is a celebrity chef, this training exercise could harm his reputation. It would have been prudent to change the name of the client in the materials.

Question 4d.

C is correct, because no exception to the confidentiality rule (1.6) applies.

A is incorrect; Alberto and Chad might decide to reveal the information as part of a plea bargain, but Alberto has no discretion to do so without Chad's authorization.

B is incorrect because Rule 1.6 does not permit a lawyer to disclose this confidential information even if a criminal investigation is ongoing.

D is incorrect. Even if Alberto had objective evidence that Chad had killed Ethan, he would not be permitted by Rule 1.6 to reveal this information without Chad's consent.

Question 4e.

B is correct. Under Rule 1.6(b)(4), a lawyer may reveal confidential information outside of the law firm for the purpose of securing advice about her ethical obligations. Jennifer could consult Isai about whether she has a duty to report under the state child abuse reporting statute and Rule 1.6(b)(6) or whether she is obliged not to report by Rule 1.6(a). Although the rule permits Jennifer to reveal confidences to obtain advice about her ethical duties, Jennifer would be well-advised not to reveal the client's identity or other identifying information to consult Isai. Instead she might frame the factual basis of the consultation as a hypothetical.

A is incorrect. Even if there were another domestic relations lawyer in her firm, Jennifer would be permitted to consult a lawyer outside the firm under Rule 1.6(b)(4).

C is incorrect because Jennifer is not required to obtain the client's permission to consult a lawyer outside the firm about her ethical obligations.

D is incorrect because Jennifer may, under Rule 1.6(b)(4), consult any other lawyer for advice about her ethical duties. The other lawyer need not have any credentials as an ethics expert.

Question 4f.

D is correct. No exception to the rule against revealing confidences applies.

A and B are accordingly not correct.

C is not correct because the fact that Oleg's son confessed is information relating to the representation, which Moira may not reveal to anyone, even Oleg's son, without Oleg's consent.

Question 4g.

D is correct. In this case, the possibility of harm to the patients does not rise to the level required by Rule 1.6(b)(1) to allow revelation.

A is incorrect. A lawyer may reveal confidential information only when permitted by the rules. Otherwise, the lawyer must keep client confidences and does not violate Rule 8.4(c) by doing so.

B is incorrect because even if Blake's conduct is fraudulent or criminal, a lawyer's non-disclosure of information protected by Rule 1.6 does not amount to "assisting" a criminal or fraudulent act. None of the exceptions in Rule 1.6 applies, so the duty to protect Blake's confidences takes precedence over any arguable duty of disclosure.

C is incorrect because no rule requires Mosi to disclose this information to the other patients.

Question 4h.

C is correct. Rule 1.6(b)(6) permits Dahlia to reveal the confidence in this situation — because revelation is required by law.

A is incorrect. Revelation is not justifiable under Rule 1.6(b)(1), but that is not dispositive, since revelation would clearly be permitted under 1.6(b)(6).

B is incorrect, because while it is true that her duty continues past the termination of representation, 1.6(b)(6) permits the disclosure in this case.

D is incorrect, because there is no exception to the confidentiality rule that permits revelation of past criminal conduct.

Question 4i.

B is correct. Rule 1.8(b) prohibits the use of confidential information to the disadvantage of the client. In this situation, however, as Rona has decided not to buy the apartment, there is no disadvantage to the client. Comment 5 explains that the rule does not prohibit uses of confidential information that do not disadvantage the client.

C and D are accordingly incorrect.

A is incorrect because the client's consent would be required only if there were some disadvantage to the client.

Question 4j.

C is correct, because Rule 1.6(b)(3) only applies when the client used the lawyer's services to commit the crime or fraud.

A is incorrect because even if the injury to Jason's financial interests was substantial, Salima may not reveal the information unless her services were used to further the crime.

B is incorrect, because lawyers may not reveal past crimes of clients except for those that fall under Rule 1.6(b)(3).

D is incorrect; the general counsel's determination is irrelevant to whether or not Salima may reveal the information.

Question 4k.

C is correct, because the duty to protect confidences learned during the course of the representation continues beyond the termination of the representation, and no exception to the duty to protect confidences applies here. See Rule 1.6, comment 20.

A is incorrect for this reason.

B is incorrect, because although the arson would cause substantial injury to property that could be prevented, Yoshi's services were not used in furtherance of the arson, so revelation is not permitted under Rule 1.6(b)(2). Cyrus informed Yoshi of his intention but did not ask for advice about this nor did he enlist Yoshi to assist in any way.

D is incorrect, because the confidentiality rule allows lawyers to reveal confidential information to prevent substantial injury to property in the circumstances listed in Rule 1.6(b)(2).

Question 4l.

B is correct. The jail identification number is not available to the general public, but jail officials and perhaps police and prosecutors could match the number with the client's identity. Even if she had omitted the number, these officials or others in the criminal justice system might be able to piece together which of her clients Ella was referring to, and would be able to learn a great deal of private information about Kenneth. Both the jail ID number and her other comments make her revelation improper.

A is incorrect because although Ella's statements about her client are highly unprofessional and disloyal, it is not clear that any rule would provide a basis for discipline if she had not revealed confidential information.

C and D are incorrect for the reasons stated above.[3]

5. The Attorney-Client Privilege and the Work Product Doctrine

Question 5a.

C is correct. The paralegal is interviewing the client as an agent of the attorney, and therefore the conversation is privileged. The other answers are incorrect.

The statements in A are not protected by the attorney-client privilege, because the client was not seeking legal advice when he made the statements.

The statements in B are not protected by attorney-client privilege because the statements were made by someone other than the client.

D is incorrect because the federal government has been able successfully to subpoena lists of clients who were advised by lawyers to purchase tax shelter investments, where, as here, the advice to purchase the investments was business advice, not legal advice. See *United States v. Jenkens & Gilchrist, P.C.*, 2005 U.S. Dist. LEXIS 10710 (N.D. Il. 2005).

Question 5b.

C is correct, because a communication is only protected by the attorney-client privilege if the communication was for the purpose of giving or receiving legal advice or legal services

3. This problem is based on an actual disciplinary case. The quotation from the blog is the actual quotation from the public defender's blog, except that we changed one digit in the jail number. The lawyer who posted this blog was suspended from practice in Illinois and Wisconsin based on multiple allegations.

(which it was) and the client reasonably believed the communication was confidential. Here, Benjamin asked his pal Rocky to help him draft the statement. Accordingly, he could not have believed the statement was confidential. The participation of a third person would not result in loss of privilege if the third person was necessary to facilitate the communication. For example, if the client did not speak English, the presence of a translator would not be a problem. In this case, however, there is no indication that Benjamin needed help. He just happened to get it. Since the privilege would be considered to be waived by the participation of a third person, either Benjamin or Rocky could be compelled to testify about its contents.

The other options are accordingly incorrect.

Question 5c.

C is correct. The statement was made by George to Damon in the course of seeking legal advice or services, and no exception to the rule against revealing privileged information applies.

A is incorrect, because this is precisely the situation in which privilege applies. The information was provided in confidence for the purpose of seeking legal advice so its disclosure should not be compelled.

B is incorrect, because a lawyer may not be compelled to testify about privileged information, even in an unrelated litigation.

D is incorrect, because the privilege applies to covered communications regardless of when those communications occur.

Question 5d.

C is correct, because opposing counsel is questioning Roland about the underlying facts, not about the statement he made to Salim. The privilege protects only communication between lawyer and client, not the facts discussed by them.

A is accordingly incorrect.

B is incorrect, because even if the conversation is protected by attorney-client privilege, the underlying information is not so protected.

D is incorrect because even communications made by a client to his lawyer by e-mail or in any other writing can be covered by attorney-client privilege.

Question 5e.

A is correct. This conversation is protected by the attorney-client privilege, because conversations between prospective clients and lawyers are privileged. The other choices are incorrect.

The statements in B are not covered by the privilege, because in order for a communication to be privileged, the client must reasonably believe that the communication is confidential.

The contract in C is not privileged, because the contract is a piece of evidence, not an attorney-client communication.

The conversation in D is not privileged because the purpose of the conversation was neither to give nor to receive legal advice.

Question 5f.

B is correct, because the communication is privileged, and the crime-fraud exception does not apply, because Lilian did not go through with the crime.

A is incorrect, because not all communications between lawyers and clients are privileged. The crime-fraud exception provides that privilege does not cover communications in which the client asks a lawyer for advice or help in committing a crime or fraud.

C and D are incorrect. Whether or not Lillian knew that reselling tickets was a crime, the crime-fraud exception does not apply, because Lillian did not ask Tommy for advice about how to commit a crime or fraud. She was seeking advice about how legally to minimize her obligation to pay taxes.

Question 5g.

B is correct. Rule 1.6 prohibits lawyers from revealing information relating to the representation of a client. The information is thus confidential. Privilege, on the other hand, only covers communications that the client reasonably believes were made in private between the client and lawyer for the purpose of seeking or delivering legal advice or legal services. As Jaya made these statements in the presence of Josh, she could not reasonably believe they were made in private. They are accordingly not privileged.

Question 5h.

C is correct. As in the *Upjohn* case, 449 U.S. 383 (1981), the lawyer is collecting information for the client so the client can mount a legal defense. It is irrelevant that a different law firm is representing the client in the lawsuit.

A is incorrect because, while it is true that the facts are not protected from disclosure, the attorneys' notes, which are a component of its report to its client, are protected.

B is incorrect, because attorney-client privilege applies to client-lawyer communications whether or not those communications are provided to litigating counsel.

D is incorrect because whether the information requested could result in a client's liability is not relevant to assessment of the applicability of the attorney-client privilege.

Question 5i.

B is correct. Pierre's presence in the meeting was necessary for Juan to be able to communicate comfortably with Alton. The presence of a third party can cause a conversation between lawyer and client not to be found privileged, but an exception exists when the third party is necessary to the conversation. See Restatement of the Law Governing Lawyers, Sec. 70.

D is accordingly incorrect.

A and C are incorrect because it does not matter whether a third party necessary to the communication was suggested or hired by the lawyer or by the client. In fact, payment is completely irrelevant to the privilege claim.

Question 5j.

B is correct. As noted by the Supreme Court in *Swidler & Berlin v. United States, 524 U.S. 399 (1998)*, there is a common law "testamentary" exception to the privilege for disputes among heirs. The court explained that the interest in settling estates outweighs the privilege that would otherwise be accorded to deceased persons who communicated with their attorneys and that revelation in estates cases furthers the effectuation of a deceased client's intent.

A is incorrect because the attorney-client privilege belongs to the client and, unless an exception applies, cannot be waived by either next of kin or by the deceased client's former lawyer.

C is incorrect because the testamentary exception applies.

D is incorrect because the application of the testamentary exception does not depend on the equities of the case.

Question 5k.

A is correct. For several reasons, the letter to Jasper is not privileged. It was directed to Jasper, who is not Martin's lawyer, rather than to a lawyer. It did not seek legal advice. And it reveals that Martin was engaged in yet another crime, attempting to involve his lawyer in subornation of perjury, so even if it were privileged, it would be subject to the crime/fraud exception.

B is incorrect because the attorney-client privilege is nearly absolute and often prevents the introduction of evidence relevant to a legal proceeding.

C is incorrect because A is correct.

D is incorrect because although prosecutors rarely subpoena lawyers, compliance by lawyers is required except as to privileged documents and testimony.

6. Conflicts of Interest: Current Clients

Question 6a.

B is correct. The conflict is a "material limitation" conflict under Rule 1.7(a)(2). The students' consent is required because there is a significant risk that Tandy's representation of them will be materially limited by her obligations to her employer. For example, she might advocate less vigorously on the students' behalf because the university might terminate her position in reaction to her "biting the hand that feeds her."

A is incorrect because although Tandy may owe some duty of loyalty to the university, the university is not a client, so she is not required by the rules to get the university's consent.

C is incorrect because the conflict is not between two clients and is not a "direct adversity" conflict. Instead, it is a conflict between the interests of a client and the lawyer's personal (i.e. employment) interests.

D is incorrect. The representation of the students would pose a conflict of interest under Rule 1.7(a)(2), but if Tandy reasonably believes that she can represent the students competently and diligently, then the conflict is consentable under Rule 1.7(b)(1). 1.7(b)(2) and (3) are inapplicable. If the students give informed consent, per Rule 1.7(b)(4), Tandy may represent them.

Question 6b.

C is correct. Under Rule 1.10, when lawyers are associated in a firm, "none of them may represent a client when one of them practicing alone would be prohibited from doing so by Rules 1.7 or 1.9. . . ." Therefore, one must ask whether one of these lawyers could reasonably believe that he could competently and diligently represent both clients. If the conflict is consentable under 1.7(b)(1) and if both clients give informed consent, then Charlie may proceed. This is unlikely on these facts, since the firm is representing Todd in a divorce suit against Suma, but might be possible if the divorce is amicable.

A is incorrect. Rule 1.10(a)(2) allows screening in limited circumstances that are not applicable here.

B is incorrect because this conflict is not "based on a personal interest of the disqualified lawyer" and therefore the language of 1.10(a)(1) has no application here. If, instead of representing Suma in a wrongful discharge case, Charlie was involved in a romance with Suma, then Rule 1.10(a)(1) would allow the firm to represent Todd despite Charlie's personal interest conflict with the divorce case.

D is incorrect because a law firm may sue a current client if the conditions stated in 1.7(b)(1) are satisfied.

Question 6c.

This question asks simply whether there is a conflict of interest. This is the question addressed by Rule 1.7(a). If there is a conflict, one would need to evaluate it using 1.7(b) to see if the lawyer could continue to represent these clients despite the conflict. This question does not require that analysis.

A is correct. Pavel must cross-examine Betty in order to represent Denny competently and diligently. This situation presents direct adversity between the two clients. Comment 6 after Rule 1.7 explains "a directly adverse conflict may arise when a lawyer is required to cross-examine a client who appears as a witness in a lawsuit involving another client, as when the testimony will be damaging to the client who is represented in the lawsuit." Betty's testimony may exculpate Denny and inculpate Betty. After the cross-examination, Denny might be acquitted on the charge and Betty indicted. Even if she is not charged with the jewelry theft, the cross-examination could negatively impact her credibility and her potential liability on the arson charge. This is not the same impact as the example in the comment, but, as in the example, the cross-examination could harm a current client.

B is incorrect because it is irrelevant whether the clients are paying for the attorney's services.

C is incorrect because there can be direct adversity even if neither party is asserting a claim against the other.

D is incorrect. Even if competent representation of Denny would require the cross-examination of Betty and is therefore impliedly authorized, Pavel may have to withdraw because of the conflict.

Question 6d.

D is correct. Laurel would be representing one client in one suit against another client whom she represents in a different matter. A lawyer may sue a current client on behalf of another client only if the lawyer reasonably believes that she can represent both clients competently and diligently, and if both clients give informed consent, confirmed in writing. Meghan does not reasonably believe that she could competently and diligently sue Walter on behalf of Laurel while simultaneously representing him on the criminal charge.

A is incorrect. The representation of Laurel in a suit against Walter would involve "direct adversity" under 1.7(a)(1). Even if the representation is not prohibited by law, the conflict is not consentable for the reasons explained above.

B is incorrect because in analyzing concurrent conflicts, the subject matters of the cases are irrelevant.

C is incorrect because Meghan is not representing both clients in the same litigation. Rule 1.7(b)(3) does not apply to these facts because Meghan is representing Walter in one matter and is considering representing Laurel in a different matter. Rule 1.7(b)(3) would apply here if Meghan represented both Laurel and Walter in Laurel's case.

Question 6e.

C is correct. A positional conflict such as the one described here can present a conflict of interest under Rule 1.7(a)(2). Comment 24 following Rule 1.7 explains:

> The mere fact that advocating a legal position on behalf of one client might create precedent adverse to the interests of a client represented by the lawyer in an unrelated matter does not create a conflict of interest. A conflict of interest exists, however, if there is a significant risk that a lawyer's action on behalf of one client will materially limit the lawyer's effectiveness in representing another client in a different case; for example, when a decision favoring

> one client will create a precedent likely to seriously weaken the position taken on behalf of the other client. Factors relevant in determining whether the clients need to be advised of the risk include: where the cases are pending, whether the issue is substantive or procedural, the temporal relationship between the matters, the significance of the issue to the immediate and long-term interests of the clients involved and the clients' reasonable expectations in retaining the lawyer. If there is significant risk of material limitation, then absent informed consent of the affected clients, the lawyer must refuse one of the representations or withdraw from one or both matters.

Restatement section 128, comment f, identifies a similar list of factors. The factor not included in either list is whether the lawyer is representing the client without charging a fee.

The factors identified in answers A, B, and D are among those listed as relevant in determining whether there is a conflict that requires client consent.

Question 6f.

D is correct. The interests of Anton's estate and Speisler are directly adverse under Rule 1.7(a). Representation of the estate would involve the assertion of a claim by Anton's estate (one client) against Speisler (another client represented by the firm in the same litigation). Under 1.7(b)(3), the conflict is not consentable. Under Rule 1.10(a)(1), if Chloe could not agree to represent Anton's estate, Matilda cannot do so either.

A is incorrect because even if Chloe and Matilda could satisfy the requirements of Rule 1.7(b)(1), they cannot satisfy Rule 1.7(b)(3).

B is incorrect because under Rule 1.10(a)(1), a lawyer may not handle a matter if her partner would be precluded from handling it. This conflict cannot be remedied by screening.

C is incorrect because this conflict is not consentable pursuant to Rule 1.7(b)(3).

Question 6g.

B is correct. There is a significant risk that the representation of Alan will be materially limited by Martha's representation of the corporation, because the corporation is paying her fee. Therefore, a concurrent conflict exists under Rule 1.7(a)(2). But Martha reasonably believes that she can provide competent and diligent representation to both, thus satisfying the requirement of Rule 1.7(b)(1), and both affected clients have given informed consent, confirmed in writing. The writing need not have originated with the clients. Nothing in these facts suggests that the representation is prohibited by law or that either client will make a claim against the other. Therefore, all of the requirements of Rule 1.7(b) are met, and the representation may be undertaken.

A is incorrect because both parties must give informed consent.

C and D are incorrect because Rule 1.7 expressly allows conflicts to be waived under these conditions.

7. Conflicts Involving Former and Prospective Clients

Question 7a.

A is correct. The prior representation was of Matthew as an individual in a matter that would not have involved "a substantial risk that confidential factual information as would normally have been obtained in the prior representation would materially advance the client's position in a subsequent matter." See Rule 1.9, comment 3. This is evident because the prior representation was not of Sharky, but of one of its officers, and the representation did not involve financial information about the corporation.

B is incorrect because the length of time a lawyer worked on a case is not relevant to the conflicts analysis. If the matters are substantially related and there is material adversity, the former client's consent may be required.

C is incorrect. Carlos' former client is Matthew, not Berry's. The work on behalf of Sharky is adverse to Berry's, not to Matthew. Even if the new matter were materially adverse to Berry's, Carlos could continue the representation without the consent of the former client unless the new matter also was the same as or substantially related to the prior matter, which is not the case here.

D is incorrect because Carlos' former client is Matthew, not Berry's. Even though Matthew owns Berry's, Inc., prior representation of an officer of a corporation in a personal matter does not create a conflict for a lawyer seeking to sue the corporation on a business matter unless the two matters are substantially related, as explained in comment 3 to Rule 1.9.

Question 7b.

C is correct. Because Sally is Mira's former client, Rule 1.9 applies. Under Rule 1.9(a), an attorney must obtain a former client's informed consent only if she plans to represent another person in the "same or a substantially related matter in which that person's interests are materially adverse to the interests of the former client." The question of substantial relationship is whether there is a substantial risk that Mira would normally have learned confidential information in her former representation of Sally that would materially advance Jose's position in the new matter. If Jose were seeking damages, Mira might have knowledge of Sally's financial situation that might be used adversely to Sally. However, since Jose is only seeking an injunction, it is unlikely that any prior confidences could be used adversely. Therefore there probably is not a substantial relationship between the prior matter and the current one, so no consent is required.

A is accordingly incorrect.

B is incorrect. For an explanation of the application of the standard articulated in Rule 1.7(a)(2), which is referenced in B, see the discussion following question 7c.

D is incorrect because Jose's interests are in fact materially adverse to Sally's.

Question 7c.

B is correct. Because Jose would become Mira's new client, Rule 1.7 applies. Under Rule 1.7(a)(2), a lawyer must obtain the consent of a prospective client if "there is a significant risk that the representation of [that client] will be materially limited by the lawyer's responsibilities to . . . a former client." Mira and Sally had a professional relationship and have had continuing social contact, so it is possible that Mira would be less vigorous in her advocacy on behalf of Jose because of her relationship to Sally.

A is not correct. Although Jose's interests are directly adverse to Sally's, Sally is not a current client, and 1.7(a)(1) refers to direct adversity between two current clients.

C is incorrect because it is irrelevant that the lawsuits are unrelated if Mira's loyalty to Sally will materially limit her representation of Jose.

D is incorrect because Jose's interests are materially adverse to Sally's.

Question 7d.

D is correct. Under Rule 1.9(a), Shawn may not represent Evelyn in drafting the new will. Adelaide is a former client of Shawn's. The new matter is the same matter as the one on which he previously represented Adelaide, and Evelyn's interests are materially adverse to Adelaide's, so his revising the will is prohibited unless Adelaide gives informed consent.

To obtain Adelaide's consent, Shawn needs to reveal confidential information to her about her mother's intentions as to the will. Shawn may not do this unless Evelyn consents to the revelation of those confidences, which she will not. (If Adelaide is a current rather than a former client, Rule 1.7 would preclude the representation because of Shawn's conflicting loyalties to two clients.)

A is incorrect because Adelaide is a former client of Shawn's. The rules do not distinguish among former clients based on the degree of the lawyer's involvement in their representation.

B is incorrect. Although Shawn owes a duty to Evelyn to protect confidences, Adelaide is a former client, so Shawn may not undertake related representation adverse to her without obtaining her informed consent.

C is incorrect because whether Adelaide is considered a current or former client, Shawn still owes her a duty not to undertake representation adverse to her without her informed consent.

Question 7e.

B is correct. 1.9(b) applies rather than 1.9(a) because Kieran himself did not represent Roxbury; it was a client of his former firm. Rule 1.9(b) would bar Kieran from working on this matter unless Roxbury gave informed consent because (1) the matters are the same or substantially related, (2) the interests of the parties are materially adverse, and (3) Kieran knows confidential information about the former matter that is material to the new matter.

However, the firm can undertake work on this matter without Roxbury's consent if the screening procedures specified in that rule are implemented. Rule 1.10 precludes a lawyer in the new firm from handling a matter if another lawyer in the firm would be precluded from doing so, unless the preclusion is based on Rule 1.9(a) or (b) and arises out of the disqualified lawyer's association with a prior firm (both are true in this case). In that instance, the conflict is not imputed to other lawyers in the firm if the firm complies with the screening procedures specified in Rule 1.10(a)(2). Therefore, the Perlmutter firm may go forward only if Kieran does not work on the matter and receives no part of the fee from it, and the firm implements all of the screening procedures required by Rule 1.10(a)(2).

A is incorrect because the nature of Kieran and Lance's relationship is irrelevant to the analysis.

C is incorrect because "substantial relationship" between the two matters does not preclude the firm from going forward so long as it implements the screening procedures listed in Rule 1.10(a)(2).

D is incorrect. The firm could in fact avoid the potential conflict by firing Kieran, but it need not do so. Instead, it can screen him from contact with the lawyers working on the new matter, as discussed in the answer to B.

Question 7f.

B is correct. Spencer is a prospective client under Rule 1.18 because he has consulted with Kai about the possibility of becoming Kai's client. Under Rule 1.18(c), Kai may not represent Max because he has received information from Spencer about his unlawful break-in. That information could be used adversely to Spencer if Spencer sues Max.

A is incorrect because there are conditions under which a lawyer may represent the adversary of someone who first requested the lawyer's representation; e.g., where the request did not include the transmission of significantly harmful information. In this case, the request did include the request of such information.

C is incorrect because although there is no conflict between two current clients, Rule 1.18(c) prohibits a lawyer from accepting representation where a lawyer has received information from a prospective client that could be used adversely to that person in the matter.

D is incorrect because Kai is precluded from representing Max because of his obligations to Spencer, who is a prospective client. The legality of Spencer's conduct is irrelevant.

Question 7g.

B is correct. Barry moved from one law firm to another. His former firm represented Panko in a similar matter. This situation is therefore governed by Rule 1.9(b), not 1.9(a). Under Rule 1.9(b):

> A lawyer shall not knowingly represent a person in the same or a substantially related matter in which a firm with which the lawyer formerly was associated had previously represented a client (1) whose interests are materially adverse to that person; and (2) about whom the lawyer had acquired information protected by Rules 1.6 and 1.9(c) that is material to the matter.

A is incorrect because even though the two matters are substantially related, Barry is not precluded from representing Panko, Inc. under 1.9(b)(2) because he did not actually acquire confidential information about the prior matter.

C and D are incorrect because even though Ted's interests *are* materially adverse to Panko's, and even though the matters *are* substantially related, Rule 1.9(b) requires the consent of the former client here only if there is substantial relationship and material adversity, *and* the lawyer actually received confidential information about the prior matter that is material to the new case.

Question 7h.

D is correct. Under Rule 1.9 a former client's lawyer may not represent a person in a substantially related matter in which the new client's interests are adverse to the former client's interests, unless the former client consents. At first blush, the two representations appear to have nothing to do with each other. But according to comment 3, a matter is "substantially related" if there is "a substantial risk that confidential factual information as would normally have been obtained in the prior representation would materially advance the new client's position in the subsequent matter." Armand would normally have learned a great deal about the extent and location of Walter's assets during the divorce proceedings. It would benefit Celia to have ready access to that information, especially because, in a punitive damages case, the recovery could well exceed the amount of Walter's malpractice insurance.

A is incorrect for this reason.

B is incorrect, because the test is what information Armand normally would have obtained in the prior representation, not what he actually knows now.

C is incorrect because a lawyer may sue a former client without consent if the former representation and the new representation involve neither the same matter nor a substantially related matter.

Question 7i.

B is correct. Sprinkles is Ash's former client. Under Rule 1.9(a), Ash need only obtain Sprinkles' informed consent if the two matters are the same or substantially related <u>and</u> if DBC's interests are materially adverse to Sprinkles'. The matters would be substantially related if, in the course of representing Sprinkles, a there is a substantial risk that confidential information that a lawyer ordinarily would have learned in the prior representation would materially advance DBC's position in the new representation. Because Ash handled only a routine license application at the inception of Sprinkles' business, Ash would not have learned confidences that would advance DBC's position in the new representation. Because the two matters are not substantially related, Ash need not obtain informed consent.

A is incorrect because the fact that a prospective client and former client are economic competitors would not exempt an attorney from the mandates of Rule 1.9.

C is not correct because attorneys may accept cases involving economic competitors if they otherwise comply with the conflicts rules.

D is incorrect because even if there is material adversity here, there is no substantial relationship. Rule 1.9 requires informed consent only if the parties' interests are materially adverse and the two matters are substantially related.

Question 7j.

B is correct. Rule 1.18 specifies the circumstances under which a lawyer owes duties to a prospective client. Ordinarily, a person who consults with a lawyer about the possibility of forming a lawyer-client relationship is a prospective client, and, under Rule 1.18(c), a lawyer may not "represent a client with interests materially adverse to those of a prospective client in the same or a substantially related matter if the lawyer received information from the prospective client that could be significantly harmful to that person in the matter." At first glance, it would appear that Roger may not represent Reva. However, comment 2 following Rule 1.18 provides that a person who communicates with a lawyer for the purpose of disqualifying the lawyer is not considered a prospective client. Therefore, Roger owes no duty to Leon. Comment 2 takes this case out from under the restrictions of Rule 1.18.

A and C are accordingly incorrect.

D is incorrect. If Leon were a prospective client, and the conflict was consentable, informed consent would be needed from both Leon and Reva. But, as explained above, Leon is not a prospective client because his consultation was not in good faith but instead was an effort to preclude Roger from representing Reva.

8. Conflicts Issues in Particular Practice Settings

Question 8a.

D is correct. Comment 25 after Rule 1.7 explains:

> When a lawyer represents or seeks to represent a class of plaintiffs or defendants in a class-action lawsuit, unnamed members of the class are ordinarily not considered to be clients of the lawyer for purposes of applying paragraph (a)(1) of this Rule. *Thus, the lawyer does not typically need to get the consent of such a person before representing a client suing the person in an unrelated matter. . . .* (emphasis added).

Accordingly, answers A, B and C are incorrect.

Question 8b.

D is correct. Joint representation of criminal co-defendants always presents a risk that representation of one client will be materially limited by the lawyer's responsibilities to the other client (for example, if the prosecutor offers one of them a deal if he testifies against the other). Virtually all authorities recommend against such representation. See, e.g. ABA, Criminal Justice Standards: Defense Function, Standard 4-3.5(c). In this instance, either defendant might get a better deal by testifying against the other, producing a genuine conflict. In particular, Bobby could benefit by confirming that Chris was the instigator and testifying or offering to testify against him.

A is incorrect because the conflict is not consentable; Meyer could not reasonably believe, under these circumstances, that he could provide diligent representation to both co-defendants. Bobby might obtain a lesser penalty by giving evidence against Chris; he arguably needs independent advice to assess his options.

B is incorrect because, while it might seem more efficient for a single lawyer to investigate one set of facts, the situation presents the possibility that it will be in the interest of each client to inculpate the other. Therefore, this situation presents a conflict under Rule 1.7(a)(2) that is not remediable under Rule 1.7(b)(1).

C is incorrect because if the standards of Rule 1.7(b)(1) are met (not the case here), a lawyer need not obtain judicial permission before engaging in representation of co-defendants.

Question 8c.

B is correct. Morton's prior relationship with Carl and the somewhat divergent interests of the siblings may create an actual or potential conflict under Rule 1.7(a)(2) (material limitation). If so, Morton may not undertake this representation without the informed consent of each of the three siblings. Comment 18 after Rule 1.7 states: "When representation of multiple clients on a single matter is undertaken, the information must include the implications of the common representation, including possible effects on loyalty, confidentiality and the attorney client privilege and the advantages and risks involved." However, if the three give consent after being fully informed, Morton may represent all three because, per Comment 28 to Rule 1.7, the siblings' interests are not "fundamentally antagonistic to each other" but are "generally aligned in interest even though there is some divergence in interest among them."

A is incorrect because a lawyer undertaking joint representation should not avoid the conflict by acting as a "mere scrivener" recording the clients' intentions, but should seek to provide each of the clients with the same range of advice as he would if he were to represent any one of them. Restatement section 130, comment b.

C is incorrect. If the siblings disagreed as to the valuation of the property, their interests might be fundamentally antagonistic. However, the sisters value preserving their good relationship with their brother and are willing to make some financial sacrifice to achieve this goal. Since the siblings agree on the most important feature of the transaction, the conflict is consentable.

D is incorrect. As explained above as to option B, there is a conflict under 1.7(a)(2), but the conflict is not so serious that Morton could not reasonably believe that he could "provide competent and diligent representation to each affected client," (1.7(b)(1)), so the siblings may waive the conflict after being fully informed.

Question 8d.

C is correct. Comment 31 following Rule 1.7 states that "continued common representation will almost certainly be inadequate if one client asks the lawyer not to disclose to the other client information relevant to the common representation." Morton owes an "equal duty of loyalty to each client, and each client has the right to be informed of anything bearing on the representation that might affect that client's interests and the right to expect that the lawyer will use that information to that client's benefit." Comment 31 following Rule 1.7.

A and B are incorrect. Morton may not withhold information from the sisters even if he believes that the benefits to Carl would be greater than the harm to the sisters from delay. See the discussion above.

D is incorrect. Morton should decline Carl's suggestion and proceed diligently with the transaction. He is not required to withdraw simply because Carl asked if Morton could secretly act for his benefit alone. So long as Morton does not participate in a crime or fraud or counsel a client to do so, he may continue the representation.

Question 8e.

C is best. Comment 10 following Rule 1.13 states:

> There are times when the organization's interest may be or become adverse to those of one or more of its constituents. In such circumstances the lawyer should advise any constituent, whose interest the lawyer finds adverse to that of the organization of the conflict or potential conflict of interest, that the lawyer cannot represent such constituent, and that such person may wish to obtain independent representation. Care must be taken to assure that the individual understands that, when there is such adversity of interest, the lawyer for the organization cannot provide legal representation for that constituent individual, and that discussions between the lawyer for the organization and the individual may not be privileged.

Rule 4.3 offers similar guidance for any lawyer in dealing with an unrepresented person.

A is incorrect because, while the conversation may be privileged, the privilege, if any, belongs to Plenum, not to Bertha, since Plenum is the client. Bertha cannot speak to Jaiden in confidence without fear of Jaiden revealing the contents of the conversation to others in the corporation.

B is incorrect. Rule 1.13(g) states that "A lawyer representing an organization may also represent any of its . . . employees . . . subject to the provisions of Rule 1.7."

D is incorrect. Jaiden does have a duty to his client Plenum to protect as confidential information relating to the representation, including the contents of this conversation, but under Rule 1.13(c), the lawyer may reveal confidential information relating to the representation of an organization outside of the organization. Jaiden may reveal Bertha's information to government officials if the conditions listed in Rule 1.13(c) are satisfied. If he reports Bertha's misfeasance to the highest authority at Plenum, Plenum fails to take action to rectify unlawful conduct, Jaiden "reasonably believes that the violation is reasonably certain to result in substantial injury to the organization," and the revelation is necessary to prevent this injury, then he may report the information outside of the corporation. Therefore, it is not accurate to describe his duty to protect confidences as absolute.

Question 8f.

A is correct. In the absence of an actual or apparent conflict, a lawyer may serve on the board of a corporation that the lawyer represents. See Rule 1.7, Comment 35. The lawyer may also own stock in the corporation. The lawyer should be aware that communications with corporate employees may not be covered by attorney-client privilege, and the lawyer should recuse himself or herself, or resign from the board, if a conflict should arise. (For example, if the lawyer is asked for a legal opinion about the validity of bonuses being paid to board members including the lawyer, he should recuse himself.)

C and D are accordingly incorrect.

B is incorrect because no law bars an attorney from being recruited to join a board because of friendship with a member.

Question 8g.

C is correct. Rule 1.13 (c)(2) provides that when the lawyer for a corporation reasonably believes that a violation is reasonably certain to result in substantial injury to the corporation she represents, and the highest authority that can act for the corporation fails to address the situation, the lawyer "may" reveal the information to prevent the injury to the corporation, but it does not require her to do so.

A is incorrect because harm to the public is not a sufficient basis for a lawyer's violation of Rule 1.6, unless the harm rises to the level of one of the exceptions in Rule 1.6(b) or elsewhere in the rules.

B is incorrect because Rule 1.13 requires "reporting up" to higher levels within the corporation but only *permits* "reporting out," rather than *requiring* it.

D is incorrect because Rule 1.13 does not require disclosure.

Question 8h.

C is correct. Under Rule 1.16, a lawyer *may* withdraw for various reasons, including if: (a) a client persists in a course of action involving the lawyer's services that the lawyer reasonably believes is criminal or fraudulent, (b) the client has used the lawyer's services to perpetrate a crime or fraud, *or* (c) the client insists upon taking action that the lawyer considers repugnant or with which the lawyer has a fundamental disagreement. The lawyer is not *required* to withdraw for any of these reasons.

A and B are therefore incorrect.

D is incorrect because she would not be *required* to withdraw even if she represented Marcus.

9. Conflicts of Interest Between Lawyers and Clients

Question 9a.

B is correct. Under Rule 1.5(b), a lawyer must communicate to the client "the basis or rate of the fee *and expenses* for which the client will be responsible" within a reasonable time after commencing representation (emphasis added). Lucille billed Basia for Magda's services, even though she had not informed her that she would do so.

A is incorrect because the rule merely states that it is "preferable" for the communication about fees to be in writing, and the rule does not require a lawyer to give an estimate of the total fee.

C is incorrect because although the lawyer's rate need not be communicated in writing, the lawyer must inform the client "whether and to what extent the client will be responsible for any costs, expenses or disbursements," such as the cost to hire an interpreter.

D is incorrect because after the bail emergency was over, Lucille did not communicate the expected expenses for which Basia would be responsible.

Question 9b.

C is correct. Rule 1.5(c) requires any contingent fee agreement to be in a writing signed by a client.

A and B are accordingly incorrect.

D is incorrect. Contingent fee rates of 33 percent are not unusual. Some scholars assert that if a lawyer works only a few hours, it is unreasonable for a lawyer to receive as much as one third of a settlement. However, this rate remains commonplace.

Question 9c.

A is correct. Under Rule 1.8(e), "[a] lawyer shall not provide financial assistance to a client in connection with pending or contemplated litigation, except that . . . a lawyer may advance court costs and expenses of litigation, the repayment of which may be contingent on the outcome of the matter." Joseph had told Cyrus that he wanted to appeal, so Cyrus was authorized to act without further consent from Joseph. Accordingly, the other answers are not correct.

Question 9d.

A is correct. Under Rule 1.8(a)(3), "[a] lawyer shall not . . . knowingly acquire an ownership, possessory, security or other pecuniary interest adverse to a client unless . . . the client gives informed consent, in a writing signed by the client, to the essential terms of the transaction. . . ." Rule 1.8(a) "does not apply to ordinary fee arrangements between client and lawyer, which are governed by Rule 1.5, although its requirements must be met when the lawyer accepts an interest in the client's business or other nonmonetary property as payment of all or part of a fee." Comment 1 to Rule 1.5. While the requirements of the rule do not apply to ordinary legal fee arrangements, where the legal fee consists of a share in the proceeds of the sale of the client's intellectual property, the transaction must comply with Rule 1.8(a). See Rule 1.8(a) for details on what is required.

B is not correct, because this is not a situation in which a contingency fee is prohibited.

C is not correct. Rule 1.8(d) states: "Prior to the conclusion of representation of a client, a lawyer shall not make or negotiate an agreement giving the lawyer literary or media rights to a portrayal or account based in substantial part on information relating to the representation." Here, the representation concerns a landlord-tenant dispute, which has nothing to do with the content of the book. Rule 1.8(d), therefore, has no application here.

D is also incorrect for that reason. If 1.8(d) applied, it would prohibit the negotiation of an arrangement to share royalties until after the representation was completed.

Question 9e.

D is correct. Under Rule 1.8(h)(1), "[a] lawyer shall not make an agreement prospectively limiting the lawyer's liability to a client for malpractice unless the client is independently represented in making the agreement." It does not matter that Morgan advised Barbara to consult another lawyer; Barbara must actually be represented by another lawyer in making the agreement.

The other answers are accordingly wrong.

Question 9f.

B is correct. Under Rule 1.8(h)(2), "[a] lawyer shall not . . . settle a claim or potential claim for such liability with an unrepresented client or former client unless that person is advised in writing of the desirability of seeking and is given a reasonable opportunity to seek the advice of independent legal counsel in connection therewith." Here, Barbara need not actually be represented by another lawyer; Morgan need only advise her of the desirability of seeking outside counsel.

C is accordingly not correct.

A is not correct, because a settlement may be considered reasonable even if the settlement amount is less than the damages. Here the settlement amount was more than the damages.

D is not correct, because while a malpractice insurance contract may require a lawyer to notify the carrier of mistakes that could result in liability, the ethics code includes no such requirement.

Question 9g.

B is correct. Under Rule 1.8(c), "[a] lawyer shall not solicit any substantial gift from a client, including a testamentary gift, or prepare on behalf of a client an instrument giving the lawyer or a person related to the lawyer any substantial gift unless the lawyer or other recipient of the gift is related to the client." In this matter, Eli did not solicit the gift nor did he prepare the gift instrument.

A is incorrect. There are restrictions, but this matter does not implicate those restrictions, as explained above.

C is incorrect, because the rules do not require a guardian ad litem to be appointed in this situation.

D is incorrect, because the rule only prohibits a lawyer from "soliciting" a substantial gift from the client; here, there is no indication that Eli solicited the gift. If the gift is unsolicited, it can be accepted even if its value is large.

Question 9h.

B is correct. Under Rule 1.15, Sebastian must keep his own funds separate from the property of clients. Until he has done the work, the $4,000 that he receives from each client is still property of the client. Accordingly, Sebastian needs one additional account: a trust account for client property. The other answers are not correct, because each client's property need not be kept separate from the other clients' property, though the lawyer must keep complete records of the account.

Question 9i.

B is correct. Under Rule 1.5(c), a lawyer may enter into a contingent fee arrangement with a client, as long as the client gives consent in a signed writing.

C is incorrect, because Rule 1.5(d)(1) only prohibits charging a fee that is "contingent upon the securing of a divorce or upon the amount of alimony or support, or property settlement in lieu thereof." Here, Maria is not helping Jillian secure a divorce or an order for support; she is merely seeking to enforce a child support order.

A is incorrect. The rules on consent for contingent fees are the same for new and former clients.

D is incorrect, because 30 percent is often considered a reasonable percentage. The rules do not make distinctions among types of cases, except that contingent fees in family law cases are prohibited as described in the answer to C, and in the representation of criminal defendants.

Question 9j.

A is correct. Rule 1.5(b) requires "the basis or rate of the fee and expenses for which the client will be responsible" to be disclosed to the client.

B is incorrect because Rule 1.5(b) only states that the basis or rate should be disclosed "preferably in writing;" a written instrument is not required.

C is incorrect because Rule 1.5 does not require an estimate of the total fee.

D is incorrect because Rule 1.5(a) only requires that legal fees be reasonable. One factor in determining reasonableness is "the fee customarily charged in the locality for similar legal services." Donna's fee is not unusual in the locality; she need not charge less than all the other lawyers in the community.

Question 9k.

B is correct. Rule 5.4(a) provides that: "A lawyer or law firm shall not share legal fees with a nonlawyer," with very limited exceptions that are not pertinent here.

A is incorrect because referral fees are prohibited whether disclosed to the client or not.

C is incorrect because the payment of referral fees is prohibited even if the referrer has no conflict of interest.

D is incorrect because even if he pays Joan only ten percent of his fee, he would be sharing his legal fee with a non-lawyer.

Question 9l.

B is correct. Rule 1.8(e) only bars financial assistance to clients "in connection with pending or contemplated litigation." Comment 10 says "Lawyers may not subsidize lawsuits or administrative proceedings brought on behalf of their clients." The lawyer in this example is assisting the client in applying for food stamps. She is not engaging in litigation. An application for emergency food stamps is not an "administrative proceeding" because, although it is an application to an administrative agency, it is not a "proceeding" which would be decided by an administrative law judge.

A is incorrect as the lawyer is charging a fee, albeit a small one. Rule 1.8(e)(3) allows lawyers to give indigent clients modest gifts for food, rent, transportation, medicine and other basic living expenses, but only if the lawyer is representing the client pro bono.

C and D are incorrect because Rule 1.8(e) does not prohibit the lawyer from providing financial assistance to the client in this situation. Also, there is no apparent conflict of interest. There is no need for the lawyer to terminate the representation before she gives the client the money.

Question 9m.

B is correct. Rule 1.8(e) prohibits lawyers from providing financial assistance to clients in connection with pending or contemplated litigation except for court costs and expenses of litigation. Geraldine is suing Mike's Counseling Service on behalf of Amber. Any financial support of Amber during this time would be considered to be "in connection with litigation." However, Rule 1.8(e)(3) allows a lawyer who is representing a client pro bono to "provide modest gifts to the client for food, rent, transportation, medicine and other basic living expenses." Under this rule, the lawyer in this problem may give the client money to rent a modest room. Accordingly, B is correct, and D is incorrect. Rule 1.8(e)(3)(ii) goes on to state that the lawyer may not seek reimbursement of the gift from the client or a relative of the client. The lawyer accordingly cannot loan the money to the client, and A and C are therefore incorrect.

Question 9n.

C is correct. Rule 1.5(d) states that "A lawyer shall not enter into an arrangement for, charge, or collect: (1) any fee in a domestic relations matter, the payment or amount of which is contingent upon the securing of a divorce or upon the amount of alimony or support, or property settlement in lieu thereof." A contingent fee is not permitted in this case because the action is a petition for child support. The support order has not yet been issued, so the amount has not yet been determined. The rule seeks to ensure that the amount of awards in domestic relations matters will not be inflated by lawyers' desire for a larger fees.

A is incorrect. Rule 1.5(d) prohibits a lawyer from charging a contingent fee for representing a defendant in a criminal case. This proposed suit, however, is an action for damages in a civil case.

B and D are incorrect because both cases are civil cases in which contingent fee agreements are allowed.

Question 9o.

A is correct. This arrangement would comply with Rule 1.5(e) on division of fees between lawyers not in the same firm, but the lawyers also must comply with Rule 1.5(c) because this is a contingent fee agreement. Comment 8 after Rule 1.5 states that "contingent fee agreements must be in a writing signed by the client and must otherwise comply with paragraph (c) of the rule."

C and D are incorrect because under 1.5(e)(1), the two lawyers may share the fee if the lawyers assume joint responsibility for the work performed. Comment 7 after Rule 1.5 says "Joint responsibility for the representation entails financial and ethical responsibility for the representation as if the lawyers were associated in a partnership." Sol's area of expertise is not relevant. Who does how much of the actual work doesn't matter either under 1.5(e), provided that they assume joint responsibility for the representation.

B is accordingly incorrect.

Question 9p.

D is correct. Rule 1.8(h) states that in general, lawyers may not limit their malpractice liability except as to clients who are independently represented in making such an agreement. However, Comment 14 to Rule 1.8 says that the rule "does not . . . prohibit a lawyer from entering into an agreement with the client to *arbitrate* legal malpractice claims, provided such agreements are enforceable and the client is fully informed of the scope and effect of the agreement" (emphasis added). The comment should be understood to mean that an arbitration clause is not a limitation on malpractice liability, and therefore the lawyer need not even advise the client of the desirability of seeking independent legal advice before signing it.

A is incorrect because a lawyer may ask a client to agree to a clause requiring arbitration of any malpractice claims without the client being independently represented.

B is incorrect because a lawyer need not advise the client of the desirability of seeking independent counsel before entering into such an agreement.

C is incorrect; the comment makes no mention of contingent fee cases.

Question 9q.

A is correct. Rule 8.4 prohibits dishonesty, fraud, deceit or misrepresentation in or outside of the practice of law. Under Rule 8.5(a), "a lawyer admitted to practice in this jurisdiction is subject to the disciplinary authority of this jurisdiction, regardless of where the lawyer's conduct occurs."

B is incorrect because Milan's relationship to this buyer is not a lawyer-client relationship so Rule 1.8(a) does not apply.

C is incorrect because Rule 8.4 allows discipline of licensed lawyers for conduct that occurs in or outside of practice.

D is incorrect because the dishonesty need not be adjudicated in a lawsuit prior to discipline.

Question 9r.

A is correct. A lawyer may not use money from a client trust account for her own purposes, even for humanitarian reasons.

B is incorrect because for a lawyer to borrow money from a client would require that the lawyer comply with the requirements of Rule 1.8(a), including getting the client's informed consent in advance of the transaction, which she has not done. No matter what the circumstances, a lawyer may not "borrow" funds from her client trust account. See Rule 1.15.

C is incorrect. Actual harm to the client is not relevant in determining disciplinary liability.

D is incorrect. Although the circumstances present a genuine medical emergency, the use of client funds for this purpose is not justifiable. "A lawyer cannot use a client's funds, no matter how noble the purpose." *In re Lenz*, 484 N.E.2d 1093 (Ill. 1985).

10. Conflicts Issues for Government Lawyers and Judges

Question 10a.

B is correct. Only Rule 1.9(a) does not apply.

A and D are incorrect. Rule 1.11(a) applies directly to evaluate conflicts of former government employees who are currently in private practice. Instead of requiring consent for a wide range of matters, the former government lawyer provision requires consent from the government only for cases in which the former government lawyer participated "personally and substantially." See Rule 1.11, comment 4. Rule 1.11(a) applies to evaluate the need for the consent of a former governmental client. It is used instead of Rule 1.9(a). Former government lawyers in private practice, then, would look at Rule 1.11(a) to assess the impact of a conflict on a former government client, and (as Comment 1 makes clear) would look at Rule 1.7, as usual, to assess the impact of that conflict on any present client. This is the reason why A is incorrect.

C is incorrect because Rule 1.11(a) explicitly provides that former government lawyers are subject to Rule 1.9(c).

Question 10b.

D is correct. 18 U.S.C. Sec. 205(a)(1) imposes criminal penalties on any officer or agent of the United States who acts as an attorney for prosecuting any claim against the United States, even if the employee works in a different part of the government. The other answers are incorrect because this law does not provide for waiver either by the United States or by a private client.

The other answers are incorrect for this reason.

Question 10c.

B is correct. Under 1.11(a), Dania's personal and substantial participation in the matter disqualifies her from working on it. Other lawyers in the firm may work on this matter if the firm notifies the SEC, erects a timely screen, and apportions no part of the fee from that work to Dania. Dania's work focused on defendants in the case who are not clients of the firm; nevertheless, the firm's work would probably be considered the same matter as the one in which Dania personally and substantially participated. Comment 10 after Rule 1.11 says "In determining whether two particular matters are the same, the lawyer should consider the extent to which the matters involve the same basic facts, the same or related parties, and the time elapsed." This is obviously the "same matter" as the one Dania worked on while at the SEC. B describes the requirements imposed by Rule 1.11(b), which explains what is necessary to allow another lawyer in the firm to work on a matter from which Dania is disqualified.

A is incorrect. Dania must comply with the mandate of 1.9(c) not to use or reveal confidential information relating to the representation of a former client, but her protecting those confidences is insufficient, by itself, to allow the firm to continue to represent the defendant.

C is incorrect because for the purpose of analyzing conflicts, all offices of a firm are considered part of the same firm, even if they are in different cities.

D is incorrect because Dania need not be fired if she is timely screened and the other requirements of Rule 1.11 are met.

Question 10d.

D is correct. The US Supreme Court has not bound itself to any formal ethics code.

Question 10e.

C is correct. The *Caperton* case, *Caperton v. A.T. Massey Coal Co. Inc.*, 556 U.S. 868 (2009), required a judge to be disqualified because he had received a very large contribution ($3 million) from a party, one that exceeded the contributions from all other persons combined. His participation was held to violate the Due Process clause of the 14th Amendment because it would impair fair adjudication. The court said in *Caperton* that the size of that contribution in comparison to the total amount contributed to the campaign was excessive and reflected on the judge's impartiality. Here, in contrast, the contribution amounted to only two percent of the candidate's funds.

A is incorrect because, as the Supreme Court said, "not every contribution by a litigant . . . creates a probability of bias," and Garner's contribution was small compared to the total fund.

B is incorrect because, given the small relative size of the contribution, recusal is not necessary, despite the lack of consent.

D is incorrect because disclosure alone could not solve the problem if the contribution was so large that it created a likelihood of bias.

Question 10f.

C is correct. Rule 1.12(b) generally prohibits lawyers who are serving as judges from negotiating for employment with lawyers for parties in matters in which the judges are participating personally and substantially. But the rule makes an explicit exception for lawyers who are serving as judicial law clerks and who notify the judge about the intended negotiation for employment.

A is incorrect because of that exemption.

B is incorrect because judicial law clerks who notify their judges as required by the rule are not barred from writing opinions favoring the client of the firm with which they were or are negotiating for employment.

D is incorrect because Evelyn would not have been subject to discipline even if she had drafted the opinion and submitted it to her judge while still negotiating for employment.

Question 10g.

A is correct. Under the U.S. Supreme Court's decision in *Williams-Yulee v. Fla. Bar*, 135 S. Ct. 1656 (2015), the Citizens United decision does not extend First Amendment protection to judicial candidates' campaigns, and this rule in the Model Code is valid. The Court held that the rule serves a state's compelling interest in preserving public confidence in the judiciary.

B is incorrect because of this exception.

C is incorrect because although federal judges may be removed from office only by impeachment, Judge DuBois is a state court judge and states may sanction judges through their own processes, as Florida did in the *Williams-Yulee* case.

D is incorrect because the Model Code has no exception for contributions from close friends or relatives.

Question 10h.

D is correct. Rule 3.5 states that a lawyer shall not communicate ex parte with a judge during the proceeding unless authorized to do so by law or court order. Rule 2.9 of the Model Code of Judicial Conduct describes the exceptional circumstances in which such ex parte communication is proper. It provides that when circumstances require it, ex parte communications for scheduling purposes, which does not address substantive matters, is permitted, provided that the judge makes provision promptly to notify all other parties of the substance of the ex parte communication and gives them an opportunity to respond. That was done here.

A is incorrect because no rule requires prior notice to Manfred, though it might have been better for her to have waited at least a day to try to reach Manfred before calling the judge's chambers.

B is incorrect because Rule 2.9 of the Model Code permits contact with a judge under the circumstances described in that rule.

C is incorrect because the tests of the propriety of these events are whether Erin's conversation with the judge was for scheduling purposes and whether Manfred was given proper notice of what was discussed and an opportunity to respond, not whose fault it was that Erin had a conversation with the judge.

Question 10i.

A is correct. Rule 3.6(A) of the Model Code of Judicial Conduct bars a judge from holding membership in any organization that practices invidious discrimination on the basis of sexual orientation. No equivalent rule applies to lawyers. Rule 8.4(g) was amended by the ABA House of Delegates in 2016 to prohibit a lawyer from engaging in conduct that the lawyer knows or reasonably should know is harassment or discrimination on the basis of "race, sex, religion, national origin, ethnicity, disability, age, ***sexual orientation***, gender identity, marital status or socioeconomic status in conduct related to the practice of law" (emphasis added). Because the purpose of the club is to facilitate social interaction, and because Leonard does not engage in conduct related to the practice of law at the Antelope Club, the rule probably does not prohibit his membership there. The report of the ABA's Standing Committee on Ethics and Professional Responsibility that urged the ABA's House of Delegates to approve the anti-discrimination language in Rule 8.4(g) stated that its scope was "narrower and more limited" than the scope of Rule 8.4(c), which prohibits dishonesty and deceit by lawyer in all of their activities, whether or not related to the practice of law. See Report at http://www.americanbar.org/content/dam/aba/administrative/professional_responsibility/final_revised_resolution_and_report_109.authcheckdam.pdf. However, comment 4 to Rule 8.4 states that the prohibition on discrimination covers "participating in bar association, business or social activities in connection with the practice of law." If Leonard's activities at the Antelope Club sometimes includes conversing with other lawyers about professional matters, membership in the club could be found to violate Rule 8.4(g). The rule is so new that its scope remains to be understood.

11. Lawyers' Duties to Courts

Question 11a.

D is correct. Rule 3.3, Comment 9 states:

Although paragraph (a)(3) only prohibits a lawyer from offering evidence the lawyer knows to be false, it permits the lawyer to refuse to offer testimony or other proof that the lawyer reasonably believes is false. . . . Because of the special protections historically provided criminal defendants, however, this Rule does not permit a lawyer to refuse to offer the testimony of such a client where the lawyer reasonably believes but does not know that the testimony will be false.

The other answers are accordingly incorrect.

Question 11b.

B is correct. According to Comment 5 to Rule 3.6, prosecutors should not comment on the defendant's guilt or innocence because such a statement is "more likely than not to have a material, prejudicial effect."

The other statements are explicitly permitted by the rule. Rule 3.6(b)(1) provides that a lawyer may publicly state "the claim, offense or defense involved and . . . the identity of the persons involved." Rule 3.6(b)(7) provides that in a criminal case, a lawyer may publicly state "the identity, residence, occupation and family status of the accused," and "the fact, time and place of arrest."

Question 11c.

B is correct. Rule 3.7 generally bars a lawyer from being an advocate at a trial at which he is likely to be a necessary witness, but an exception permits a lawyer to testify if his disqualification would work substantial hardship on the client.

A is incorrect. Rule 3.7 allows a lawyer to testify on an uncontested issue in a matter in which the lawyer is representing one of the parties. The issue on which Tito needs to testify, however, is whether the necklace was stolen or given. That issue is highly contested, so the uncontested issue exception does not apply.

C is incorrect because the rule allows Tito to testify to avoid substantial hardship.

D is incorrect because no judicial ruling is required.

Question 11d.

C is correct. Vojtech is in the awkward position of knowing of an impending fraud on the court but not being able to prevent it. Rule 1.6(a) bars a lawyer from revealing confidential information relating to representation of a client, unless an exception applies. No exception applies here. 1.6(b)(2) only allows revelation of client fraud to prevent reasonably certain substantial financial injury to another if the lawyer's services were used in the perpetration of the fraud. Vojtech's services have not been used to perpetrate a fraud. Rule 3.3(b) does not apply because Vojtech is no longer representing a client in an adjudicative proceeding. Perhaps the rule should allow a lawyer to reveal information in this setting, but it provides no latitude with respect to a former client.

A is incorrect because Vojtech's silence does not constitute assistance to a client's commission of a crime or fraud.

B is incorrect because the confidentiality rules provide no exception that would allow Vojtech to reveal the information to the new counsel or the court, even when a lawyer is aware of a fraud that affects a judicial proceeding.

D is incorrect because there is no exception to confidentiality based on financial harm to a person unless the lawyer's services were used to commit a crime or fraud.

Question 11e.

D is correct. Rule 3.7 would bar Athena from acting as an advocate in the proceeding and also testifying as a witness. The rule allows a lawyer to serve as both advocate and witness where the subject matter of a lawyer's testimony is uncontested. But in this case, Athena may not serve as both advocate and witness, because the issue on which she would testify is contested. No other exception applies because the matter does not involve legal fees, and the advocate/witness rule imposes no substantial hardship imposed on a client, since Ernest is not yet a client and he can retain a different lawyer.

A is incorrect because the problem involves her serving as both advocate and witness for the estate, and the fact that her testimony would be truthful is not an exception to the rule.

B is incorrect because a lack of previous representation is also not an exception to the prohibition on serving as an advocate and a witness.

C is incorrect. Serving as an advocate and a witness as to a contested issue is impermissible for the reasons explained above. Therefore, Athena may not represent Ernest and testify even though her testimony is at not odds with her Ernest's position in the matter.

Question 11f.

D is correct. Rule 3.3(a)(3) bars a lawyer from counseling a client to testify falsely, but it does not bar a lawyer from coaching a client to tell the truth in a way that is most favorable to the client.

A and B are incorrect because Mort did not counsel Julio to give evidence that is false.

C is incorrect because Rule 3.3 is applicable to depositions as well as to trials. Comment 1.

Question 11g.

D is correct. Libby knows that Ira's statement was material to the case and false, and that Ira deliberately concealed the complaint record from the jury. Under Rule 3.3(a)(3), "If a lawyer, the lawyer's client, or a witness called by the lawyer has offered material evidence and the lawyer comes to know of its falsity, the lawyer shall take reasonable remedial measures, including, if necessary, disclosure to the tribunal." Comment 10 explains that she must remonstrate with her client, but if the client will not correct the false evidence, she must take further action, including disclosure to the tribunal if withdrawal from representation "will not undo the effect of the false evidence." The disclosure must be that which "is reasonably necessary to remedy the situation" even if this "requires the lawyer to reveal information that otherwise would be protected by Rule 1.6."

A is incorrect because the evidence was false. It is possible that Ira could avoid a perjury conviction because of the way he phrased his answer, because the standard for perjury convictions under *Bronston v. United States*, 409 U.S. 352 (1973), is extremely strict. But the standard of falsity in Rule 3.3 is not the same as the standard applied in criminal prosecutions for perjury.

B is incorrect because the duty to correct false testimony continues until the end of the proceeding, including any appeal. Rule 3.3, Comment 13. This case is still on appeal.

C is incorrect because Libby's duty to take remedial measures under Rule 3.3 includes the duty to undo the effect of the false evidence if her client will not do so.

Question 11h.

A is correct. Percy violated Rule 3.6(a) by communicating about his investigation of a matter when he reasonably should have known that his communication would have a substantial likelihood of materially prejudicing an adjudicative proceeding in the matter. Moreover, by claiming that Dr. Belknap had a history of failing to report abortions, he went beyond stating, pursuant to Rule 3.6(b)(3), that an investigation was in progress. He also violated Rule 4.4(a) by using means (the television show) that had no substantial purpose other than embarrassing or burdening Dr. Belknap. And he violated Rule 8.4(d) by engaging in conduct prejudicial to the administration of justice by publicly prejudging a case without any evidence of wrongdoing.

B is incorrect because Percy did violate a Rule of Professional Conduct.

C is incorrect because no lawyer is immune from ethical discipline.

D is incorrect because Percy's statement was false and defamatory, and he had made no effort to ascertain the truth of the statement. The statement was therefore not constitutionally protected.[4]

12. Lawyers' Duties to Adversaries and Third Parties

Question 12a.

D is correct. Rule 4.2 bars a lawyer from communicating about the subject of a representation with a person the lawyer knows to be represented by another lawyer in the matter without that lawyer's consent. Comment 7 explains that in the case of a represented organization such as a corporation, this Rule "prohibits communications with a constituent of the organization who supervises, directs or regularly consults with the organization's lawyer concerning the matter or has authority to obligate the organization with respect to the matter or *whose act or omission in connection with the matter may be imputed to the organization for purposes of civil or criminal liability*" (emphasis added). Because Xavier's acts or omissions may be imputed to the organization for purposes of liability, Maude needs Peter's permission before interviewing him.

The other answers are accordingly incorrect.

Question 12b.

B is correct. Rule 4.2 prohibits communication about the subject of the representation with a person the lawyer knows to be represented "in the matter" unless the lawyer has the consent of that person's lawyer. If Tom does not know that Manuel has a lawyer in connection with his non-payment of rent, he may communicate with Manuel. Comment 8 says that a lawyer may not "evade the requirement of obtaining the consent of counsel by closing his eyes to the obvious," but the rule does not require the lawyer to ask if Manuel has a lawyer in the matter.

A is incorrect because if Manuel does not have representation in the matter, he is an unrepresented person and Rule 4.3 applies. Rule 4.3 imposes some restrictions even when no proceeding is pending, such as the duty not to state that the lawyer is disinterested. Comment 2 to Rule 4.3 advises that if a lawyer negotiates the settlement of a dispute with an unrepresented person, the lawyer should identify himself as the attorney for an adverse party.

4. This question is based on the discipline administered by the Supreme Court of Indiana to Todd Rokita, the Attorney General of Indiana, *In re Rokita*, 219 N.E. 3d 733 (2023).

C is incorrect because if Tom knows that Manuel has a lawyer but does not know that the lawyer is representing him in the landlord-tenant matter, Rule 4.2 does not impose obligations.

D is incorrect because neither Rule 4.2 nor Rule 4.3 imposes an obligation to make inquiries to ascertain whether Manuel has a lawyer, or to advise Manuel of his rights, although Rule 4.3 would permit Tom to advise Manuel to retain counsel. Despite the absence of an obligation, Tom would be well-advised to start this conversation by asking Tom if he is represented in this matter. This would avoid future controversy about what Tom knew and when he knew it, if it turned out that Manuel had, after all, retained a lawyer about a possible eviction.

Question 12c.

B is correct. Toby is evidently under the misimpression that Sam is a police investigator, as evidenced by the phrase "your station." Sam must clarify his role to correct Toby's misimpression. See the second sentence of Rule 4.3.

A is incorrect; while a lawyer may advise a witness of his right to obtain legal counsel, he has no obligation to do so under these circumstances, where the person being interviewed does not appear to have interests adverse to those of the lawyer's client.

C is incorrect. Sam owes to Toby the duty to correct his misunderstanding of Sam's role, even though Toby does not have interests adverse to those of Alan.

D is incorrect; Sam did identify himself as Alan's lawyer, but after that, it became clear that Toby misunderstood his role, so Sam was obliged to say more to correct Toby's misunderstanding.

Question 12d.

C is correct. Rule 4.4(b) is very narrowly drafted, requiring disclosure of electronically stored information relating to the representation of the lawyer's client only if the information was inadvertently sent. Also, ABA Formal Op. 11-460 notes that information that is deliberately sent rather than inadvertently sent is not covered by Rule 4.4(b).

A is incorrect for that reason.

B is incorrect because the handbook warned that e-mails sent over the company's system could be read and disclosed by others, so Celinda was on notice, even if she did not read the handbook, that she had no expectation of privacy.

D is incorrect because the rules make no distinction between litigation and arbitration with respect to the duty to disclose.

Question 12e.

A is correct. Comment 7 following Rule 4.2 explains that a lawyer may not contact an employee of a corporation who "has authority to obligate the organization with respect to the matter or whose act or omission in connection with the matter may be imputed to the organization. . . ." However, the comment continues: "Consent of the organization's lawyer is not required for communication with a former constituent." The comment means that a lawyer may contact any *former* employee without Talmart's consent.

Most courts that have considered the issue have said that a lawyer may contact former corporate employees without the consent of the corporation's lawyer even if those employees had relevant managerial authority.[5]

5. See the cases collected at Lexis Hub, Ex Parte Communications with Former Managers/Employees of Adverse Corporate Parties Are Generally Permitted, https://perma.cc/D58C-D7SP.

B is incorrect because even if litigation already had been instituted, Ashley could speak with a former employee.

C is incorrect because although Rule 4.2 would require consent of Talmart's counsel if Chi were still a Talmart employee, the rule does not bar communications with former employees.

D is incorrect because Rule 4.2 does not distinguish between former employees who had managerial authority or were directly involved in the transaction leading to the claim and those who had no managerial authority or relationship to the claim.

Question 12f.

A is correct. Rule 4.2 requires consent of opposing counsel before a lawyer, including a prosecutor, talks to an opposing party known to be represented by counsel in the matter.

B is incorrect, because Brenda was required to refrain from questioning Donald without getting permission from his attorney; her notifying Donald of his right to have his lawyer present would not have satisfied this obligation.

C is incorrect because although Brenda did not violate Rule 4.1, barring false statements, she did violate Rule 4.2.

D is incorrect because according to comment 5 following Rule 4.2, the "authorized by law" exception in Rule 4.2, as applied to prosecutors, only permits investigative communications with a represented criminal defendant "prior to the commencement of criminal or civil enforcement proceedings."

Question 12g.

C is correct. Rule 3.8(g) requires:

> When a prosecutor knows of new, credible and material evidence creating a reasonable likelihood that a convicted defendant did not commit an offense of which the defendant was convicted, the prosecutor shall:
> (1) promptly disclose that evidence to an appropriate court or authority, and
> (2) if the conviction was obtained in the prosecutor's jurisdiction,
> (i) promptly disclose that evidence to the defendant unless a court authorizes delay....

Comment 7 following Rule 3.8 requires that the defendant be informed through his lawyer. Burt's confession, combined with the evidence of his blood at the scene of the crime, would give Daniel knowledge of "new, credible and material evidence creating a reasonable likelihood" that Ray did not murder Tammy. This triggers the duties spelled out in Rule 3.8(g).

A and B are incorrect for this reason. B is incorrect because the rule requires disclosure to the court or other authority as well as disclosure to the defendant.

D is incorrect because the prosecutor has no obligation to move to reopen the case, though "when a prosecutor knows of clear and convincing evidence establishing that a defendant in the prosecutor's jurisdiction was convicted of an offense that the defendant did not commit, the prosecutor shall seek to remedy the conviction." Rule 3.8(h). Comment 8 lists steps that may be needed to remedy the situation. A motion to reopen is not one of the listed steps.

Question 12h.

B is correct. Rule 3.8(a) bars a prosecutor from moving forward with a charge that the prosecutor "knows" is not supported by probable cause. "Knows" "denotes actual knowledge of the fact in question." Rule 1.0(f). Marcella is uncertain about whether the probable cause standard is met, so she does not "know" that the charge would be unsupported by probable cause.

A is incorrect because the standard is not whether she believes that John is guilty, but whether she knows that the charge is unsupported by probable cause.

C and D are incorrect because Rule 3.8 imposes only the very low standard of probable cause.

Question 12i.

D is correct. Rule 4.2 bars communications between lawyers and persons known to be represented with respect to a matter, without consent of that person's lawyer.

A and B are incorrect because Comment 3 provides that the rule applies even if the person known to be represented initiates or consents to the communication.

C is incorrect because even written consent from the adverse party, as opposed to that party's lawyer, is insufficient to permit the conversation.

Question 12j.

A is correct. Comment 7 following Rule 4.2 explains that a lawyer may not, without consent of opposing counsel for a corporation, contact an employee of a corporation who "has authority to obligate the organization with respect to the matter or whose act or omission in connection with the matter may be imputed to the organization. . . ." But, as in *Messing, Rudavsky & Weliky, P.C. v. President & Fellows of Harvard College*, 764 N.E. 2d 825 (Mass. 2002), a lawyer may, without such consent, contact a present employee who has no managing authority and who is not alleged to have committed wrongful acts at issue in the litigation.

B is incorrect for this reason.

C and D are incorrect because a lawyer in this situation has no obligation to notify a witness of her right to seek independent legal advice.

Question 12k.

B is correct. While the state courts and the other federal courts have adopted versions of the Model Code of Judicial Conduct or another ethics code to govern the conduct of sitting judges, the United States Supreme Court has declined to adopt an ethics code to govern the justices. This means, for example, that no articulated standard guides the justices in deciding whether to recuse themselves in the face of possible conflicts of interest.

A is incorrect. The ABA Model Rules of Professional Conduct does not have the force of law. Each state adopts an ethics code; lawyers admitted in that state must comply with that code or face discipline. The state ethics codes are most often based on the ABA Model Rules of Professional Conduct.

C is incorrect. The Restatement of the Law Governing Lawyers does synthesize the state ethics codes and the case law interpreting them, but it also synthesizes all other state and federal civil and criminal law governing lawyers. For example, the Restatement includes the standards for legal malpractice liability and for the disqualification of lawyers based on conflicts of interest.

D is incorrect. Lawyers who work for the federal government are admitted to the practice of law by one or more states, and compliance with the state ethics code is a condition of maintaining a license to practice. The McDade Amendment makes clear that the state ethics codes bind federal government lawyers. Because it is statutory, the McDade Amendment overrides any contrary federal agency regulations. Therefore, federal government lawyers are not exempt from compliance with the state ethics codes.

Question 12l.

D is correct. Under Rule 4.1, lawyers may not make false statements of material fact, but Comment 2 to Rule 4.1 states that "under generally accepted conventions in negotiation," a party's intentions as to an acceptable settlement of a claim are "not taken as statements of material fact."

The other answers are accordingly incorrect.

13. The Changing Landscape of Law Practice

Question 13a.

C is correct. Under amendments adopted by the ABA House of Delegates in August of 2018, Rule 7.3(a) prohibits a lawyer from soliciting professional employment "by live, person-to-person contact" if a significant motive for doing so is pecuniary gain. The rule makes exceptions where the prospective client is a lawyer, "has a family, close personal, or prior business or professional relationship with the lawyer or law firm," or where the prospective client "routinely uses for business purposes the type of legal service offered by the lawyer."

A is not prohibited by Rule 7.3 because in the rule prohibits solicitation by live, person-to-person contact, but does not prohibit use of electronic (or telephonic) contact with prospective clients.

B is not prohibited because in the situation described, the lawyer has a prior professional relationship with the client.

D is not prohibited because no rule prohibits mailed solicitation of business from prospective clients.

Question 13b.

D is correct. Rule 5.4 prohibits lawyers from allowing non-lawyers to invest in their firms. Rule 5.4(d) provides: "A lawyer shall not practice with or in the form of a professional corporation or association authorized to practice law for a profit, if: (1) a nonlawyer owns any interest therein . . ." (The rule mentions an exception that is not relevant to this example.)

A is incorrect, because the rule makes no exception for a familial relationship between the lawyer and a prospective partner.

B is incorrect. The purpose of the prohibition is to protect the independent professional judgment of the lawyer, but the investment is prohibited regardless of steps taken to that end by Betsy.

C is incorrect because Rule 5.4(b) states "A lawyer shall not form a partnership with a nonlawyer if any of the activities of the partnership consist of the practice of law." It does not matter whether the lawyer's partner is a general partner or a limited partner.

Question 13c.

C is correct. Under Rule 5.5(c), a lawyer "may provide temporary legal services" in a jurisdiction in which he is not admitted if the services "arise out of or are reasonably related to the lawyer's practice in a jurisdiction in which the lawyer is admitted to practice." Esteban's advice is "temporary" because Esteban is providing it only to help Patrick start up his business rather than on an ongoing basis. Rule 5.5, Comment 6 explains that "services may be temporary, even though the lawyer provides services in this jurisdiction on a recurring basis, or for an extended period of time. . . ." This example clearly qualifies as "temporary" legal services. It is related to his practice in State A because he already provides business advice to Patrick in State A.

A is incorrect because the rules do not require a lawyer to disclose where the lawyer is licensed to practice law.

B is incorrect because under Rule 5.5, Esteban may provide certain temporary legal services in State B without being admitted to practice there.

D is incorrect because Rule 5.5 imposes restrictions on out-of-state practice even for lawyers who are competent and licensed.

Question 13d.

C is correct. Rule 7.3 prohibits in-person solicitation by lawyers if a significant motive for the solicitation is pecuniary gain. The rule allows in-person solicitation even motivated by a desire for income if the person contacted by the lawyer is herself a lawyer, is a person with whom the lawyer or the law firm has a prior close personal or business relationship, or the person is a regular user of legal services of the type offered. Pedestrian accident victims would not be "regular users" of such services, so C correctly states that this type of contact is forbidden.

A is incorrect. Ethical rules against in-person solicitation were upheld in *Ohralik v. Ohio State Bar Ass'n,* 436 U.S. 447 (1978) (upholding a total ban of in-person solicitation when the primary motivation behind the contact is the attorney's pecuniary gain). The Court found that in-person solicitation was protected by the Constitution if the goal was to benefit the public rather than to generate private income for the lawyer. *In re* Primus, 436 U.S. 412 (1978) (holding that direct in-person solicitation is entitled to greater constitutional protection against state regulation when the attorney is motivated by the desire to promote political goals rather than pecuniary gain).

B is incorrect; lawyers and insurance adjusters are regulated by different entities, and no court has held that the same solicitation rules have to apply to both.

D is incorrect; a lawyer may challenge the validity of an ethics rule by violating the rule and raising the objection as a defense to a disciplinary proceeding. Therefore, Ian might deliberately violate the rule to invoke discipline and test its validity. That was the procedure followed by Dominic Gentile in *Gentile v. State Bar of Nevada*, 501 U.S. 1030 (1991).

Question 13e.

C is correct. Although Rule 7.2 states that "a lawyer shall not compensate, give or promise anything of value to a person for recommending the lawyer's services," Comment 4 to Rule 7.2 explains that "[p]aragraph (b)(5) permits lawyers to give nominal gifts as an expression of appreciation to a person for recommending the lawyer's services or referring a prospective client. The gift may not be more than a token item as might be given for holidays, or other ordinary social hospitality."

A is incorrect for the same reason.

B is incorrect. Comment 4 to Rule 7.2 states: "A gift is prohibited if offered or given in consideration of any promise, agreement or understanding that such a gift would be forthcoming or that referrals would be made or encouraged in the future." However, Margery's intention is not to pay people for the referrals but to thank them.

D is incorrect because although a lawyer may give a thank-you gift to another lawyer, the value of permissible gifts is restricted by Rule 7.2.

Question 13f.

D is correct. The advertisement does not include any false or misleading information, so there is no violation of Rule 7.1.

A is incorrect because Comment 9 to Rule 7.2 states: "Paragraph (c) of this Rule permits a lawyer to communicate that the lawyer does or does not practice in particular areas of law. A lawyer is generally permitted to state that the lawyer 'concentrates in' or is a 'specialist,' practices a 'specialty,' or 'specializes in' particular fields based on the lawyer's experience, specialized training or education. . . ."

B is incorrect. Under Rule 7.2(c), any communication to a prospective client must include the name and contact information of at least one lawyer or law firm responsible for its content. Suzette includes her phone numbers so this requirement in the rule is met. Rule 7.2 used to require that a lawyer list her office address in an ad. This rule was amended by the ABA in 2018 to eliminate that requirement.

C is incorrect. The Supreme Court decided in *Bates v. State Bar of Arizona*, 433 U.S. 350 (1977), that a complete ban on lawyer advertising would be unconstitutional, but it explicitly recognized that some regulation of advertising by states was acceptable.

Question 13g.

D is correct. Rule 5.4 prevents a lawyer from forming a partnership with a non-lawyer, regardless of how the fees are divided or what disclosures are made to clients. Rule 5.4(b) states "A lawyer shall not form a partnership with a nonlawyer if any of the activities of the partnership consist of the practice of law."

A is incorrect; Rule 5.3 requires that a lawyer make reasonable efforts to ensure that non-lawyers in a firm comply with the Rules of Professional Conduct, but compliance with Rule 5.3 does not overcome the bar imposed by Rule 5.4 on having a non-lawyer partner.

B is incorrect; lawyers may share fees with other lawyers not in the same firm if the fee is divided in proportion to the amount of service rendered (Rule 1.5(e)), but proportional division does not overcome the bar of Rule 5.4.

C is incorrect; even if notice were to be given, the partnership is impermissible.

14. Access to Justice: The Lawyer's Role

Question 14a.

D is correct. A lawyer is not subject to discipline even if he fails to comply with the guidelines for pro bono work listed in Rule 6.1. The rule says "A lawyer *should aspire to* render at least (50) hours of pro bono publico legal services per year." The less-than mandatory language of the rule indicates that lawyers have discretion as to whether and how they comply. If the language of the rule were mandatory, Duncan would be subject to discipline. Rule 6.1(a) provides that lawyers should provide at least 50 hours of pro bono services annually and that "a substantial majority" of the 50 hours of pro bono service should be provided "without fee or expectation of fee." Duncan is not providing any hours of service at no fee.

A is incorrect because of the non-mandatory language of the rule.

B is incorrect for that reason and is also incorrect because the standard in the rule does not require that the recipients of the service be destitute, but only that they be persons "of limited means." People whose families are below the poverty line are "of limited means." Comment 3 specifies that persons who qualify for participation in programs funded by the Legal Services Corporation are eligible under Rule 6.1(a), and persons in families below the poverty level are among those who qualify even if they are not utterly destitute.

C is incorrect because of the non-mandatory language of the rule and also because if the rule were mandatory, a substantial majority of the 50 hours should be provided without fee, not at a discounted rate.

Question 14b.

D is correct. With some exceptions, there is no due process right to counsel in civil cases. The *Kras* case, 409 U.S. 434 (1973), is widely cited for the origin of that rule. *Lassiter v. Department of Social Services*, 452 U.S. 18 (1981) rejected any presumption that there is a right to counsel in civil cases, but it opened the door to the possibility that under some circumstances, a court could require counsel for an indigent who was threatened with the loss of fundamental rights. The courts have rarely found that those factors warranted appointment of counsel for indigents, but some courts have appointed counsel for indigents in some particularly compelling cases, especially when the government was seeking to terminate parental rights or to commit a person to a mental institution involuntarily. See John Pollack, Walking Before Running: Implementation of a Right to Counsel in Civil Cases, 14 MIE J. 6 (2010), http://papers.ssrn.com/sol3/papers.cfm?abstract_id=2560620. See also *Turner v. Rogers*, 131 S. Ct. 2507 (2011) (suggesting that appointment of counsel for indigents in civil matters is not constitutionally required, but if an indigent party's ability to pay is a key substantive issue in the case, and counsel is not provided, "substitute procedural safeguards" are necessary.

The other answers are therefore incorrect.

Question 14c.

B is correct. Comment 5 to Rule 6.1 allows employees who are barred from performing pro bono services to individuals and organizations to satisfy the obligation by engaging in the activities specified in Rule 6.1(b). One of those activities is "participation in activities for improving the law, the legal system or the legal profession."

A is incorrect. A lawyer who is unable to provide direct pro bono services to persons of limited means may satisfy the aspirational requirement by contributing money to organizations that provide free legal services to persons of limited means. See Comment 9 to Rule 6.1. However, the Environmental Law Awareness Council provides legal information to the public generally and does not focus its resources on persons of limited means.

C is incorrect because government lawyers need not represent individual clients to fulfill the aspirational obligations of Rule 6.1. They may do so by engaging in any of the activities listed in Rule 6.1(b). See Comment 5.

D is incorrect. It is true that the agency regulations take precedence over a merely aspirational professional conduct rule, but she may comply with both Rule 6.1 and her agency's regulations by participating in law reform efforts.

Question 14d.

A is correct. This problem is similar to *Evans v. Jeff D.*, 475 U.S. 717 (1986), in which the Supreme Court held that the Fees Act did not bar a settlement offer that was conditioned on the plaintiff's lawyer waiving attorney's fees to which the lawyer would otherwise be entitled. The Truth in Lending Act is similar to the Fees Act in that it provides that a prevailing plaintiff's lawyer can recover attorney fees from a defendant.

B is incorrect because nothing in *Jeff D.* or other law requires the defendant's lawyer to waive fees, even if that lawyer is requiring her adversary to do so as a condition of settlement.

C is incorrect because no rule prohibits a party from making a settlement offer whose effect is to create a conflict of interest for a plaintiff. Such an offer may have been made, for example, in *Fiandaca v. Cunningham*, 827 F. 2d 825 (1st Cir. 1987).

D is incorrect because in *Jeff D.*, the majority opinion did not accept an argument made by the dissent that the attorney fee provision in the Fees Act should override the judicially created policy of encouraging settlements.

Question 14e.

B is correct. The Fees Act allows plaintiffs' lawyers who prevail in federal civil rights litigation against state agencies to be awarded counsel fees to be paid by the defendant. But under the Supreme Court's decision in *Buckhannon Bd. & Care Home v. West Virginia*, 532 U.S. 598 (2001), a plaintiff is not deemed to prevail unless the case results in a court order in the plaintiff's favor. An out-of-court settlement or a voluntary change in the defendant's practices will not suffice.

A is incorrect because *Buckhannon* requires a court order embodying the changed practice before fees can be awarded.

C is incorrect because the Fees Act has never been held unconstitutional and is often the basis for fee shifting when plaintiffs prevail in cases like this, provided that the plaintiffs obtain a court decree or order sustaining their claims.

D is incorrect because the Fees Act abrogates the American rule for federal civil rights cases against state actors.

Question 14f.

C describes his best option. Amar would like to work in the public sector indefinitely. If he stays at legal aid or works at any "501(c)(3)" non-profit or government agency and makes 120 monthly on-time payments while in income-based repayment, he will not only lower his monthly payments substantially, but he will also qualify to have his loan balance forgiven, tax-free, after he makes the 120th payment. The rising balance due will not affect him; it is only a measure of the amount of debt to be forgiven.

A is not a good option, because if he is sued, he will stand to lose not only whatever money or other assets he has or may later accumulate, and he could also suffer severe damage to his professional reputation.

B is not a good option because with very rare exceptions, student loans are not dischargeable in bankruptcy.

D is not a good option because he would be trading work that he enjoys for drudgery. In the private firm, his income would still be relatively low, and he could still use income-based repayment to lower his monthly payments. But because he would be working in the private sector rather than the public sector, he would not qualify for forgiveness before repaying for 25 years, and any forgiveness at that point would be taxable.

Question 14g.

C is correct. Rule 5.5(a) provides that a lawyer may not assist another in practicing law in violation of the regulation of the legal profession in the jurisdiction in question. With very limited exceptions, such as Washington State's program of licensing legal technicians, all jurisdictions prohibit non-lawyers from giving legal advice, so Ann should not assist Pablo in giving legal advice, no matter how well-intentioned either Pablo or Ann is.

A is incorrect for that reason.

B is incorrect because lawyers may give legal advice to undocumented persons—but nonlawyers may not.

D is incorrect. Assuring that Pablo's services are competent does not solve the problem because by giving this answer, Ann disclaims responsibility (e.g., malpractice and disciplinary liability) for whatever errors or malfeasance Pablo might commit.